T0390470

War, Race, and Culture

ASIAN AMERICA

Edited by Gordon H. Chang

War, Race, and Culture
Journeys in Trans-Pacific and
Asian American Histories

Gordon H. Chang

STANFORD UNIVERSITY PRESS
STANFORD, CALIFORNIA

Stanford University Press
Stanford, California

© 2025 by the Board of Trustees of the Leland Stanford Jr. University. All rights reserved.

No part of this book may be reproduced or transmitted in any form or by any means, electronic or mechanical, including photocopying and recording, or in any information storage or retrieval system, without the prior written permission of Stanford University Press.

Library of Congress Cataloging-in-Publication Data

Names: Chang, Gordon H., author.
Title: War, race, and culture : journeys in trans-Pacific and Asian
   American histories / Gordon H. Chang.
Other titles: Asian America.
Description: Stanford, California : Stanford University Press, 2025. |
   Series: Asian America | Includes bibliographical references.
Identifiers: LCCN 2024055935 (print) | LCCN 2024055936 (ebook) | ISBN
   9781503642591 (cloth) | ISBN 9781503642775 (ebook)
Subjects: LCSH: East Asian Americans—History. | Asian American
   arts—History. | United States—Relations—East Asia. | East
   Asia—Relations—United States. | United States—Race
   relations—History. | LCGFT: Essays.
Classification: LCC E184.E15 (print) | LCC E184.E15 (ebook)
LC record available at https://lccn.loc.gov/2024055935
LC ebook record available at https://lccn.loc.gov/2024055936

Cover design: Michele Wetherbee
Cover art: Alan Lau, *Sierra Tracks (for the Railroad Builders)*, 1980; Sumi and mixed media on rice paper, 5′ × 5′; Eden Arts courtesy of Francine Seders Gallery, Seattle, Washington
Typeset by Newgen in 11/14 Adobe Garamond Pro

To the many, many teachers through the years, in and beyond schools, who've taught me about history and life

Contents

Introduction: Toward an Intellectual Memoir 1

Part I: War

1   JFK, China, and the Bomb 25

2   Eisenhower and Mao's China 49

3   Chinese Americans and China: A Troubled and
Complicated Relationship 65

4   Whose "Barbarism"? Whose "Treachery"?: Race
and Civilization in the Unknown United States–Korea
War of 1871 79

5   China and the Pursuit of America's Destiny:
Nineteenth-Century Imagining and Why Immigration
Restriction Took So Long 119

Part II: Race

6   "Superman Is About to Visit the Relocation Centers"
and the Limits of Wartime Liberalism 143

7   Social Darwinism Versus Social Engineering: The
"Education" of Japanese Americans During World War II 163

vii

viii *Contents*

8 Asian Americans and Politics: Some Perspectives
from History 183

9 Chinese Railroad Workers and the U.S. Transcontinental
Railroad in Global Perspective 205

10 History and Postmodernism 223

Part III: Culture

11 Emerging from the Shadows: The Visual Arts and Asian
American History 231

12 Chinese Painting Comes to America: Zhang Shuqi
and the Diplomacy of Art 241

13 America's Dong Kingman—Dong Kingman's America 255

14 The Many Sides of Happy Lim: aka Hom Ah Wing,
Lin Jian Fu, Happy Lum, Lin Chien Fu, Hom Yen Chuck,
Lam Kin Foo, Lum Kin Foo, Hom, Lim Goon Wing,
Lim Gin Foo, Gin Foo Lin, Koon Wing Lim, Henry Chin,
Lim Ying Chuck, Lim Ah Wing, et al. 261

15 The Life and Death of Dhan Gopal Mukerji 291

Appendix: Selected Work 327

Acknowledgments 333

Notes 337

Biographical Note 399

INTRODUCTION

Toward an Intellectual Memoir

Writing history, the systematic effort to understand the human past, is a demanding intellectual endeavor. For me, it has also been a personal and moral enterprise inextricably connected to my commitment to realizing a better world. The ideal of "scholarly detachment," which some maintain is essential for serious scholarship with the presumption that interpretation can exist independent of a point of view, was never persuasive to me. History has always been an engaged practice informed by visions of social equality and global justice.

I grew up in the San Francisco East Bay during the height of the Cold War. Vivid memories of practicing "duck and cover" in my primary school classrooms and contemplating how I might react if I saw an immense, orange-colored mushroom cloud cover the magnificent harbor, with its array of military bases and industrial centers, remain very much with me to this day. Our family was comfortable, with my father being an artist who had an accomplished and distinguished career in China before and after World War II. During the war years, when he lived in the United States, he attracted wide public attention for his efforts in promoting goodwill between China and the United States. He engaged in what we now call cultural diplomacy to inspire American sympathy for the Chinese people through an appreciation of their art and civilization. His unique career, with his live painting demonstrations at art museums, galleries, public spaces, and universities across the country, served as an alternative life model for me as one who was never attracted to conventional professional or business tracks.

I

2   *Introduction*

Dad went back to China at the conclusion of the war, and a few years later I was born in Hong Kong. After the founding of the People's Republic of China in 1949, the family returned to the United States and watched the relationship between the two countries deteriorate into mutual animosity. The brutal fighting in Korea was an especially raw point. The once-great American affection for Chinese civilization plummeted, replaced by a hostility stoked by the emotions of war and anticommunism. The racially alien Chinese in America became suspect. My father and our family could not escape the uneasiness imposed by global politics, which steadily diminished his once-illustrious career. We felt vulnerable. Though he passed when I was just nine years old, he remained a formidable presence throughout my life.

Inheriting my father's attention to international relations and, as an adolescent during the escalation of the U.S. intervention into the Vietnamese civil war, I developed a youthful curiosity about American involvement in Asia. Fighting in Southeast Asia escalated soon after the war in Northeast Asia ended. The Vietnam War would shadow the country for years. In a high school competition for a college scholarship provided by a Chinese American civic organization, I had to answer the question: did I support or not support the war and why? Evading taking a stand in the increasingly polarized political climate, I offered a mealy-mouthed answer that straddled both positions. Avoiding taking a stand on the criminality of the war soon became untenable.

My mother was a third-generation Chinese American, with her roots in the California Gold Country and the San Francisco region. Her siblings, my aunts and uncles, formed part of the small emerging Chinese American middle class. Their parents, Fong Chow and Lonnie Tom, had been prominent members of the Chinese community in the heart of the gold country in the Sierra Nevada foothills and in Vallejo at the north end of San Francisco Bay. Grandfather had managed the legendary Omega Mine, located near the town of Washington, California. It was one of the most productive gold mines in the state, with many of the Chinese workers who worked it veterans of railroad construction in earlier years. *China Gold* (1954), one of the first books about Chinese American lives, tells his and Lonnie's moving story of trials and joys. The account, along with handed-down family photos showing them to be vigorous, affectionate, proud, and comedic as well as heart-broken and resigned when they faced tragedies, touched the

Toward an Intellectual Memoir   3

soul of the incipient historian within me. I thought about what it is that we leave behind with our lives.[1]

Their many children went to college and were among the first of their backgrounds to become teachers, nurses, office employees, entertainers, and shopkeepers. My mother's elder sister, later better known by her married name of Alice Fong Yu, was the first Chinese American schoolteacher employed in San Francisco and a leading community activist. She considered herself a champion of Chinese Americans and Chinese American women in particular. Today, a Cantonese immersion school in San Francisco carries her name to honor her pioneering efforts. My own mother, Helen Fong, majored in physical education at UC Berkeley, thinking that she would also become a teacher, a profession that was within reach. She and her siblings were proud of their heritage and contributions to American life through their military service and sacrifice in World War II, dedicated public service, and devoted family lives. They inspired pride in Chinese American history. I consumed the many books on Chinese civilization and culture around the family house (other than *China Gold,* there was nothing to read about Chinese Americans) and always took note of the rare story about a Chinese American that appeared in the press or television. Chinese Americans in the 1950s were largely unseen, unheard, and of little interest to the rest of the American public. My mother, a hard-working single parent who raised my brother and me after our father died, modeled self-reliance, dignity, and respect toward people of all races and backgrounds.

Growing up, unlike friends who knew what they wanted to be early in life, I did not know what I wanted. I never considered the study of history, or academia for that matter, as a serious career objective. In fact, the study of American history was one of the least interesting subjects for me in high school because of the emphasis on rote memorization and the myopic attention to business and government elites. I can't remember whether we even had "world civilization" history.[2] I was ambitious and wanted to make a mark on society in some way, and becoming a teacher of names and chronologies wasn't for me. My future would be elsewhere, I thought, but I lacked any clear vision.

I performed well at my high school, where only two of us in my senior class were students of color. I was therefore a conspicuous, and unusual, valedictorian at graduation, and I challenged the politically conservative audience of parents and friends to heed the turbulent times in the mid-1960s.

4   *Introduction*

Far-reaching changes were in the making, I declared, and we all needed to open our eyes and confront the new realities of a society in turmoil. I then went off to Princeton, far from home on the other side of the country. Elite universities were then beginning to open up to students from nondominant backgrounds, and I am sure that what became known as "affirmative action" opened the way to an education I sincerely appreciated. With a scholarship, I joined just a few other Asian Americans and students of color in a class of eight hundred men. Princeton then did not admit any women. The place, because of its elitism, white supremacy, and other objectionable social features, was profoundly alienating, but I decided to tough it out and stayed. I would not be driven away.

As for classes, taking college-level history courses at first didn't change my opinion about the subject. Long-standing conventions still ruled much of the discipline, especially in U.S. history. The definition of subject fields mirrored the established, contemporary nation-state and the perspectives of the male power elite. There was no gender, ethnic, or environmental history that was offered. The study of governmentality and the uses of formal power, otherwise known as political history, ruled the day. Historical study, which explored transnational or global study not tethered to nation-based perspectives, only slowly entered my studies.

My own mindset about the world when I entered college had not been much different from what I encountered in high school civics class. John F. Kennedy had celebrated government and public service, and I heeded the call. I knew about the scholar/diplomat George F. Kennan, whose memoir I consumed during the long train ride across the country to get to college. Involvement in international relations, as Kennan had exemplified, could have been where I concentrated my studies. Might the times accept someone who specialized in China as it had with the Russian specialist Kennan, whose career spanned government and academia? But then the brutal war in Southeast Asia became ever-present. Ensconced in isolated Princeton, I watched as the war relentlessly escalated to horrific levels. By 1968, half a million U.S. soldiers were fighting on the ground in south Vietnam. Millions of Vietnamese, Cambodians, and Laotians died. Atrocities mounted, and I could no longer look away. I developed a pan-ethnic Asian or racial identity oppositional to a perceived white imperialism.

China, seen by many as the ultimate enemy in the Southeast Asia war, was far distant and there were no formal relations between Beijing and

Toward an Intellectual Memoir 5

Washington. There were virtually no diplomatic contacts, travel, business, educational or cultural exchange, or other avenues of contact. Much of the rest of Asia was distant, unknown, and in ferment, which piqued my curiosity all the more. Might the world's future lie in Asia?[3] But thoughts about a future in government work fell away as my revulsion against the war steadily grew and then exploded into anger against what I saw was American aggression and the genocidal destruction of Asian peoples. From wanting to serve Washington, I concluded that Washington was itself the world's problem and the source of unjust wars. As an anxious, alienated college student, I did not know what I was going to do with my life.[4]

I concerned myself with the immediate challenge of opposing the war and imperialism. I helped organize protests, formed a "third world liberation front," and co-founded and edited *Prism*, an independent, radical newspaper. I tried to find common cause with other Asian American and minority students at Princeton and, with activists from other colleges, advance the fledgling Asian American movement on the East Coast.

Alongside my political activism, I spent my time studying Chinese and East Asian history, language, and culture and took courses with scholars, whose politics did not necessarily parallel my own soaring radicalism but whose learning I nevertheless admired. I discovered the possibilities of understanding the human experience that historical study provided and gravitated toward a history major. I studied with an array of distinguished historians and Asia specialists at Princeton, including Wen Fong, Marius Jansen, James T. C. Liu, Frederick Mote, John Schrecker, Weiming Tu, and others. Modern European revolutions, culture, and diplomacy also spoke to me, and I studied with Europeanists Stephen Cohen, Arno Mayer, and Carl Schorske. I owe them all a debt of intellectual gratitude. Though I still found American history unengaging, a class with Martin Duberman, a pioneering historian of social history, opened new vistas. But it was Mayer who made the deepest impression on me with his expansive, dynamic interpretation of the international history of the end of World War I and his structuralist approach to Great Power politics. I left with a degree in History and East Asian Studies and acceptances to pursue doctoral study in graduate school.[5]

Because of social upheaval and my own involvement in radical politics, I entered Stanford in 1970 with great ambivalence. I was to study modern Chinese history with the historians Harold Kahn and Lyman Van Slyke,

6   *Introduction*

and my focus would be on the history of early Marxist thought in China before the founding of the Communist Party. My senior thesis at Princeton had been on Chen Duxiu, a leading revolutionary intellectual and a founder of the Chinese Communist Party. I would continue to explore the Sinicization of Marxist thought by studying the life and writing of Ai Siqi, one of the most prominent early Marxists in China and an interlocutor with Mao Zedong, but I quickly learned that my hesitance to pursue graduate studies had been well founded. My commitment to realize radical change made it impossible to stay on the long, sequestered path of becoming a professional historian. I left the doctoral program, assuming that it would be highly unlikely I would ever return to the relative quiet of academia. I once naively thought that the academic study of revolution and modern communism might prove helpful in finding a way to advance contemporary movements for social liberation, but came to conclude that university life was for me too removed from the world of social protest. Though I had taught the first Asian American history course at Stanford and had even traveled to China in 1971 on an American delegation that preceded the Nixon trip, I concluded that pursuing a doctoral degree was not for me then, and I departed. I thought it highly unlikely I'd ever return to graduate studies. I pursued my social activism, waited on tables, wrote about politics, tried to apply radical theory to analyze American conditions, worked in the labor and community organizing movements, and taught at local community colleges in Oakland. For ten years, I taught Chinese history, East Asian civilization, Asian American history, and even English as a second language at Laney Community College in downtown Oakland. The experience was rewarding and transformative, as I interacted with recent immigrants from around the world, factory workers, retirees, army veterans, and young people of every color and belief. Their determination, aspirations, and curiosity impressed me. I have never forgotten them when I think of the audiences for my own writing.

The future, however, rarely develops as one wishes, or seeks to construct, and ten years later, it became evident that the social revolution I once envisioned would be a long time in realizing, if at all in my lifetime. The existing socialist world was in turmoil and liberation movements around the world were floundering. America had moved from the radical possibilities of the 1960s, and the sense that the capitalist world was in terminal crisis, to the triumphalist national chauvinism of Ronald Reagan. I remained active in movements for social justice and empowerment but returned to Stanford in 1982 with a longer view on my life's purposes.

Though modern Chinese history continued to fascinate me, I moved my area of concentration to the study of modern American history, surprisingly enough. Being involved in political activism and teaching in the inner city brought me a new appreciation of the vitality of American life and its past. New scholarship, especially in social history, was invigorating and changing the field. I searched for ways to connect Chinese and American histories and found an agreeable place in the sub-field of East Asia–America relations history. Its embrace of cultural dimensions, ideologies, social interactions, migration, and race offered new ways forward. The war in Southeast Asia had inspired young academics to rethink America's long experience in Asia beyond the war itself, and they opened fresh perspectives on the past.[6]

In my second stint at Stanford, I studied with historians who worked along established lines in U.S. political history, such as Bart Bernstein, David Kennedy, Jack Rakove, and others who were opening the way to new appreciations of domestic ethnic and social histories. Especially influential were Al Camarillo, Clay Carson, Carl Degler, Estelle Freedman, and George Fredrickson. For a moment, I thought I might complete a study of my aunt Alice, the educator and community leader, for my dissertation. She was still healthy and eager to help and had collected a huge archive of her papers, but the professional prospects for what would become known as Asian American Studies were murky and failed to resonate with the faculty. I turned instead to the conventional field of diplomatic history, which spoke to my longstanding interest in international relations.[7] The result of my graduate work became my dissertation and first book, *Friends and Enemies: The United States, China, and the Soviet Union: 1948–1972* (1990). At the age of forty, when most other academics would be in mid-career, I received my doctoral degree and became a professional historian.

I remained at Stanford for two further years as a researcher in a project dedicated to understanding war and peace in the Asia-Pacific region. Once again, I found myself in unfamiliar circumstances, as my immediate colleagues were political scientists who focused on international security, such as Coit Blacker, David Holloway, and John W. Lewis. They were also interested in influencing Washington policymaking. I had to learn new vocabularies about crisis management, signaling, and confidence-building measures. For one who had condemned U.S. war-making, I found myself

8   *Introduction*

having to think about constructing plausible security alternatives for Washington's consideration. The experience was short-lived, as I realized that I missed the analytical, political, and moral, possibilities provided by distance from the contemporary moment and establishment politics. I began to search for positions in university history departments.

Developments beyond history also opened intellectual possibilities for me. Community-based practitioners had long championed the recovery of Chinese and Japanese American pasts, but their efforts had largely remained outside academe.[8] In the 1970s and 1980s, however, scholars such as Sucheng Chan, Roger Daniels, Yuji Ichioka, Gary Okihiro, and Ron Takaki began to establish a new field of study, now known as Asian American Studies. These scholars made it possible to think about ethnicity and race in new and important ways and bridge the foreign and domestic spheres in American history. Having never taken a course that mentioned Asian Americans, I developed my own understanding of Asian American history largely through my own study and research. With student activists around the country demanding that universities establish Asian American Studies programs, positions slowly began to appear, and I became a beneficiary of their advocacy.

I wound up at the University of California, Irvine and had a rewarding two-year stay. But in 1990, Stanford invited me to present a lecture on my developing scholarship. I spoke about race, the Korean and Cold Wars, and anticommunism. The talk went well, and I received an offer to join the Stanford history faculty. Stanford students had conducted sit-ins and hunger strikes to diversify the curriculum, and the administration, after years of resistance, finally relented and accepted the idea. Student activism had made my return to Stanford possible, and the university soon became a leader in minority studies among private institutions.[9]

The twists and turns in my career, however, were not over.

When word got out that the Stanford History Department had offered me a faculty position, right-wing students went on a rampage to demand that the university retract the offer. The campus conservative newspaper, citing my social activism and leftist politics, condemned me as unacceptable for Stanford. It had never attacked a faculty candidate in such a vicious way before. It ignored my scholarship and teaching record, which had persuaded the department, but focused on my political views. I wavered in accepting the Stanford offer, worrying about what I might encounter if I were to return to campus in such a heated environment. Several good colleagues within the Department, however, reached out to support me. Just ignore the rightist agitators, the faculty urged, and I took a leave from UCI, which gave me tenure after just a year on campus to counter the Stanford offer.

After I returned to Stanford, however, I found that some Stanford faculty did not know how to think about, let alone fully respect, the different kinds of work I pursued. My work in diplomatic history was respected and helped legitimate me as a scholar, but Asian American Studies as a field of study was novel. Many at Stanford were skeptical at best. A senior Americanist ignorantly declared, I later heard, that Asian Americans had "no history." By that he meant that because there were no real archives and documentation to study, there could be no legitimate history, at least that a research institution such as Stanford could acknowledge. (He was grievously wrong about the lack of documentation.) And working to intersect the two fields was even more challenging for reviewers. Advancing my work was not easy. The intellectual atmosphere at Irvine, a public institution with many minority students, had been more receptive to work in ethnic studies than Stanford, which was tethered to a safe and established approach to the study of the past.

I arrived without tenure at Stanford, and several years later, at the time of promotion review, the University balked. Though the History Department supported my case, the upper administration, which was not prepared to acknowledge, let alone fully appreciate, the value of my efforts, did not approve tenure. I was made "associate professor, untenured" and told I could come up for tenure review again in a few years. I had to produce more work to prove my worthiness before I could advance. I almost left Stanford again but stayed, worked hard, and celebrated promotion when it finally came several years later. I have been at Stanford ever since. Going through tenure review three times was enough!

The story of my life and career given above should help a reader see connections in the chapters that comprise this volume. A search for more profound themes would be in vain, however. These essays and chapters are not a product of a well-thought-out effort to address a discrete intellectual problem, but rather are largely products of opportunities and unplanned circumstances that explore topics which aligned with my overarching curiosity about the interconnections of race and foreign and domestic realms of history.

My unconventional career trajectory helps to explain, at least in part, the intellectual choices of my subject matter. I entered the academy relatively

10   *Introduction*

late in life. I lived for many years as a dedicated activist with values and commitments to social change that deeply grounded me and continued to influence me as a professional historian. In more than thirty years of political activism, I developed lifelong ties with many dedicated activists with a wide array of class, racial, national, and work backgrounds. The learning experiences, and engagements with them, became formative elements in my life outlook and intellect. Life itself was also challenging, having to live on modest means, make many personal sacrifices, and work in the knowledge that state authorities were closely monitoring my activities. At times it was perilous, as when I was knifed in the back over politics by rightist New York Chinatown street gang members and sent to the hospital. Despite the difficulties and disappointments, I've never regretted my activism.

Even after entering academia, I did not always take the conventional route in my writing choices or in maximizing career opportunities and professional advancement. I was not especially active in the professional circuit. Enjoying family life late in life and handling acute family health challenges profoundly shaped my agendas. Less important to me were the worlds of professional associations and academic controversies. All this is to say that the following chapters are the product of an unusual intellectual and professional life.[10]

One further observation needs to be made. The influence of social theory in postmodernist, Marxist, or cultural studies variations played less upon me in my scholarship. From one who had been deeply involved in the movements for radical change, this may be an unexpected, even surprising, disclosure. As part of my social activism and within a Marxist framework, I had written about race and ethnicity in contemporary America, class structures, international politics, cultural production, and movements for social transformation. I had wanted to contribute to an activism that was rooted in, and meaningful for, specific American conditions. A creative application of Marxism was necessary, I believed, to build a movement for effective social change. But none of that activist writing appears in this volume.

Early in my academic studies, I concluded that Marxism in its various given forms, including what I call academic Marxism, provided only a generalized vision for university scholarship that required respect for evidence and the complexity of the human experience. Thinking and writing about radically transforming the present, which required connecting theory and active political practice, was one challenge. Understanding the past as a scholar was another, and an effort to merge the two realms of radical change and scholarship within academia never strongly appealed to me, especially as one interested in the subject of race, which has always challenged the traditional tenets of Marxist theory. What did stay with me was an abiding interest in the systemic workings of social and political power, an appreciation of the inequalities of class and racial hierarchies, and sympathy with the marginalized of the world.

My work has moved in tandem with dramatic changes in society and in the historical profession itself. The work of other colleagues, especially in recent years, has also confronted assumptions about what constitutes acceptable scholarly fields, topics, source material, and framing. Our work has contributed to what some have aptly called the democratizing of American history writing. Today, the histories of racial minorities, women, other marginalized communities, iconoclasts and activists, and others who were often sidelined in the past are moving beyond the narrow spaces that privileged the points of view of elites and the powerful in historical study and are assuming their own rightful places in intellectual importance. We can comprehend and appreciate a broader range of human agency.

Over the years of my professional career, I have been fortunate to have engaged consummate colleagues, librarians, curators, and generous scholars from around world. I have learned and received inestimable help from them. Historical scholarship is the product of collaboration in archives and libraries, organized exchange, and serendipitous conversations. I have enjoyed the generous support of educational institutions, academic societies, and foundations. My work with undergraduate and graduate students has also been especially rewarding. Their energy, advocacy, and intelligence in thinking through historical problems and identifying new directions for scholarship constantly inspire me. They are forging new paths forward in understanding the dynamic and boundless human past.

I am grateful for the rich diversity of pursuits I have been able to pursue in academia, a realm that can offer precious spaces for thought and reflection. I have been able to research, write, teach, and serve the greater university community, including serving as the Senior Associate Vice Provost for Undergraduate Education for several years, the Director of the Center for East Asian Studies, the founding director of the Program in Asian American Studies, and the inaugural director of the Asian American Research Center at Stanford. These experiences have influenced my scholarship, as I have

12 *Introduction*

had to think about the close relationship of pedagogy, research, and institutional administration. Since 1993 I have also been the academic editor for the Stanford University Press book series in Asian American Studies. Our list, with works in history, literary criticism, anthropology, sociology, politics, cultural studies, and other interdisciplinary methodologies from more than fifty authors, many with their first book, has contributed to advancing careers and heightened respect for Asian American Studies nationally.[11]

At the start of my graduate studies, conventional scholarship in American history was largely divided into discrete fields known either as foreign or domestic, political or social, minority or dominant. It is sometimes said that academic fields are "siloed." Organized in such a metaphoric way, scholarship is focused but it also means that writing can be constricted and have difficulty breaking with established approaches. Uncomfortable with trying to understand the past through rigid binaries, I aspired to pursue scholarship that challenged assumptions about what constituted proper, even legitimate, fields, topics, and framing. Specifically, I wanted to study race, broadly construed as a social construct, and its place in diplomatic, social, and cultural histories, especially about Asia-America relations and about Asian Americans. I explored the deep connections of race with power in its political, cultural, and social forms. Race is intimately connected to power and is not simply a circumstance. I wrote about racial thinking in presidential decision-making, the incarceration of Japanese Americans during the Second World War, Chinese railroad workers in nineteenth-century America, Chinese American lives, and Asian American art, among other subjects. These and other interests appear in the following pages.

Chapters in this volume, some published years ago early in my career, were pioneering in subject matter and approach when they appeared and challenged established academic conventions. They presented new ways of thinking about important episodes in East Asia–America relations and Asian American history and helped establish the importance of race in ways now more widely accepted in the profession, though much more remains to be done to examine its centrality throughout American history.

Toward an Intellectual Memoir   13

I wrote these essays over the long arc of my professional life. They are not a full compilation of my writing in academia and beyond. Some are chapters from books I authored or coauthored. Others originally appeared in professional journals or in editions of scholarship edited by others. Two have not been widely or publicly circulated before.[12] Some major pieces of my writing, which appeared in *American Historical Review, International Security,* or *South Atlantic Quarterly,* for example, are not included as they did not fit well or were intended for audiences other than for the ones at hand. But this is the first time that an array of my university-based work appears together to provide access to essays from different sources as well as an opportunity to consider multiple pieces of my writing together in conversation. This book's contents are wide-ranging, even sprawling and eclectic, compared to other typical volumes of selected scholarship. Each chapter begins with a brief headnote that reflects on the circumstances of the essay in question, as well as the new resonances for our present moment.

As the reader will see, my writing spans the academic categories of diplomacy, international relations, Asian American history, labor studies, and even art history. I have written about war, politics, individual experience and biography, and cultural expression. Interconnected concerns, such as the relationship of geopolitical conflict and race, or of cultural production and power, link the different chapters. The reader might see the chapters not as disjointed efforts but as evidence of an abiding curiosity to produce knowledge on important episodes from the past in America and Asia.

One of the reasons for the unusual diversity in the choices of my scholarship was that the pursuit of historical knowledge was never an endeavor solely of intellectual choice. My professional efforts have followed my moral compass, by which I mean my work engaged with, and expressed, core values and elements that form my identity as an Asian American sensitive to racial injustice in America and dedicated to seeking a more humane world. Such a commitment has not contradicted standards and rigor of academic inquiry, which I firmly uphold, but has guided what I write and think about and, very importantly, inspired my efforts to better understand the past in ways that advanced conversations about race and minority experiences into the historical mainstream.

The chapters in this volume are not presented in chronological order according to publication date. The material is organized thematically, with three general sections structuring the book: "War," "Race," and "Culture." The sections, however, are not mutually exclusive. The ideas and perspectives in the essays entwine and engage with each other. Race is deeply

14   *Introduction*

relevant to the work on international relations, while international dimensions inform much of my work on Asian American topics. These categories in turn inform my interest in culture. The chapters can be read separately or as connected efforts in exploring episodes in late nineteenth- and twentieth-century history.

The title of this volume, *War, Race, and Culture*, identifies the broad rubrics that connect the chapters. War, encompassing the drama, tragedy, and importance of geopolitical conflict that has fundamentally shaped East Asia–America relations, has long preoccupied me ever since my college days when I became active in protest against the war in Vietnam. This disquiet lies at the heart of the first book I published, *Friends and Enemies: The United States, China, and the Soviet Union, 1948–1972*, which studies the history of U.S. policy toward its perceived communist adversaries in the first decades of the Cold War and what has been called the "strategic triangle." In its approach to questions of war and peace and in its presentation, it was a rather conventional work, being the debut book of a young academic venturing into a long-established field. Discussion of the racial thinking of U.S. leaders as related to policy occupies only a few pages in the monograph, but the importance I placed on the connection of their racial attitudes to policy and decision-making was fundamental to the book's overall approach and upset former top officials. They wanted to keep such discreditable realities obscure and attacked my work.[13]

My concern with race and foreign relations is evident in Chapters 1 and 2, both of which consider U.S.-China policy at the presidential level. In Chapter 3, I examine the ways that global racial thinking in America has affected everyday contemporary Chinese Americans, as the relationship between the two global powers returns to Cold War patterns and even to American fears of the Yellow Peril as first seen in the nineteenth century. The terrible upsurge in anti-Asian violence during the Covid pandemic in the twenty-first century resembled earlier episodes in American history when Asians were targeted as antithetical to the physical health and domestic security of the nation.

Several of the essays in this volume further explore this critical dimension of racial thinking beyond America-China relations per se and complicate traditional diplomatic history approaches that do not go beyond reconstructions of the formal making of policy. One of the clearest expressions of my interest in race and war is found in Chapter 4, which uses the study of one brutal encounter in East Asia, the U.S. war against the

Kingdom of Korea in 1871, to consider the ways racial thinking was thoroughly imbricated in its conception, conduct, and received meaning. It encourages other scholars to think about the close relationship of race and war and to write about what is called "America in the world." These histories continue to speak to the ongoing U.S. war-making in the twenty-first century. Military conflict has become an indelible stain in the tapestry of the nation and an element in its core identity.[14]

My 2015 book, *Fateful Ties: A History of America's Preoccupation with China,* expanded the scope of my writing about America and China relations temporally and methodologically. It presents the "long view" of the America-China relationship, from colonial America to the recent past, and identifies enduring patterns of fascination, dread, curiosity, and ambition in American culture and thinking that have connected the two countries from the beginnings of America itself. The book argues that Americans, especially those I call those with "creative imaginations," have historically held peculiar sentiments about China and its connections to the imagined destiny of the "youngest empire," long before the phenomenal economic rise of the "oldest empire." For good or ill, many Americans today continue to see China as especially consequential for their future.

Chapter 5, which considers the complex history of the effort to exclude Chinese from the United States, establishes its important place in late nineteenth-century diplomacy and expansive American thinking about race and national development. A variety of factors, including economic ambitions and the complexity of passing exclusion legislation, continue to be questions of major importance in immigration studies.

Describing my work as being concerned with "ideology" would not be unfair, though a suggestion that it was epiphenomenal to the ways hard power has been wielded and geopolitics pursued would be deeply mistaken. Rather, I see what can be called mental dimensions, or mindsets, as imperative to consider alongside the functioning of the formal structures of power. Power cannot be separated from thought. Ideology, in turn, is embedded in social and historical structures, including assumptions about racial selves, enemies, and "others" that are held by those at the highest levels of politics. Another way to characterize the development of my work is to understand it as focusing on race to explicate racial thinking in a global way, as a history of an expansive empire with racial dimensions that interweave through the spheres customarily labeled "foreign" and "domestic."

16   *Introduction*

"Race" became an ineradicable part of my being ever since the explosions of black rebellion and protest in the 1960s awakened me to American racism at home and abroad. Those turbulent years when I was in college dramatized the realities of white supremacy and racial inequality in ways that the movements for justice and against state and social racial violence continue to remind us today. Our present requires that we go back and think about our past with greater sensitivity, if not awareness, about the pervasive place of what we call race in American life and government policy.

One writer who especially inspired me was W.E.B. Du Bois, the great scholar who maintained that race fundamentally shaped the totality of American life. Though Du Bois didn't elaborate on his famous early twentieth century declaration that the "color line" was a global problem, his words highlighted the deep importance of race in the world.[15] His insight was cogent then and remains so today. My perspective has been on Asian Americans, defined as those Americans whose ancestry lies in the huge sweep of Asia, historically defined. Race has been an inescapable part of their histories, with the chapters in this collection emphasizing the international dimensions of their experiences. Indeed, it can be argued that global conditions influenced the lives of Asian Americans in unique, even singular ways, especially in the ways that the violence of war and military experiences affect American life and society. Those profound overseas encounters are indelibly linked to the construction of racial ideas about Asians *within* the boundaries formally delineating the country. The past, seen in this way, necessarily challenges the approach of strictly distinguishing between the "foreign" and "domestic" in Asian American history.

Morning Glory, Evening Shadow: Yamato Ichihashi and His Internment Writings, 1942–1945 (1997), my second book, bridges the study of international relations and American ethnic history.[16] Ichihashi, one of the first professors of Japanese ancestry in the United States, received his bachelor's and master's degrees from Stanford in the early twentieth century. After completing his doctoral degree in political economy at Harvard, where he worked with Frederick Jackson Turner, he returned to Stanford and stayed for his entire career. His published scholarship examined pre–World War II U.S.-Japan relations as well as the lives of Japanese immigrants in America. Then in 1942, federal authorities required him to leave the quiet campus to languish in one of the ten desolate prison camps that incarcerated Japanese

Toward an Intellectual Memoir   17

Americans during the war. He eventually returned to campus intellectually depleted, personally exhausted, and his family ruined.

Ichihashi's scholarship that addressed international and domestic spheres of history and his career path eerily resonated with my own—even my departmental office is located near where his once was. His archive in Stanford Special Collections of largely unexplored personal papers composed during the war years provided me the opportunity, even the felt obligation, to recover his unique life experiences and contributions. By the 1990s, he had been largely forgotten, though a few historians referenced his scholarship when they wrote about the Asian American past. But his life was of singular importance, as he was among the most notable Japanese Americans of his generation and his private journals provide an unrivaled personal record of the wartime experience. Drawing substantially on Ichihashi's own words written during incarceration, my book is the only full, first-person account of those years in a prison camp. Examining Ichihashi's scholarship also helped establish the subfield of intellectual history within Asian American Studies. My effort, in drawing attention to his life, prompted the university to establish the Ichihashi Chair in Japanese History and Civilization, now described as the first endowed chair at Stanford because of the money that he helped bring to the University in 1919.[17]

The work on Ichihashi led me to study the histories of other Asian Americans in the war era and beyond and resulted in the work in Chapters 6 and 7, which consider the incarceration of Japanese Americans in the contexts of popular culture, politics, and social science-thinking about mass population control. In these essays, I seek to explicate the multiple ways that racial thinking was expressed in history and how ideas, even cultural expression, had profound social and political implications.

In Chapter 8, I focus on political thinking, pan-ethnic experiences, and race-making. I use the term "Asia America" to explore the ways that shared histories of experienced racism created commonalities among very different peoples whose ancestries lay in Asia. The term has always been awkwardly used, as it blurs ethnic distinctiveness. But the term has endured because of its utility in understanding the past, the present, and the continuing "functional reality" of identity in a country that maintains a highly confused and unsystematic understanding of race. As the notion has evolved, "Asia America" is simultaneously an imprecise designation for a collective social identity as well as a broad category comprising many distinct ethnicities.

18   *Introduction*

A focus on specifically recovering Chinese American history led me to a high point in my career. In the mid-1990s, I collaborated with the great scholar of Chinese American studies, Him Mark Lai, and Judy Yung, who was a San Francisco public librarian before she became an accomplished historian, to compile an annotated selection of primary writing by Chinese Americans about their lives in America. We met regularly over several years to share our understanding of the past, select meaningful writings, and produce a volume that would tell the story of Chinese Americans to a popular audience through the words of Chinese Americans themselves. *Chinese American Voices: From the Gold Rush to the Present* remains, as has been described, a "compelling volume that offers a panoramic perspective on the Chinese American experience and opens new vistas on American social, cultural, and political history."[18]

My interest in neglected histories of Asian Americans eventually guided me in 2012 to co-found, with Shelley Fisher Fishkin, along with the contributions of Hilton Obenzinger and Roland Hsu, a large-scale research project that aimed to recover the lived experiences of Chinese railroad workers who toiled to complete the western portion of the first transcontinental railroad in the late nineteenth century. Although it was one of the foundational episodes in Chinese American life, and in American western history generally, little was known of what I call the "Railroad Chinese" and their extraordinary work and sacrifices. One of the reasons for this neglect was the limited source materials from the Chinese themselves, but another was the general inattention, until relatively recently, given to marginalized and working people in American history. Material uncovered by the project came together in two path-breaking publications, my book *Ghosts of Gold Mountain: The Epic Story of the Chinese Who Built the Transcontinental* (2019) and a scholarly volume, *The Chinese and the Iron Road: Building the Transcontinental* (2019), co-edited with Shelley Fishkin. The two books contributed to awakening popular and academic understanding of the early Chinese who came to America and toiled to build the country's railway infrastructure in the West and beyond. The Chinese railroad workers project was the largest collaboration of scholarship on any topic in Asian American history, and the responses—public, academic, and even official—were gratifying. The prodigious efforts of more than one hundred scholars and researchers worldwide made Chapter 9 possible. It considers the history of Chinese railroad workers beyond the region or nation and in global perspective.[19]

Toward an Intellectual Memoir 19

Chapter 10 presents thoughts about history and social theory. It was published early in my career and was aimed at those who at the time were enamored by postmodernism, a radical intellectual skepticism that questioned truth claims. The postmodernists held that my views were an old-fashioned, even retrograde, approach to writing history. The essay's perspective, however, has largely passed the test of time with its insistence on historical substantiation, evidence, and the value of the historical enterprise. After all these years, it still largely describes my approach to history-writing.

The third section of this book, "Culture," contains writing inspired by my lifelong interest in art history, especially painting, and the now-emerging field of Asian American visual arts. I appreciate the arts as forming a central element in the human experience but also as a prism to understand minority lives and cultures, especially those populations who have lived under regimes of prejudice and restriction. My interest also originates from my own family's connection to the arts. Chapter 11, my introduction to the first book-length exploration of the history of Asian American art, provides an overview on this now-burgeoning field of study. *Asian American Art: A History, 1850–1970* (2008) was the product of an ambitious research project, founded in 2003 by Mark Johnson, Paul Karlstrom, Sharon Spain, and myself, to recover the then largely unknown history of artwork produced by persons of Asian descent in America. The project eventually involved a score of scholars and researchers and also led to a major art exhibition at the DeYoung Art Museum in San Francisco in 2008. The rich archive of our project resides in Stanford Special Collections.[20]

Chapter 12 considers my father's own art career, which complicates the categories of what constitutes formal Chinese and American art histories, and the ways the American public in his time encountered his artwork. It emerged from rich conversations sponsored by the Smithsonian Institution about the complexity of what was called East-West cultural interaction. Chapters 13 and 14 explore the work of two other very different Chinese American creative individuals. Dong Kingman was among the most successful and well-known artists of Chinese ancestry who worked in mid-twentieth-century America. Major Hollywood productions, including *The Sand Pebbles* and *Flower Drum Song*, projected his work in their film credits, and he became commercially successful in the art market. But his life, as discussed

20   *Introduction*

in the chapter, reveals the uncomfortable place that even prominent Chinese Americans occupied in those years.

"Happy Lim" was a very different sort of cultural worker. In the 1930s, he emerged as a leading Chinese American labor activist and self-taught writer in the socialist arts tradition. My life study of him and translations of several of his poems from Chinese provide unique insight into the lived experiences and personal sentiments of radical members of his generation in the early and mid-twentieth century. Asian American art and political activists today are very much his descendants. The last selection, Chapter 15, is a biographical essay about one of the earliest South Asian writers in the United States, Dhan Gopal Mukerji, who enjoyed a celebrated and peripatetic writing career in India and America but whose life ultimately resulted in tragedy. The chapter forms part of the reissuing of his long out-of-print classic, *Caste and Outcast*, first published in 1923. In this memoir, Mukerji reflects on his life growing up in India and his encounters with America after he came to the country. My collaboration with anthropology colleagues Purnima Mankekar and Akhil Gupta, who contributed their study to the reissue, exemplifies the value of interdisciplinary effort. Our work contributes to retrieving the history of early Asian American writers and artists, whose creativity and art production continue to be underappreciated in the history of modern American culture.

This volume of a wide-ranging array of essays, though historical in perspective, speaks to our twenty-first-century moment when relations between Asia and America are taking center stage in global geopolitics, culture, and economics. Americans fixate on the rise of China and its implications for the future of the global hegemonic position of the United States. So too are American political leaders across the political spectrum occupied about war dangers on the Korean Peninsula, the Taiwan Strait, and the vast, important region of Southeast Asia and its seas. Korean popular culture floods the country, along with a panoply of consumer goods from food to clothing. Japanese cars, technology, and cultural products abound, along with the ubiquity of *kanji* tattoos, among other visible expressions of the myriad influences of Asia on America. Asian immigration, from India, China, and beyond, into the United States occupies a central position in political debate and social change. The literal complexion of the country is transforming, to the deep discomfort of those who hold to a racialized, mythical American pageant.

Toward an Intellectual Memoir 21

Much has changed in global matters since the end of the Cold War, when several of the essays in this volume were first published. The economic and geopolitical rise of East and South Asia has continued unabated, but many of the issues in today's world continue to appear in the historical essays in this volume. The extreme, palpable fear of China seen in the height of the Cold War never disappeared and indeed has erupted again in American political discourse and culture. The complex position of the Asian immigrant in American life, welcomed as well as reviled, continues today. Asians almost overnight went from being celebrated as a putative "model minority" to becoming a popular public target for hate and violence. They never escaped the burden of being a perpetual foreigner in American life, despite their visible presence in the worlds of business, academia, professions, and even sports. Being eternally alien is part and parcel of the inheritance of American empire in Asia, where its people have been mortal, deadly enemies as well as uneasy allies in American expansionism. Consequential wars, "incursions," and threats of brutal conflict characterize the relationship from its earliest times. Asians in America inherit the racialized imperial experience and can become what I call "transposed enemies": the threat from without becomes the threat from within in the form of an "enemy race," an inassimilable migrant deluge, or an invasive medical peril within the borders of the country. The notion of the "transposed enemy" points to the experiential origin, and historical source, of being seen as eternally foreign, the social stigma which Asian Americans bear.

Racial identities over time have not lessened or blurred but have soared in relevance for everyday life. The involvement of Asian Americans, for example, in the cultural and artistic worlds of the country, in cinema, fine arts, literature, and music, has been remarkable despite their vexed position in the history of the country. Asian Americans are also increasingly engaged in politics, even at the highest levels in the country. At the same time, hate crimes against Asians and federal suspicion of Asian-ancestry scientists, engineers, and technical workers stubbornly persist. The position of Asian Americans in American life is as complex as ever.

The essays in this volume do not provide a seamless narrative of precedent and evolution to understand our present moment but offer glimpses into the multifarious, spasmodic, and uneven past in trans-Pacific relations and in Asian American history. They are products of a

22   *Introduction*

historian whose scholarship engaged the past as he watched the dynamic trans-Pacific and Asian American worlds rise in national and global import. These fields are as intriguing and inviting as ever. And more is to come.

An abiding commitment to explore the intersections of race, international relations, and American history will continue to guide my scholarship. The study of the past is a never-ending conversation and for me will always be inextricably connected to my aspirations of realizing a more humane world. Writing history is never far from my present. It is always proximate to my life journey to seek a more just and peaceful world.

PART I

War

ONE

JFK, China, and the Bomb

This essay, my first publication in an academic journal, appeared in the *Journal of American History* in 1988 as the recipient of that year's Louis Pelzer Memorial Award from the Organization of American Historians. Its content sparked heated controversy because several senior members of the Kennedy administration, most prominently McGeorge Bundy, took strong exception to the claim that the president, with his intense fear and animosity toward China, seriously explored conducting a preemptive strike against China to destroy its nuclear weapons facilities. The possibility of enlisting the Soviet Union in the attack was included in John F. Kennedy's approach to Premier Nikita Khrushchev. The article contributed to the developing reassessment of President Kennedy's reputation as a prudent chief executive.

My article was built on documentation that a former government official shared with me completely by chance over a lunch when we were both at the Lyndon B. Johnson Presidential Library. Control of classified documents, even high-level ones, was less strict in the 1980s, and my fellow researcher had retained copies of the sensitive material when he left his

"JFK, China, and the Bomb," *Journal of American History* 1988, 74, 4, 1287–1310, by permission of the Organization of American Historians. (Illustrations accompanying the original article are not included in this volume.)

26   *Chapter One*

Washington work even though they had not been formally declassified. When he shared them with me, I was astonished at what they revealed.

Further documentation that was declassified and then released after the publication of the article corroborated its findings on JFK. The article highlights the importance of appreciating racial thinking at the highest levels of American geopolitical thinking and policy.[1]

*

William F. Buckley, Jr.'s *National Review* started 1965 with a startling proposal: The United States should "destroy—destroy literally, physically—the present Chinese nuclear capability" to guarantee that China could not become a nuclear power "for a good many years ahead." The magazine's editorial "Should We Bomb Red China's Bomb?" advocated an American air strike against atomic installations in China to protect Asia and the United States. Such a "mission," according to "an unimpeachable, fully qualified source within our military command structure," would be entirely feasible from a "military-technological standpoint."[2]

The conservative journal contended that the interests of national security required radical action. China had exploded its first nuclear device just months before, in October 1964, and was expected to begin stockpiling weapons. Although the Chinese had no intercontinental missiles, *National Review* warned that China already had planes that could drop atomic bombs on all of Asia and that "even today a ship can carry a Chinese bomb into the harbors of New Orleans, San Francisco, New York or London." With such a frightening prospect before the nation, the United States could not sit passively "like a man who merely watches and waits while the guillotine is constructed to chop his head off." While the magazine's editors conceded the possibility that they had not addressed "every relevant doubt and question that may legitimately be raised" about the plan, they professed complete sincerity; they were convinced "that this proposal deserves serious discussion by serious men."[3]

Buckley probably presumed that only the political right wing had sufficient anticommunist mettle to advance a proposal of such audacity. His presumption was mistaken. As will be shown, the liberal president John F. Kennedy and his closest advisers, in their quest for a nuclear test ban, not only seriously discussed but also actively pursued the possibility of taking military action *with the Soviet Union* against China's nuclear installations at least a year and a half earlier.

From the start of Kennedy's administration, government researchers and officials devoted close attention to China's weapons development and concluded that China would soon join the nuclear club. In January 1961 the commander in chief of the United States forces in the Pacific advised Washington that China might explode an atomic device by the end of 1962 and construct a small arsenal of nuclear weapons by 1965. Such a prospect chilled the president, who, according to the recollection of Walt Whitman Rostow, believed that "the biggest event of the 1960s [might] well be the Chinese explosion of a nuclear weapon." Under Secretary of State Chester B. Bowles shared Kennedy's concern and in fall 1961 publicly warned that Communist China was "far more dangerous, in many ways, than even the [pro-Nationalist Chinese] Committee of One Million would have us think."[4]

Members of the Kennedy administration were also certain that the prospect of a nuclear China weighed heavily on the Soviets, whose own ideological and political differences with the Chinese had steadily widened since the late 1950s. The Soviets had torn up contracts and withdrawn thousands of their technicians from China in 1960 in retaliation for Communist Party of China (CPC) criticisms. Beijing, challenging the Kremlin's leadership of the international Communist movement, accused the Soviets of "revisionism" and capitulation to American imperialism. On February 11, 1961, soon after taking office, President Kennedy, met with Vice President Lyndon B. Johnson, Secretary of State Dean Rusk, Ambassador W. Averell Harriman, Ambassador to the Soviet Union Llewellyn E. Thompson, former ambassadors Charles E. Bohlen and George F. Kennan, and Special Assistant for National Security Affairs McGeorge Bundy in the White House to review the "thinking of the Soviet leadership." Kennedy already knew that Harriman, who had sent the president-elect reports of his conversations with Soviet leaders about their differences with Beijing, was deeply interested in having the United States exploit Sino-Soviet tensions. Kennan, too, wanted to take advantage of Sino-Soviet discord. "The main target of our diplomacy," wrote Kennan to then Senator Kennedy in August 1960, "should be to heighten the divisive tendencies within the Soviet bloc. The best means to do this lies in the improvement in our relations with Moscow." That trend of thought shaped the entire February 11 White House meeting. Discussing

28   *Chapter One*

Soviet attitudes on foreign affairs, the men speculated that Nikita Khrushchev might be eager for some diplomatic success with the West, perhaps on arms control. "Soviet interest in this area appears real." They also concluded that in addition to the United States, Germany and China represented "the great long-run worries of the Soviet Union." "These are the countries whose relation to the atomic problem seems an important one to the Soviet Union, and indeed effective restraint of the Chinese Communists is a continuing task of the Soviet government." The participants discussed the merits of an early meeting between Kennedy and Khrushchev, which soon was scheduled for June at Vienna. The acute interest in the Sino-Soviet division that the administration exhibited in private contrasted sharply with its public inattention to the subject.[5]

During the preparations for the Vienna summit, Kennedy's advisers recommended that the president exploit Sino-Soviet tensions and seek a common understanding with Khrushchev about China, including the need to prevent it from becoming a nuclear power. By emphasizing the Chinese threat to both Washington and Moscow, it was suggested, Kennedy might gain Soviet agreement to restrain Chinese aggressiveness and encourage a condominium of interests in what was called a "stable viable world order" dominated by the two superpowers. Kennedy's advisers suggested that the president inform Khrushchev that "so long as Peiping adheres to a doctrine of 'unremitting struggle' against the United States and our allies, we will have no recourse but to maintain our systems of individual and collective security arrangements." Thus, if the Soviet Union "sincerely desires peace throughout the world, it should urge Communist China to renounce the use of force in the conduct of its foreign relations." The president should stress that "it is neither in the interests of the USSR nor of the United States to allow Communist China to pursue policies which risk touching off a general war." The president should take the initiative in calling for a halt to nuclear proliferation. "Does the USSR really believe that the chances of avoiding a nuclear war will not be lessened after [Communist China] becomes a nuclear power? Can the USSR safely conclude that its espousal of the policies of a militant, expansionist [China] is fully consistent with Soviet national interests?" Kennedy's advisers were already convinced that the Soviet Union's fear of a nuclear China helped explain its interest in arms control, but they wanted to elicit the Soviet leader's ideas on what actually could be done about Beijing's nuclear development. Other background papers for the Vienna meeting speculated that the Soviet Union might want to utilize a nuclear nonproliferation treaty to frustrate the Chinese atomic program.[6]

But Khrushchev's behavior at Vienna disappointed and disturbed Kennedy. The atmosphere was grim throughout the meetings. The two men sparred over practically every issue, including China, with Khrushchev unwavering in his support for China's recovery of both its United Nations (UN) seat and Taiwan. The Soviet leader failed to lunge for the "China bait" when Kennedy invoked the specter of an expanded nuclear community. At one point in the meetings, Kennedy cited the Chinese proverb that a long journey begins with a single step and tried to persuade the Soviets to take that step toward an arms agreement with the United States. But Khrushchev rebuffed the president and quipped that Kennedy seemed to know the Chinese well but that he, too, knew them well. Kennedy, in turn, needled Khrushchev, saying that the Soviets might get to know the Chinese "even better." Khrushchev ended the verbal duel by saying that he was already quite familiar with them.[7]

Kennedy discovered at Vienna that, although the Soviets were sensitive about China's growing power, they were not yet ready to reject their former partner and enter into a marriage of convenience with the United States. Khrushchev evidently did not want to lend further credence to the charge that he was conciliating imperialism. As some of Kennedy's advisers had observed, Moscow's behavior was ambivalent: Khrushchev wanted to pursue détente with the United States but could not appear overeager for fear of validating Chinese accusations that he was "soft" on the United States. Sections of the international Communist movement were already leaning toward Beijing in the internecine dispute. Bohlen, Kennedy's close adviser on the Soviet Union, had warned before the Vienna meeting that Khrushchev might act more "Bolshevik" to avoid being outflanked by the Chinese from the left.[8]

Kennedy, however, was undeterred by the lack of substantive progress in American-Soviet relations at Vienna and continued to seek a modus vivendi with Khrushchev to prevent the spread of nuclear weapons. The president's concern about Beijing, in particular, mounted. He gloomily told *New York Times* columnist Arthur Krock in October 1961 that the "domino theory" had lost its validity: China was bound to develop an atomic bomb, and when it did, all of Southeast Asia would fall to the Chinese Communists.

30   *Chapter One*

In January 1962 Kennedy directed the National Security Council (NSC) to confront and resolve the "special unsolved problem" of a China with nuclear weapons and its effect "on our dispositions in Southeast Asia."[9]

Kennedy was not resigned to watching Beijing assemble its nuclear capability and decided to devote more of his own attention to achieving a nuclear test ban treaty with the Soviet Union. This was a significant change in attitude for Kennedy, since he had not been serious about a test ban during the first year and a half of his administration – his interest in disarmament, according to Theodore C. Sorensen, had been limited mainly to its "propaganda" effect on world public opinion.[10] But during the late summer of 1962, months before the Cuban missile crisis, Kennedy's growing consternation about China's atomic program stimulated his search for a test ban, which he hoped might somehow prevent the Chinese from developing their atomic weapons. What the administration thought the negotiation of a test ban treaty could do to achieve such an end took clearer form in the months ahead.

A ban on nuclear weapons tests was not a new idea. During the last years of the Eisenhower administration, Washington had sought understandings with Moscow about ending nuclear testing, and in mid-1958, the United States, the Soviet Union, and the United Kingdom, the three nuclear powers at the time, agreed to a moratorium on all testing. But the downing of a United States U-2 spy plane over the Soviet Union in May 1960 scuttled prospects for a formal agreement, and negotiations at a trilateral Geneva Conference on the Discontinuance of Nuclear Weapons Tests bogged down in recriminations. Conflicts over technical issues, such as methods of detecting clandestine testing, obscured the contention and the underlying political suspicions. Discussions with the Russians after Kennedy assumed office also made little headway. Neither side found compelling reasons— even the threat of China—to override the perceived disadvantages of a formal treaty forbidding testing. The trilateral meetings in Geneva collapsed in January 1962.[11]

In mid-1962, however, Kennedy ordered a review of the western position on nuclear testing and the drafting of new treaty proposals. Several factors have been advanced as explanations of Kennedy's heightened interest in negotiations: the pressure of adverse world opinion following the Soviet resumption of atmospheric testing in 1961 (followed by the American resumption in 1962), a changing American strategic doctrine that deemphasized nuclear weaponry, and technological breakthroughs in the detection of distant underground nuclear explosions. But excerpts from the private journal of Glenn T. Seaborg, head of the Atomic Energy Commission (AEC) under Kennedy, provide some new insights. His notes of a series of meetings Kennedy held with his top arms control and national security advisers at the end of July and early August 1962 reveal that the administration was profoundly dismayed about the imminent acquisition of nuclear weapons by China and other countries. Assistant Secretary of Defense Paul Nitze, in a meeting with the president and his top advisers on July 30, 1962, presented a report commissioned by Kennedy on the potential spread of nuclear weapons in the absence of a comprehensive test ban treaty. Nitze said that a "test ban would be a necessary, but not a sufficient, condition for inhibiting this proliferation, and that to prevent it would require collaboration by the U.S. and USSR." Soon afterwards, Washington presented two major new draft test ban treaties to the Soviets at a newly established Eighteen-Nation Disarmament Committee at Geneva.[12]

The first treaty, presented by United States Ambassador Arthur H. Dean on August 27, called for a comprehensive ban. The outlook for the proposal was not bright as the administration expected the Soviets to reject the provisions for installation of monitoring stations and inspections to detect violations. The Soviets argued that a verification system was unnecessary and would be used for espionage purposes. Dean said he knew, even before he presented the two treaties, that the Soviets would reject any plan requiring on-site inspections. But the second, backup treaty seemed more promising. It proposed a partial test ban, which would outlaw testing only in the atmosphere, in outer space, and under water, and sidestep the sticky problem of underground explosions. That too was turned down by the Soviets. However, the rejected draft was virtually identical to the Limited Test Ban Treaty, which the Soviets did agree to less than one year later. Moscow's change of mind was inseparable from its own widening rupture with Beijing.[13]

Even though the Soviets rejected both August 1962 treaties, saying they gave unfair advantages to the United States, Kennedy remained convinced that a test ban agreement might help end nuclear proliferation. He thought that if the four existing nuclear powers—the United States, the Soviet Union, Great Britain, and France, which had exploded its first atomic

32   *Chapter One*

device in February 1960—could all agree on a test ban, they could pressure other countries to follow suit and sign. The result would be the end of nuclear proliferation since, the thinking went, no additional country could develop a bomb without testing. The nuclear powers would also conveniently retain their monopoly.

The Cuban missile crisis in October 1962 seemed further to impress both Kennedy and Khrushchev with the importance of arms control and reduction of tensions. Following the showdown, the two leaders drew closer to one another, while Sino-Soviet relations continued to deteriorate. China accused Khrushchev of recklessness in installing the missiles in the first place and of weakness in withdrawing them when confronted by the United States. As the Central Intelligence Agency (CIA) reported in January 1963, Sino-Soviet relations had reached a "new crisis." Ideological and national differences had become so fundamental, the report argued, "for most practical purposes, a 'split' has already occurred. . . . the USSR and China are now two separate powers whose interests conflict on almost every major issue." According to the CIA, that development would "obviously have many important advantages for the West," although a separate "Asian Communist Bloc" under Beijing could have grave implications for the United States in the Far East.[14]

The CIA report made an additional observation, which must have caught the eye of any reader on the American side who was contemplating a possible military clash with China. The CIA believed that the Sino-Soviet breach would continue to widen and that, although the "public military alliance between the two countries probably would not be openly repudiated," this was "not really a key question." "Already, neither side can consider treaty obligations as an important element in future calculations; each recognizes that, in crises which raise the possibility of nuclear war, for example in the Taiwan Strait, neither can expect its 'ally' to expose itself to major military risks unless the 'ally' itself feels its vital interests to be threatened." The CIA report concluded that in all matters "short of survival," "China and the USSR will increasingly view each other as hostile rivals and competing powers."[15]

Other problems, however, complicated agreement between the United States and the Soviet Union on a test ban. One was the position of France. Its entry into the nuclear club and its adamant refusal to limit its program had confounded Kennedy, as it appeared that only if he could bring the

French to subscribe to a test ban would the Soviets be willing to exert pressure on the Chinese. The Soviet Union also seemed unlikely to accede to a test ban unless Great Britain and France, regardless of their avowed independence from the United States, did so.

In early January 1963, Kennedy tried to send a message to President Charles de Gaulle of France through Minister of Culture André Malraux, who was visiting the United States to present the *Mona Lisa* for exhibition. Hoping to convince the French government to join arms talks, Kennedy drew a terrifying picture of a world imperiled by a China armed with atomic weapons. Over dinner in the White House with Malraux, as William R. Tyler, assistant secretary of state for European affairs, recalled, Kennedy stressed that a nuclear China would be the "great menace in the future to humanity, the free world, and freedom on earth." Revealing his own alarm and racial bias, Kennedy claimed that the Chinese "would be perfectly prepared to sacrifice hundreds of millions of their own lives" to carry out their "aggressive and militant policies." De Gaulle and other European leaders had to realize that the differences within the western alliance paled in the face of such a threat. Kennedy, recalled Tyler, believed that the Chinese attached a "lower value" to human life.[16]

William C. Foster, the head of the Arms Control and Disarmament Agency (ACDA) under Kennedy, later recalled that Kennedy was certain that the United States had to do "something about ostracizing or containing China. He felt that somehow there must be a way in which the rest of the world can prevent China from becoming a [nuclear threat]." Preventing China from acquiring the bomb loomed in Kennedy's thoughts about a test ban, as his remarks to his closest advisers revealed. At a NSC meeting on January 22, 1963, Kennedy emphasized that "the test ban treaty is important for one reason. Chicom [Chinese Communists]." The declassified notes of Roger Hilsman, director of the State Department's Intelligence Bureau, indicate that Kennedy observed, "If the Soviets want this and if it can help in keeping the Chinese Communists from getting a full nuclear capacity, then it is worth it. Can't foresee what the world would be like with this. Chinese Communists are a grave danger. Ban is good if it does prevent them from becoming a nuclear power. Can't afford to let them do this. Important if it has potential affect on Chicoms."[17]

Two weeks later on February 8, Kennedy reiterated this theme to his top arms control officials—Johnson, Rusk, Bundy, Seaborg of the AEC, Foster

34   *Chapter One*

of ACDA, and Secretary of Defense Robert S. McNamara. Kennedy asserted that "the principal reason" for seeking a treaty was its possible effect in preventing the spread of nuclear weapons to other countries, "particularly China." If it were not for that possible gain, the treaty would not be worth the struggle with Congress and the political disruption. To press his point, Kennedy said that he would even accept some cheating by the Soviets on a comprehensive test ban if the Chinese could be denied the bomb.[18]

But how would a test ban stop the Chinese from developing a nuclear capacity if Beijing refused to sign a treaty? Seaborg recalls that he was never clear how this would happen, and conservative members of Congress who were closely monitoring the test ban negotiations also wondered. Foster confronted the problem in May 1963 during his testimony before the Senate Preparedness Investigating Subcommittee (popularly known as the Stennis Committee after its chairman, Sen. John Stennis), which questioned the value of a test ban. Foster argued that a treaty would slow the arms race, help maintain United States military superiority by stopping the testing needed to improve Soviet weaponry, reduce nuclear fallout, and end nuclear proliferation. Foster admitted that the administration had "no illusions that China would sign a test ban treaty in the near future. Its leaders have made it clear that they have no such intentions." He then posed the obvious question: Why did the administration think a treaty would have any effect on China? Foster suggested that a test ban would give added force to the Soviets, whose policy had been to frustrate the Chinese nuclear program. If there was a treaty, the Chinese could not point to American or Soviet testing to justify their own program. The Soviet Union and other countries trading with China might also exert more economic and political pressures on Beijing. In any event, Foster added a not insignificant consideration: "The treaty would have a divisive effect on Sino-Soviet relations." The senators remained unconvinced by Foster's vague contention that seemed to rely largely on trusting the Soviets to turn on their erstwhile ally. To many in the Senate who were unsure about the nature and depth of the Sino-Soviet division, Foster must have appeared wishful, at best. If the Soviets were so interested in stopping China's nuclear program, they wondered, why were they stalling on the test ban negotiations?[19]

Progress toward a test ban, in fact, was slow during the spring of 1963. Kennedy had no success with de Gaulle, and the American press focused on the differences between the United States and the Soviet Union over methods of detecting violations of a test ban. But the real block to an agreement was Soviet leaders' preoccupation with the worsening conflict with Beijing. The Soviets hestitated to reach an accommodation with the West until they resolved what to do about their eastern flank.

The Chinese, in increasingly shrill terms, charged Khrushchev with abandoning communism in exchange for improved relations with United States imperialism. Throughout the first months of 1963, the Communist Party of China openly polemicized with many of the major communist parties of the world, including those in France, Italy, and the United States, that had been especially supportive of Moscow's views. To undercut the Chinese, Khrushchev temporarily hardened his position toward Washington and tried to rally as much of the international Communist movement as possible against the CPC. Foy Kohler, the United States ambassador to the Soviet Union, described the chill in American-Soviet relations in a long telegram in March 1963. He predicted that there would be no progress on the test ban, Germany, and other outstanding matters until the Soviet leadership "decides how to deal with Chicoms and starts to do so." Open hostilities between Moscow and Beijing already seemed a distinct possibility. United States intelligence agencies reported extensive troop movements along the Soviet-Chinese border and military clashes between the two sides.[20]

But as late as May 22, President Kennedy still publicly admitted that he had seen no interest on the part of the Soviets in a test ban treaty. Their position had remained unchanged for five months, he lamented, and the prospects were not bright. He was afraid the nuclear "genie," in his words, might soon escape from the bottle. Secretary of State Rusk expressed similar pessimism the following week at his press conference.[21]

Then suddenly it appeared that the volatile Khrushchev had made up his mind to shift direction. On June 7 Khrushchev accepted a secret proposal from Kennedy and British prime minister Harold Macmillan for a high-level tripartite conference on a test ban treaty. Kennedy quickly followed with his American University speech on June 10 in which he revealed the Khrushchev communication and reemphasized the urgent need for U.S.-Soviet cooperation in reducing tensions in the world. The Soviets responded glowingly to Kennedy's conciliatory address, disseminating it in its entirety on the Soviet media. American intelligence experts wondered if Khrushchev's *volte-face* was aimed at using the test ban negotiations as a lever or even as an implied threat against the Chinese.[22]

36   Chapter One

In contrast to Kennedy's overture to the Soviets was the letter that the Chinese delivered on June 14, just four days after the American University speech, to a meeting of the Central Committee of the Communist party of the Soviet Union. The communication detailed comprehensive, fundamental differences dividing the two parties. The tone and content of the letter virtually foreclosed any possibility that a high-level bilateral party meeting scheduled to begin on July 5 would be able to close the rift. A study conducted by the American embassy in Moscow after the Limited Test Ban Treaty had been signed in August concluded that "it was the outbreak of virtually undeclared war between Moscow and Peiping [in the] spring which explained Soviet acceptance of a partial test ban agreement which it could have had at any time during the past year."[23]

The Sino-Soviet split was a mixed blessing for Kennedy. He, of course, welcomed the splintering of the Communist world. Ever since the Chinese Revolution of 1949, Washington had longed for such a development. But now, even if the Soviets themselves would agree to a treaty, it was highly unlikely that they could pressure the Chinese to sign, as Foster had tried to convince Congress they would. The two countries were simply too distant from one another. In late June Kennedy himself told Chancellor Konrad Adenauer of West Germany that Khrushchev had a real problem with the Chinese and no way to bring them into a test ban.[24] Members of the Kennedy administration could have asked an ironic question: Where was the "Sino-Soviet bloc" now that it was "needed" by the United States?

The president gave few public hints of how he would resolve his quandary, but at a press conference in Bonn, West Germany, on June 24, he dropped a vague threat. In response to a question asking how the proposed test ban treaty would prevent China or others from gaining the bomb, Kennedy pointed out that one provision might be that signatories would "use all the influence that they had in their possession to persuade others not to grasp the nuclear nettle." Kennedy quickly added, "quite obviously" countries seeking the bomb "may not accept this persuasion and then, as I say, they will get the false security which goes with nuclear diffusion." Was Kennedy implying that the acquisition of a nuclear capability did not lessen, but instead heightened, the threat to a nation's well-being and invited possible retaliation from other powers?[25]

The president selected the veteran diplomat and Soviet expert W. Averell Harriman as the representative of the United States at the tripartite Moscow meeting. Harriman had closely followed the Sino-Soviet split for years and was convinced that it was genuine and profound. Harriman confided to the Danish ambassador on July 1 that "Khrushchev's main preoccupation is with the Chinese." "There has never been close confidence between Moscow and Peiping," he said. In preparing for the Moscow meeting, Kennedy and his people were buoyed by Khrushchev's surprise announcement on July 2 that he was ready to accept a limited test ban treaty if a nonaggression pact between the North Atlantic Treaty Organization (NATO) and the Warsaw Pact nations was also signed at the same time. Still, the administration remained outwardly cautious, for there was always the possibility that the Soviets might sacrifice an East-West accord for a resolution of the Sino-Soviet dispute.[26]

As the date for the Moscow conference approached, the administration busily formulated its position. Invariably, the recommendations called for Harriman to approach the Soviets to see if they would cooperate in taking action against the Chinese nuclear program. Using phrases such as "removing the potential capability" or "action to deny the Chicoms a nuclear capability," advisers in the administration made clear they were willing to go far to stop China's nuclear development, although Harriman doubted that Khrushchev would want to talk with him about China. According to Arthur M. Schlesinger, Jr.'s cryptic later description, Kennedy nonetheless told Harriman as he left for Moscow that he "could go as far as he wished in exploring the possibility of a Soviet-American understanding with regard to China." What Schlesinger only dared to hint, declassified documents begin to reveal.[27]

On July 14 Soviet Deputy Foreign Minister Valerian Zorin warmly welcomed Harriman and his delegation to Moscow. The Soviets gave the British team, headed by Lord Hailsham (Quentin Hogg), an equally hospitable reception. In contrast, the front page of the day's *Pravda* prominently displayed a Soviet party letter blasting the Chinese Communists. That publicity boosted the hopes of United States officials for a successful outcome of the talks, according to American newspaper reports. Harriman publicly declared that he would be prepared to discuss any matter that Khrushchev might raise. The next day Khrushchev himself opened the negotiations. In a mood described by the press as "relaxed and jovial," he bantered with the United States and British delegations for three and a half hours about the test ban and related matters, including China. Across town the Chinese

38   *Chapter One*

and Soviet party showdown remained under a cloud. Deng Xiaoping, the general secretary of the CPC and leader of Chinese delegation, was making no progress in resolving the differences with the Soviets and the Soviet press virtually ignored the party conference. The *People's Daily* of Beijing charged that Kennedy's strategy was one of "wooing the Soviet Union, opposing China, and poisoning Sino-Soviet relations." Moscow, according to Beijing, was falling into Washington's trap.[28]

Kennedy personally monitored the discussions in Moscow and required unusual precautions to ensure complete secrecy in the communications between Washington and Harriman. Restricting the customary wide circulation of cable traffic during a negotiation, Kennedy arranged that only six top officials outside the White House read the messages from Moscow. Only Rusk, Thompson, Foster, McNamara, Under Secretary of State George Ball, and John McCone, the director of the CIA, were permitted to read the cables on a hand-delivered, "for-your-eyes-only" basis. All messages from Washington to the American delegation in Moscow were cleared through the president. Kennedy followed the negotiations with "a devouring interest," according to Assistant Secretary of State Benjamin H. Read, who was responsible for communications during the Moscow talks.[29]

The opening session in Moscow greatly encouraged Harriman, and he immediately reported the good news to the president. Kennedy, revealing his preoccupation with the Chinese, responded to Harriman the same evening. Kennedy was determined to use the test ban talks to find a way to stop China's development of nuclear weapons. On July 15 he gave Read a provocative directive for Harriman, which the president himself had drafted in longhand. The cable read, in part:

> I remain convinced that Chinese problem is more serious than Khrushchev comments in first meeting suggest, and believe you should press question in private meeting with him. I agree that large stockpiles are characteristic of US and USSR only, but consider that relatively small forces in hands of people like CHICOMS could be very dangerous to us all. Further believe even limited test ban can and should be means to limit diffusion. *You should try to elicit Khrushchev's view of means of limiting or preventing Chinese nuclear development and his willingness either to take Soviet action or to accept US action aimed in this direction.*[30]

Kennedy did not spell out exactly what kind of Soviet or American "action" he had in mind, but it is clear that he was suggesting more than political methods. He knew that the Soviet ability to persuade China to abandon development of the bomb was negligible. As he had dejectedly confessed to Adenauer in late June, the Soviets had no way of bringing China into a test ban.[31]

Could the Soviets coerce the Chinese into abandoning their quest for the bomb? That, too, was unlikely since Moscow had little remaining leverage to use against Beijing. Moscow, top administration officials were almost certain, had ended its assistance to China's atomic program as early as 1960 or 1961. By 1963 China's effort was wholly independent. And whatever economic and political weapons the Soviets might have had, they had largely been expended in the futile counterattack against the Chinese ideological offensive. The Soviet attempt at economic coercion had failed to bring Beijing into line in 1960, trade between China and the Soviet bloc had fallen precipitously, and the recent effort to isolate Beijing in the international Communist movement had not intimidated the Chinese Communists. If anything, Beijing had become more antagonistic to the Soviets.[32]

The United States possessed even fewer means to influence China. Trade and normal diplomatic relations between the two countries did not exist. And in any case, China's economy was autarkic—even world economic sanctions against Beijing would hardly have been decisive. China's leaders had invested so much material and political capital in the nuclear program that it was unlikely they would surrender to external pressures. Unless there was a total prohibition of nuclear weapons throughout the world, Beijing had announced, it would reject a test ban treaty and continue to develop its own capability in order to break the atomic monopoly.[33] With the Chinese on the verge of exploding an atomic device, Kennedy must have understood that only force, only military "action," would have any chance of "preventing" China from becoming the fifth nuclear power in the world.

The option of taking military action to stop the proliferation of nuclear weapons had, in fact, been discussed in the administration for months before the Moscow meeting. In February 1963, Secretary of Defense McNamara drafted a memorandum for Kennedy on the prospects and implications of the "diffusion of nuclear weapons." He concluded that the spread of nuclear weapons was "clearly not in the interest of the US." While he thought that a test ban would help slow proliferation, a more important

40   *Chapter One*

factor would be "the pressures the US, the USSR and others are willing to employ in restraining others from testing." "The cooperation that may develop between the US and USSR, as a result, has a potential importance," McNamara wrote. "In some cases, we, and others, would probably have to employ stronger incentives and sanctions than has seriously been considered so far. However, a comprehensive test ban would make it more likely that stronger steps could be taken and would be effective." McNamara listed the "sharing of weapons information" with countries such as France or Israel as an example of "positive incentives" and mentioned "penalties (economic or military)" for use against uncooperative states.[34]

More explicit were the "top secret" briefing books prepared just before the July Moscow meeting. Although much is still classified, including a section labelled "Military and Other Sanctions Against Communist China," one paper discussed at length possible Soviet responses to a United States proposal "to take radical steps, in cooperation with the USSR, to prevent the further proliferation of nuclear capabilities." The paper reviewed the principal factors that would influence Soviet acceptance of a "joint program" with the United States, including the national security of the Soviet Union, the concept of United States–Soviet Union partnership in the world, and the impact on the Communist world. With regard to China, the paper indicated that if the Soviets accepted the American proposal, they would understand that "they would be obliged to see it through to the very end," which might require "Soviet, or possibly joint US-USSR, use of military force" against China. The ramifications of using "military force against a Communist nation" on the position of the Soviet Union as "leader of the Communist world" would "assume significant, perhaps overriding, weight in determining whether or not to accept the US proposal." The paper did not speculate as to what the Soviet decision might be.[35]

What kind of military force the administration may have contemplated is not made explicit in the documents that have been declassified so far. But the most likely option was an air strike on China's facilities, which were located far in the western part of the country. According to one former high-level official in the Kennedy administration, a joint American-Soviet preemptive nuclear attack was actually discussed. One idea was to have a Soviet and an American bomber fly over the facilities at Lop Nor, with each dropping a bomb, only one of which would be set to go off. The official, who wished to remain unidentified, maintains that the idea did not get to the planning stage. However, in 1973 Joseph Alsop reported that the Kremlin had been well aware of Kennedy's interest in collaborating in an attack to destroy China's nuclear program. Alsop did not reveal how the Soviets learned such information.[36]

In Moscow, the test ban talks proceeded swiftly. General agreement on a limited treaty was reached within the first two days, although Foreign Minister Andrei Gromyko, who represented the Soviet side, continued to press for a nonaggression pact. By July 18, Secretary of State Rusk instructed the United States ambassador to West Germany to inform the Bonn government that a three-environment test ban "is likely to be agreed upon" and that no commitment to a "nonaggression arrangement" would be made without consultation. On July 20 the United States, the Soviet Union, and Great Britain announced that they had tentatively concluded an agreement on a limited test ban treaty, exempting undergound testing. It was not linked to any other agreement. That same day Beijing's *People's Daily* condemned the Moscow talks with a statement by Chairman Mao Zedong exhorting the people of the world to defy nuclear blackmail. The Chinese denounced the test ban treaty as a fraud aimed at maintaining American nuclear superiority and at preventing China from acquiring its own capability. Deng Xiaoping's delegation left Moscow the same evening, ending the obviously unsuccessful party summit. In a rare move, the entire top leadership of the CPC came out to give Deng a hero's welcome at the Beijing airport. In a slap back at China, the Soviet Communist party accused Beijing of wanting to "build Communism on corpses."[37]

Since Gromyko handled the negotiations for the Soviets while Khrushchev was busy with visiting Premier János Kádár of Hungary, Harriman did not have a chance to talk with the Soviet leader for several days. But Washington did not give up hope that something could be done with the Russians about the Chinese. Harriman believed that the Soviets wanted the treaty "to obtain leverage on Peking," but he doubted that the Soviets would entertain more radical solutions. On July 23 he cabled Washington that while it had become "crystal clear" the Soviets wanted to isolate China in the world, Khrushchev wanted the "pressure to appear to come on Chicoms from other countries, particularly the underdeveloped," rather than from Moscow. Another Harriman message later in the day reiterated that Khrushchev and Gromyko "have clearly shown that their way of

42   *Chapter One*

getting nondissemination is through adherence of maximum number of states to test ban treaty, thus isolating and bringing pressure on Chicoms."[38]

Kennedy was still not satisfied. That night he again pressed Harriman to raise the China issue with Khrushchev. The president, the directive read, "still hopes very much you will find an opportunity for private discussion with Khrushchev on China." When Harriman finally succeeded in cornering Khrushchev, he did raise the subject of China's acquisition of nuclear weapons and asked the Soviet leader what he would do if Chinese missiles were targeted at Russia. But Khrushchev did not respond. It is not clear whether Harriman actually presented Kennedy's proposal for joint action against China, but Khrushchev was evidently not yet ready to take action with Washington.[39]

Kennedy must have been sorely disappointed at the failure to gain Khrushchev's cooperation in stopping China's nuclear development, and the president could not resist taking some public swipes at the Chinese. In his announcement of the test ban treaty to the American people, Kennedy referred to China several times, even quoting from one of Khrushchev's diatribes against Beijing the gibe that the Chinese Communists "would envy the dead" in the event of a nuclear war. In one last deliberate affront, Kennedy concluded his address with the Chinese proverb that "a journey of 1,000 miles must begin with a single step."[40]

William Buckley's *National Review* condemned the Moscow treaty as a "diplomatic Pearl Harbor for America."[41] But the magazine had it wrong: the treaty could have been the avenue for a surprise attack on China. Would Washington now accept the inevitability of China's acquiring the bomb, even though one of Kennedy's principal reasons in seeking the test ban had been to frustrate China's nuclear program? Apparently not. As Rusk had informed the United States ambassador to West Germany just after agreement had been reached on a ban, wide acceptance of the treaty would place "powerful pressures on Peiping not to go down the nuclear path." But if China persisted, Rusk stated, "other action might have to be taken to prevent this."[42]

Khrushchev's own attitude remained one principal consideration in deciding what might be done. At the July meetings in Moscow, he had not been receptive to the suggestion of taking action against China, but he could always change his mind. Administration officials believed that was a real possibility, depending on the course of the Sino-Soviet split. As Rusk testified in executive session before the Senate Foreign Relations Committee, which was reviewing the treaty, the Sino-Soviet split was "getting wider and deeper."[43] The test ban treaty and subsequent amicable United States-Soviet relations could so aggravate the division in the Communist world that a variety of advantageous possibilities might develop for Washington. The prospect appeared sufficiently plausible and attractive that it helped win the military's endorsement of the negotiated treaty.

In June, during preparations for Harriman's trip to Moscow, top military personnel who testified before executive sessions of the Stennis Committee questioned the wisdom of a test ban treaty. Gen. Curtis E. LeMay, air force chief of staff, doubted a treaty would stop the spread of nuclear weapons, particularly to China. Responding to a question about common American-Soviet interests in opposing China, LeMay discounted the possibility of reaching agreements and argued that at some point the Soviet Union might actually provide China with nuclear weapons. As late as two days before Harriman left for Moscow, at a White House meeting with the president, the chairman of the Joint Chiefs of Staff OCS), Gen. Maxwell D. Taylor, questioned even a limited test ban treaty. The JCS wanted further study as to whether an atmospheric test ban was in American interests, but Kennedy rebuffed Taylor.[44]

In contrast, during the August Senate hearings on ratification of the treaty, the JCS rallied behind the Moscow agreement, endorsing it as in the national interest. Following the Moscow meeting, Kennedy, Rusk, and others had met repeatedly with JCS members to report on the Moscow events and current Soviet attitudes. The administration, in addition to using promises of weapons procurements to calm the military, also convinced them of the *political* desirability of the treaty. General Taylor admitted that, although the treaty contained certain military disadvantages, it also represented "major political achievements" having "important and favorable military implications." Taylor vaguely listed restraining nuclear proliferation and reducing causes of world tension as positive aspects. But General LeMay, with his characteristic bluntness, better clarified what the "political advantages" were. He said he had spoken with Rusk and Harriman "at great length." They had pointed out that the United States would reap the largest advantage "if we could really divide the Chinese and Russians." Although he was less optimistic about achieving such division than they, LeMay agreed that if it occurred, it would be significant, and he was

44   *Chapter One*

clearly more persuaded of the possibility of a Sino-Soviet split than before the Moscow meeting. Gen. Earle G. Wheeler, chief of staff of the army, and Adm. David L. McDonald, chief of naval operations, expressed similar points of view. Wheeler observed that it was "always a sound military principle to divide your enemies if you can, or to contribute to any division that there may be between them." If the United States could do so, "this is a solid military advantage." He added that the Soviets would not like to see the replacement of the Communists in China, but Khrushchev "would enjoy seeing the Chinese Communists get a bloody nose." What kind of punch Wheeler envisioned, he kept to himself.[45]

The Limited Test Ban Treaty sparked an explosion, exactly as the administration wanted: It split the Sino-Soviet rift wide open. Through the rest of 1963 and into 1964 the Soviet and Chinese Communist parties exchanged the most strident polemics in the history of the international Communist movement. American officials closely watched the unfolding battle and nervously monitored the development of China's nuclear program. Yet Washington, worried that a United States strike against China might still reunite the two Communist giants, hesitated to take unilateral action against Beijing. The United States continued its strategy of playing toward the Soviets and waiting for Khrushchev to change his mind about possible joint action against China.

On September 15, 1964, shortly before China's first atomic test (which American intelligence accurately predicted to within days of the explosion), President Johnson and the same advisers who had counseled Kennedy again discussed the problem of China's nuclear weapons. The confident and concrete tenor of the conclusions indicates that the subject was a familiar one. Special Assistant for National Security Affairs McGeorge Bundy recorded the decisions:

> We discussed the question of Chinese nuclear weapons today, first in a lunch at the State Department given by Secretary Rusk for McNamara, McCone, and myself, and later at a meeting with the President. . . .
>
> At the luncheon we developed the following position:
>
> 1. We are not in favor of unprovoked unilateral U.S. military action against Chinese nuclear installations at this time. We would prefer to have a Chinese test take place than to initiate such action now. If for other reasons we should find ourselves in military hostilities at any level

with the Chinese Communists, we would expect to give very close attention to the possibility of an appropriate military action against Chinese nuclear facilities.

2. We believe that there are many possibilities for joint action with the Soviet Government if that Government is interested. Such possibilities include a warning to the Chinese against tests, a possible undertaking to give up underground testing and to hold the Chinese accountable if they test in any way, and even a possible agreement to cooperate in preventive military action. We therefore agreed that it would be most desirable for the Secretary of State to explore this matter very privately with Ambassador Dobrynin as soon as possible. . . . [here several sentences have been "sanitized" from the memorandum]

These preliminary decisions were reported to the President in the Cabinet Room, and he indicated his approval. The Secretary of State now intends to consult promptly with the Soviet Ambassador.[46]

It seems that a United States overture again came to naught. The Chinese detonated their first atomic device on October 16, 1964. At almost the same time, the Communist party of the Soviet Union replaced Nikita Khrushchev for reasons still not completely known, but which some observers believed were linked to the conflict with China.

Was Kennedy's extreme alarm about China justified?

Others in the Kennedy administration did not share the president's dread. Some junior officials in the White House and State Department wanted the United States to adopt a less, not a more, hostile stance toward China. Roger Hilsman, director of the State Department's Bureau of Intelligence and Research, commented in public in 1962 that as "dramatic" as the prospect of China's exploding a nuclear device might seem, "it [would] not change the balance of power in Asia, much less throughout the world." He pointed out that the Chinese had actually been rather cautious in the Taiwan Strait. In late July 1963, after the Limited Test Ban Treaty had been concluded, a CIA report on China's anticipated response to the agreement observed that "over the past few years, in spite of their warlike oratory, they have followed a generally cautious policy." "The Chinese have thus far shown marked respect for US power, and we do not expect them to change this basic attitude." The CIA discounted the possibility of increased Chinese aggressiveness. During the Senate ratification hearings, General Taylor

46   Chapter One

stated that he had seen no evidence showing that the Chinese believed they would gain from a nuclear war, a claim both Kennedy and Khrushchev had made to scare the world. Taylor also observed that there was "a pretty hard-headed group of Chinese in Peking" who would not do something reckless. The military generally downplayed the significance of China's acquisition of nuclear weapons.[47]

The administration had even received overtures from Beijing not long after Kennedy had taken office in 1961. Ambassador Wang Bingnan of the People's Republic of China, who was meeting with American representatives at ongoing bilateral talks, made "friendly gestures" at Geneva and Warsaw. In 1962, Kennedy received reports showing a Chinese belief that the United States was not necessarily wedded to a policy of hostility toward China. But the United States discounted those tentative approaches and pursued its policy of siding with the Soviets and further estranging China.[48]

Kennedy's foreign policy was touted as a "strategy of peace," a phrase from the title of his 1960 campaign book. Kennedy's boosters, too, promoted the Limited Test Ban Treaty as a breakthrough in the struggle to make the world stable and to end the threat of war. But behind the rhetoric, Kennedy and his associates sought to aggravate tensions between the Soviet Union and China to the point that the Soviets might possibly join with the United States even in military action against China, an action that certainly would have thrown Asia into greater turmoil than any other single act since the Korean War.

The United States could have tried to improve relations simultaneously with both the Chinese and the Soviets, but there is no evidence that the Kennedy administration seriously considered that possibility. That was something that Richard M. Nixon would attempt in the next decade. Instead, Kennedy's policies sharpened the Sino-Soviet split, which eventually resulted in armed clashes between the two states. His policies increased the pressures on the Soviets by a provoked Chinese leadership, and began to construct a United States-Soviet stewardship over the world. Administration officials clearly understood those would be among the results of the Limited Test Ban Treaty.[49] While it might be argued that Kennedy's policies toward China, the Soviet Union, and the bomb were sophisticated and in the imperial interests of the United States, it is doubtful that they were consistent with the interests of international peace. Indeed, the Kennedy administration came dangerously close to giving an affirmative answer to the question posed by the *National Review*: "Should we bomb Red China's bomb?"

Notes

The author would like to thank Bart Bernstein, David Kennedy, Benjamin Loeb, and Rebecca Lowen for their helpful comments in writing this essay and the MacArthur Foundation and the Lyndon B. Johnson Foundation for financial support.

TWO

Eisenhower and Mao's China

An invitation from the historian Stephen E. Ambrose, who was a leading scholar on the life and career of Dwight D. Eisenhower, initiated this essay. Ambrose had read and liked my work on Kennedy and the bomb. Ambrose wanted new thinking about President Eisenhower, especially from a younger generation in the 1990s. Ambrose had been known for his characterization of Eisenhower as a more restrained and capable leader than other scholars had previously seen. My piece took Ambrose to task, at least as regards China.

The essay examined the prominent place China occupied in his thinking, especially in his Cold War fears. The story of the Cold War was told, and continues to be presented, very much as an U.S. and Soviet confrontation over Europe, but Eisenhower's views, including his private musings about Chinese communism, show great concern about Asia and his fear of the region falling to communism. This and Chapter 1 suggest that Kennedy's and Eisenhower's racial fears should be appreciated to understand their special dread of Asian communism and the extreme measures they were willing to consider to counter their perceived threat. The eventual full involvement of the United States in Vietnam directly flowed from their view of the danger of the combination of the red and yellow

"Eisenhower and Mao's China," in *Eisenhower: A Centenary Assessment*, edited by Günter Bischof and Stephen E. Ambrose (Louisiana State University Press), 1995: 191–205.

49

50   *Chapter Two*

perils that communism represented in their minds in Asia. Scholarship published since this chapter appeared largely sustains its interpretation.

*

At his last meeting with the press as president of the United States, Dwight Eisenhower was asked what his greatest disappointment had been in office. Eisenhower confessed that it was the failure to achieve a "permanent peace with justice." He went on to explain. He did not rue initiatives he had failed to take nor lament decisions perhaps unwisely made during his eight years in office. Rather, Eisenhower attributed the continuing high level of tension in the world to the bellicosity of Mao Tse-tung and his fellow Chinese Communists. He said: "During the entire first four years, I think, the Red Chinese were constantly threatening war, saying they were and they were not only threatening, but often making moves in that direction and at the same time the Russians were saying, 'We are going to support our Red China allies.'"[1]

Indeed, the Chinese Communists had frustrated the Eisenhower administration from beginning to end. From Korea—Eisenhower's top problem upon entering office in 1953—to the defeat of the French at Dien Bien Phu, Vietnam and the rising Communist insurgency in Southeast Asia, through two crises in the Taiwan Strait, and finally to rising turbulence in the international Communist movement as a result of the militancy of the Chinese in the emerging Sino-Soviet split, China had been an especially vexing and dangerous adversary for the administration of President Dwight David Eisenhower. During the 1950s, the Eisenhower administration repeatedly discussed the possibility of general war with China and the use of nuclear weapons. If he had been asked at his last press conference what was America's number-one enemy, the answer would likely have been, "Communist China."

Thus, it is fitting to devote some attention to assessing Eisenhower's experience with China. I will focus mainly on his presidency and refer just in passing to his pre-presidential experiences with China. First, I will examine some of the traditional historical views about Eisenhower and China and then review what the new documentary evidence has revealed that has allowed us to have a more sophisticated understanding. And last, I would like to launch into a somewhat speculative but hopefully intriguing endeavor: I

Eisenhower and Mao's China   51

will compare Dwight Eisenhower with his chief adversary, Mao Tse-tung, especially as political-military strategists.

There is one thing that the Eisenhower public record, the traditional, somewhat partisan critical view of his presidency that emerged during and immediately after his administration, and the more recent revisionist reinterpretation of Eisenhower all share in common—that is, the conviction that the former president had a particular dislike of the Chinese Communists.

Even before he became president, Eisenhower seemed to accept the conservative Republican position on China that was voiced in the late 1940s during the defeat of Nationalist leader Chiang Kai-shek in the Chinese civil war. Before a group of legislators in June, 1951, Eisenhower stated that he considered the fall of China to the Communists in 1949 to be "the greatest diplomatic defeat in this nation's history."[2] During the 1952 presidential campaign, he frequently condemned the Truman administration for "losing" China.[3] Eisenhower's view was not simply partisan, however, for he did personally harbor a special dread of Chinese communism. His image of China under communism, he privately told his cabinet during discussion of his inaugural address, was "one of claws reaching out to grab anyone who looked as though he had five cents."[4] His imagery was typical of those days in America, when Asian villains appeared as fiendish demons. From his first state of the union address, where he announced what appeared to be a major change in foreign policy, that is, the "unleashing of Chiang Kai-shek" to harass the mainland, to his visit to Taiwan where he engaged in a public love-fest with Chiang in the last months of his administration. Eisenhower gave the impression that he was a steadfast supporter of the Chinese Nationalists and implacable foe of Chinese communism.[5]

The administration's actions and statements gave no substantive hint of a contrary opinion. In his first months in office, Eisenhower ordered that word be passed to Beijing that he was considering use of atomic weapons if an armistice was not soon reached in Korea. Then in 1954, after the ceasefire, his principal national security advisers repeatedly recommended—five times in one year—that he militarily intervene again in Asia, even with the use of nuclear weapons against the Chinese mainland or along its periphery.[6] Eisenhower did not adopt these bellicose recommendations, for he was sensitive to the dangers of becoming involved in a land war in Asia once again, and instead he pursued other anti-Communist courses of action to maintain American interests. Still, his administration quickly gained the

Chapter Two

reputation that it was prepared to use all the weapons at its disposal to deter the threat of Chinese aggression in Asia.[7]

The two offshore island crises involving Quemoy and Matsu, in the Taiwan Strait off the China mainland, brought the United States closer to general war than perhaps any other incidents during the Eisenhower administration and became symbolic of the intransigence of the administration's general China policy. The two crises, the first lasting eight months from the fall of 1954 through the spring of 1955, and the second occurring over several weeks in 1958, had eerie similarities.[8] From the U.S. perspective, both crises were initiated by Beijing, with the probable intention of seizing clusters of islands off the mainland shore that were held by Chinese Nationalist forces. The islands were not more than a few miles away from important harbors and sea routes. In both cases, Washington feared that Communist shelling of the small bits of land presaged a possible all-out attack on Taiwan, the last redoubt of Chiang Kai-shek and his defeated remnants from the Chinese revolution. And in both cases, the United States publicly and fully committed its forces to the support of Chiang s defense of Taiwan and territories related to the defense of the island. The Eisenhower administration, in both cases, came under severe domestic and work criticism for apparently injecting the United States back into the Chinese civil war and bringing the country to the brink of war over territory of extremely dubious value. And in both cases, Eisenhower concluded that because of American resolve and display of military might, war did not occur. During the 1955 crisis, Eisenhower announced in public his opinion that he did not see why atomic weapons couldn't be used like a bullet or any other munition. It was also during this crisis that the administration gained from Congress what became known as the Formosa Resolution, which gave the president a virtual blank check for the use of American military forces in the defense of Taiwan and the related Pescadores Islands. This was a precedent-setting move that substantially eroded Congress' responsibility for committing the United States to war and opened the way for the disastrous Gulf of Tonkin Resolution in 1964.

These incidents, combined with such highly publicized events as the refusal of John Foster Dulles, Eisenhower's secretary of state, to shake Chinese premier Chou En-lai's hand at the 1954 Geneva Conference, the administration's prohibition of American reporters from visiting China in 1956 and 1957, and Dulles' public judgment that Chinese communism was a "passing and not perpetual phase." created the impression that Eisenhower was obdurately hostile toward the Peoples Republic of China.[9] In contrast to the Soviet Union, with which Eisenhower had pursued serious arms control measures and with whose top leaders he had met at several summits, China seemed to be an illegitimate international pariah. It expressed no indication of a willingness to lessen its hostility, let alone consider any change from the policy of recognizing the Chiang Kai-shek government as the sole, legitimate government of the Chinese people.

Critics of the Eisenhower administration charged that its China policy was unrealistic toward the most populous country on earth and dangerously attached to an unpredictable ally in the person of Chiang Kai-shek, whose only hope to regain his former glory was through war between China and the United States. Moreover, critics, Democrats as well as some Republicans, believed that the Eisenhower hard line toward China only helped cement the Sino-Soviet alliance, a strained partnership in the eyes of some. American flexibility toward China, it was suggested, might erode the Sino-Soviet alliance by showing the Chinese there was a Western alternative to dependence upon the Soviet Union.

Historians in the 1960s and 1970s arrived at similar conclusions about the Eisenhower record on China. They interpreted the hostility as based upon an emotional and myopic anti-communism. If it had not been for Eisenhower's hard line toward China, it was charged, the United States might have been able to reduce tensions in Asia, which could have led to an earlier exploitation of Sino-Soviet tensions, an interest in which helped lead Richard Nixon to Beijing in 1972, and possibly even an avoidance of the Vietnam tragedy—America's entrance into the quagmire was to stop alleged Chinese Communist expansionism in Southeast Asia. Arthur Schlesinger, Jr., respected historian and confidant of John F. Kennedy, suggests that Eisenhower's inflexibility on China even prevented the Kennedy administration from seeking a new China policy. According to Schlesinger, Eisenhower told President-elect Kennedy, in their last meeting before the inauguration, that he hoped to support the new administration on all foreign policy issues. Eisenhower warned the new president, however, that he would return to public life if Communist China threatened to enter the United Nations.[10]

But as more of the documentation about the internal life of the Eisenhower administration becomes known, we are developing a deeper and more complex sense of Dwight Eisenhower's views of China.

54   *Chapter Two*

Take, for example, his policy toward Nationalist China. Despite all outward appearances, the Eisenhower administration did not have an untroubled relationship with Chiang Kai-shek. In fact, Eisenhower had little regard for the Nationalist leader and found him a troubling gadfly rather than a loyal ally.[11] Eisenhower did not trust Chiang, disdained his abilities, and doubted that he would ever return to the mainland. Eisenhower's support for the Nationalists on Taiwan was unwavering, but Eisenhower never labored under the illusion, dear to the Republican conservatives and Chiang himself, that the Nationalists would soon, if ever, reverse the verdict of the Chinese revolution.

Moreover, Eisenhower carefully controlled Chiang's machinations in the offshore island area. He tried to get Chiang to reduce his garrisons on the offshore islands or withdraw from them entirely when conditions permitted. Despite his early rhetoric about "unleashing Chiang," Eisenhower kept the reins tightly on Chiang to ensure that the United States would not be drawn into a wider conflict in the region. Eisenhower's support for Chiang was part of the general policy of containment of communism but reflected no special love for the Nationalists. In turn, the evidence now shows that Chiang and the Nationalists were never at ease with Eisenhower.

As regards the Communists on the mainland, Eisenhower actually toyed with thoughts about possibly less rigid policies toward them as early as the end of the Korean War. In late 1953, he reviewed U.S. policies and mused about the seating of the Chinese Communists in the United Nations, and U.S. recognition.[12] Throughout the 1950s, he favorably discussed among his advisers the advisability of opening limited Japanese and other non-Communist trade with the mainland. Western trade might help undermine the ruling Communist group, in Ike's view, by exposing the Chinese masses to the riches of the capitalist world. Moreover, trade might also encourage fissures in the Sino-Soviet alliance.[13] The Republican line on China trade at this time was complete embargo.

What is even more interesting is that the documentary evidence now confirms what had only been quietly rumored during the Eisenhower presidency: that Eisenhower himself believed it might have been possible for the United States to encourage Communist China to break away from the Soviets. He was convinced that the Communist alliance was an unnatural one and that under the right conditions China might end its ties with the Soviets. He wondered what might bring about such a split.[14] Other immediate considerations, such as the need to continue to sustain the Chiang Kai-shek regime and the perceived threat of the growing Communist movement in Southeast Asia, blocked progress toward an improvement in U.S.-China relations. Nevertheless, Eisenhower's confirmed anti-communism did not blind him to the possibilities of exploiting intra-Communist tensions in the long run. Despite his administration's constant public railings about "international communism," Eisenhower did not assume that China and the Soviet Union composed a monolithic bloc.[15]

Regardless of its relationship with Moscow, however, Eisenhower was still deeply worried about Communist China's independent threat to American interests. Discussions in the National Security Council in March, 1959, reflected the difficulty the Eisenhower administration had with China as an independent adversary. The record of these dramatic top-level meetings has only recently been declassified.

The National Security Council was the most important body in the Eisenhower administration, and its discussions helped the president determine fundamental policies regarding war and peace. In March, 1959, the NSC discussed the wording of a major draft policy paper entitled NSC-5904, "U.S. Policy in the Event of War." The discussion centered around the question of what the United States should do in the event of general war with the Soviet Union. The State Department objected to proposed language that seemed to commit the United States to waging war automatically against the eastern bloc countries and China in the event of hostilities between the United States and the Soviet Union. Christian Herter, who had taken over the State Department after Dulles' death, argued that some of the eastern bloc countries might actually take the opportunity of general war to rebel against Soviet domination.[16]

Eisenhower, according to the record of the meeting, "immediately expressed disagreement with Secretary Herter." Eisenhower conceded that Herter might be right about the eastern bloc countries, but not about Communist China at all. According to the record, Eisenhower said, "If the U.S. got into *a* disastrous nuclear war with the Soviet Union and in the course of the war simply ignored Communist China, we would end up in a 'hell of a fix.'" He continued later in the meeting, saying that he could not foresee the United States becoming involved in an all-out nuclear war with Moscow and permitting Beijing to stay on the sidelines to "develop, after perhaps forty years, into another Soviet Union." Eisenhower drew a

56   *Chapter Two*

sharp distinction between the eastern bloc countries and China, which was a "willing partner" in international communism, in his view. Even if China sat out a war between the United States and the Soviet Union, the president said, the United States would have to "disarm and remove the threat of Communist China. We simply could not just ignore a Communist China which remained untouched and intact. . . . To do so would be unrealistic in the extreme." The essential thing, Eisenhower pointed out, was that in the event of general war, the United States had to ensure that both the USSR and China were "incapable of further harming the U.S. after the end of hostilities." Eisenhower's argument did not assume that China would automatically enter hostilities with the Soviets against the United States; rather, he assumed its independence from Moscow.

Even though Eisenhower had thought he had made himself clear, the discussion continued at the next NSC meeting on the same topic. Again, Eisenhower made the same points as he had in the earlier meeting. The result of these harrowing discussions was that U.S. policy drew a clear distinction between the Soviet Union and China on the one hand and the eastern bloc countries on the other. The final position paper included a notation that was sanguinary in its implications: "It is assumed that the peoples of the Bloc countries other than the USSR and Communist China are not responsible for the acts of their governments and accordingly so far as consistent with military objectives military action against these countries should avoid non-military destruction and casualties." Unstated but obvious, however, is that the U.S. military would not be hampered by concerns for civilian death and destruction in war against the Soviet Union and China.[17]

This discussion helps explain, if Eisenhower was privately willing to consider more flexible policies toward the mainland, why there was no change in the implacable policy toward China. For one, Eisenhower's comments about a change in China policy among his associates within the administration never amounted to more than musings, and much more on Eisenhower's mind was the independent threat China represented to American interests. There were also other important interests and concerns. The United States could not simply jettison Chiang on Taiwan, and mainland China itself seemed wedded to a policy of hostility toward the United States. Eisenhower knew it took two to tango, and Beijing was still in no mood to dance.

Nevertheless, Eisenhower kept open the possibility for an eventual two-China solution, a solution whereby the United States would be able to deal with the Communist government on the mainland of China and the Nationalist government on Taiwan as separate entities. Eisenhower did not believe that Chiang Kai-shek represented the Chinese people and even anticipated eventual recognition of the mainland government. A so-called two-China solution was anathema to both the Communists and Nationalists (each claimed it was the sole, legitimate government of the Chinese people), but it was what the Eisenhower administration quietly prepared the way for.[18]

All in all, Eisenhower remained wary of both Chinese and Nationalist Chinese. One suspects that this caution profoundly colored his assessment of U.S.-China relations and made him reluctant to take initiatives relating to the China area. Eisenhower's suspicion was itself rooted in an American attitude of superiority that looked down upon nonwhite peoples of the world. Eisenhower was at best insensitive to the condition of blacks in America, and was known to engage in racial jokes as president. He believed in a racial hierarchy of humankind.[19] On a number of occasions he expressed his belief that Orientals were devious and thought in ways profoundly different than Westerners.[20] Eisenhower's attitudes were linked, in fact, to his close association with Asia during the first part of his military career, and here it might be useful to review some of Eisenhower's early experiences with Asia.

Although Eisenhower is better known for his career in Europe, he had become familiar with much of Asia before World War II. Near the end of his life, Eisenhower recalled that it was an event in Asia that first awakened him to the reality beyond his home and Kansas. He remembered his uncle Abraham Lincoln Eisenhower's "glee" in hearing the news of Commodore Perry's victory over the Spanish fleet in Manila Bay during the Spanish-American War. As Eisenhower wrote, "I do not know just what day we got the news in Abilene but the smell of gunpowder and victory was in Uncle Abe's nostrils."[21] Perhaps it was that memory that inspired the West Point cadet Eisenhower to seek a post in the Philippines, perhaps the lowest priority in terms of preference among cadets. In 1935, at the age of forty-five, he finally got his wish and was stationed for four years in the Philippines with the staff of Douglas MacArthur.[22] These years were the heyday of American colonialism in the Philippines, and Eisenhower was

58 Chapter Two

likely affected by the attendant racism. His personal diaries at the time contain expressions of impatient frustration with Filipinos. He observed with exasperation that while in the Philippines he had "learned to expect from the Filipinos ... a minimum of performance from a maximum of promise."[23]

While in Asia, he also had the opportunity to visit China itself in 1938 and again in 1946. From January to March, 1942, he was deputy chief for the Pacific and Far East, a position which was concerned with strategic planning and operations of the war in Asia. After the war, as chief of staff of the Army, he was well aware of the difficulties of the Marshall mission to China and visited Nanking in May, 1946.[24] During these trips it seems that Eisenhower developed impressions he kept for life. For one, he was struck by China's huge population. He, like many of his generation, saw China's masses as an ominous and threatening horde, a yellow peril. "China is a great mass of human beings, hundreds of millions," he observed as president. "Those of you who have traveled through China I know have been as astonished as I have that so many people could live in such a space." As he later stated in his memoirs, China's leaders were "absolutely indifferent to the prospect of losing millions of people" and that the Chinese held "peculiar attitudes" toward human life.[25] With such beliefs about the Chinese, it is no wonder that Eisenhower expected the worst from Asia throughout his life.

In closing, I want to explore a topic that might sound offbeat, but which I think may be intriguing. I want to compare Dwight Eisenhower and Mao Tse-tung. protagonists in the 1950s. Historians often compare leaders like Churchill and Roosevelt, Stalin and Hitler, but as far as I know there has been no effort to compare Ike and Chairman Mao; perhaps the immense contrast between the two men appears so great that one might assume that an effort at comparison would be futile if not facile.[26] The popular image of Ike is that he was rather bland, colorless, a company man, unlike Mao, who is thought of as a charismatic revolutionary and messianic tyrant. But a comparison of the two helps highlight the qualities of the two leaders and may even help explain why the two countries under their respective leadership became such bitter enemies.

To begin with, one finds some remarkable parallels in their early personal lives. They were of almost the same age: Ike was born in 1890 and died in 1969; Mao was born in 1893 and died in 1976. They were both products of small communities in their countries' heartlands: Kansas and its wheat, Mao's Hunan Province and its rice. Their families were linked to the land, frugal, and somewhat better off than many others in their communities. They were not poor but neither were they prosperous. Their fathers were authoritarian, distant, prone to beating their children, and apparently unliked. Their mothers were kindly and, in the recollections of the two men, the greater parental influence on them.[27] As young men, both were preoccupied with their physical strength, exercised assiduously, and associated early with the military. Mao was a private in a revolutionary army at the age of eighteen, two years younger than Ike when he entered West Point.[28] Both men then devoted the rest of their lives to what one might loosely call public life: For Ike, it was the U.S. Army, supreme command of European Allied forces in World War II, and then the presidency of the United States in 1952; for Mao it was the Communist party, the Chinese revolution, which was mainly a military struggle, and then the chairman of the People's Republic of China in 1949. Both men coincidentally also had brief but important experiences with university life, Ike with Columbia and Mao with Peking University.

One could go on to compare further their upbringings, marriages, personal lives, military careers, associations with friends and colleagues, work methods, and so on. There are some fascinating comparisons, in fact. I was intrigued, for example, by Stephen Ambrose's description of Ike in the introduction of the second volume of his two-volume biography of Eisenhower. Ambrose writes (one might mentally substitute "Mao" for Ike's name in the following passage):

> Eisenhower is at the center of events. Just as in Overlord, when he was the funnel through which everything had to pass, the one man who was responsible for the whole operation, so too as President, he was the one man who could weigh all the factors in any one decision—the political repercussions, the effect on foreign policy, the economic consequences, and the myriad of other considerations involved—before acting. . . .
>
> [Eisenhower] wanted to be in the position in which he could have a maximum influence on events. He liked making decisions. The primary reason was that lie had such complete self-confidence that he was certain he was the best man in the country to make the decisions.[29]

60   *Chapter Two*

But what I would like to focus on here is some comparison of Ike and Mao as strategists. By strategist I mean one who is concerned with the relationship of military means and national political ends. The extraordinary military careers of the two men gave them unique qualities as political leaders and later as adversaries when they were the leaders of their countries.[30] Roosevelt, Truman, Kennedy, and all other modern-day presidents of the United States had no comparable military experience to Eisenhower's; nor did Churchill, Stalin, or Khrushchev have either Ike's or Mao's field, organizational, and command experience leading millions of soldiers.

What we know about Mao and his work as the leader of China is rather limited, certainly considerably less than what we know about Ike. Nevertheless, some general comparisons of the men as strategists can be advanced. First, perhaps one obvious but not trivial observation can be made: Neither man was mystified by the military and what military force could and could not do. Both clearly understood that military considerations were always subordinate to political ends. One of Mao's best-known aphorisms was that the party always commands the gun.[31] Throughout his career, he frequently had to oppose what was called the purely military point of view in the revolution. Ike too was never intimidated by his military advisers during his administration. He felt no hesitation in rejecting their advice—a man with less military experience might not have been as confident in his own opinion and decisions to buck the military professional.[32] Both men refused to accept the recommendations of their military commanders during confrontations in the Taiwan Strait, for example, and kept decisions about the operations in their own hands.[33]

All the same, both men understood the efficacy of the use of military means to achieve specific national security purposes and were not hesitant to use military force or the threat of military force to achieve specific ends. One thinks of Ike's threatened use of the atomic bomb to end the Korean War, his deployment of the Marines in Lebanon, and the CIA in Iran, Guatemala, and elsewhere. Of the evidence we now have, we also know that Mao employed military force in the Taiwan Strait less to achieve traditional military ends, such as gaining territory, than as a political instrument to probe the state of Nationalist China–U.S. relations.

Ike and Mao, as strategists, were also both keenly sensitive to popular opinion and actively sought in their own ways to cultivate domestic support and influence world public opinion. In the 1950s, both generally remained widely popular at home, which permitted them to pursue foreign policy aims with fewer constraints than other leaders would later face in China and in the United States. But Ike and Mao understood they were international leaders, who by their spoken word and gesture could influence millions around the world. Mao had messianic claims, and Eisenhower too was acutely sensitive about his public image, his legacy to history, and his responsibility as leader of the "free world."

Closely linked to this sensitivity to public opinion was their attention to what one might call the psychological aspect of international politics. Mao was a master in conducting psychological-political warfare during the revolution—his writings are full of essays concerning propaganda, ideological, and cultural work. Mao's concern for these areas came from his conviction that the human element was central in the conduct of war, both in leading one's own forces and in defeating the enemy. On his part, Ike was the first American president to make psychological warfare a regular and high-level instrument of foreign policy.

And perhaps because of this sensitivity to the psychology of politics, both Mao and Ike favored cultivating deliberate ambiguity in their military and political campaigns, especially in the several crises between the United States and China in the 1950s. It has never been completely clear why and for what purposes Beijing initiated the two offshore island crises in 1955 and 1958. On the other hand, Eisenhower also tried to maintain a degree of ambiguity in America's commitment to Chiang Kai-shek. Ike maintained this flexibility in opposition to the almost universal opinion of his military and political advisers, who wanted the president to define explicitly what the United States would or would not do given certain conditions.

There is another fascinating comparison of the two leaders concerning the basic relationship of war and peace. The Eisenhower administration is known for practicing what was called "brinkmanship," taking the country to the verge of war to achieve political ends and, paradoxically, it seemed, to maintain peace. Dulles explained this philosophy: "The ability to get to the verge without getting into war is the necessary art. If you cannot master it, you inevitably get into war. If you try to run away from it, if you are scared to go to the brink, you are lost."[34]

Mao's statement about imperialism and the atom bomb being "paper tigers" is similarly inspired. By paper tigers, Mao meant that war and the atom bomb were real threats and could kill people; one had to take them

62   *Chapter Two*

seriously *tactically.* But Mao encouraged his followers to despise war and the enemy *strategically,* firmly believing such an attitude was necessary to deflate the arrogance of the enemy and deter his threat. If, on the other hand, one is intimidated by the enemy and the threat of war, one is already defeated.[35] The conduct of the two offshore island crises, which brought the two countries to the edge of war but were both firmly controlled by their leaders, is evidence of this philosophy. In a sense, their strategic sensibilities were mirror images of one another.[36]

One, of course, can overstate the parallels of Ike and Mao as strategists. Ike's strategic approach was largely characteristic of Western traditions in strategy. He emphasized the massing of immense firepower and the efficacy of weaponry, nuclear or conventional, in war. As he stated on several occasions, one should avoid war, but if one must go to war, one should go into it with no holds barred, believing that firepower was decisive.[37] As president, he tended to make firm distinctions between war and peace, offense and defense, and enemy and friendly positions. He tended to see the holding and winning of territory as decisive and a zero-sum game.

Mao, in the Asian tradition of strategy, emphasized man over weapons, deception, and fluidity. Chinese strategists historically blurred the distinctions between war and peace, offense and defense, and interior and exterior lines. Territory was less important than time and psychological advantage.

The differences between Ike and Mao reflect in many ways the different philosophies of Clausewitz, the most famous Western thinker of war and strategy who lived in the nineteenth century, and Sun-tzu, Chinas most important strategist, who lived around 500 b.c., the time of Confucius. Mao was familiar with both. To give you just a taste of the philosophy of Sun-tzu, let me quote a brief passage from his treatise, *The Art of War:* "Now an army may be likened to water, for just as flowing water avoids the heights and hastens to the lowlands, so an army avoids strength and strikes weakness. And as water shapes its flow in accordance with the ground, so an army manages its victory in accordance with the situation of the enemy. And as water has no constant form, there are in war no constant conditions."[38] Water is the metaphor for the army in Asian military thought, while steel is usually the metaphor in Western conceptions.

Lastly, I also wonder if the differences between the two men derive from the fundamentally different strategic positions of the United States and China. Eisenhower's responsibility in World War II was to restore the

Eisenhower and Mao's China 63

predominance of the United States and then as president to maintain its global hegemony. Mao was a revolutionary his entire life; he devoted the first half of his life to seizing power and then to constructing a radical socialist society and elevating China in the family of nations. Eisenhower was preeminently a leader of the status quo; Mao was never content with the status quo, even after the revolution.

Despite these immense differences in military tradition, strategic position, and personal temperament, there are some intriguing comparisons, as I have tried to point out. One wonders to what extent these parallels contributed to the animosity in U.S.–China relations in the 1950s. The legacy of Korea, the foment in Indochina, and the continuing Chinese civil war in the Taiwan Strait were fundamental sources of conflict, certainly. But Mao and Ike were also strangely contrasting and certainly capable adversaries. Their strategic approaches, similar as they may have been in odd ways, may have unwittingly heightened tensions and frustrations on both sides. And yet, with good fortune, after Korea, neither Dwight Eisenhower or Mao Tse-tung again committed his armed forces to wage war against those of his formidable opponent.

There is one last thing the two men shared and which linked them in an ironic way: They both played a major role in the life of another man who helped change the geopolitical complexion of the world. Eisenhower and Mao both contributed to building the career of a man named Richard M. Nixon.

THREE

Chinese Americans and China: A Troubled and Complicated Relationship[1]

In January 2019, the Carter Center at Emory University convened a major conference on the fortieth anniversary of the normalization of U.S.-China diplomatic relations to reflect on the history and present state of the bilateral relationship. The recognition of the People's Republic of China by the United States when Jimmy Carter was president was one of the signal achievements of his administration and marked the formal end of thirty years of Cold War hostility. The historic visit of Richard Nixon to Beijing in 1972 started the process that resulted in the 1979 watershed moment. By any measure, it was a transformative event in global politics.

The conference surveyed the history and current relationship, which at the time appeared robust, especially in economics, but was still troubled by tensions over issues such as Taiwan, human rights, and intellectual property rights, among others. My own contribution to the conference was a historical reflection on what normalization meant for Chinese Americans and the variety of sentiments they held about their land of ancestry. This chapter has not been published previously.

"Chinese Americans and China: A Troubled and Complicated Relationship," from a paper presented to The Carter Center, *United States and China at 40: Seeking a New Framework to Manage Bilateral Relations*, Emory University, January 2019.

China has long occupied a prominent place in the politics and personal feelings of Chinese Americans and has strongly influenced how they have been viewed by the wider American public. Many have been unfair and even prejudicial in not recognizing much distinction between China and Chinese Americans. China historically also connects and deeply divides Chinese Americans, more so than ever because of deep differences of opinion about Taiwan, Hong Kong, the treatment of family members, and the governance of China itself. But the deeply negative perceptions of China, and Chinese, held by many Americans cause great ill ease among the Chinese American community regardless of political views.

The essay is published largely as it was presented in 2019.

January 1, 1979, for many Chinese Americans (those of Chinese ancestry who are U.S. citizens or permanent residents) was a joyous moment. They enthusiastically welcomed the normalization of relations between the United States and the People's Republic of China as it ended the politically charged and long-hostile relationship between the two countries: one, their land of ancestry—no matter that for some it was four or five generations past—and the other, their land of nationality for themselves and their families for now and the future.

Few saw the moment as validating the politics of either the PRC or the U.S.—politics *per se* was not the reason for celebration. A major step toward full social and cultural acceptance in American life was the reason for Chinese American hopefulness. For the backers of the Republic of China (ROC) on Taiwan who had watched as their ranks had steadily shrunk over the years, the day was dismal, of course, but they had been prepared for it. That the ROC claimed that Taipei was the capital city of the country of China had become difficult to maintain even for many of them. For most Chinese Americans, a bright new day of respect seemed to have arrived.

During the many years from the early 1850s, when Chinese began to arrive in the U.S. in significant numbers, to that moment in 1979, Chinese believed that their land of ancestry, regardless of the form of its government—imperial, warlord, nominally republican, and communist—had been disrespected and treated unfairly. Social discrimination and the prejudice Chinese Americans suffered was part and parcel of what they believed was the global insult and oppression of China. The relatively brief rule of the Republic of China on the mainland had been a high point in both the Sino-American relationship and in Chinese American history. Unprecedented mutuality and public affection between the two countries accompanied the alliance during World War II. The putative friendship between the two countries, however, was more a product of sharing a common enemy than anything else. During the war, the dismantling of the Chinese Exclusion Acts that started in 1882 began. Marginalization of Chinese Americans moderated, albeit slowly. Hatred of imperial Japan was a forceful, though ephemeral, adhesive. Soon after the end of World War II, the United States reconstructed its relationship with Japan in the early the Cold War and began to distance itself from the ROC as Chiang Kai-shek's regime lost the Chinese Civil War.

After the Communist victory in 1949 and then the Korean War from 1950 to 1953, China and the United States confronted one another in what became seen by many as the coldest front in the Cold War. For many in the United States, the racial "Yellow Peril" merged with the political "Red Peril" to form an especially dangerous and unpredictable enemy. Chinese Americans, especially those with liberal politics, came under intense scrutiny and surveillance. Geopolitics served to isolate Chinese Americans generally and perpetuate their second-class status. Chinese in the United States had virtually no contact with family, friends, or anyone in their land of ancestry. News about China for them and the American public was filtered through the prism of Cold War attitudes. "Free China" on Taiwan, for many Chinese Americans and other Americans, was largely a political expedient. The possibility of the return of its control over the mainland steadily eroded over the years and its desperate efforts to retain the support of Chinese in America actually alienated many. ROC efforts to retain the loyalty of Chinese Americans served to separate them from the mainstream of American life. Trying to continue to perpetuate the Chinese Civil War on American soil found fewer and fewer sympathizers. Moreover, the regime on Taiwan, despite its vigorous efforts to claim itself as the inheritor of cultural China, the land of ancestry that transcended regimes and ideologies, always had a difficult time relating to the Chinese Americans whose descent was from

68   Chapter Three

the southern Pearl River Delta, far from the historical centers of Chinese civilization and culture to the north.

The historic, and globally transformative, normalization of relations in 1979 was thus a watershed for Chinese Americans. It appeared to end the effort to avoid reality, as well as signal, finally, U.S. acceptance of China on the basis of formally expressed equality and mutual respect. Even more, as everyone knew, normalization had been made possible by the visit of the first sitting U.S. president to visit China. (Ulysses S. Grant had been the first to visit, but it was after he had left office.) None other than conservative Richard Nixon, the erstwhile ardent defender of Chiang Kai-shek and the Nationalists, had gone to Beijing, toasted Zhou Enlai, shaken Mao Zedong's hand, and visited the Great Wall, the symbol of timeless China.

It was "indeed a great wall," the never eloquent Nixon is said to have announced. Chinese in America had long believed that if their land of ancestry was disrespected as poor and weak, their own fates would also be bleak. Conversely, a united, modern, and strong China that enjoyed international respect was essential for Chinese Americans, in their view, to be able to enjoy their own rightful place in America. This was a core assumption of Chinese through the years, whether they were followers of Sun Yat-sen, Chiang Kai-shek, or Mao Zedong (though very quietly). Some ROC followers in the U.S. even celebrated China's atomic bomb test in 1964. *China* now had the bomb! And thus January 1, 1979, seemed to be the start of a promising new era, even for many who had once backed the ROC. China had stood up, demanded respect, and finally received it. U.S. President Jimmy Carter acknowledged the reality of China as an international power.

If nothing else, it was evident that the PRC was here to stay and the United States had committed itself to building a long-term relationship with it.

The national flag of the ROC that had flown over the family and civic associations of Chinese communities throughout the United States for decades gradually came down over the years, replaced with the red and yellow five-star banner of the PRC. Some Chinese American merchants saw the possibility of economic advantages in the opening, but these were less the reason for celebration than what normalization seemed to mean for the place of Chinese in American life and the ability to reconnect with the land of ancestry for social or family reasons.

Today, forty years later, those rosy hopes are long gone and remembered by few. The optimism of that time now appears to have been naïve, or certainly short-sighted. The consequences of normalization were enormously positive for many Chinese Americans, no doubt about it, but their attitudes toward China today, and their positions in American life, are far more complex, and vexed, than one would have anticipated following 1979.

One might wonder why this is the case, given the soaring rise of China's market-oriented economy, its rapidly expanding stature and presence in international affairs, and the exuberance of many of its people overseas. The rigidity, austerity, and isolation of Mao's China is long past. The reasons are in part because the demographics and social profile of the Chinese population in America have changed in far-reaching and profound ways and geopolitics.

Forty years ago, there were approximately 800,000 persons of Chinese ancestry in the country, the majority being American-born of Cantonese background, the rest permanent residents waiting to adjust their status. Today, there may be more than 400,000 citizens of the People's Republic of China in the U.S. here as students, tourists, undocumented residents, and temporary resident workers and professionals. Hundreds of thousands of others from China are here waiting to become American citizens. The Chinese American population today is officially over five million, the result largely of a vast immigration of people of Chinese ancestry not only from the mainland, Hong Kong, and Taiwan but from Southeast Asia and other parts of Asia. America has never seen so many "Chinese" before. Southern Chinese no longer predominate; Mandarin-speakers do.

Chinese Americans are no longer a modest-income, residentially segregated, and politically unimportant part of the U.S. population. Today, Chinese Americans can be found in the ranks of the wealthiest Americans; they are in aggregate among the most highly educated and successful in many professions; and they have become a political and philanthropic force that is not ignored but courted. They live in high-income suburban areas throughout the country, no longer relegated to urban enclaves. Since 1979, Chinese Americans are occupying seats in presidential cabinets and gubernatorial and mayoral offices. Chinese Americans populate newsrooms, Hollywood director's chairs, and editorial boards of leading newspapers and opinion-influencing periodicals. They are building a presence in sports and the arts. They travel back and forth from China with ease.

70   *Chapter Three*

Despite the notable progress of Chinese in American life, however, all is not well in Chinese America. Far from it.

Income inequality among Chinese Americans, as with other Asian Americans, is the widest among all social groups in the country. Attention to the well-to-do Chinese and the hundreds of thousands who arrived in the past several decades with H-1B visas that privilege highly educated professional immigrants overlooks the still significant numbers of Chinese Americans struggling to establish a permanent place for themselves and their children in America.[2]

The relationship between Chinese Americans and the People's Republic of China is as fraught and complicated today as it has been since normalization. The relationship has never been simple, unemotional, or without significance but political, economic, and social developments in recent years have created not only opportunities but also highly troubling challenges. Popular reactions to the "tiger mom" included expressions of respect toward Chinese parenting approaches but also widespread resentment and hostility toward aggressive and driven Chinese Americans who were allegedly taking over suburban schools and communities once reserved for whites. One hears all around the country not welcome, but condemnations, of monied Chinese buying choice property and driving up land values. Anti-immigrant sentiment is stimulating racial prejudice against Chinese and other Asians perceived as inassimilable foreigners. Most ominously, loud voices in America link Chinese Americans to a putative geopolitical China threat. Demonizing certain domestic ethnic communities because of international tension has a long tradition in American life, from German Americans in World War I to Japanese Americans in World War II and Middle Eastern Americans today. Might Chinese Americans be next?

In these troubled circumstances, Chinese Americans themselves are presenting themselves in a variety of ways. They are deeply divided in their attitudes toward their land of ancestry and the rise of China since normalization. Two prominent examples illustrate this tension. The religious group from China known as Falun Gong (also known as Falun Dafa), with a branch founded in the U.S. around the turn of the twenty-first century, has become a familiar presence in American public spaces thanks to its performance of meditation practices and energetic demonstrations against visiting Chinese officials and Chinese diplomatic offices in the U.S. Holding bright banners and displaying gruesome photographs of alleged communist atrocities and persecution of their movement in China, their members have become the most visible expression of Chinese American hostility toward Beijing. The leader of the group, Li Hongzhi, moved out of China and has lived in the United States since 1996. Ostensibly focused on attaining spiritual enlightenment, the organization sits at the core of a fiercely anti-Beijing movement and has become the most vociferous social force against Beijing, perhaps even surpassing the public influence of the ROC-linked anti-communist crusade in the U.S. in the 1950s and 1960s.[3]

Perhaps the most prominent and visible expression of the Falun Gong movement is a cultural troupe, Shen Yun Performing Arts, whose connections with Falun Gong are not widely known but also not hidden. Based in the Hudson River Valley, the large troupe has staged hundreds of elaborate performances of Chinese dance and music at high-profile venues throughout the United States and other countries since 2006. It boldly declares that its intention is to reclaim China's "5,000 years of civilization." Echoing the ROC's claim in the 1950s, it maintains that it presents "traditional Chinese culture," which "cannot be seen anywhere else in the world—*not even in China.*" It claims that "the ruling communist regime has viewed China's rich spiritual and artistic heritage as a threat to its ideology, and for decades sought to erase it. Chinese artists have suffered untold ordeals over the past century." Politics is never far from their performances: the troupe says that it draws "from their shared practice of Falun Gong" and its "repertoire regularly includes important works shedding light on the plight of believers like themselves in communist China today." It also engages in noncultural activities including condemning "Chinese student associations" on college campuses and "Chinese business associations" in the U.S. as being covert agencies for Chinese communist-related activities.[4]

Another wing of the Falun Gong movement is a well-funded media group best known for its publication of *Epoch Times*, which has print and online editions in two dozen languages.

Founded in 2000 by what it says was a "group of Chinese-Americans" and based in New York City, it is a registered nonprofit organization that declares its purpose is to "bring honest and uncensored news to people oppressed by the lies and violence of communism." It distributes full editions in English and Chinese five days a week for the New York and Washington, D.C., area and shorter versions throughout the rest of the United States. It maintains professionally produced online versions. The media group claims

72   Chapter Three

that it produces the largest Chinese-language newspaper outside of "mainland China and Taiwan."[5]

Its content is full-range, from reportage to cultural and life-style features, but its focus is on developments in China and the U.S.-China relationship. On American politics, it assumes an unabashedly pro-Trump position and supports the administration's array of policies on immigration, business, and economics and international affairs. It is militantly anti-Beijing, condemnatory of Beijing in all of its China coverage. Articles are from a range of sources, including mainstream commercial outlets, staff writers, and far-right independent authors. Identification of its ownership, editorial board, and sources of income is murky. The paper's editor in chief refuses to share the identity of its owners and main funders.

Among the most troubling of its coverage is its regular reportage of alleged Chinese spying in the United States, including implicating Chinese working and living in the country. In this, the newspaper echoes one of the most disturbing developments under the Trump administration: the drumbeat about Chinese agents as a national security threat living within the country. In February 2018, the director of the FBI, in a highly publicized statement, described Chinese spies as a "whole-of-society threat" to America. *Epoch Times*, in its zealousness, echoes unfounded claims about the danger that Chinese, and Chinese American agents, pose to the United States and has impugned the integrity, and even loyalty, of those of liberal to middle-of-the-road position, including Chinese Americans involved in the Democratic Party.

The significance of the Falun Gong movement, especially its cultural and media wings, lies in its efforts to influence public opinion, rather than on credible opinion or policy-makers, who do not generally appear to hold the movement in high regard.

Diametrically opposed to this unremitting hostility toward Beijing is the position of the Committee of 100, a member-by-invitation organization of now approximately one hundred and fifty Americans of Chinese descent who have achieved high distinction and recognition in their careers.[6] The organization's stated dual purpose is to "promote full participation of all Chinese Americans in American society" and advance "constructive dialog and relationships between the peoples and leaders of the United States and China." The idea for the nonpartisan organization of elite voices came a few years after normalization from the renowned architect I. M. Pei and Henry

Kissinger, who saw the need for an organized expression of the views of accomplished Chinese Americans that could address developments in United States–China relations. Among its members today are business leaders such as Jerry Yang of Silicon Valley, former U.S. ambassador to China, and Washington State governor Gary Locke, actor Lucy Liu, and artist Maya Lin. In its ranks are among the wealthiest and most influential Chinese Americans. All are American citizens.[7]

Unlike the highly visible Falun Gong and its related organizations, the C-100 takes a low public profile. It quietly organizes venues for meetings of Chinese and American political and business leaders to address issues of common concern, organizes public forums, and occasionally issues statements on current developments. It commissions studies on American public opinion toward China and Chinese Americans to gauge the social climate.

One of its concerns has been the excesses in the U.S. government efforts against Chinese espionage in the U.S. For example, in 2018 the C-100 declared its support for justice for Sherry Chen, a U.S. citizen employed by the Department of Commerce who was accused of espionage for China in 2014. Though charges against her were completely dropped a year later, she was dismissed from her position. She sought to resume her employment but was blocked by the Department of Justice in 2018. In contrast, *Epoch Times* reported on her arrest and the incendiary charges against her but never ran follow-up reports on the clearing of her name.

In the view of many C-100 members, the treatment of Chen recalled that of the earlier mistreatment of nuclear engineer Wen Ho Lee, who worked for the University of California at the Los Alamos National Laboratory. In 1999, when he was in his sixties, authorities arrested Lee and accused of him of spying for Beijing. His name and reputation were smeared and he lost his job. He was jailed and placed into solitary confinement for nine months before he was cleared of all spying charges. Lee was a Taiwanese-American U.S. citizen and had been in the country since 1965 when he arrived as an international student. Federal mistreatment of Lee had been abominable.

For many C-100 members, the cases of Chen, Lee, and other Chinese American scientists who have been arrested and accused of espionage and then had their charges dropped are troubling evidence of racial profiling. They fear a worsening of a climate of suspicion and mistrust of Chinese Americans. Remarkably, the professional success of the elite members of the C-100 has not left them insensitive to social injustice and they are keenly

74 *Chapter Three*

aware that the advances Chinese Americans have made since normalization of relations cannot be taken for granted.

As with the diplomacy of the PRC generally over the past several decades, China's attitude toward those of Chinese ancestry in America has become more sophisticated. In 1971, when I visited the PRC, I entered the country from Hong Kong. I crossed over the territorial boundary via a small bridge, where, in mid-span, a PLA soldier stood. He gave me a stern disapproving look when he saw that my passport had an ROC visa stamp. He then announced that I, as a returned *"tongbao"* (fellow countryman), was nevertheless warmly welcomed back to the "motherland," the People's Republic of China, "the one and only China." For a few years after normalization, PRC representatives in the U.S. viewed Chinese Americans similarly, making little distinction between Chinese nationals and Americans of Chinese ancestry.

Today, that confusion is no longer made, or is rarely made, in China or by its diplomatic representatives in the United States. They try to make clear distinctions between Chinese nationals who hold Chinese passports (*zhongguo gongmin*), overseas Chinese who reside long-term overseas either as immigrants or permanent residents (*huaqiao*) and Americans of Chinese ancestry (*huayi*).

There is little question that the PRC is concerned about, and monitors, the behavior of Chinese nationals in the U.S., especially its students and visiting professionals, whether government officials, scientists, or researchers. In recent years, it has increased its surveillance and efforts to secure the support and affection of its nationals overseas. And Beijing seeks to positively influence its general image and reputation through its Confucius Institutes, the language training facilities it has funded on American campuses in recent years, as well as through other "soft power" instruments such as promoting traditional cultural practices, sports competitions, and media. But there is little evidence that Beijing seeks to involve itself directly in Chinese American (*huayi*) communities to serve immediate interests. It seems, at least to this writer, that Beijing tries to avoid even the perception of meddling in the lives of Chinese Americans and their communities, let alone seeking to recruit them to become agents of the mainland. The once-common presence of representatives of the ROC in the community life of Chinese in America has been replaced by that of the PRC on occasion and, sometimes by the uneasy, but not impossible, presence of both.

What of the future?

Normalization of relations between China and the United States has resulted in enormous benefits for Chinese Americans. Their numbers alone have grown tremendously because of more favorable immigration policies. They have become an undeniable and accepted fact of everyday life in communities and walks of life throughout the country. The economic relationship between China and the United States, though now in deep trouble, has created tremendous opportunities for their own entrepreneurial activity. Chinese and American companies have also turned to Chinese Americans for their cultural and professional expertise in business and as capable researchers, scientists, and academics. Everyday families have enjoyed reunions, thanks to immigration and to the ease of travel across the Pacific. The huge success of leading Chinese American bankers and investors, as well as businesses such as the popular Panda Express, whose owners rank among the wealthiest of Americans, would not have been possible without normalization.

But visible success has also inspired new insecurity and worry, not unalloyed confidence. There is fear of new forms of racial discrimination against Chinese and other Asian Americans in education, in hiring, and in everyday community life. *Backlash* is a word often heard locally as Chinese Americans, seeking their place in local life, encounter resistance from established populations. And above all, there is the looming fear of catastrophe as tensions continue to rise in the global U.S.-China relationship. Might Chinese Americans be caught in the middle of a conflagration between the two countries?

Among Chinese Americans, discord, not unity or agreement, is likely to continue to rise as their political differences over Beijing and Washington sharpen. In recent years, a growing number of newcomers from China (sometimes called the "new Chinese immigrants") have become a loud and visible element within the Chinese American community. Though they may have had a good education in China and are professionals and middle class here, many are indifferent to learning about American life and history, especially regarding racial prejudice and right-wing extremism. They often are antagonistic toward other immigrants of color and racial minorities, and even other Chinese Americans whose families go back generations in

76   *Chapter Three*

the U.S. Inexperienced in the politics of a pluralist democracy and civic engagement, they eschew collaboration and coalition building, the hallmarks of American politics. Their style is confrontational and combative. Many are also disdainful of China and hope for radical change there. As such, they have found a home in the Trump movement and proudly proclaim that they are "Chinese Americans for Trump." They like his belligerence toward Beijing.

Other recently arrived Chinese strongly identify with the mainland and vociferously advocate for it, in a manner similar to the way that supporters of the ROC did in the years before normalization. The specter of fighting over "homeland politics," which divided Chinese American communities during the Cold War, is rising and complicates efforts to forge ethnic solidarity.

Differences among those identifying with Taiwan and those with China are also deepening, as the relationship between Taipei and Beijing continues unresolved. Identification with Taiwan among those from Taiwan has grown markedly and confidently since the 1970s. PRC efforts to discourage such sentiment has resulted in strengthening rather than weakening resolve. More than ever, many from Taiwan forcefully reject Chinese ethnic identity. A similar trend, though still early, is emerging among younger people from Hong Kong in the United States.

Heterogeneity within Chinese America is therefore growing, not diminishing. Differences in generation, socioeconomic position, religious belief (many more Chinese are evangelical Christians than before), regional origin in Asia, education, American party identification, and attitude toward Beijing are widening among Chinese Americans, even though many in the larger American population see little nuance.

And thus, the dilemma or challenge for Chinese Americans who seek to make a difference in U.S.-China matters: common ground will be more difficult than ever to establish among Chinese Americans, despite the persistence in America of seeing racial sameness and the PRC's growing effort to cultivate the good favor of overseas Chinese. Agreement among Chinese and Chinese Americans is becoming more difficult because of the scrutiny of the two state powers, the United States and China. Regardless of internal differences in the communities that are identified as Chinese American, their members will continue to live under the long shadow of the darkening U.S.-China geopolitical relationship. Not long ago, political leaders of both countries spoke of seeking a constructive engagement and defying the odds that conflict was inevitable between the two states. Now, clouds are gathering and there is little that Chinese Americans will be able to do to clear the horizon. That is the reason for the growing worry within Chinese American communities throughout the country. Will the mounting anti-China sentiment among the American public stoke anti-Chinese fear, including of Chinese Americans? Will they be caught in the middle of global geopolitics? Might they be the ones to suffer severe, unintended consequences that come from U.S.-China conflict?

FOUR

Whose "Barbarism"? Whose "Treachery"?: Race and Civilization in the Unknown United States–Korea War of 1871

The genesis of my scholarship has often been serendipitous. I might stumble across unusual primary material that speaks to my interests in war and racial thinking and starts me on a journey of intellectual discovery that culminates in advancing our understanding of important dimensions of the past in trans-Pacific relations. This essay is exactly such a piece.

The essay did not originate from a particular interest in the topic. In fact, I had not even known about this war until after I discovered rich documentation from the episode that I found by chance in the Library of Congress.

The core of this essay is the correspondence sent by Admiral John Rodgers, who commanded the U.S. expeditionary force sent to initiate formal U.S. relations with the Kingdom of Korea in 1871. His failure to do so led him to initiate a bloody military attack on Korea to try to force open its doors. Even though the mini-war was seen in the United States as a major event when it occurred, it slipped into obscurity and misunderstanding as the years passed. The documentation of its conduct and experiences of those

"Whose 'Barbarism'? Whose 'Treachery'?: Race and Civilization in the Unknown United States–Korea War of 1871," *Journal of American History* 2003, 89, 4, 1331–1365, by permission of the Organization of American Historians.

80   *Chapter Four*

who fought on both the U.S. and Korean sides also highlight the power of notions of race and civilization in geopolitical conflict. Racial ideas from home for the Americans were very much applied overseas. The Koreans themselves harbored very strong views about the civilization of others as well. The war-making experiences of Americans in Asia, in this and other occasions, contributed mightily to the development of white American racial ideas about Asians, not just in Asia but at "home" as well. The striking visual imagery from the encounter continues to influence popular understanding of the past.

This essay contributed to the development of a field now known as "America in the World," which broadly describes the study of American interaction with other countries beyond political diplomatic history and embrace other approaches including social, cultural, ideological, and other dimensions.

Unstated in the published essay was the influence of the buildup to the Second Persian Gulf War, which Washington initiated in March 2003, the same time as the publication of this essay as the cover piece for the *Journal of American History.* The timing was a coincidence, as far as I know, but the connections were not lost on me. In both cases, important explanations for the wars focused on the economic dimensions which played upon American leadership: in 1871, the commercial possibilities for the country and, in 2003, oil. But in my view, ideological views must be appreciated to help explain the expedition leaders' decisions, motivations, and public support. I ended my 1871 essay concluding that "civilization and humanity, not the prospects of profits, had been the main reason [expedition leadership] had risked life and limb in demanding that Korea open its door." In 2003, the neoconservative blind passion to spread what it called democracy and American anti-Arabism had to be appreciated to see the war's origins beyond the need for petroleum.

*

Whose "Barbarism"? Whose "Treachery"? 81

Barbarism will still respect nothing but power, and barbaric civilization repels alike interference, association, and instruction.
> —United States secretary of the navy George M. Robeson, 1871

Western barbarians foully attack! Should we not fight, accord must be made! To urge accord is to betray the country!
> —Korea's prince regent, the Taewon'gun, 1871

An anecdote that diplomatic historians sometimes use to illustrate the national prejudices infusing popular historical understanding describes a French schoolboy's first visit to Trafalgar Square in the heart of London. He learns from his British host that the mighty column in the public space celebrates the great naval battle of 1805 near the Rock of Gibraltar, at the entry to the Mediterranean Sea. "My, how curious," the impressed but perplexed youngster exclaims, "to erect a monument to a terrible defeat!"

The following account of a battle between American and Korean military forces in June 1871 near Korea's Rock of Gibraltar, during an American expedition to "open" Korea as Matthew C. Perry had opened Japan in 1853, in some ways confirms the truth of that tale. The standard American interpretation of the war differs dramatically from the Korean, with the differences having everything to do with national perspective rather than with "facts" alone. The nationality of the storyteller commonly predicts which side will be identified as the "aggressor" and which the "defender" in the conflict. But in other ways, the national accounts of the United States-Korea War of 1871 depart from the simple wisdom of the Trafalgar Square anecdote. For one, there is no consensus over who was the "victor" and who the "vanquished"— whereas most French youngsters concede that Trafalgar was a French defeat. In the Korean case, each side has claimed glorious victory over a demoralized enemy. Each side has built its own version of a victory column at home and honored its martyrs as national heroes. And while every English and French youngster knows that the battle of Trafalgar ended with the defeat of Napoleon Bonaparte's navy, few, if any, American students (and only a small minority of American diplomatic historians) know anything about

82   *Chapter Four*

the 1871 events in Korea. It is, for Americans today, an unknown war. (Those who know of the incident may have read articles entitled "'Our Little War with the Heathen,'" "America's War with the Hermits," or perhaps "When We Trounced Korea," the dismissive titles themselves reflecting a common historical attitude toward the Asian enemy.) In contrast to their American counterparts, most Koreans, in the south as well as the north, are familiar with the outlines of the *Shin-mi Yang-yo* (the barbarian incursion of 1871, a name suggestive of attitudes toward the Western adversary) and with the valiant Korean resistance to the aggression.[1] A respected Korean scholar, Dae-Sook Suh, eulogizes the war as "one of the bloodiest battles that Koreans have fought to defend their country."[2]

But why have Americans relegated this conflict to the margins of historical importance?

It was not always that way. From the events themselves through the first several decades of the twentieth century, American diplomatic historians and journalists regularly wrote about the episode as a pivotal event in nineteenth-century U.S.–East Asian relations. Tyler Dennett in his foundational 1922 work on U.S. diplomacy in East Asia describes the American effort to engage Korea as "by far the most important political action undertaken by the United States in Asia until the occupation of the Philippines in 1898."[3] But the "real" Korean War of 1950–1953 now overshadows that earlier history, and few American scholars devote much attention to the 1871 events. When the incident has made its way into recent American historical literature, the account typically is misleading or incomplete, fundamentally wrong factually, or blatantly chauvinistic and one-sided.[4] Only a handful of studies, most of them from the early twentieth century or obscure, offer more informed and thoughtful perspectives on the events.[5] For Americans today, the 1871 clash recalls a decidedly unpleasant period in U.S.–East Asian relations, Korean relations in particular, whereas the story of mid-twentieth-century American sacrifices in Korea in the common battle against Communism is a far more congenial story. That war now dominates American popular and scholarly understanding of all modern Korean history, obscuring what came before.

But the 1871 clash was a major historical event by any standard. The American public widely appreciated its significance at the time. The war was one of the largest, if not the largest, and bloodiest uses of military force overseas by the United States in the fifty years between the

Perhaps the first photographic image of a Korean, taken by Felice Beato during the 1871 U.S. military expedition to "open" Korea. The man holds empty bottles of Bass Ale, with its trademark triangle symbol—nicknamed the "entering wedge of civilization"—and other spirit and wine bottles. He also holds a copy of *Every Sunday*, with a front-page picture of Charles Sumner. *Courtesy Special Collections and University Archives, Stanford University Libraries, RBCDS915.P4f.*

84   *Chapter Four*

Mexican-American War of 1846–1848 and the Spanish-American War of 1898.[6] American officers claimed they had killed some 250 Korean soldiers; the number may have been twice as high. Included in the Korean casualties was a high-ranking military commander who was posthumously appointed minister of war and is still honored today as a national hero in Korea. It was also the first time that American ground forces actually seized, held, and raised the American flag over territory in Asia, initiating a long and traumatic tradition of American military involvement there.[7]

One purpose of this study is to recapture the historical importance of the war for the broader history of American diplomatic relations in East Asia by offering a more accurate and fuller narrative. A second, related objective is to interpret the ways American ideas about race and civilization decisively shaped American decision making. Those ideas, informal and formal, shaped what the leaders of the expedition wanted, how they interpreted their encounters with Koreans, how they responded to Korean actions, and why they decided to go to war. The ideas were not peripheral to the main events, but central in determining their outcome. And fully appreciating the power of those ideas is necessary to understanding the wider story of nineteenth-century American involvement in Asia. The standard historical accounts of U.S. diplomatic activity in nineteenth-century East Asia—such as the classic works by Tyler Dennett, Michael H. Hunt, Walter LaFeber, and William A. Williams—emphasize the interest in obtaining commercial rights and privileges, especially in establishing trade with China, Japan, and Korea. Dennett characterized the pursuit of trade and markets, embodied in what is popularly known as the most-favored-nation or Open Door policy, as "the tap-root of American policy" in East Asia for the entire century.[8] But alongside the general interest in commercial opportunity, American assumptions about races and civilizations, about their own as well as those of others, powerfully influenced behavior. Americans went to Korea in 1871 not only to open the way for trade but also, in the telling words of Secretary of the Navy George M. Robeson, to instruct "barbarism." The 1871 American war against Korea illustrates how ideas about race and civilization helped shape the nineteenth-century American approach to East Asia.[9]

Official American interest in developing formal relations with the kingdom of Korea dates from the 1840s at the latest, but little was done until William H. Seward's tenure as secretary of state in the mid-1860s. The expansionist

Seward wanted to advance American influence in the Asia-Pacific region and to open Korea to American commercial interests. Korea, like China and Japan before they were forced to accept the Western international system, had been closed to foreign powers, other than China and, to a lesser extent, Japan, since the early seventeenth century. Those and several other East Asian countries had formed an East Asian regional system that was based on shared Confucian norms of diplomacy, etiquette, and cultural values; they were uninterested in developing extensive contacts with westerners. Seward had authorized efforts to approach the Korean government, but they never got underway. Korea was left for Seward's successor, Hamilton Fish.

In early spring 1870 Fish directed the newly appointed minister to China, Frederick F. Low, a wealthy businessman, former U.S. congressman, and former governor of California, to proceed to Korea with a naval expedition to negotiate a treaty ensuring the protection and good treatment of shipwrecked American seamen, a concern the United States commonly raised with other powers in the Pacific region during these years of expanded American naval activity.[10] Commercial interests were high on the American agenda but took second place to what Washington identified as its general "humanitarian" concerns, specifically the regularized acceptable treatment of stranded nationals. Other than formulating general objectives for the mission, Fish could provide little diplomatic guidance to his emissary. "Little is known," Fish admitted to Low, of Korean waters "or of the people who inhabit that country." American contact with Korea had been limited to a handful of unofficial encounters, the most prominent being the experiences of two private vessels flying American flags that had ventured into Korean waters in 1866. Korean authorities had treated the shipwrecked crew of the *Surprise* well, but Washington believed that Korean soldiers had killed the entire crew of the *General Sherman,* an American ship with a mainly Chinese and Malay crew that had entered Korea under murky circumstances and for dubious purposes. Washington also knew about the few interactions between Koreans and Europeans, especially the French, who had sent a large punitive force in 1866 to avenge the killing of Catholic missionaries who had secretly entered Korea to proselytize, which the royal court had outlawed. Korean forces bloodied the French expedition after several days of fighting and forced them to withdraw.[11] Adm. John Rodgers, commander of the expedition's forces, condensed about all that he knew of Korea in a couple of sentences in a letter to his wife. "The Coreans are a stiff

86   Chapter Four

necked people," he wrote, "but there are said to be two parties, the liberals and tory's. Those who wish their rules relaxed and those who would not give anything—but really we know very little about them."[12]

Despite their declared ignorance of the country, American officials nevertheless formed quick and firm opinions of Korea based on their meager intelligence reports and negative impressions of the racial character of Asians. Their attitudes toward Asians as a "race" were an unsystematic mix of ideas about character, behavior, ethics, and intelligence, based on a perceived similarity in physical appearance and a conflation of specific cultures into an "Oriental" type of civilization. And Asians, compared to white Americans and Europeans, were not just different, but morally and socially deficient. With these notions, Washington officials, even when there was clearly contradictory evidence, assumed the worst about the Koreans and minimized or discounted information that suggested a more positive characterization of the people and the reasons for their suspicion of westerners. The dominant American attitude, as expressed in official as well as personal records, was that the Koreans were mendacious, backward, and simply barbaric.[13]

Low himself had no previous diplomatic experience and little intimate knowledge of Asians, other than what he had picked up as a young employee of Russell, Sturgis, and Company, one of the first American firms in the China trade, and recently as governor of a state with many Chinese residents. But perhaps because of those experiences, he was confident in his own opinions about race and civilization, and they made him pessimistic about the prospects for his mission. While the expedition's goals were, in his view, eminently reasonable and honorable, he was convinced that the Koreans would resist the American effort. "I apprehend that all the cunning and sophistry which enter so largely into oriental character," Low wrote his superior on May 13, 1871, just as the expedition got underway, "will be brought to bear to defeat the object of our visit, and if that fails it is not unlikely that we may be met with a display of force." Anticipating what the mission might encounter was even more complicated, in Low's view, since the Koreans' emotions were unpredictable. Who knew, as he put it, what the "temper and disposition of the Corean officials" would be? But Low assured his superior that he was prepared for all possibilities, including responding to any attack or insult, and he insisted that Washington appreciate the perverse Asian mind. "It is mistaken policy when dealing with oriental governments and people," Low informed his superiors, "to allow insults and injuries to go unredressed. Such lenity leads them to believe that fear alone prevents retaliation, and adds to their arrogance, conceit, and hostility."[14]

During the winter of 1870–1871, Low repeatedly approached Chinese officials in the Zongli Yamen, the imperial bureau responsible for foreign relations, for their help in forwarding a letter to the king of Korea describing his mission, the questions he wished to discuss, and the mission's objectives. The Chinese rebuffed him, believing it improper to act as a channel

Soon after the U.S. fleet entered Korean waters in May 1871, Felice Beato took this picture, probably the first photograph of Korea ever taken. *Courtesy Special Collections and University Archives, Stanford University Libraries, RBCDS915.P4f.*

88   Chapter Four

of communication for the United States. Because of his insistence, however, the Chinese finally agreed to forward Low's message in March 1871. An internal memorial drafted by court officials about the American message reveals concern about the American activities as well as their own awkward position. "We have done our best," the Chinese officials wrote, "to prevent America's plan to send warships to Korea. Now, in view of her firm determination, the question does not depend on whether or not we forward this letter. If we do not, we are afraid that Korea may not know the reason for their coming, and consequently, may be unable to meet the situation."[15]

Though it received the American message from the Chinese, the Korean government did not reply to Low, since such a response would have violated its own nonintercourse policy. Moreover, the Korean regent and de facto ruler of the country, the Taewon'gun (Yi Ha-Eung), the father of the teenage King Kojong, was personally anti-Western, anti-Christian, and opposed to changing the long-standing seclusion policy. He and others at the court believed that Korea was the last bastion of true Confucian morality and order, China and Japan having been corrupted when they were forced to engage in regularized relations with the westerners. To uphold civilization, in their view, required resisting the westerners and isolating virtue.[16]

Although they had heard nothing from Seoul, Low and Rodgers believed that they had successfully communicated their peaceful intent to the Korean court. Convinced that the Koreans had no legitimate reason to fear their expedition and not sharing the consternation of the Chinese, Low and Rodgers assembled their expeditionary force. Although the American flotilla might not have been a match for the advanced French or British navies, it was still formidable. It included five heavily armed warships carrying eighty-five cannons and 1,230 marines and sailors, the largest Western military force to enter Korean territory until the twentieth century. (The French had sent 600 men in 1866.) Rodgers, the fleet's commander, was one of the most distinguished officers in the U.S. Navy—he was commander in chief of its Asiatic squadron, son of a celebrated American commodore in the early republic, and father of an even more important naval leader of the early twentieth century. John Rodgers, like many of the officers and men beneath him, had extensive battle experience, including fighting Seminoles in Florida, Mexicans during the 1846 war, and Confederates during the Civil War. He also knew Commodore Matthew C. Perry well professionally and personally—Rodgers had carefully studied Perry's efforts in Japan,

Whose "Barbarism"? Whose "Treachery"?   89

and the Perry and Rodgers families were related by marriage. Indeed, in Korea Low and Rodgers would adopt tactics virtually identical to those Perry had used in Japan: the visible display of force, the provocative use of soundings in shore waters to increase pressure on local officials, the refusal to meet with low level representatives, and the insistence on communication with the highest authorities.[17]

Although Rodgers, like Low, knew virtually nothing about the Koreans, he too had strong feelings about Koreans and Asians generally. He revealed these in letters to his wife and his child, William Ledyard Rodgers (1860–1944). Admiral Rodgers found Asians, whether in Singapore, Hong Kong, Japan, or Shanghai, physically repugnant and their ways either disagreeable or childishly quaint. He and other expedition members saw Asia (other than Japan) as weak and needing domination. From Beijing, for example, he described China as "effete—worn out—decaying." The country, in his view, needed "the infusion of new ideas from some conquering race." Everything, he said, was "dilapidated." But Asians were also brutal—favoring torture and decapitation for punishments—untrustworthy, and stupidly anti-Western. He saw himself as on a mission both to secure specific American national interests and to advance civilization in general in East Asia.[18]

He colorfully expressed his own sense of racial and cultural superiority in a letter sent home from China just two weeks before he departed for Korea. He informed his wife that he and "Shanghai" (meaning, of course, the westerners in Shanghai) were reading Bret Harte's "The Heathen Chinee" with great enjoyment. The recently published verse by the popular poet was a demeaning portrait of Chinese immigrants in California, embodied in the character of Ah Sin. According to Rodgers, the poem marvelously captured the "astuteness" of the Chinese, "coupled with his knavery and apparent simplicity." It reads, in part:

> That for ways that are dark,
> And for tricks that are vain
> The Heathen Chinee is peculiar
>
> Ah Sin was his name;
> And I shall not deny
> In regard to the same
> What that name might imply.

90 *Chapter Four*

"Ah Sin" and "the heathen Chinee" quickly became popular metonyms for the Chinese in the United States and Chinese generally. The poem describes the trickery of a Chinese cardplayer, who bests his opponents through feigned naivete and cheating. Only after he is physically beaten is his deception unmasked, and the poem quickly became symbolic of the proper and efficacious way to handle Orientals. As the *North China Herald,* the major English-language newspaper published in Shanghai, observed at the time, the moral of Harte's poem is that Chinese "double-dealing must be met by physical force."[19]

"It is very amusing to a man—but much less so, I fancy, to a lady," Rodgers wrote. Trying to end his letter home on a light note, he informed his wife that a Shanghai racehorse had recently been named the Heathen Chinee.[20]

For their part, Chinese imperial officials found the ways of the Americans difficult to comprehend, especially their newfound, intense interest in Korea, which by the late nineteenth century was Beijing's most important and closest tributary state. The two countries had constructed a close relationship over centuries of contact, and although the Koreans acknowledged the supremacy of the emperor in Beijing, Korea was considered fully independent in its internal and external affairs. The Chinese and Korean courts assumed certain obligations and responsibilities toward each other, and their political and cultural stability and well-being were of mutual concern. Both adhered to a Confucian world view, with prescribed, hierarchical codes of personal and official conduct, strict social moralities, and formal modes of conduct in interstate relations. Adherence to such belief and behavior, it was held, separated the civilized from the barbarian.[21]

In Beijing's view the Americans had only base, acquisitive interests in Korea and, like the other Western powers, had no respect for the established East Asian moral order, which placed great value on ethics and proper behavior. Chinese officials sensed that heightened U.S. interest in Korea, an area previously peripheral to China's own troubled contact with the West, presaged further possible conflict; they therefore closely monitored American preparations for the mission. The more the Chinese learned, the more concerned they became. Their record of the 1871 expedition offers a unique third-party perspective on the American actions.

Writing from Shanghai, the day before Rodgers wrote his amused letter about the "heathen Chinee," Li Hongzhang, the powerful and famous

Whose "Barbarism"? Whose "Treachery"? 91

governor-general of the Hebei area responsible for security in China's northeastern region, alerted Beijing that Japanese ships might accompany the American fleet. The prospect was disturbing since the Chinese especially feared Japanese territorial ambitions on the Asian mainland. If the Koreans did not establish trade relations with the United States, Li wrote, there might be war. He warned that "if the Koreans treat the Americans . . . as they did the French, I really do not dare anticipate what would happen." He had hoped that the Koreans might find a way to accommodate the Americans, who might then counterbalance the Japanese on the Korean peninsula. Other Chinese reports suggested that British and French ships might join the American fleet. Although the rumors never materialized, the Chinese court accurately learned the number of ships, types of armament, and combat strength of the American force. The *Colorado,* flagship of the Asiatic fleet, left Shanghai on May 8, 1871, with China and other powers closely monitoring the outcome of the American venture.[22]

The *Colorado* stopped for several days at Nagasaki, Japan, where it met other American vessels for the mission. While in port, the leaders of the expedition conferred with officers and officials from several European countries. The expedition also picked up news reporters, including Felice Beato, a British citizen perhaps born in Venice, resident of Yokohama, one of the earliest professional photographers in the world, and correspondent for *Harper's Weekly.* Beato's presence suggests Rodgers and Low's awareness of the importance of their mission—after all, Perry's trip had already assumed heroic proportions in the American imagination, and a photographer on board could record their efforts for posterity. The U.S. minister to Japan urged Rodgers to take Beato on the expedition, since his activities "would result in a work of very great interest to the world as well as of exceeding usefulness to you." (Beato and the enduring legacy of his expedition photographs are discussed in an afterword to this essay.) The Americans also met with commanders of French naval forces who provided navigation and other logistical information gained from their Korea experience.[23]

After a short cruise from Japanese waters, the U.S. flotilla arrived at Korea's Taeyong Islands on May 19. (At the start of the expedition, the Americans called the islands the "Ferrieres," the French designation. Later, they began to replace French names with American ones. This essay will use the Korean names, which have been in continuous use.) Over the next several

92   *Chapter Four*

days, because of dense fog, uncertain navigation charts received from the French, and strong tides (the Americans estimated that the tides rose and fell twenty-five to thirty feet), the U.S. fleet slowly ventured into Korean waters off the coast from Inch'on. The expedition observed a few Korean fishing boats late on May 21, but it was not until May 30 that the fleet finally anchored off Chagyak, near the mouth of the Yomha River, which led directly to the Han River. This site, which became the fleet's operations base, was one of the most strategically sensitive in Korea, with Seoul, the capital, only fifty miles up the Han from the coast. The French had begun their own 1866 attack from this very location, and Gen. Douglas MacArthur would do the same in his famous landing at Inch'on in 1950.[24]

The arrival of the American fleet immediately attracted the attention of local Koreans. The physical presence of the flotilla startled onlookers: the *Colorado* was a steam frigate, with sail and engine, that displaced 4,772 tons, reached 264 feet at the water line, and carried 47 cannons, 47 officers, and 571 men. Three other ships were each at least 250 feet long. The fifth was an iron gunboat measuring 137 feet. After the fleet came in sight off the coast, beacon fires appeared on prominent hilltops near the anchorage. Local residents abandoned villages and took everything they could carry. But after a few days tensions quieted, and the Americans, using a Korean interpreter accompanying the expedition, engaged in casual conversation with a few of the remaining locals on shore. When the expedition sent out surveying parties in quickly moving steam launches to chart the coast and river channels, however, the Koreans again became agitated. Low recorded in his diary that as the launches proceeded "large numbers of people could be seen fleeing from the coast towards the country taking many cattle with them." John P. Cowles, an interpreter and acting assistant secretary of the U.S. legation in Beijing who accompanied one of the surveying parties, reported that on several occasions the "natives" shouted at the boats, displayed guns and other weapons, and "showed alarm" by retreating to hilltops overlooking the river. After several days of taking soundings, the surveying boats came alongside fortified locations and observed hundreds of agitated, armed Koreans under the command of uniformed military officials. "The plying to and fro of the launches speedily," Cowles wrote, "creates excitement." He also reported that if the boats had gone within "bow-shot" of a river village, "it is probable they would have run great risk of being fired into." Cowles thought that the chances of armed conflict

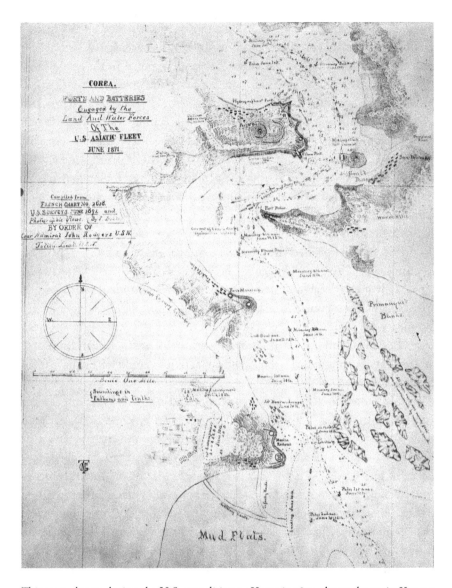

This map, drawn during the U.S. expedition to Korea in 1871, shows the main Korean fortifications along the Yomha River and the routes taken by American land and naval forces to engage the Koreans. Fighting centered on the forts overlooking the river passageway. The map legend states that Felice Beato was responsible for the expedition's "photographic views." *Courtesy Special Collections and University Archives, Stanford University Libraries, RBCDS915.P4f.*

94   *Chapter Four*

had been high, and he was thankful the Koreans did not, in his words, "shoot whoever lands—cold blood or hot blood matters not," an action that the Americans "might have anticipated." Unknown to the Americans, the Korean king had ordered all officials along the coastal areas to avoid provoking any conflict with the Americans.[25]

Capt. McLane Tilton, a Civil War veteran and commander of the marine detachment assigned to the fleet, was also nervous about the mission. Pessimistically, Tilton wrote his wife just before entering Korean waters, "My impression at this moment is, that the people will have no intercourse with us, and our journey will be so much love's labor lost." Though he hoped trouble could be avoided, he feared conflict. Rumor had it, he wrote, that some Westerners had recently come to Korea for trade, but "the natives" "cut them up, and pickled them, took them in the interior and set them up as curiosities!" "You may imagine," he wrote his wife back in Annapolis, "it is with not a great pleasure I anticipate landing with the small force we have, against a populous country containing 10,000,000 savages." Still, his men were "quite jolly," he wrote, and everyday the men on board were "exercised in the infantry drill & firing with small arms," which the Koreans presumably observed.[26] The American activities could hardly have been more provocative.

But nowhere in all the existing official and unofficial documentation generated by Cowles, Tilton, and their superiors are any questions, let alone doubts, expressed about the purpose of the mission and their behavior in Korean waters. The Americans were confident in the sincerity of their own peaceful intent and high purpose: they were acting in the interests of advanced civilization, not just for commercial or other narrow interests. They did not entertain the possibility that any truly civilized people could view their purposes in any other way. But this was the challenge for the Americans, for they assumed that the Koreans were not civilized. They made that assumption because of popular racial prejudices, but also because they, like most others in the West, believed that a central expression of civilization was a country's acceptance of treaty obligations and other formally negotiated diplomatic arrangements. Korea, which refused to accept such arrangements, was by definition savage and barbarian. But short of conquest and occupation, which the Americans did not seek, how could a resistant Korean government be brought to civilization? Contemporary Western practice had an answer: The threat, and even the limited exercise, of military force could compel the backward to accept the more advanced notions of the Western international system.

Assumptions that rationalized the intimidating and provocative display of force, along with popular hearsay and prejudices about the savage and treacherous nature of Asians, encouraged an aggressiveness among the Americans that would have dire consequences, leading to the failure of the expedition's avowed purposes. What the Americans encountered over the next several days only seemed to affirm the conviction of their own superior civilization and of their Asian adversaries' moral inferiority.

As the Chinese officials in Beijing had feared, the arrival of the American fleet alarmed Korean central authorities. The court in Seoul, which had received Low's message through China, was nonetheless unsettled by the imposing American flotilla. The court immediately dispatched a special military commander, O Chae-yon, to Kanghwa Island, Korea's Rock of Gibraltar and the key strategic island guarding the river passageway that the Americans were exploring. The court also sent military supplies and hundreds of troop reinforcements to the local fortresses.[27]

Several days after the Americans' arrival in Korean waters, local officials tried to make contact with them, but because of rough waters and translation problems, the two sides were unable to speak to each other. Through written correspondence, the officials asked about the nationality of the visitors and their reason for coming to Korea. The Americans replied by formally announcing the arrival of "an envoy and an admiral from the Great United States of America for negotiations with a Korean envoy of high rank" and their interest in negotiations with the court. The American message also stated that the fleet would "remain until all the business was completed." On May 30, three Koreans of unclear rank and a clerk came on board the *Colorado* and asked again about the fleet's business. Low refused to meet them because of their inferior status and repeated through an intermediary that he would meet only with high-ranking Korean officials. The Korean emissaries were also told that the expedition would continue to send out coastal surveying parties. The Americans informed the Koreans that "the smaller vessels of the fleet will make explorations further on, in order that the large ships may move nearer the capital, in case the [U.S.] minister deems it necessary." This less-than-veiled threat was coupled with an assurance that nothing would happen as long as the American vessels

96   *Chapter Four*

were "treated with civility and kindness." The Americans again proclaimed their "peaceful disposition" and their desire to avoid any conflict.[28]

On May 31, three Korean officials visited the *Colorado,* but they were apparently still of a minor rank. Low refused to meet them. The Korean emissaries informed the Americans that the king had read Low's letter from China and that, although he desired friendly relations with the United States, he had no interest in meeting or negotiating any treaties. Unpersuaded (Low privately recorded that he had "little confidence in oriental professions of friendliness"), unsatisfied, and undeterred, the American officials repeated their terms and reminded the Koreans about the surveying parties that would go further up the river. The surveyors meant no harm to anyone, the Koreans were told, but if the boats were attacked, "force would be met by force." Low recorded that the Koreans gave what he later described to his superiors in Washington as "tacit" approval of the surveying. The Koreans were notified that the surveying would begin in twenty-four hours. Low never explained why, on the one hand, he refused to meet the Korean envoys because of their supposed low rank, yet, on the other hand, he presumed they could authorize the American advance into sensitive waters.[29]

Less than a day later, at noon on June 1, the U.S. expedition dispatched two gunboats and four steam launches. But whereas on previous days the surveying had been limited to the offshore sea area, the vessels entered the mouth of the Yomha and proceeded upriver. The Yomha, as described by Admiral Rodgers, led directly to the "River Seoul [Han] which passes near the city of Seoul, the capital and residence of the Sovereign." As the party sailed north in the river, which separated Kanghwa from the mainland, it encountered "numerous forts" festooned with military banners and official flags. The parapets were fully and visibly manned. Some ten miles from the base anchorage and two hours into the journey, the party entered a sharp bend in the river, with a "whirl, as bad that of Hell Gate, New York, full of eddies and ledges."[30] The river bend, Sondolmok, known as "the gateway to the capital," was the key entry into the interior of the country. The French labeled it "Passage difficile." According to the American official reports, when the U.S. ships approached Kwangsong, the main fort that controlled Sondolmok, Korean cannons suddenly opened fire. Guns also opened up from Tokchin and Tokp'o, other strategically located forts along the sides of the river. The shelling was ferocious but inaccurate, and the

Whose "Barbarism"? Whose "Treachery"? 97

American ships escaped damage. They immediately counterfired, apparently with considerable accuracy and consequence. The incident lasted no more than fifteen minutes, with some five hundred rounds exchanged. The untouched American ships then returned to their base anchorage, with just two wounded and no loss of life. Reports that the Americans later received put the number of Korean deaths at 30, with many more wounded. The Americans had knowingly ventured into one of the most sensitive sites of the country.[31]

The Korean bombardment infuriated the Americans and confirmed their assumptions about Korean perfidy. Low officially described the attack as "unprovoked and wanton, and without the slightest shadow of excuse." Low wrote that he was now convinced that the Korean government would resist "all innovation and intercourse with all the power at its command" whether the overtures concerned trade or the humane treatment of shipwrecked sailors. The Koreans, he concluded, were simply a "semi-barbarous and hostile race." They had without reason attacked "a peaceful mission in the interest of humanity." Rodgers described the events similarly—the act was "sudden" and "treacherous." The king of Korea, Rodgers wrote his wife, "has declared war against a peaceable expedition." It was "premeditated treachery," in Rodgers's words.[32]

Evidence from sources other than the official U.S. record suggests a very different interpretation. The Korean attack was not as sudden, unexpected, and unprovoked as Low and Rodgers reported. One purpose of the surveying parties was to unsettle the Koreans. Fifteen years after the expedition, an unidentified junior officer who was on the surveying mission published his recollection of the events, still controversial after many years. The vessels were originally unarmed, he recalled, but before setting out, the men outfitted the launches with howitzers (small cannon), highly visible on their bows, and were given rifles, all in anticipation of a possible clash. The two large gunboats that accompanied the launches were also heavily armed. Moreover, this memoir reconstructed the timing of events differently from the official reports. According to his detailed recollection, many moments passed from the time that the Americans first saw the massed Korean armed forces, with their guns trained down on the river, and the first shot. The Americans could clearly see the Korean "dark faces and the artillerists blowing their fuses [to keep them lit]." The officer recalled that he "trembled like a leaf" in seeing all this. He told his superior, "These Coreans are

98   *Chapter Four*

certainly going to fire upon us." His superiors laughed him off, but they ordered the men to load the howitzers and their rifles. The vessels continued upstream. A Korean soldier captured during later fighting, when asked why his compatriots had opened fire, told his interrogators that fighting began only after the Americans violated the Korean "fortified zone." After that point, "the only thing left for us to do as patriots," he said, "was to fire upon the vessels, and try to prevent them from passing our nation's gateway. We only did our duty."[33] According to an article that appeared just days after the June 1 incident in a Western-language newspaper published in China, the American surveying party ignored signs of trouble along their way up the river channel. When the party entered the sensitive area, the paper reported, some 2,000 Korean soldiers appeared, putting on a "demonstration [that] seemed intended to induce the surveying party to retire." But the American officers did not heed the signal. And at least one American diplomatic official quietly questioned the wisdom of the expedition's actions. George F. Seward, the U.S. consul general in Shanghai and later minister to China, formally rallied behind his embattled colleagues when he learned about the June 1 clash, but he also confidentially criticized the expedition's decisions in his communications with the State Department. "I do not know why the surveying should have been pushed forward so rapidly," he wrote. He cited precedents for the violent Korean reaction, which he suggested might have been defensive. But Seward's objection changed nothing and was never made public.[34]

After the surveying party's return, Low and Rodgers quickly decided how to respond to the Korean attack. They immediately began assembling a large landing force, which was to set out the next morning to destroy the offending fortifications. But after considering the dangerous currents, Low and Rodgers decided to postpone the mission for ten days, until the waters were calmer. More interesting is their analysis of the events. Low and Rodgers concluded that the Koreans had deliberately ambushed the innocent American party: The Koreans had never intended to negotiate but had lured the Americans upriver where they would be vulnerable to attack. Such "treachery" had been in the Korean plans from the beginning, in Low's view. Now something must be done to redress the insult since the events had to be understood from the "oriental stand-point," "rather than [from] the more advanced one of Christian civilization." Even though the American forces had handily rebuked the Korean attack, Low wrote, the Koreans were undoubtedly claiming victory. He argued that leaving the Koreans with this misimpression would be "injurious, if not disastrous" to American interests, not only in Korea but also in China, where anti-Western sentiments were running high. The Koreans and possibly even the Chinese might conclude that they could successfully defy the West. Low therefore concluded that the American forces had to avenge "the wrongs and insults which our flag has suffered." Destroying the Korean fortifications would also leave the Americans in control of the Yomha and the entry to the Han, which they could blockade until the president sent further orders. Under such circumstances the Korean government might feel compelled to negotiate, Low speculated. After giving thought to an attempt to advance all the way to Seoul, the expedition's leaders reluctantly concluded that, although Western international law would sanction such an action, they had inadequate forces "to conquer this people and compel the government to enter into proper treaty engagements." In a private note to himself, Rodgers calculatedthat 5,000 men would be needed to take Seoul and subdue the surrounding fortresses.[35]

Although the Marine, Captain Tilton, had not been eager to engage the Koreans on the battlefield before June 1, he too was now itching for a fight. He had not been with the assaulted surveying party, but he agreed that the Koreans had dishonored the United States. "We are all 'hearty as bucks,'" he wrote his wife, "and *full* of having a *bang* at the Koreans before very long." He was looking forward to venturing forth to attack the Koreans and demolish their offending forts. Tilton's truculence also seems to have been stirred by reports of the lethal accuracy of American weaponry and the corresponding ineffectiveness of the Korean guns. He no longer seemed to be worried about engaging ten million "savages," as he had earlier confided to his wife. He described the Korean cannons as being "very *rude*"; they were apparently "*lashed* to *logs,* and cannot be trained except on a point before hand." The Koreans' small arms were "jing-galls," which "two men carry on their shoulders & touch off with a match!" The Koreans could not return fire after the American guns, with great accuracy and power, scattered the Korean soldiers from their positions. Imagine, he boasted to his wife, "how unable they are to cope with us, armed as we are with the latest improvements." Indeed, when the Americans occupied the forts, they found antiquated weaponry, with many pieces dating from the sixteenth and seventeenth centuries. One captured cannon had been cast in 1313.[36]

100   *Chapter Four*

Within days of the June 1 clash, Western newspapers in Asia carried sensational articles based on expedition reports sent to China. The English paper, the *Shanghai Evening Courier,* threw its full support behind the Americans. The "Coreans, with the faithlessness of the barbarian," the newspaper reported, "opened fire on the U.S. flotilla." Though it said it usually rejected warmongering, the newspaper declared that in this case "the good of the civilised world must come before the good of a horde of semi-savages." It looked forward to American actions against the Koreans and expected "that now America is about to take her share in opening up the East to the peaceful and beneficent action of western civilization." The newspaper saw the United States as an ally in advancing a higher moral order, not as a commercial rival. Other Western papers in China and the press in the United States and Japan joined in praising the bravery of the American mission and eagerly anticipated an aggressive American response in the name of humanity.[37]

The Korean government's deliberations after learning of the June 1 incident are not known in detail, but scholars of Korea have suggested that Low and Rodgers were terribly wrong in assuming that the surveying party had been lured into an ambush. It appears that Korean officials believed the American surveying party was a prelude to an invasion similar to the French attack in 1866, which had taken the same route in an effort to reach Seoul. William Elliot Griffis, one of the earliest American scholars of Korea, later argued that the Koreans probably thought the American party was "nothing more than a treacherous beginning of war in the face of assurances of peace. To enter into their waters seemed to them an invasion of their country." Advancing as the Americans did, after speaking words of "friendship," must have seemed the "basest treachery" to the Koreans.[38]

Evidence in Korean archives shows that the court reacted hurriedly in ways that support Griffis's interpretation, rather than the assumption that the Koreans had prepared a trap. Immediately following the clash, the court's military council dispatched several hundred additional soldiers and supplies to the Kanghwa area, especially strengthening Kwangsong. Military units around the capital were also mobilized. But the most interesting evidence of official Korean thinking is contained in communications sent to the American forces following the June 1 clash. In the messages the Koreans presented their view of what had transpired and an explanation for their actions. Not surprisingly, the Korean interpretation of events

Whose "Barbarism"? Whose "Treachery"? 101

differed dramatically from the American. It was, however, fully consistent with Western notions about national rights and territorial integrity. But the Korean argument, though it revealed some familiarity with Western concepts of international relations, made no impression on the leadership of the American expedition—it was then commonly held that the principles of international law, such as respect for national boundaries, applied in full only to "civilized," Christian nations that accepted the rights and responsibilities of regularized diplomacy as practiced in the Western international system. Nations that did not, such as Korea, were by definition less civilized, morally inferior, and subject to treatment appropriate to their backwardness. The Korean court's appeal to universal standards of international behavior therefore fell on deaf ears.[39]

For several days after the June 1 clash, the Americans exchanged messages first with local and then with regional Korean officials, although at first this proved difficult. After the outbreak of hostilities, local villagers had abandoned the coast, leaving the areas near the American anchorage deserted. The Americans could find no one to transmit letters to the authorities. The American and Korean sides therefore resorted to an odd but functional procedure to exchange messages. Communications were affixed to a pole stuck in the mud flats near the fleet. Under cover of darkness, the Koreans left messages, which the Americans retrieved at this "post office," as it was called, the next morning. The Koreans picked up the American notes in reverse manner.[40]

The Koreans informed the Americans that they wanted friendly relations with the United States and did not understand why the Americans had acted so aggressively. The Koreans asked: Were the Americans interested in seizing Korean territory or valuables? How could the Americans ignore four thousand years of Korean culture and ways and try to intrude into their life? One message wondered why the United States came from "afar the vast ocean to penetrate another country. Even though you disclaim all purpose of killing or harming us, who can help being puzzled and suspicious." Invoking what should have been a familiar tenet about a country's security, a Korean official argued that the "barriers of defense of a country are important places, within which it is not allowable for foreign vessels to make their way. This is the fixed rule of all nations." It was therefore the advance of the American surveying party that provoked the engagement. Once the vessels violated an important passageway, how could

Western publications widely reproduced Felice Beato's images of Koreans in staged, subordinate positions, including this one, which he claimed showed "Corean officer & soldiers with dispatches on board the *Colorado*," the flagship of the 1871 U.S. expedition. Beato's own captions on other photographs, however, identify these men as wounded prisoners, captured during fighting in June 1871. *Courtesy Special Collections and University Archives, Stanford University Libraries, RBCDS915.P4f.*

the officers, "appointed to guard the frontier, whose duty it is to take measures of defense, calmly let it go by as of no consequence?" The whole world knows of Korean's policy of "non-intercourse," so "why do you then wait for a high official to meet you?" The official also offered as a gift from the local governor three bullocks, fifty chickens, and one thousand eggs to succor, or possibly appease, the Americans. The Americans declined the beneficence, which symbolized, of course, Koreans' magnanimity toward the unruly guests to their country.[41]

Whose "Barbarism"? Whose "Treachery"? 103

The Americans in turn sent the Korean court their version of the events and their new demands. They had come in peace, Edward B. Drew, the acting secretary of the American legation in China, wrote for Low as head of the American expedition, but Korea had responded with "an unprovoked and wanton attack." While that act might have been committed by local people and subordinates, the Korean king could now send "an apology for this outrage," disavow it, and "send a high officer to meet and consult" with the American minister. If there was no such meeting, Drew advised, the American minister and admiral would "pursue such a course as they may deem proper to obtain redress for the wrongs done to us." The Americans gave the Korean authorities no more than six days to respond positively. In closing, Drew pointed out that the fleet in Korean waters was just part of a larger and more powerful navy in the region. Those ships, the Koreans were informed, "are constantly within two or three days' sail of your country, and if they choose, can destroy your towns and annoy your districts and departments for an unlimited number of years." But that was not what the United States wanted, Drew claimed: "We desire peace and friendly feelings to exist between our country and all others."[42]

Two days later the Americans, again under Drew's signature, sent another note. It was brief and blunt. The Americans said they had received no apologies from the Koreans but only rationalizations. This disappointed the expedition's admiral, who repeated his hope that the Korean king would send a high emissary to meet him. "Three or four days of the time allowed still remain," Drew reminded the Koreans. But he again threatened that if the Americans were not satisfied, "the admiral and minister will then feel at liberty to pursue such a course as they may deem proper."[43]

Less than three days later, on the morning of June 10, with the tides more cooperative, an American punitive force set out from the fleet. It consisted of twenty-two vessels, including two of the large gunboats, several launches with cannon, and many troop transports. The total force contingent was 950 men, 650 of them ground troops, many with extensive Civil War battlefield experience. McLane Tilton led 105 marines. Winfield Scott Schley, celebrated in the Spanish-American War and eventually a rear admiral, was among the naval officers. As the force made its way toward the river channel, a Korean boat bearing a white flag came up to the American vessels in one last effort to forestall further violence. The boat carried a message from a high Korean official replying to Drew's latest note. The official

104 *Chapter Four*

again tried to show the wisdom of his country's point of view. He argued that by sending heavily armed vessels of war up the river the Americans had provoked the Koreans. "I apprehend that the way of concord and the rule of propriety of entering another country," he wrote, appealing to a universal sense of national rights and privileges, "do not justify this." He expressed regret for the Korean firing but argued that what the Koreans had done was "what you would do were the case your own." Unsatisfied, the American forces resumed their advance.[44]

The refusal or inability of the leadership of the American forces to appreciate the Korean point of view, as persuasive as it might seem in historical hindsight, reveals the Americans' assumptions about Korean barbarism and American moral superiority. The very premise of the mission, which aimed to force Korea to join the "civilized" nations of the world in regularized intercourse, was that Korea occupied not just a backward legal position, but an inferior moral position. Conversely, it was assumed that the United States represented advanced civilization and a system of international relations in accord with the natural order. The need to end Korea's self-imposed isolation from the international system took precedence over respect for its sovereignty, since such sovereignty only protected and perpetuated an unnatural exclusivity. Korean invocation of a national right to self-defense therefore only served to *confirm* the country's barbaric backwardness in the eyes of the Americans. Decades earlier, John Quincy Adams had made the same argument in supporting the British in the Opium War against China in 1840: national exclusivity was selfish and arrogantly defied natural law by artificially impeding others' pursuit of wealth and happiness. In the 1840s Adams had persuaded few Americans to support the British, but by the 1870s few Americans denied that the Western international system embodied natural law.[45]

Nowhere in the official documentation is there any indication that the American leadership considered any explanation for the hostilities other than Korean treachery. No thought was given to the possibility of misunderstanding, for example, even though the records show considerable American frustration over communications. Although they had brought along a Korean sailor to help interpret, formal communications, including those in writing, were in Chinese. Two of Low's American secretaries understood Chinese, but Low also used the services of a Chinese interpreter, whom he derisively referred to as "Confucius." Often the Americans could

Whose "Barbarism"? Whose "Treachery"? 105

not even infer the status of the Korean officials they did meet. Nevertheless, the expedition leadership believed that the Koreans had ambushed their vessels after approving the upriver surveying. The Americans had assumed they might encounter oriental deceit and treachery, and the events simply confirmed their suspicions.[46]

The punitive expedition advanced upriver, and when it reached the first of the defending forts, the vessels opened with artillery fire, destroying the ramparts and scattering the defenders. Then the American ground forces,

Within minutes after the fall of Kwangsong, the main Korean fort overlooking the Yomha River, Felice Beato photographed the destruction, labeling the image the "interior of Fort McKee." American forces renamed the site after its conquest to honor one of their casualties in the United States–Korea War of 1871. The Korean dead lying before their conquerors is typical of images by Beato, who was keen on displaying battlefield "still lifes." Beato sometimes rearranged elements, including corpses—even on occasion exhuming them—to create a dramatic moment. *Courtesy Special Collections and University Archives, Stanford University Libraries, RBCDS915.P4f.*

106   *Chapter Four*

with seven advanced howitzers in tow, landed under covering fire from the gunboats. Soldiers ransacked a nearby village for provisions, taking stores of grain and beans. With their vastly superior power, the Americans then easily captured the first of the five forts that fell over two days of fighting. Fires started by the attacking forces spread to nearby villages, which burned to the ground. But the high point of the engagement for the Americans was the battle for Kwangsong, the principal fortification overlooking the strategic turn in the Yomha. After tremendous shelling from land and water, the American forces stormed what they called the "citadel." Accounts tell of ferocious hand-to-hand combat, with the Korean soldiers fighting virtually to the last man. Schley recalled that the American field commanders had decided to make war employing "the most approved modern methods, and to spare nothing that might be reached by shot, shell, fire or sword." After the fighting was over, the Americans counted some 250 bodies, with many more assumed killed with their remains lost in the river, ravines, and burning rubble of the forts. The Americans spiked cannons, seized banners and supplies, destroyed fortifications, and took 15 prisoners. They reported that the scene inside Kwangsong was horrendous, with piles of burning and dismembered bodies two and three deep. The bodies of Korean soldiers, who had clothed themselves in protective vestments constructed of layers of tough, thick cotton, now lay smoldering in the dirt. The stench of roasting flesh was everywhere. American casualties, on the other hand, were just 3 killed and 9 wounded. The American leaders pointed to the disparity in human loss between the two sides (the nineteenth-century equivalent of the Vietnam War's "body count") as evidence of their victory and, of course, their superior civilization.[47]

The intense fighting with the Koreans left a strong impression on the Americans, even the hardened veterans of the Civil War and Indian campaigns. All their accounts tell of brutal combat. Low himself reported to Washington that the ferocity of the Koreans in combat was "rarely equaled and never excelled by any people." But why did they fight with such "desperation," in his words? Low was at a loss for an explanation. Was it because they believed neither escape nor surrender was an option, and so they fought to the death? Low did not even consider whether something so familiar and understandable such as loyalty to king or country was the explanation. No, there was something irrational in their fighting, in his view. The Korean tenacity was fanatical or bestial, other American soldiers concluded. McLane Tilton said the Koreans "fought like tigers." One combatant described the Korean soldiers as "wild beasts," and another said they fought "more like demons than men." Recalling brutal wars familiar to many of the American soldiers, another witness described the Koreans as fighting with the "coolness and immobility of Indians." Another man reported that before battle the Koreans chanted a war cry or a death wail—he knew not which, but it was not like anything he had ever heard. "The awful cadence of that blood-curdling strain. It was like nothing human!" Other comments betrayed disdain for the enemy, even in their resistance. Adm. John Rodgers described the fighting to his wife: "the Coreans fought desperately—if no weapon was at hand they picked up stones and threw them—some who were pinioned to the earth with bayonets threw dust on their conquerors." But then he quickly added, "the greater part however ran away—some of them falling head over heels upon the steep descent." Others graphically described the enemy as bleeding "like pigs," presenting an especially dreadful sight in their white uniforms. Tilton said that when he looked upon the dead enemy, to his own surprise, he felt little emotion. "It didn't affect me more than looking at so many dead hogs," he wrote his wife. Others made allusions to dogs and rabbits in describing how the fleeing enemy flew heels over head when shot from behind. Several days after the fighting had ended, Low inspected the Korean prisoners and reflected on the Asian enemy in his diary. Korean autocracy had reduced the common people to "serfs or slaves," he wrote. They were ignorant and craven and the soldiers "mere automatons," their tenacious fighting mistakenly called "courage." In reality, Low wrote, it was "mere stolidity and indifference to death." Low ended his diary entry, "Human life is considered of little value, and soldiers, educated as they have been, meet death with the same indifference as the Indians of North America."[48]

The record from the Korean side also tells of terrible fighting and slaughter. Field reports describe the "fierce fighting of the Western enemy" and the inability of the Korean forces to stop their advance. "The shells of the foreign ships fell like rain," one report read, "and the bullets from the foreign guns on land came down like hail." Commanders reported being completely routed. When the Koreans reoccupied the forts after the American withdrawal, they found horrible ruin, with mangled bodies everywhere. They discovered the remains of Gen. O Chae-yon and other Korean

108   *Chapter Four*

commanders embedded in the Kwangsong moat and river mud flats. "The invasion of the country by a foreign enemy," the king of Korea reportedly said during a meeting at the Korean court following the clash, "is a most painful thing." "The barbarians said they wanted peace, [but] we do not know what they want to do with us." The court decided to continue to have nothing to do with the Americans. Convinced that the events confirmed Korean righteousness and moral purity, the court reaffirmed its seclusion policy to protect its own civilization.[49]

After the American attack force triumphantly returned to the fleet on June 12, the two sides resumed their verbal war. Each accused the other of treachery and barbarism. On June 14 Low sent a long dispatch to the Korean king summarizing the American view of the events. After the Koreans had "wantonly fired" on the American surveying team and when the Americans received no apology for the insult, the Americans could take no other course "than to seek redress by arms, as is usual among all civilised nations." That had now been done, Low pointed out, and "the events of the past few days afford convincing proofs of our power whenever we choose to exert it." Although "well-established precedent would sanction the moving of our forces against any and all places of the kingdom" and although the U.S. forces were "possessed of the power," Low assured the king that the United States had no interest in war or conquest. It wanted only to cultivate friendly relations with Korea and to establish formal arrangements, similar to those with its Asian neighbors. Low reiterated his demand that the Korean king send a "speedy and frank reply" and "a person of suitable rank" to negotiate. Two days later, the Korean official who received the message informed Low that he would *not* forward the insulting message to the king. Low had his assistant threaten the local official for obstructing communications and inform him that the leadership of the U.S. expedition now "contemplates a prolonged stay in the vicinity of the capital," while waiting for the king's response.[50]

Not surprisingly, Low never heard from the Korean king, the court, or any other high-ranking Korean official. Early in the morning of July 3, three long weeks after Korean and American forces had battled one another, the U.S. fleet pulled up anchor and withdrew from Korean waters. Tilton was glad to leave. "We are heartily sick of this place," he wrote his wife a few days before sailing away. Before departing, Low took a parting shot at the Korean authorities. In one last letter he warned, "it can scarcely

In the United States–Korea War of 1871, Felice Beato portrayed the Americans, in contrast to the Koreans, in heroic light. Beato's caption for this photo describes it as a "council of war" on board the U.S. flagship after fighting broke out with the Koreans on June 1, 1871. The expedition's military leader, Adm. John Rodgers, is second from the right, among his officers. In fact, Beato probably took this photograph on June 23, almost two weeks after major hostilities ended. *Courtesy Special Collections and University Archives, Stanford University Libraries, RBCDS915.P4f.*

be expected that the United States, or the governments of Europe, will continue to submit tamely to the haughty dictum of His Majesty, or rest content with his persistent refusal to hold direct communication with the ministers that may be sent on public business." The Western governments, Low informed the Korean sovereign, possessed ample grounds for using "power necessary to enforce compliance with their reasonable demands." In the meantime, Low would "withdraw temporarily to some other point on the coast of Corea or China."[51]

110   *Chapter Four*

After he returned to China, away from the heat of battle, Low reviewed his course of action in a report to his superiors in Washington. His lengthy communication reveals that he remained wedded to the cultural assumptions that had produced the disastrous outcome of the mission. Low thought that "civilized and Christian governments" might be able to learn from his effort. He began by characterizing Korea as presumptuous, ridiculing it as the "only nation on earth claiming to be civilized," when in fact it refused to "hold intercourse of any sort with the Christian countries of Europe and America." In addition to the matter of principle, there was also the matter of power: Low argued that the June 10 attack was required to establish who had won the June 1 clash. If the United States had not severely punished the Koreans, they would have claimed victory, spreading the news of their supposed success, "enlarged and embellished as orientals only can do." For the future, Low argued for a combined Western effort against Korea. The Korean central government would "feel the force of foreign arms" only when westerners "menaced or occupied" Seoul. "Foreign governments should decide," Low argued, "either to let Corea alone, and allow her to burn, pillage, destroy, and massacre all that come within her reach" or "organize and send such a force as will be able to insure success . . . in breaking down the barriers that stand in the way of intercourse." Delay would only worsen the situation. "If no adequate measures be taken to avert the impending storm in the East, the result will, I fear, be disastrous." Admiral Rodgers more succinctly expressed the same sentiments when he reported to his superior, Secretary of the Navy George M. Robeson. "Christiandom," he wrote, required a formal treaty, not "the word of a semi-barbarous, irresponsible and perfidious monarch." Might and virtue had to make right.[52]

In the United States, the public generally supported and endorsed the expedition's actions. Most major newspapers echoed the official reports, accepting without question the Grant administration's version of events. The periodicals duly repeated the demeaning racial and cultural characterizations. The *New York Times*'s headlines promised to deliver a "Detailed Account of the Treacherous Attack of the Coreans on Our Launches" and news of the "Speedy and Effective Punishment of the Barbarians." The *New York Herald* labeled the conflict "Our Little War with the Heathen."[53]

But there were exceptions to the chorus of support, and they indicate that not all Americans accepted a political logic that rationalized aggression by self-proclaimed civilized nations. Edward B. Drew, Low's chief assistant,

Whose "Barbarism"? Whose "Treachery"? III

seems to have been privately critical of his superiors' attitude and course of action, but he waited more than a decade before he revealed his feelings. The Americans, he stated at a public lecture in China, "having trailed their coats before the faces of the Coreans, and having at last persuaded the Coreans to step on them, demanded an apology for the insult." At the time of the expedition, Horace Greeley's *New York Tribune,* which was generally critical of the Grant administration, condemned the expedition and its pretensions. The paper mocked the American claims of superior morality and justice and turned the idea of civilization back upon the United States. Under the sarcastic title "Civilizing the Coreans," an editorial focused on the arrogance of the Low-Rodgers mission's declaration that it only wanted to have the Koreans "partake of the sweets of American civilization." What else could be expected but armed clashes, the paper argued, when "armed foreigners [the Americans] [went] poking about [the Korean] coast?" And after the Koreans attacked, the paper continued, the American admiral took "such measures as the interests of 'civilization required'": "the taking of the Corean forts, guns numberless, and the slaughter of all the natives who did not get to the tall timber." The newspaper ended its editorial with rhetorical questions that would be repeated many years later during other American conflicts in Asia: "What right [do] we have in Corean waters, what [are] we to gain by killing these people, how many more are to be killed, and where [is] this fierce diplomacy to land us—all these questions will become interesting as we find how much easier it is to go to war than to get out of it."[54]

But in the highest circles, Low and Rodgers were only praised for their service, and their recommendations for further action against Korea received serious consideration. In his annual message to Congress on December 4, 1871, President Ulysses S. Grant fully backed the Low-Rodgers mission and asked Congress to consider taking further action against Korea, perhaps even declaring war. But Congress did not act, and Korea gradually faded from national attention.[55]

Neither Low nor Rodgers ever went back to Korea. Both returned to the United States more hostile toward Asians than before. Although as governor of California Low had had a reputation as being somewhat liberal on Chinese immigration, he now feared that an East-West conflict, rooted in racial difference and standards of civilization, was inevitable. After he returned to the United States, Low wrote, "The Chinese and the Oriental civilization is as distinct from our's as darkness is from light. There is no similarity in our

112   *Chapter Four*

language or modes of thought." He saw no chance of amalgamation of the Chinese in America without deterioration of the superior race. He too now found wisdom in Bret Harte's "The Heathen Chinee," quoting it in correspondence to illustrate the unintelligibility of Chinese ways. Both he and Admiral Rodgers, after going to war ostensibly to "open" Korea's door to the West, now endorsed *closing* the doors of the United States to Asians. Lending their names and prestige as ones who well knew the inferior and dangerous Asian, they joined the growing domestic chorus calling for Chinese exclusion from the United States. In fall 1876, both men appeared as expert witnesses before a special joint congressional committee investigating Chinese immigration. Low, now a leading businessman in San Francisco, and Rodgers, superintendent of the navy's Mare Island shipyard in Vallejo, California, both strongly endorsed legislation restricting further Chinese entry into the country. The Chinese, Low testified, were unable to "assimilate, amalgamate, and become part of [this] Government and its people." They, like "negros and Malays," were "incapable" of amalgamation with the "Anglo-Saxon race."[56]

In Asia, the Korean king got the last word. In the winter of 1871–1872, months after the U.S. forces had departed, he sent Chinese officials a detailed explanation of the conflict with the United States. Its apparent purpose was to allay any suspicions the Chinese may have had about the wisdom of the Koreans' actions. The country had acted honorably and consistent with past practices, according to the king. It was the Americans who from the start had acted aggressively and arrogantly, raising Korean concerns. They waved away messengers and officials sent by the court; they then entered a highly sensitive river passage. How could "foreign armed men-of-war, which have not yet apprized us of their intentions, be allowed to go rushing about?" "Weighing all the reasons for our proceedings," he wrote, "any other country would have acted in just the same manner."[57]

The king's analysis of American thinking revealed a keen insight into the expedition's contradictory behavior. The Americans forwarded messages "bragging," in the king's words, "that they had come with peaceful intentions, that nobody need harbor suspicion, that they certainly would hurt no one, and there was therefore no ground of fear." Why then, the king asked rhetorically, did "they come in ships full of soldiers?" Why did they refuse to meet with the officials sent to them? Why did they enter an important passage that they should have known would be well guarded?

Whose "Barbarism"? Whose "Treachery"?   113

Therefore, he concluded, all the American talk about peaceful intent "was simply a device to put us off our guard, a crafty scheme to take advantage of our negligence, and get into the interior." Yet, even if that had not been the true purpose of the Americans, he continued, their behavior at least displayed "utter contempt" for Korea, "as if this was a country without anybody to take care of it." How could the Americans have had genuinely friendly feelings toward the Koreans when they acted so insistently and in disregard of the authorities? Their basic purpose was to conclude a treaty, something that the Americans knew the Korean court did not want.[58]

The king's interpretation was only partly correct: It was true that the Americans had hoped to compel the resistant Koreans to do something they did not want to do, that is, to begin formal relations with the West. What the king did not fully appreciate, however, is that the words and actions of the Americans were not part of a secret plan to invade his country, seizing territory or making war to conquer the country. Unlike the Europeans, the Americans did not covet territory and special privileges in Asia. The Americans sincerely believed they had come in peace and harbored no malice toward Korea. Representing the purposes of a greater civilization, however, the Americans also believed they were in Korean waters only to raise the barbarous and inferior Koreans to a higher standard of behavior in international relations. The American display of force and its actual use had been fully justified and even necessary, in their view. It is no wonder that, from the king's point of view, the American behavior had been contemptuous toward Korea.

Although Low believed that the expedition had taught the Koreans a lesson, the Korean court concluded that the nation had again defeated Western encroachment. The policy of seclusion was vindicated and officially reaffirmed. Immediately following the departure of the Americans from Korean waters, the Korean court ordered the prominent display of special steles around the country carrying the Taewon'gun's declaration, "Western barbarians foully attack! Should we not fight, accord must be made! To urge accord is to betray the country!" The court even ordered that makers of ink sticks imprint the Taewon'gun's declaration on every slab, and it showered honors on the fallen and surviving defenders of the Kanghwa forts. The Taewon'gun composed a flamboyant couplet to celebrate the victory: "The smoke and dust of the vessels of Westerners cover the world with darkness, but the great light of the East enlightens it throughout eternity." The leaders of the 1871 American expedition to Korea were not the only ones guilty of

114   *Chapter Four*

egoism and moral arrogance—the Korean court used the successful repulse of the Americans to elevate its prestige among the Korean officialdom and intelligentsia. Korean Confucian virtue and moral determination, it seemed to many in the country, had triumphed over the unruly Western barbarians, confirming the rightness of the state's policy. For the next ten years, the Korean court held that a state of war existed between Korea and America.[59]

In China, court officials concluded that Korea had acted with just cause. In May, before the U.S. expedition had left China, leading officials had hoped that the Americans might succeed. The Chinese thought that an American presence in Korea might serve as a counterweight to the Japanese, whose territorial ambitions caused the Chinese greater concern. But after reviewing the record of the war, court officials concluded that the Koreans had been reasonable to resist the American demands. The case made by Korea's king persuaded the officials of the Zongli Yamen. Korea, not the United States, had acted in a civilized and proper way. Prince Gong, China's top official for foreign affairs, asked the Americans to back off. "The reasonable view of the whole case," he wrote Low, was to "respect the free action" of Korea and not try to force it "to comply with your demands respecting things which it may be unwilling to carry out. This would be the way to consolidate peaceful and harmonious [U.S.-China] relations."[60]

Avoiding Korea for a decade, the United States returned in 1882 and successfully concluded a treaty of "amity and commerce" with the kingdom. It was the first between Korea and a Western power. Changes in the personnel and attitude at Korea's court and reconfigured regional politics helped produce a very different outcome. But perhaps an equally important reason for the accord was the attitude taken by Adm. Robert Shufeldt, the leader of the 1882 effort. Shufeldt was conciliatory toward King Kojong from the very start of the overture. In a letter to the king, Shufeldt expressed his wish to bring about an "amicable intercourse" between the two countries, which "owing to a misunderstanding [had] been unfortunately interrupted," as he wrote in oblique reference to the 1871 conflict. In a private note to himself, Shufeldt went further and blamed the historic exclusion of the West from Japan, China, and Korea "entirely to their [Westerners] own acts & machinations." Perhaps thinking specifically about Low and Rodgers in 1871, Shufeldt criticized Western behavior in Asia. "Our prejudices are continually finding arguments wherewith to advance our interests," he wrote sarcastically, "these people, we say, have no right, natural, or acquired to this haughty, contemptuous, indifference to our

Whose "Barbarism"? Whose "Treachery"? 115

commerce or to our civilization." It was not that Shufeldt was averse to the use of force or that he accepted Asians as racial equals—like Low and Rodgers, he believed that Asians were inferior and supported legislation to control Chinese immigration into the United States. But Shufeldt did not want what he considered prejudiced cultural attitudes to interfere with the advancement of vital U.S. commercial interests. East-West interaction and trade were too important an end. The result for Shufeldt was diplomatic success, not war.[61]

This essay has in part been about clashing moralities and the conflict between different nineteenth-century international systems, but in the main it has been about the influence of American attitudes about race and civilization on diplomacy and war making in a specific historical instance. Those ideas powerfully affected the entire conduct of the Low-Rodgers expedition, from conception to execution to evaluation. At each point, Americans' denigration of the Koreans and their belief in Korean treachery and barbarism deeply influenced thinking and helped create a self-fulfilling prophecy: expecting trouble from the Koreans, Low and Rodgers provoked it. As Secretary of the Navy George Robeson reflected upon the events of June 1871, barbarism respected "nothing but power" and repelled any outside "interference, association, and instruction." Concurrently and conversely, the expedition leadership, convinced of its own goodwill, benevolence, and superiority, never entertained the possibility that the Koreans might perceive its designs or actions as threatening. The expedition, in the leadership's eyes, could do no wrong.[62] Popular prejudices reinforced by assumptions about international relations and natural law encouraged the provocative American behavior. Though ostensibly privileging the nation-state through formal negotiated treaty arrangements and diplomatic procedures, the Western international system in fact did not recognize the equality of nations. Only those that accepted the tenets of the system would enjoy its rights. Political entities that did not, such as the kingdom of Korea, occupied a position that was inferior not only diplomatically but also morally. Threatening the use of force and then actually waging war against a Korea that arrogantly stood apart and therefore above this system thus seemed fully justified to the American expeditionary leadership.

Beyond interpreting the specific events of 1871, this essay also suggests that American racial ideologies, at least as regards Asians, had powerful international as well as domestic historical sources and implications. Low and others on the expedition held racial prejudices acquired from life in the

116   *Chapter Four*

United States; they drew on "The Heathen Chinee" and similar wisdom to help guide them in Asia. They returned with deeper appreciation of the savage ways of the Orient and the threat it posed to their homeland. Life and combat in Asia helped establish them as authorities on the racial character of the Asian, and they returned to the United States to lend their voices to the growing anti-Asian movement.

Lastly, this essay also engages the historiographic emphasis on the search for economic opportunity as the motive force in American efforts to open Asia (the Open Door policy as the taproot of nineteenth-century American diplomacy in Asia). While economics occupied a preeminent place in Washington's thinking about Asia, and Korea in particular, the leadership of the 1871 expedition believed that the mission's purpose was of a higher order, nobler than the expansion of American commercial frontiers alone. Diplomatic personnel, military officers, and fighting men alike believed their efforts served "humanitarian concerns," human progress, and civilization. Even after the savage fighting of June 10–12, American leaders maintained that their presence was for the Korean people's own good, to seek an end to their country's backward isolation. Low stressed these high-minded purposes repeatedly in his summary report to Secretary of State Hamilton Fish. He clearly acknowledged the commercial potential of Korea but maintained that concerns for the good of civilized society had guided his entire enterprise. This attitude was not a new one, he said, and he denied being defensive about his recent decisions. The secretary well understood, Low wrote, that he was "opposed to making war upon Corea or any other country for the sole purpose of opening them to foreign trade." His efforts, he declared, were based on considerations "of greater importance than mere mercantile advantages." Korea's exclusiveness violated the natural order and trampled the rights of other nations to regularized interaction. For Low and other members of the 1871 American expedition to Korea, civilization and humanity, not the prospects of profits, had been the main reason they had risked life and limb in demanding that Korea open its door.[63]

Images from the Expedition

War leaves emotional, durable legacies. Mythologies about battles and the apotheosis of heroes immediately appear and become deeply embedded in national identities. Though the 1871 war is unknown to most Americans, it is nevertheless embedded in the celebration of the U.S. military heritage.

The captured Korean artifacts, banners, flags, cannons, and guns have been on public display at the museums of the United States Naval Academy at Annapolis since they were deposited there after the expedition. The Annapolis chapel contains a memorial plaque to one of the fallen American heroes, Hugh McKee, the eponym for all U.S. ships named McKee. Six American soldiers on the expedition were immortalized with the congressional Medal of Honor. Military historians have even studied the 1871 events for its lessons regarding coordinated amphibious operations.[64]

But the most enduring legacy of the 1871 expedition does not reside in its memorabilia or in the story of battle; it lies in the stunning visual imagery captured during the month that the American expedition occupied Korean waters and territory. Felice Beato, who accompanied the expedition, compiled a portfolio on Korea that contains the very first photographic images of the country and people. Several of them, some rendered as etchings, accompanied contemporary accounts of the expedition and subsequent articles on this period of Korean history. Long after the events passed and the written accounts were placed aside, the images continued to circulate uncoupled from the historical events, and they have taken on a life of their own. They continue to influence current understandings of nineteenth-century Korea and early American contact with that country. Beato's images, which are often unattributed, appear today in pictorial books on modern Korean history, on subway station walls in Seoul, and even in the hallways of the Korean embassy in Washington, D.C. That the images are entwined with war and that the photographer occupied the position of an intruder into Korea is often understood only vaguely, if at all. Yet this victor's nineteenth-century photographic eye continues to influence the way historical Korea is viewed today.[65]

Felice Beato, one of the world's first great photographers, made his career largely on the basis of his images of the work of the British army in Africa, the Holy Land, the Near East, India, and China. In the latter years of his life, when he lived in Asia, he was celebrated for his delicate photography of Japan. But it was his association with British colonialism and his images of war from the vantage point of the conqueror that made his name and for which he is chiefly remembered. He is credited with being the first photographer to show the dead on a battlefield (in images of Indian soldiers killed during the Sepoy Rebellion of 1857–1858). His work continues to circulate widely—in 1999 the Santa Barbara Museum of Art, in California, held a

118 *Chapter Four*

major exhibition of his images depicting the destruction wrought by the British and French invasion of north China in 1860.[66]

Beato's early life is somewhat of a mystery; perhaps Venetian by birth, he became an English subject as an adult. After many years of travel with the British army, he settled in Yokohama, Japan, in 1863. He joined the Low-Rodgers expedition at Nagasaki and took scores of photographs of the U.S. ships and personnel and of Korean vessels, common people, scenery, officials who visited the American fleet, and prisoners. His most dramatic photos are of the aftermath of battle in Kwangsong.

On June 24, 1871, Beato left the American fleet and sailed for China on board the supply ship *Millet*. Just one week later an advertisement in a Shanghai newspaper announced the sale of Beato's Korea photographs. He later marketed them widely in the United States as well. The July 22, 1871, edition of the *New York Times* described and listed forty-seven of the views collected in bound volumes. Apparently one wound up in the collection of Ulysses S. Grant. The president's grandson speculated that Adm. John Rodgers presented the volume to the president. It remained in the Grant family until it was donated to the National Archives in 1953. As part of the public domain, the photographs have been even more widely reproduced, acquiring yet greater influence.[67]

FIVE

China and the Pursuit of America's Destiny: Nineteenth-Century Imagining and Why Immigration Restriction Took So Long

In this essay, I turn from racial thinking in international relations to a topic traditionally considered an American "domestic" issue: the rise of virulent anti-Chinese sentiment and the campaign to prevent Chinese entry into the country toward the end of the nineteenth century. The result was Congressional passage of the Chinese Restriction Act of 1882, later known as the first of many Chinese Exclusion Acts that dramatically limited the entry of persons of Chinese ancestry into the country for more than sixty years. Enforcement of the racial acts is seen as the historical beginning of national immigration control and enforcement.

Explanation of exclusion typically focuses on prejudice directed against the Chinese from their early arrival in the United States after the California Gold Rush of 1849, with the Chinese seen as racially and culturally unassimilable and undesirable, or perceived competition with white workers for jobs. The march toward formalized hostility seems irresistible and inevitable. The following essay, however, challenges that narrative by arguing

"China and the Pursuit of America's Destiny: Nineteenth-Century Imagining and Why Immigration Restriction Took So Long," *Journal of Asian American Studies* (15:2) June 2012: 145–169. Copyright © 2012 The Johns Hopkins University Press. This article first appeared in *Journal of Asian American Studies* 15, 2, June 2012. Published with permission by Johns Hopkins University Press.

120   *Chapter Five*

that American attitudes toward incoming Chinese were inextricably tied to thinking about the importance of China for American commerce and trade and of Chinese workers for the construction of the West and complicated efforts at formal exclusion. The essay maintains that the global setting must be appreciated to understanding domestic developments in this case. The "global" and "national" were highly intertwined. Exclusion was contingent upon different factors, including the sentiments of mercantile forces in the United States who wanted access to China and trade and the big capitalists in the American West seeking labor for their projects.

$*$

The completion of the Pacific road, the opening trade with the East, and the vast emigration from China, are the grand events which follow our terrible war, and reveal something of our great destiny.
—Jurist Edwards Pierrepont at a banquet honoring Anson Burlingame and the U.S.-China Treaty of 1868 that bears his name, New York City, June 23, 1868[1]

The day will soon come when we shall be the east and China the west . . . and the western passage—the long-lost hope and desire of the ancient navigators—shall be accomplished.
—Boston mayor Nathaniel B. Shurtleff, at a banquet honoring Burlingame, Boston, August 21, 1868[2]

A familiar narrative goes something like this: Chinese immigrants to the United States faced considerable hostility from the moment they arrived in large numbers in the early 1850s. Racial prejudice, a common feature of nineteenth-century America, white labor fears of unfree Chinese competition, and popular dread of Chinese heathenism, immorality, and foreignness combined to produce powerful anti-Chinese sentiment among whites that led ultimately to the passage of the Chinese Restriction Act of 1882 (only later did it become known as the Exclusion Act) and even more stringent subsequent legislation.[3] Few voices opposed this reactionary movement, which appeared to be consistent with other nineteenth-century

China and the Pursuit of America's Destiny   121

white supremacist and nativist ideologies and movements. Hence, it was relatively easy for demagogues such as Denis Kearney and ambitious presidential aspirants such as James G. Blaine to overwhelm the voices of those like Charles Crocker, who championed the economic benefits of Chinese labor, or Charles Sumner after the Civil War, who defended their political rights. According to this narrative, Chinese exclusion was a foregone conclusion, an inevitability.

There is considerable evidence that sustains this narrative, so much so that the narrative seems clear and without challenge.[4] But let me offer a question that shakes its stability. Why did it take *so long* for Washington to pass anti-Chinese immigration legislation?

Thirty years passed between the arrival of more than 20,000 Chinese in the single year of 1852 and the passage of the Restriction Act in 1882. Some 300,000 Chinese landed in America during these three decades, though some anti-Chinese agitators believed many more had actually arrived. Most of the Chinese did not stay, but 100,000 did. Certainly, national political leaders had a lot on their plates at the time—the sectional crisis, slavery, civil war, and reconstruction—but we know that anti-Chinese sentiment, especially on the West Coast, soared in these years supported by white southern forces. We can ask, why did Chinese immigration restriction, as embodied in the 1882 legislation, fail to become law sooner than it did?

This is not the place to offer a full counterexplanation to the dominant narrative. Factors one would have to consider include the preoccupations before the nation mentioned above, the confusion between the states and the federal government over who and what was responsible for immigration law, and the weak political position of the West, where anti-Chinese sentiment was strongest, among other matters, but here I want to focus on one particular arena of social thought that can help explain why the restriction legislation was actually late in passage. Many at the time had agitated for years to rid the country of Chinese and stop their further arrival. Bills in Congress to end the importation of alleged involuntary labor did pass, but efforts to stop the entry of Chinese altogether repeatedly failed in the 1870s and early 1880s, and even the 1882 act was denounced by ardent exclusionists at the time as inadequate. Another decade passed before the United States actually effectively barred most Chinese from the country.[5]

I suggest that the strength and pervasiveness of thinking among many Americans about the central importance of China for America's future

Chapter Five

was critical in encouraging a positive reception of Chinese immigrants to America through much of the nineteenth century. Access to China, and Pacific commerce more generally, free Chinese immigration, and America's future welfare formed one integrated vision in the minds of important Americans—business, political, and religious leaders among them—through much of the nineteenth century. This vision inspired their powerful opposition to immigration restriction and frustrated exclusionists until altered national and international diplomatic landscapes created the conditions for successful exclusion. The two epigraphs that begin this essay are emblematic of this positive vision of Chinese immigration and the entwined imagined destinies of the two nations.

America's early contacts with China and Chinese immigration are intimately linked to a chapter of American history that has occupied a grand place in the telling of the American pageant—the story of discovery, westward expansion, and the realization of "Manifest Destiny." Leading figures in the early republic held audacious, bold visions about a continental empire that spanned North America. From the beginning of the republic, Americans believed that the defense of their treasured political independence required economic well-being. Their vision of national greatness required economic self-sufficiency, and they pursued every possible opportunity for commercial advantage. The subsequent realization of "Manifest Destiny" became national myth. The rapid and seemingly irresistible westward expansion of the United States from east to west, to go past the Alleghenies and then the Missouri and Mississippi Valleys, to cross the Great Plains and Rocky Mountains, and then to reach the Pacific, became the national epic immortalized in countless cultural forms, from music, drama, and literature to the textbooks read by every school student for the past 150 years. Plentiful land, adventure and discovery, and boundless resources are said to have been the attractions for the restless and ambitious Euro-Americans. Often overlooked in the mythologizing of the westward movement however is the lure that lay beyond the continent and the Pacific Coast—China, the object of national desire.

For many Americans in the eighteenth and nineteenth centuries, China, and the Far East more generally, was *the* reason to go to the Far West. The Far West was not an end, but a means. Seeking a waterway through the continent was a prime reason that the English even settled in America. The 1607 Jamestown, Virginia, colonists were to enrich London backers

China and the Pursuit of America's Destiny   123

and locate a passage that would link the Atlantic to the Pacific and thus open the way to the markets of the East. Early Americans and Europeans took the existence of such a route as a matter of literal faith. None believed that the Holy Father would have created the New World as an impassable barrier to their capacious ambitions to reach the Far East. English, Spanish, and French explorers all were convinced that such a route existed, and they incessantly sought to locate it. After independence, the dream of the passage to the East, through the West, continued to inspire Americans to explore the continent, to covet the expansive Oregon Country, to help justify the war with Mexico, and then to annex golden California with its vital harbors. Spanning the continent was America's given fate, and controlling the West would bring America closer to the East. When the eminent historian and articulator of American nationalism Frederick Jackson Turner declared that the westward movement had been *the* "fundamental process" in American life, he also said that Americans were people of the Pacific who shared a "common destiny" with those across the great ocean.[6]

The lure of the Pacific in great part inspired the acquisition of the Louisiana Territory from France in 1803, whose acquisition in turn further encouraged Americans to think about their future as irresistibly linked to Asia and China. Early Americans, among them Thomas Jefferson, dreamed of a continental empire. Such an immense territory would not only embrace vast lands and natural wealth but also physically and territorially link the world's vast oceans, the Atlantic and the Pacific, giving America an insurmountable commercial advantage over the Old World, constrained by the unruly Atlantic. Within weeks after finalizing the purchase of Louisiana from France, Jefferson received congressional support for what would become known as the Lewis and Clark expedition, whose primary objective was to locate a water route across the continent. "The object of your mission," Jefferson instructed Meriwether Lewis, "is to explore the Missouri River and such principal streams of it as by its course and communication with the waters of the Pacific Ocean may offer the most direct and practical water communication across the continent for the purpose of commerce."[7]

After obtaining much of the central territory of the continent, American leaders turned their attention to the Far West and what it might mean to the young country. They frequently invoked the importance of China to America in the public debates and discussions about the occupation of Oregon and California as early as the 1820s. One of the most vocal of these

124   *Chapter Five*

expansionists was Congressman John Floyd of Virginia, whose cousin had been with Lewis and Clark. Floyd later became Virginia's governor and a presidential contender, but in the 1820s he distinguished himself as the first in Congress to urge that the United States occupy the Oregon Country, an immense swatch of land that reached from what is today's northern California to southern Alaska and east into Wyoming. Its ownership was in dispute, he maintained, and America should seize control of the Northwest to enable it to exploit the great trading potential of Asia. Asia, he declared, was the goal "which the West has been seeking ever since Solomon sent out his ships in search of the gold of Ophir." He conjured the prospect of an American Tyre, the fabled Phoenician trading city that commanded the wealth of the ancient world, at the mouth of the Columbia River that could supply China's millions with American flour, cotton, and tobacco. His biblical and Old World references emphasized the grandeur of the possibility.[8] Political figures from the southerner John C. Calhoun to New Englander Daniel Webster in the antebellum years similarly trumpeted the importance of the China trade for America. Ardent expansionist Senator Thomas Hart Benton of Missouri envisioned the Columbia River Valley becoming the granary of Asia. Others declared that American tobacco could replace British opium in China and that American wheat would replace Chinese rice. The possibilities were limitless in their imaginations. Asa Whitney, the first booster for the construction of the transcontinental railway, dismissed the Atlantic as "a petty and petulant sea" compared to the vast commercial potential of the inviting Pacific.[9]

The desire to acquire the port of San Francisco and control the Pacific Coast more generally inspired expansionists such as President James K. Polk to wage the predatory war on Mexico and seize its northern territories. Midway through the Mexican-American War of 1846–48, Polk spoke to Congress to rally support for the plan to annex what is now called California. The region, said the president, would soon be settled by Americans, and San Francisco Bay and other ports along the coast would harbor an American navy, whalers, and other "merchant vessels," and these ports would soon "become the marts of an extensive and profitable commerce with China and other countries of the East." In other addresses, Polk repeatedly spoke about the importance of California and the China trade for America.[10]

These ideas linking continental expansion, Manifest Destiny, and the China trade came together in the fertile and ambitious imagination of Asa

China and the Pursuit of America's Destiny   125

Whitney. Whitney came from a comfortable New England family (he was distantly related to the inventor of the cotton gin) and had made a fortune in the China trade around the time of the 1839–1842 Opium War. During his two years of living in China, he studied the economies and societies of China, the rest of Asia, and the Pacific Islands and concluded that America was singularly positioned between "Europe, with a starving, destitute population of 250,000,000" and Asia with a population of "700,000,000 of souls still more destitute." This position placed an immense responsibility (and opportunity) upon America, he believed, a responsibility that required the construction of the transcontinental link. Convinced that "vast commercial, moral, and political results" resided in the project, he returned to America from China resolved, as he said, "to devote my life to the work which I believed promised so much good to all mankind." As he immodestly but piously claimed, "nature's God" had made absolutely clear that the rail route he proposed across the continent was "the grand highway, to civilize and Christianize all mankind." Whitney rejected the idea he would personally gain from the proposal, declaring he was willing to risk his very life and fortune for his historic vision. As with many other Americans when they thought about their country's future welfare, Whitney presented arguments of commercial advantage, control of the continent and seas, and divine moral purpose that seamlessly reinforced one another.[11]

For much of the rest of his life, Whitney lobbied for government support for his vision, repeatedly memorializing Congress and the president with his idea. Whitney's plan combined exacting detail with epic vision. He calculated ocean and land distances, defined the best overland routes, consulted business and political leaders across the country, and argued that a rail link from the shores of Lake Michigan to the Pacific Northwest or San Francisco was not only feasible but essential to advance the transcendent goal of bringing the East and the West (America and Europe) together. The rail line would open "an unlimited market for our cotton, rice, tobacco, hemp, corn, flour, beef, pork, manufactured goods, and all our various and vast products." But more importantly, it was America's own singular, historic purpose to construct this link that would bring together human history, natural geography, practical economics, military security, and providential design.

Whitney anticipated challenges to his audacious proposal. What of a canal through the Panama Isthmus, another approach to linking the two

126   *Chapter Five*

great oceans that some favored? Whitney argued that a canal had huge logistical and political problems and would require a much longer ocean run from the north Atlantic and then through the Pacific to China than transporting goods and people from the East Coast ports along a rail line to the West Coast ports. But what or who would populate the great western reaches of the United States? Whitney believed the poor masses of Europe would flock to America with its plentiful land now within reach because of the rail line. And as for the peopling of the Pacific? Why, "millions of Chinese would emigrate" and it would be American ships that would move them. "What a field, then, would there not be here opened for industry and enterprise—for the humane, for the missionary, and for the philanthropist!"

Whitney's most powerful argument drew not from economics but from a dramatic, historical imagination that bordered on the millenarian. Echoing the sentiments of the Virginian Floyd, Whitney declared,

> The change of the route for the commerce with Asia has, since before the time of Solomon even, changed the destinies of Empires and States. It has, and does to this day control the world. Its march has always been westward, and can never go back to its old routes. . . . Through us must be the route to Asia, and the change to our continent will be the last, the final change.
>
> We see the commerce of Asia, with civilization, has marched west. Each nation, from the Phoenicians to proud England, when supplanted, or forced to relinquish it, has declined, and dwindled into almost nothingness, and a new nation, west, risen up, with vigor and life, to control all. When this road shall have been completed, that commerce, with civilization, will have encircled the globe. It can go no further. Here, then would be the consummation of all things; and here it would be as fixed, as fast, as time and earth itself. Here we should stand forever, reaching out one hand to all Asia and the other to all Europe . . . seeking not to subjugate any; but all, the entire, the whole, tributary, and at our will, subject to us.[12]

Whitney received wide support for his visionary but compelling proposal. State legislatures and many in Congress enthusiastically endorsed his effort, though he failed to obtain full federal backing. That went, ultimately, to another, much more powerful and better positioned group a decade later. Leland Stanford and the other "Big Four," who controlled the Central Pacific Railroad that employed Chinese railway workers, also played, of course, an important role in the story of Chinese immigration. Whitney, however, had succeeded not only in popularizing the idea of binding America's newly acquired lands with iron but also of linking continental expansion with American connections with the Pacific and Asia beyond.

And in the minds of some, America's "Manifest Destiny" was not limited to a contiguous land mass, but to an even grander destinarian imagination. As *DeBow's Review,* an influential businessman's periodical from New Orleans, declared in a long, elaborate article, published not long after the United States had realized its Northern American *continental* expansion, China and the Indies were to be "Our 'Manifest Destiny' in the East." China had special significance for America, the journal pointed out. It was "more important to us than to Europe; and more important to Europe than all Southern Asia besides." It was therefore essential for America to control that area of the world for commercial advantage, for security, and for its general well-being. The Far West had moved to the Far East.[13]

The lure of Asia went far beyond mere words and ambitious dreams, for the China trade had produced immense, real profits since the mid-eighteenth century. American merchants had brought goods from China in huge amounts and sold them in England and America, amassing some of the largest early fortunes in the colonies. The port cities of Salem, Boston, New York, Philadelphia, and Baltimore all depended on the lucrative China trade, and the American commercial elite—the Cabots, Lowells, Browns, Perkins, Delanos, Astors, and Forbes, among others—all thrived from the tea, furs, textiles, ceramics, housewares, and other goods that the Yankee traders plied across the seas. Trade in African slaves and that in Chinese goods were the pillars of the early American economy. It was not a coincidence that the first, or at least one of the first, ships to fly the new Stars and Stripes after the of winning independence was the *Empress of China,* a three-mast sailing ship outfitted by Robert Morris, "the financier of the American revolution" and one of the wealthiest men in America. It departed New York harbor on February 22, 1784, George Washington's birthday, bound for China with a hold full of American ginseng that was to appeal to the Chinese male market.

Destinarian thinking was not limited to territorial or commercial expansionists. Evangelical Americans, numerous and influential in nineteenth-century America, also looked beyond the shores of the country for the release of their pious energies. China was a land of commercial

128   *Chapter Five*

opportunity, but it was also a place that desperately needed Christian salvation. China, for tens of thousands of Americans, became the location where they, devout Americans, would find their own salvation in helping others find theirs. American Protestant missionaries began to travel to distant and mysterious China in the early years of the nineteenth century.

What inspired them to face a life of hardship, even possible mortal sacrifice, in that faraway land? For Peter Parker, one of the prominent early missionaries, the attraction of China ran parallel to what the merchants and territorial expansionists felt: the belief that China would play an especially important role in the future not just of America but of the entire world. For Parker, though, it would be China's salvation through Christianity, not commerce, that would be transformative. In 1832, just before he made his way to China, Parker confided in his diary,

> But O Lord by what process have I come to the preference of China as the destined field of my labor? Is it not because there are these millions on millions who are perishing for want of the Gospel and the faithful heralds of salvation, forerunners of the Holy Spirit, which other fields have but thousands or perhaps hundreds? The Celestial Empire shall become Christian, will not her influence on the civilization of the remainder of the Earth be greater.[14]

After returning from two years in China, David Abeel, another of the early American missionaries to China, wrote about his experiences to enlighten fellow Americans about the importance of the missionary's task in China. The elevation of his vision surpassed the ambition of the merchant. The conversion of China, he wrote, was of a historic immensity that could hardly be fathomed: "[H]ow infinitely vast, how worthy of all sacrifice—all hazard, all experiment—does the moral elevation of this nation appear, when viewed in its connection with the Redeemer's glory. Here is a triumph and a trophy for His victorious grace, a gem, the purest and brightest which earth can offer, to deck His mediatorial crown!" Abeel called forth missionaries to go to every possible place in China: "[T]he coasts should be invaded, and the sea-ports entered . . . every opening should be searched out, every tenable post occupied." "Look where we may, beneath the wide expanse of the heavens, we can find no distinct enterprise so laudable, so imperious, so inconceivable in its results, as the conversion of China."[15] Pious churchgoers at home could not help but be inspired by the glorious challenge before the self-sacrificing, visionary, and militant missionary.

What explained this zeal? In part, it was the identification of their *own* salvation, and the moral regeneration of American itself, with the effort to win China, and other heathen lands, to Christianity. The missionaries understood their sacrifice in China as a response to God's calling and as an integral part of the recovery of a genuinely moral America. Even more, toward the end of the nineteenth century through the early twentieth century, millenarian thought surged again and was embraced by many American evangelicals. They concluded that the coming of the millennium—the second advent of Jesus Christ on earth—was imminent, but only on the condition that the gospel was spread through all the lands of the world. Christ's appearance would inaugurate a thousand-year reign of his peace on earth and the fulfillment of biblical prophecies. This belief emphasized the foreign missionary enterprise as an urgent, if not the foremost, duty of the church, and spreading the Word to the vast masses of China, the hundreds of millions of them, became one of the central concerns of American Christians for decades. The spiritual revival at home, therefore, became dependent on the propagation of the Word abroad and would help realize transcendent American purposes. As the Reverend J. H. Barlow, secretary of the American Board of Foreign Missions, pungently declared in an effort to gain support for American missionaries in China later in the century, "Wherever on pagan shores the voice of the American missionary and teacher is heard, there is fulfilled the manifest destiny of the Christian Republic." Thousands of ministers, their families, and many more volunteer church workers and lay evangelicals made their way to China through the nineteenth century and well into the twentieth century, making it the largest American missionary effort in the world. Sherwood Eddy, the commanding leader of the YMCA, described China in the early twentieth century as "the goal, the lodestar, the great magnet that drew us all."[16] The mystery of China beckoned, certainly, and even more compelling was the magnitude of the challenge. As the Reverend Charles Ernest Scott, an American missionary in Qingtao filled with "apostolic enthusiasm," declared in a lecture at Princeton Theological Seminary in 1914,

Verily the vastest prize on this planet for continued mastery over which Satan contends is China. And verily the most stupendous single task that faces the Christian Church till Christ shall come again is the bringing of the knowledge of the True and Living God to China.[17]

130   *Chapter Five*

Many Americans through much of the nineteenth century assumed that opening China to American commerce and the Bible required the reciprocal American reception of Chinese here. Many believed that the mingling of Chinese with others on North American soil was a historic inevitability and, in the minds of some, the actual culmination of a human drama that began in the earliest moments of human civilization. This was not about real immigrants so much as it was about an idealized vision of migration and heavenly intentions. In the thinking of many prominent Americans in the early nineteenth century, the white and yellow "races," separated in the distant past, were destined to meet again and amalgamate in America.

The idea that the native people of North America originated in Asia was already popular among the first English settlers in North America. Columbus, of course, never surrendered his belief that he had successfully navigated to Asia and the people he encountered in the Caribbean were Asian. They were misnamed "Indians," and the name continued to link New World native peoples to Asia, at least etymologically. (A curious side note: a nineteenth-century missionary to China and Sinophile once claimed that, in actual fact, "Columbus meant *Chinese*" but called the people he encountered "Indians" only because Europeans in the fifteenth century commonly called all Eastern Asia the "Indies." Only the "mere use of a general for a particular appellation," according to the minister, prevented "our Indians from being called by us 'Chinese.'" The minister was right in his characterization of Europe's old naming practice, but why he assumed that Columbus meant Chinese, as opposed to, say, Japanese, is unclear.) English settlers in Jamestown in the early seventeenth century believed that the "Indians" they met either were descendents from ancient migrants who had come from Asia or were somehow recently closely connected to traders from China.[18]

The Spanish and British brought small numbers of people from China as they colonized North America. Chinese settlements appeared in Mexico in the late sixteenth century. American explorers to the Pacific Northwest in the late eighteenth century found Chinese "carpenters" brought by the British. Other Chinese arrived in America as deckhands on ships and were seen in the port cities along the Atlantic. Some stayed and even formed unions with white women and had families as early as the 1820s. Merchants who returned from China sometimes brought back their servants to New York or Philadelphia, and missionaries facilitated the travel of a score of young Chinese to America for education beginning as early as 1818.[19]

In their exhortations to have Americans move across the continent, expansionists in the early nineteenth century often argued that Chinese settlers could help populate the regions of the Far West, distant from the eastern centers of population. John Floyd, who advocated seizing the Oregon Country, predicted that Chinese would immigrate to the region and help settle the wild land. The Chinese, he maintained in his widely circulated 1821 report to Congress on Oregon, "would willingly, nay, gladly, embrace the opportunity of a home in America, where they have no prejudice, no fears, no restraint in opinion, labor, or religion." Floyd may have been misinformed or simply naive, but he clearly believed that the prospect of Chinese immigration was a positive one and would help win public support for his controversial proposal. The public response to his proposal was wildly supportive.[20]

Thomas Hart Benton also welcomed the possibility of large-scale Asian immigration to the western part of the country. Anticipating doubters who thought the idea of taking distant Oregon was an expensive and unrealistic ambition, Benton argued that Americans could transform the Columbia Valley into a great granary and sell the bounty, with good profit, to the vast markets of Asia. The Oregon Country, Benton forecast, would also become an outlet for Asia's "imprisoned and exuberant population," presumably providing the agricultural labor needed to farm the granary.[21]

Benton's expansionism was also intimately linked to his version of grand history where race determined and explained all great human developments. By many decades, he anticipated the white supremacist arguments of the race theorists at the end of the nineteenth century. In Benton's version, in the ancient, dimly seen human past, the "Caucasian race (the Celtic-Anglo-Saxon division)" "alone received the divine command, to subdue and replenish the earth." This "race" started from western Asia (presumably the Caucasus), followed the sun and went west, left "the Mongolians" behind, and eventually inhabited the shores of the Atlantic, where it lit the lights of science, religion, and arts. In time, "in obedience to the great command," the white race, he wrote, "arrived in the New World, and found new lands to subdue and replenish." It then arrived on the Pacific, "the sea which washes the shore of eastern Asia." On the other side of the ocean was "the Mongolian," or "Yellow race," "once the foremost of the human

132   *Chapter Five*

family in the arts of civilization, but torpid and stationary for thousands of years." Though "far below the White," the Yellow was "far above" "the Black," "the Malay, or Brown," and "Red," and inevitably the white would uplift eastern Asia. "The sun of civilization," Benton pronounced, "must shine across the sea" and the white and yellow "must intermix." The two races would once again unite. And in what must have shocked many of his fellow senators, he declared, "They must talk together, and trade together and marry together. Commerce is a great civilizer—social intercourse as great—and marriage greater. The White and Yellow races can marry together, as well as eat and trade together." There was no doubt in Benton's mind that the result would be salutary for the world: the advanced white race would help rejuvenate the stagnant yellow. "The moral and intellectual superiority of the White race will do the rest: and thus the youngest people, and the newest land, will become the reviver and the regenerator of the oldest." Benton's words conjured a stupendous human drama, if not divine plan.[22]

Other leading Americans shared Benton's vision of the West as the meeting ground of grand racial history. William H. Seward, U.S. senator from New York in the 1840s and 1850s and later secretary of state for Abraham Lincoln and Andrew Johnson, was also a passionate expansionist and saw the Pacific as the natural center of American interests. Controlling the China trade was essential for America's future, as would be the acquisition of islands and strategic points all along the Pacific. His lead later as secretary of state in acquiring Alaska in 1867 was just the most audacious expression of this ambition. But he too believed that human flows attended what he saw as the inexorable shift of power toward the Pacific. In 1852, he declared from the floor of the Senate, "[T]he commercial, social, political movements of the world, are now in the direction of California," and in turn California was the gateway to the grand Pacific. Da Gama, Columbus, Americus, Cabot, Hudson, and even the discovery of the entire New World and its settlement, he believed, "were but conditional, preliminary, and ancillary to the more sublime result, now in the act of consummation—the reunion of the two civilizations, which, having parted on the plains of Asia four thousand years ago, and having travelled ever afterward in opposite directions around the world, now meet again on the coasts and islands of the Pacific Ocean. Certainly, no mere human event of equal dignity and importance has ever occurred upon the earth."[23]

China and the Pursuit of America's Destiny   133

Benton and Seward's largely secular visions of the mission of America drew from the religious, complementing those of the missionary. In a curious twist, religious figures presented views similar to Benton's but drew from the secular to support the biblical. The most prominent of these was Reverend William Speer (1822–1904), who lived from 1846 to 1851 in Guangzhou, China, as a medical missionary and became one of the most famous of the returned missionaries in America in the nineteenth century. His young wife and child died of ill health while in China, and he had to return to America to recover his own strength. He decided, however, to spend his time with the Chinese here. He lived for six years among the Chinese migrants in San Francisco and founded what is now known as the Chinatown Presbyterian Church, which claims today to be the oldest Asian Christian church in North America. In San Francisco, he also founded the first Chinese-language newspaper in the country, *The Oriental,* and a school and dispensary for the local Chinese. He devoted himself to evangelical work throughout the country afterward and served as an officer for the Presbyterian Board of Education for many years. He wrote several books, the most important being the highly regarded and influential 700-page study, *The Oldest and the Newest Empire: China and the United States,* published in 1870.

Unlike other missionaries who disdained the Chinese for their heathenism, Speer was an unabashed Sinophile. He admired China's long civilization and culture, praising China the way Voltaire and other Enlightenment figures did in eighteenth-century Europe. He devoted much of his life to what he called the regeneration of the great Chinese people, who had slipped into backwardness, with Christianity and modern knowledge. The Chinese needed Jesus, certainly, but they deserved none of the prejudice heaped upon them—the Romans, he argued, were a "far more depraved and cruel people than the Chinese," and yet they were routinely praised in the West. According to Speer, there was no more urgent task before the Christian church and the American nation than the rejuvenation of "the Oldest Empire" by the new, as such "consummating work" had to be performed "to prepare the earth for the Kingdom of the Messiah."[24]

Much like Benton, Speer believed Americans, as representatives of the great white race, and the Chinese were destined to be reunited after many centuries of separation. Speer drew from his study of scriptures and ancient history to argue that the Chinese may very well have been one of the

134   *Chapter Five*

tribes from the Ark who dispersed after the great flood. Historical evidence and sacred literature suggested that it was actually Noah, Speer wrote, who founded the colony along the Yellow River that became the core of the country of China. Speer was convinced that the contact of Americans and Chinese on the shores of the Pacific was therefore bringing history full circle, the "termination of that westward course of empire which began in the first period of the history of man." It was nothing less than "the completion of one great cycle of the Divine government on earth," according to Speer, and "the commencement of another—the glorious and golden age of mankind." Grandly, he declared, "[T]he coming of the Chinese to America is excelled in importance by no other event since the discovery of the New World."[25]

Beyond the metahistorical, Speer highlighted other evidence to support his conviction. For instance, the Americans and Chinese, though very different in respects, were much alike, which suggested something more than mere accident. Indeed, their countries resembled each other more than any others on earth: they both enjoyed great stretches of land of similar size, geographies, and climates; their national personalities had much in common (both peoples were "naturally thoughtful, earnest, acquisitive and enterprising"); and they were analogous even politically, with neither ruled by a nobility (Speer must have been thinking of the Chinese administration staffed by those who passed the imperial examination system) and each country "now in the travail of a change from old bondage and feebleness to new power, light and influence" (Speer might have been thinking about the aftermaths of the Civil War and Taiping Rebellion). All in all, Speer predicted that a wonderful day was coming "when many millions of Chinese will be dispersed over the Pacific coast, the Mississippi Valley," Mexico, Central America, South America, and all the islands of the Pacific. He pointed out that Americans needed to learn from the tragic experience with the African, which eventuated in a "stupendous and calamitous civil war," and embrace "the race whom He is now bringing to our shores." The Chinese, Speer warned, are "so incomparably greater than the negro in numbers, in civilization, in capacity to bestow immense benefits on our land or to inflict upon it evils which may end in its ruin." He hoped his book would help prepare his audience for this new racial group—God's divine plan would bring great changes to America, to the rest of Asia, to the islands of the Pacific, and to all the peoples of the whole New World. Their "destiny," he wrote "is to be decided by the influences that shall proceed from the United States and China."[26]

Speer devoted most of his book to recounting China's long history, its arts, habits, and ways, drawing from existing scholarship and his own ethnographic investigation and personal experiences, but the emotional and intellectual heart of his work was a sympathetic discussion of the actual arrival of the Chinese in America. He conceded that much was unfortunate and tragic in that history, and he maintained that the Chinese, for whom he clearly had affection and respect, deserved none of the brutal mistreatment and political approbation heaped upon them by white Americans. Their behavior was unchristian, un-American, and, in Speer's view, likely to be harmful ultimately to America itself. The Chinese would accept only so much abuse before they would rise to correct the injustice, he wrote. Speer reminded his readers that Napoleon Bonaparte himself warned of such a development, if the West continued to mistreat the Chinese. "In the course of time," Napoleon once declared, the Chinese will take up the battle and "defeat you." But the heart of Speer's effort to win favor for the Chinese immigrant was his argument, which he reiterated throughout his book, that the arrival of the Chinese to America must be seen as the working of God's will. The Chinese appearance was actually their *return* to the North American continent, which their ancestors, in God's plan, had settled in the distant eons. They had been sent "to occupy the New World until the appointed time" when "the Protestant Christian nations" came to transform the continent. Now the Chinese immigrant signaled the great reunion of the "two great streams of civilization" that had separated long ago when one went west and the other east. The "peculiar glory," "the great Ruler of nations," had made America the place where the unification of humankind would occur![27]

Speer's support of the Chinese immigrant had the support of many of his fellow church leaders who wanted as much access as possible to the Chinese, be they in China or in America, to further their evangelical mission. They possessed a confidence from their ensured belief that the Chinese could be as Christianized and elevated as other Americans as long as they had access to the Word. It seemed that God was physically bringing Chinese to Christian America for their conversion and through them would effect the transformation of their homeland and verily the rest of the world.

136   *Chapter Five*

The ideas of commerce, evangelism, power, moral purpose, and immigration all came together in the fertile thinking of William H. Seward. After retiring as secretary of state in 1869, Seward left for a grand tour around the globe. Notably, he traveled westward from the East overland to the Pacific Coast, as he wanted to see America's Far West himself before he traveled to the Far East. He visited Japan and China and then stayed in Hong Kong from late December 1870 to mid-January 1871. He offered fascinating comments about American-Chinese relations at the U.S. consulate that are worthwhile reproducing here at length.

At the time, Seward was one of America's most senior and respected political figures. He had been an early, firm abolitionist, had opposed slavery and racial prejudice on moral and ethical grounds, and had himself nearly been martyred in a vicious attempt on his life in his own home that was part of the plot against President Lincoln. Seward favored free Chinese immigration and was the actual, secret author of the 1868 Burlingame Treaty, the most equitable and favorable treaty China concluded with any Western nation in the nineteenth century. (See the epigraphs that begin this essay.) Free immigration was one of the central elements of the treaty but was eviscerated by the legislation of the 1880s.[28] His comments in Hong Kong focused on the great importance of the Pacific for America, with particular reference to the place of China in America's future, and were substantially reproduced by the *New York Times* back in the States:

> I do not undervalue missionary laborers in China, but I look for the practical advancement of civilization in China chiefly to commerce—commerce across the Pacific Ocean, commerce by steam across the American Continent and across the Atlantic Ocean. . . . Say what they may the whole world cannot prevent the commerce from regenerating China and Japan. There is no measure to its expansion and enlargement, because a trade that is firmly established must be destined to great increase. The free emigration of the Chinese to the American and other foreign continents will tend to increase the wealth and strength of all Western nations; while, at the same time, the removal of the surplus population of China will tend much to take away the obstructions which now impede the introduction into China of art, science, morality, religion. . . . [The policy of the United States has been] the practice of equal and exact justice toward China and the Chinese. When that shall have been completed and we are able to show ourselves

willing to render justice, it will be in our right to make increased demands for an extension of commercial facilities. The railroads, a telegraph, a free Press, all may be attained by foreign nations who are just to China, and who leave mankind to decide.[29]

Seward and many other powerful, elite Americans who shared his vision opposed restricting Chinese immigration to America. Restriction was unjust *and* self-destructive. Immigration restriction, in the view of Seward and others, would damage American ambitions in Asia. Indeed, U.S. efforts to advance its interests in Asia were on the ascendancy.[30] Many capitalists, traders, entrepreneurs, boosters of westward expansion and Pacific commerce, and religious leaders, like Seward, accepted, and even promoted, Chinese entry into America. It was all part of America's destiny in Asia, at least in their view. In 1876, William W. Hollister, one of California's wealthiest men, represented this commercial viewpoint. Before a state commission investigating Chinese immigration, he openly declared, "I say, fully, freely, and emphatically, that the Chinese should be allowed to come" to California without restriction if the state was to enjoy prosperity![31]

Throughout the 1870s, proponents of Chinese immigration at the local and regional levels, led by powerful employers and landowners such as Hollister, repeatedly thwarted the efforts of anti-Chinese forces, but then in the late 1870s, widespread social unrest and political disaffection in the West fueled the belief that the Chinese were labor competitors and louder demands for federal efforts to control their entry into the country. But even then, exclusionist efforts were still repeatedly frustrated. In 1879, a coalition of politicians from western and southern states succeeded in passing the so-called Fifteen Passenger Bill to limit the number of Chinese passengers an American ship would be permitted to carry to the United States, but President Rutherford B. Hayes vetoed the bill, maintaining that the unilateral action on the part of the United States would contradict the provisions of the Burlingame Treaty and could harm Americans, "merchants or missionaries," who were then in China. Hayes pointedly reminded the public that the existing relationship with China was one of "peace and amity" and of "growing commerce and prosperity."[32]

In early 1882, Congress again passed an anti-Chinese immigration bill, but President Chester Arthur also vetoed it, using language even stronger than that of Hayes. In the public explanation for his action, Arthur

138   *Chapter Five*

emphasized the importance of upholding the country's treaty obligations with China but also reminded the nation that Chinese labor had brought great benefit to the country. The Chinese "were largely instrumental in constructing the railways which connect the Atlantic with the Pacific," he wrote in his long veto message. The tremendous growth of the states on the Pacific slope was further evidence of the importance of the Chinese to the American domestic economy, he declared, and limiting their numbers might harm regions of the country where the Chinese could still be "advantageously employed." And more, "Experience has shown," Arthur lectured, "the trade of the East is the key to national wealth and influence," and it was the American West that had gained the most from that trade. "San Francisco has before it an incalculable future if our friendly and amicable relations with Asia remain undisturbed." Arthur warned that imprudent legislation against Chinese immigration could drive Asia's "trade and commerce" away from America and toward others more friendly to the Chinese. Proponents of the anti-Chinese measures could not muster enough support to override the veto.[33]

Arthur's reasoning closely followed that of George F. Seward, William Seward's nephew, who had spent twenty years as a representative of the United States in China. In 1881, he also publicly condemned the anti-Chinese sentiment that was growing in the West. George Seward, like his uncle, was passionately antirestrictionist, and in 1881 he published one of the longest and most reasoned rebuttals against the restriction movement. In his more than 400-page study, he argued, "Is it not time then, in view of the qualities exhibited by Chinamen on our own soil, in view of the illiberality which has characterized our treatment of them, in view of the progress which China is herself making, and in view of our common humanity, to drop this cry that the Chinese do not assimilate, and to devote ourselves to a policy which will be more just at the moment and which will conduce to build up relations of enduring respect and profit between the two great nations of the opposite coasts of the Pacific?"[34]

Sympathy for the points of view of William and George Seward had helped defeat repeated efforts to pass anti-Chinese legislation. But changing political conditions in the country were tipping the scales against those who favored continued open immigration from China. The Compromise of 1877 ending federal Reconstruction marked the resurrection of racist politics nationally, represented largely by the Democratic Party and the return of a white South to national prominence. The anti-black South was becoming a powerful political ally of the anti-Chinese elements in the West—West-South coalitions formed the heart of restriction efforts in Congress.[35] The Democrats would actually take the White House in 1884—the previous presidential victory of the Democratic Party had been way back in 1856. Economic depression and white labor unrest also swept the country in the late 1870s. Paradoxically, it was the fulfillment of the dreams of Manifest Destiny boosters and developers that created conditions that anti-Chinese agitators exploited. Chinese had begun to populate the West; the railroads, built with Chinese labor, enabled whites to populate the Far West; and the very growth of the West, which had been encouraged by the lure of the Far East and trade, enhanced the domestic political importance of California, Oregon, and the Washington Territory. Now that section could not be ignored by the eastern establishment, which had formed the bulwark of sentiment supporting open immigration.

And importantly, the predatory ambitions of European nations and Japan, which were then actually seizing Chinese territory and eroding regional prerogatives, heightened the security concerns of the Chinese elite. Beijing believed America's goodwill was needed to counterbalance the other aggressive foreign powers. Worried that the rising sentiment against Chinese laborers, whose welfare was of little concern to the imperial court, might jeopardize American friendship, Beijing signaled its willingness to accept immigration restriction. This new attitude was expressed in the Angell Treaty of 1880, in which Beijing expressed it might accept moderate immigration limitations while keeping its own doors open to American traders and missionaries. The issues of immigration to America and pursuit of trade began to decouple, and in May 1882 President Arthur finally signed revised legislation that *suspended* the entry of Chinese laborers into the country for the next ten years. The bill also had other provisions acknowledging the rights of reentry of Chinese already in the country, exempting ten "classes" of other Chinese, such as merchants, teachers, and travelers, from exclusion, and explicitly recognizing other allowances and important protections for the Chinese. The bill was seen as a compromise between diplomacy and domestic political sentiment, but it still failed to mollify the exclusionists. For more than the next two decades, they agitated for more stringent restrictions against the continued entry of Chinese into the country. Washington did take further efforts in 1884, 1888, 1893, 1894, 1902,

140   *Chapter Five*

and 1904, the number of efforts as much an indication of the persistence of the exclusionists as of the difficulty in getting what they wanted. Actual Chinese exclusion was constructed over a long period of time and was far from ever being a foregone conclusion, let alone an inevitability.[36]

Acknowledgments

A version of this article was presented at the Asia-Pacific and the Making of the Americas Symposium, Brown University, April 7 and 8, 2011 and the Stanford–UC Davis Workshop on the American West, November 5, 2011. The author thanks the participants for their helpful comments. Beth Lew-Williams also provided valuable help.

PART II
Race

SIX

"Superman Is About to Visit the Relocation Centers" and the Limits of Wartime Liberalism

After I joined the History Department at Stanford in 1991, I explored the libraries to locate research material related to Asian American history. One of the most exciting finds was the archive of Yamato Ichihashi, a Japan-born scholar who had graduated from Stanford in 1906 and received his doctoral degree in political economy at Harvard. He was recruited to return to Stanford, but as one who would teach and research Japanese Studies, an area the university wanted to develop. He also studied Japanese immigrants to America and produced one of the earliest books on his compatriots.

Using his rich collection of diaries, correspondence, and research notes from his years of incarceration during World War II, I published *Morning Glory, Evening Shadow: Yamato Ichihashi and His Internment Writings, 1942–1945*. The book presents much of Ichihashi's own words, but I also

"'Superman is about to visit the relocation centers' & the Limits of Wartime Liberalism," *Amerasia Journal* (19:1) 1993: 37–59. © 2019 The Regents of the University of California, reprinted by permission of Informa UK Limited, trading as Taylor & Francis Group, www .tandfonline.com, on behalf of The Regents of the University of California. (Illustrations accompanying the original article are not included in this volume.)

144   *Chapter Six*

offer my own narrative of incarceration, using his life as an entry into recovering personal, felt experience. The book remains unique in documenting an individual's entire experience of three years of life in incarceration. Ichihashi languished in several federal camps from 1942 to 1945 before returning to Stanford, where he lived the rest of his life.

Though there was a growing literature on incarceration, a subject that had been avoided for many years after the war because of the attendant trauma and shame, much was still understudied. The following chapter came from research I had conducted related to the Ichihashi project. At the Truman Presidential Library, I stumbled across the papers of a mid-level official in the Roosevelt administration. The file contained material documenting his efforts to monitor public opinion about the incarceration of Japanese Americans.

The essay presents insights into wartime popular culture but also into the connections, and responsibilities, of political liberalism for the brutal mistreatment of 120,000 Japanese Americans in the war years.

*

In late June 1943, advanced notice of a story line that would appear in the daily newspaper version of the Superman comic strip alarmed the Office of War Information, the Roosevelt administration's wartime propaganda bureau. "Superman is about to visit the relocation centers," Philleo Nash, an OWI media analyst who monitored minority relations in America during the Second World War, alerted his superiors. Nash described what was soon to appear before millions of readers across the country. In the story, according to Nash, "subversive and disloyal Japanese in the centers will perpetrate an act of destruction which will be stopped by Superman, who will then leave the center and will prevent further sabotage by Japanese *outside* the centers."[1]

Nash's report touched off a flurry of activity among those responsible for the relocation camps in the Roosevelt administration. Their response and the bizarre story line that finally did appear in the Superman strip provide insight into the complex of often self-contradictory public as well as official attitudes toward Japanese Americans during the Second World War. In particular, the incident exposes the limits, even bankruptcy, of liberals who thought themselves passionate opponents of racism but who also endorsed mass forced relocation of aliens and citizens alike solely on the basis of race.

In the short span of a year or two since the character first appeared in book and strip form in 1938–1939, Superman had become one of the most popular comic features in the United States. By 1941, it surpassed in readership long-established cartoons like Little Orphan Annie, Dick Tracy, and Popeye and appeared in 230 newspapers across the country with a combined following of an estimated twenty-five million persons. Magazine editions of Superman's exploits ran into a million and half copies and countless listeners followed his radio program. Superman was on his way to becoming the most important comic strip character in American history and to ensuring the success of the comic book as a central genre of mass culture.[2]

The spectacular adoration of Superman in the late 1930s and early 1940s, however, befuddled cultural observers at the time, as difficult as that may seem for those in the late twentieth century who have grown up with Superman comics, television shows, and movies. Fifty years ago, Superman was a genuine novelty as he was the first "super-hero" in popular science fiction, inspiring the birth of countless other characters. His creators actually had failed to sell their idea to publishers for years, so Superman's sudden success provoked commentators to try to make sense of the mass phenomenon. According to a writer for the liberal periodical *The New Republic,* the explanation for Superman's popularity lay in the power of "primitive myth" or "the blacker arts of modern demagogy." Superman embodied all the traditional attributes of a "Hero's God"; he was a "protective deity" who was to be the "savior of the helpless and oppressed." Superman filled "some symptomatic desire for a primitive religion." The German philosopher Friedrich Nietzsche's *Ubermensch* and his notion of a "will to power" were even invoked as possible inspirations for the character's creators. Whatever the explanation, Superman would endure over the years with only slight modifications in appearance, cast of characters, and plot.[3]

The outbreak of World War II provided Superman with an opportunity to bring his Manichean battle with evil out from removed make-believe into a more emotionally engaged "real world." Genuine human monsters replaced petty criminals and fantasy adversaries. Superman joined other detective and military comic strip characters to fight the wartime enemies of America at home and abroad. The Nazis and "Japs" were frequent and predictably portrayed as villains in the pulps, although the Pacific War received much

146   Chapter Six

greater attention than the war in Europe, according to a 1942 OWI survey of the comics. The grotesquely racist caricatures of the enemy—Japanese in particular were routinely portrayed as vermin, sub-human, or simian—were as simple and unproblematic as the American patriotism that was promoted. These images, moreover, were highly influential since the comics had become a powerful media form in the United States among people of all ages, not just the young. The Advertising Research Foundation in 1942 discovered that the comics page of the daily newspaper, other than advertising, was the most widely read feature among adult readers. The OWI itself determined that approximately 83 percent of all adults in the U.S. read at least one comic strip daily.[4] The simplistic messages and crude images sometimes disturbed the media watchdogs at the OWI who believed the anti-fascist aims of the war were being insufficiently communicated to the public. To counter blatant white chauvinism, for example, the OWI encouraged a nonracialist under-standing of the Pacific War in some radio scripts it released for consideration by broadcasters. In one of these, the OWI observed,

> Men and women who foster racial prejudices are fighting for the enemy. . . . To pepper [the Japanese] with epithets like yellow Japs . . . is not the way to win battles.[5]

On the whole, however, the federal government devoted little effort toward trying to dictate the specific content of strips produced by the private sector. The OWI's actual authority was limited; it had no censorship powers and its charge was mainly to monitor the media, disseminate war-related informa-tion, and produce morale-boosting features for public consumption.[6] The intensity of government activity provoked by Superman's impending visit to a relocation camp holding Japanese Americans was therefore unique. Because the Superman strip would imply criticism of an actual, not ficti-tious, government program and controversial domestic policy, the strip had more direct relevance to bureaucratic concerns than the usual war story. Washington officials evidently believed that the story line would make their efforts to implement war-necessitated measures on the home front more difficult. (In contrast, the cover of the March 1943 Superman comic book that declared "SUPERMAN SAYS: YOU CAN SLAP A JAP," replete with a racist caricature, failed to generate similar concern at the OWI.)[7]

Philleo Nash, who had first brought the Superman comic strip story line to the attention of the leading officials in the OWI, was like many other New

Deal intellectuals who wanted to devote their professional skills to social improvement. He had received his doctorate from the University of Chicago in anthropology in the early 1930s, and by the 1940s had broadened his expertise from his early attention to Indian life to race relations generally in the U.S. In 1942 he joined the domestic branch of the OWI to study public opinion and minority issues. He later became a special assistant to President Harry Truman on minority affairs, lieutenant government of Wisconsin in the late 1950s, and Commissioner of Indian Affairs during the Kennedy and Johnson administrations. The red-baiting Senator Joseph McCarthy charged Nash as being a "communist" when he was an adviser in the White House in the early 1950s. On the other hand, Supreme Court Justice Thurgood Marshall fondly wrote to Nash's widow upon his death in 1987, that Nash "will always be remembered for his great contribution to civil rights and civil liberties during the trying days. I remember too well that he was always there when needed." Through his long public career, Nash forged a distinguished intellectual reputation and established firm liberal credentials.[8]

Back in June 1943, though, Nash worried that the Superman story line would make running the relocation camps more difficult for federal authorities because of the story's suggestion that the camps were hotbeds of disloyal, even subversive, activity and that the War Relocation Authority, charged with responsibility for camp administration, was negligent in its security measures. Nash anticipated that the story would fuel public pressures for *more* stringent measures against the internees, measures which were contrary to administration efforts to implement what it considered was a legitimate policy, that is relocation, carried out humanely and cognizant that many Japanese Americans were indeed loyal.

The Superman story could not have come out at a worse time, from Nash's and the WRA's point of view. In September 1942, newspapers carried lurid stories about alleged Japanese spy rings operating in the U.S. The Chicago *Herald American,* with a two and one-half inch headline, declared "BIG JAP PLOT HERE! G-MEN JAIL 81." In articles that foreshadowed the Superman story line, the paper described the breakup of the leadership of a supposed "Jap-inspired fifth column" that advocated "exterminating the white race." Under the direction of the "powerful Japanese Black Dragon Society," and "Jap intelligence ace," Major Satakata Takahashi, whose "English was perfect, without accent," the subversive "army" supposedly numbered up to 100,000 throughout the United States.

148   *Chapter Six*

(The arrested were apparently African-Americans who opposed the war.)[9] Then in November 1942, internees at the Poston camp, largest of the relocation camps, conducted a mass strike for self-government rights. In December, a violent riot over camp conditions at Manzanar left two internees dead and a dozen wounded. Exploiting the sensational publicity generated by these events and the widespread racist attitudes toward Japanese Americans, zealots within and without the government in early 1943 began publicly accusing the Roosevelt administration of coddling Japanese Americans and of endangering domestic security.[10]

This adverse public attention threatened to disrupt "resettlement," what the WRA considered to be one its "fundamental" policies. In early 1943, the WRA had begun a screening process to try to determine the loyalties of internees and stepped up a program of release and resettlement of those the government deemed free of suspicion. By May 1943, 4186 internees had been granted "indefinite leave" from the camps.[11] Along with the formation of the army team that became known as the 442nd Combat Unit, the resettlement program had raised the ire of men such as General John L. DeWitt, military commander of the Western Region and a prime instigator of relocation in the first place, who rejected any notion that the loyalty of Japanese Americans could be determined. DeWitt flatly opposed the formation of the 442nd and the screening process on racialist grounds that even the Assistant Secretary of War, John J. McCloy, no liberal himself and the highest government official concerned with the running of the camps, found unacceptable.[12]

From Capitol Hill, the Administration was under attack from Texas Congressman Martin Dies, head of the notorious House Committee on Un-American Activities. Dies was an anti-Black, anti-Asian chauvinist who even before Pearl Harbor had purported to have evidence showing that Japanese in America were engaged in widespread propaganda and espionage. After the outbreak of the war, Dies, convinced that "racial characteristics" made all persons of Japanese ancestry in America security threats, continued to call for repressive measures against them. In June 1943, at virtually the same moment that Philleo Nash learned of the Superman story line, Dies prompted the convening of a special subcommittee under Representative John M. Costello of Hollywood, California to investigate camp administration and the entire resettlement program. Costello publicly accused the WRA of permitting "pro-Japan" elements to seize virtual control of the relocation camps and undertake "subversive activities." Costello charged that "native-born and alien troublemakers have been permitted to leave the camps" due to the "lack of aggressive leadership" by the WRA.[13]

Aside from Nash and the OWI, the WRA itself had become concerned about the planned Superman story and on its own raised the issue to the McClure Syndicate, distributor of the strip. The WRA, however, received an unsatisfying response. The McClure people saw nothing in the strip that would require the retraction of the panels that had already been sent out to newspapers across the country by late June. Philleo Nash dejectedly acknowledged on June 28,1943, the day the story line began appearing, that time made it "impossible for the syndicate to withdraw the next two weeks strip now even if they wanted to."[14]

Nash recommended the OWI urge the McClure Syndicate to point out to Jerry Siegel and Joe Shuster, Superman's creators who themselves may have had Jewish relatives in the concentration camps of Nazi Germany, that "This story about disloyal Japanese, with only *a* passing mention of loyal Japanese, works a severe hardship on the 5,000 Japanese who are already in the Army, the Japanese who have never been placed in the centers, and on the loyal Japanese who have been released from the centers to work on farms and in war production plants."

Nash's neglect to mention the tens of thousands of persons of Japanese ancestry who continued to languish in the relocation centers was not an oversight, for whatever personal concern he may have had for the rights of the Japanese, he expressed interest in this instance only in what effect the strip would have on the government's ability to implement relocation and resettlement. Nash explained to his superiors:

> The Superman reference will create new hostility to the work of the War Relocation Authority program. The centers have to be run. No one suggests that there should be *no* Japanese relocation program. Even the severest critics of the War Relocation Authority admit that there are very large numbers of loyal Japanese in the centers. The task of segregating them is enormously difficult. It will only be made more acute by the portrayal of incidents like this in such a popular medium as comic strips.

Nash's assertion that "no one" opposed the relocation program betrayed the limits of his liberalism. He obviously ignored the public opposition, albeit weak, to the camps that did exist and, of course, the sentiments of

150   *Chapter Six*

the internees themselves. Nash, however, like many of those who ran the WRA, as Richard Drinnon has pointed out, likely believed he was opposing racists who refused to appreciate the conscientious work of the WRA.[15] Nash wanted the OWI and the WRA to inform the McClure Syndicate that the federal agencies "strongly feel that an episode should be *added to the present Superman sequence, or later episodes should be created, in which loyal Japanese assist Superman; in which the Japanese Combat Team is mentioned; and in which the absence of sabotage accredited to Japanese both in Hawaii and on the Mainland is mentioned.*" (emphasis in original)[16]

Instead of pursuing the recommendation immediately, however, Nash's superior directed him to explore whether the government's Office of Censorship could handle the matter.[17] Nash inquired but found that the censorship people believed the matter was "strictly not censorship business." Nash then suggested that the OWI get Assistant Secretary of War, John J. McCloy, involved and have him contact the artists, their agents, and the McClure Syndicate. McCloy, aside from his official position, was already a powerful man on Wall Street and in Washington and on his way to becoming known in the post-war era as the chairman of "The Establishment." Nash was probably right to assume that representations from a man of McCloy's stature would have an effect on the Superman people.[18]

In the meantime, McCloy independently became drawn into the controversy. The start of the Superman story line on June 28 prompted immediate protests from the public, including cables and letters to McCloy from leading liberal voices such as Read Lewis and M. Margaret Anderson of the Common Council for American Unity. They wrote McCloy that Superman was "inciting" "race hatred against Japanese Americans." By spreading misinformation and creating distrust of all Japanese Americans, these strips "unless discontinued or altered, threaten to extend disunity and present wave of race hatred and also handicap [the] Army's special combat unit of Japanese Americans." Since the comic strip misrepresented Japanese Americans as "prisoners of war under the jurisdiction of the Army and implies the Army is lax enough to allow concealed weapons to the evacuees," the protesters believed McCloy's War Department should have "definite concern." References were also made to the concurrent investigations of the relocation program by the House Committee on Un-American Activities. "It would be a sad day for us to have the resettlement program bog down now because of national distrust."[19] (In their letters, Read and Anderson did not object to

"Superman Is About to Visit the Relocation Centers" 151

the existence of the camps themselves and the relocation program, but limited their protest to the hostile public attitudes toward Japanese Americans. The Common Council itself had had conflicting views on the legitimacy of the relocation program which will be addressed below.)

McCloy himself, before the OWI had made contact with him, inquired whether the OWI could do something about the Superman strip. According to McCloy, the military had an interest in the matter since, if, as a result of anti-Japanese American agitation, there were "untoward incidents arising on the West Coast" against the former internees who were being resettled from the camps, "it will probably reflect against our prisoners in the hands of the Japanese." McCloy also argued that even from the perspective of the "most native of Native Sons," the comic strip was damaging to their aims, since "If the country through the Superman cartoons feels that the Japanese Relocation Centers are hotbeds of disloyalty and conspiracy, the efforts to redistribute the Japanese population throughout the country, thus relieving California and the other western states of some of their Japanese population, will be frustrated."

McCloy asked whether "there is anything that OWI could do" about the Man of Steel.[20]

The OWI's response, apparently from Milton Eisenhower, brother of General Dwight D. Eisenhower and director of the WRA before he moved to the OWI, acknowledged that the OWI too had received telegrams and letters in connection with "Superman's exploits in the Relocation Centers," although it had been somewhat at a loss as to how to formulate an official response. McCloy was told that Philleo Nash had had an informal discussion with people connected to "Superman, Inc." in which he suggested that story lines be added to the strip to balance the negative portrayal of Japanese Americans, and that he apparently had some success. The "editor of Superman" agreed to work on the matter. The OWI asked McCloy to forward "factual material on the Japanese combat team and on the absence of Japanese sabotage in Hawaii and on the West Coast." The WRA would then send it along with information on the relocation centers directly to Superman, Inc. for possible use in future strips. Some days later, McCloy had a long letter sent to Eisenhower detailing "displays on the part of the evacuees in the centers of their loyalty to the United States."[21]

Philleo Nash, of course, had mistakenly argued that "no one" believed there should be no relocation program, but he was, in truth, not far off the

152   *Chapter Six*

mark. Other than the Japanese victims themselves, few Americans publicly opposed relocation. While the socialist leader Norman Thomas and the Quakers were notable dissenters to the federal policy, even the Communist Party, USA and others of the identifiable left openly endorsed relocation.

In June 1942, *People's World,* the CPUSA's West Coast newspaper, lauded the Army round-up of Japanese Americans and wholly accepted Washington's rationale—forced evacuation "was a job well-done which was dictated by military necessity." The editorial praised the action as having "eliminated the possibility of free operation of fifth-column elements among the Japanese" on the West Coast. And while it was "regrettable" that many "loyal Japanese-Americans" had to be evacuated, their experience was "unavoidable under the circumstances." "On the whole," the Party concluded, "the Japanese evacuees are being treated in a fair and democratic manner." Later in the year, the Party again endorsed relocation. The Manzanar riot, the Party maintained, proved the correctness of its opinion. The protest, by pro-fascist elements according to the CPUSA, demonstrated that forced relocation "was justified." After all, the Party argued, there had not been time to "sort the sheep from the goats" after Pearl Harbor, and thus the Army had been right to move all Japanese away from the coastal area "where they could do mischief." The Party did not clarify which animals represented which political tendencies. The CPUSA also suspended the membership of its Japanese American cadres for the duration of the war.[22]

The response of the Common Council for American Unity to relocation also illustrates the extent to which racial prejudice had infected the American left. The Council expressed its views in *Common Ground,* which first appeared in 1940, and was one of the leading liberal periodicals of the day. Its agenda was a forerunner of what is today known as "multiculturalism." *Common Ground* promoted appreciation of the ethnic and racial diversity of American life, anti-racism, anti-nativism, and vigorous and full extension of democracy to all peoples. Those affiliated with the publication ran the gamut from established liberals like Eleanor Roosevelt and Pearl Buck to leftwing intellectuals such as Langston Hughes, Louis Adamic, and Woody Guthrie. The publication was notably strong in its attention to Asian Americans, and had published the work of Younghill Kang, Toshio Mori, and Jade Snow Wong, among others. The liberalism of *Common Ground,* however, initially foundered on the rocks of the relocation program.

The inconsistency of *Common Ground*'s liberalism is specifically seen in the views of Carey McWilliams, chief of the Division of Immigration and Housing for the State of California in 1942, and later prolific and leading author on American minority and labor affairs and editor of *The Nation*. McWilliams was a frequent contributor to *Common Ground* and his article "Japanese Evacuation: Policy and Perspective" was the lead piece of the Summer 1942 issue and was distributed as a special reprint.

In his essay, McWilliams accepted the essential legitimacy of the camps as a wartime necessity, although he tried to distance himself from the overt racists. The Japanese, in his view, were removed *"not* because they are suspect en masse," but "primarily to allay popular uneasiness created by their presence on the West Coast in large numbers in strategic areas," an uneasiness that might have grown out of hand and interfered with the war effort. McWilliams, writing between the time of evacuation and assembly and the establishment of the actual relocation camps, saw the policy as a great challenge to American democracy but also an opportunity: "Here is a task which can be handled democratically and fairly for the attainment of highly desirable social objectives, or mishandled and botched in a manner that will gravely reflect upon the ideals and standards which now, as never before, we are proudly emblazoning to the world."

McWilliams believed that the relocation camps could become great demonstrations of democracy and the resettlement of Japanese away from the West Coast a help to their economic progress and social integration, if only the whole matter was "soundly conceived," "liberally construed," and if "the American nation decides it should be done, and will not capitulate to demagogic harangues and discreditable race-baiting." McWilliams wanted a "humane" relocation. Addressing the obviously touchy question of the constitutionality of forced relocation based on race, McWilliams stretched far to rationalize that some sort of group "due compensation" could be offered to the Japanese American community "as we have always provided ... when an individual's property is taken or his rights impaired *for a public purpose*." (emphasis in original)

Later issues of *Common Ground* also carried favorable articles from the government's public relations officer at Manzanar and an essay describing the relocation program from Dillon Myer himself, chief of the WRA. Only later in its Summer 1943 issue did the magazine completely

154   *Chapter Six*

reverse its position on the camps and begin to condemn the program. A powerfully worded article by M. Margaret Anderson signaled the reversal in position. In "Get the Evacuees Out," she condemned relocation as a "deep wrong," characterized the centers as "uncomfortably close to concentration camps," and demanded that America must either "really mean democracy—at home and abroad—or we don't." She called for the resettlement of Japanese Americans as quickly as possible. By mid-1943, McWilliams changed his opinion and also criticized relocation.[23]

Carey McWilliams, it seemed, realized he could not continue to rationalize the contradiction between support for forced relocation, with its anti-democratic premises, and his liberal principles. Others, however, refused to undertake a similar intellectual self-examination. For decades following World War II, the CPUSA, for example, continued to waffle on its endorsement of the camps as well as its discrimination against its own Japanese American members.[24] Such political inconsistency can be explained, at least in part, by appreciating the depth of anti-Japanese prejudices that ran (and continue to run) deeply and pervasively in American culture. (The virulence of "Japan-bashing" in recent years indicate that such sentiments never disappeared but remained a subcurrent in American life.) The strangely revealing story line in the Superman strip helps illuminate the particular nature of this racism and aspects of the cultural assumptions that underlay relocation.

A description and assessment of the strip that ran six days a week (Sunday's strip ran a different story line) for more than eight weeks from June 28, 1943 to August 21, 1943 (much longer than the two weeks originally anticipated by Philleo Nash) is in order here. While the OWI and WRA in 1943 tried to pressure the Superman people behind the scenes, the cartoon story line unfolded in daily papers around the country, apparently unaffected by the political tumult.

The reader should note the presence of several traditional racist themes and assumptions in the strip—negative and demeaning portrayals of Asians had a long history in American cartoon art. Prominent themes include the suggestion of widespread disloyalty among Japanese Americans, the sinister and especially arrogant nature of the Japanese enemy, stereotypic Orientalia, dialogue, and slurs, and the implication that, for the United States, race formed a basis for nationality and loyalty (and conversely disloyalty).

"Superman Is About to Visit the Relocation Centers" 155

(These themes are even more evident in the published illustrated panels. The reader's imagination will have to substitute for the actual illustrations.) The following narrative is presented with minimal editorial comment (material enclosed in " " are direct quotes from either the strip's omniscient narrator or characters themselves):

Panel 1 (all bold in original)[25]

Daily Planet editor Perry White directs Clark Kent and Lois Lane to what Kent describes as an "unusual assignment."

White says: "The public is interested in knowing the full details of what goes on inside a typical Jap relocation camp where alien Japs, as well as American citizens of Japanese ancestry have been sent after being evacuated from the West Coast and elsewhere."

Visiting "Camp Carok," Kent and Lane are hosted by "Major Munsey" who informs the reporters that "Our main difficulty is that loyal Americans of Jap ancestry are indiscriminately mingled with enemy sympathizers who would be glad to sabotage our national welfare at the first opportunity. It's a delicate and difficult situation. Our government has done all but lean over backwards in its desire to be humane and fair."

Lane praises the work, adding "the Jap government should have absolutely no excuse for not showing their prisoners of war as much consideration." Clark Kent (Superman) however senses that trouble lurks beneath the superficial calm.

Panel 2

"Clark's amazing x-ray vision reveals to him that serious trouble is brewing within a woodworking shop they are approaching."

A group of swarthy, sinister-looking Japanese internees, all male, secretly plan an escape with the aid of smuggled firearms.

"A visiting party approaches, Masu Watasuki!"

"Let them come! Hostages will assure our unhindered departure!"

Clark Kent ducks out of the tour, leaving Lane and the Major to be captured by the Japanese conspirators. Kent strips off his outer garments revealing "the super-dynamic MAN OF STEEL!"

156   *Chapter Six*

Panel 3

Masu Watasuki, planning to abduct Lois Lane, finds Major Munsey an uncooperative hostage and is about to execute him.

"But even as the cruel-faced son of Nippon fires at the major, a stream-lined human form hurtles into the shop."

Panel 4

Faster than the eye can see, Superman rescues Munsey and Lois Lane, whisks them away to safety, and returns to deal with the shocked internees.

"Superman!"

Panels 5, 6, 7

The internees find that bullets and electric saws cannot stop Superman. Frustrated and bashed against a wall, a villain cries out "Feat renders Jap-boys velly unhappy!!"

But Masu Watasuki drops a booby-trap of lumber on Superman, bury-ing him.

"Behold—the highly vaunted Superman falls victim to Japanese inge-nuity."

"Verree clever."

"Added proof that America is destined to become a vassal state of Japan!"

Panels 8, 9, 10, 11

Masu Watasuki's victory is short-lived. Superman breaks out of the lumber pile and imprisons the Japanese themselves in a wooden jail cell. He won-ders, though, about the source of the smuggled weapons. His X-ray vision shows two white thugs lurking in the nearby forest wondering whether something has gone wrong with the escape attempt.

Superman strips off the clothes of Masu Watasuki and dons them. "Then with the aid of his amazing muscular control and makeshift mate-rials, Superman disguises himself as... " "A Jap." "Takea lookee at the new Watasuki!" Superman says.

"Superman Is About to Visit the Relocation Centers" 157

Panels *12, 13, 14, 15*

The disguised Superman tells the thugs he was the only one to escape. He thinks to himself: "White men co-operating with the enemy! There are always renegades who will sell their country and their souls for money. We must beware of these hidden enemies in our midst."

Camps guards try to stop the truck of the fleeing thugs and disguised Superman, but the superhero frustrates their efforts since he wants to uncover the headquarters of the subversives.

The truck arrives at the garage of a "large Oriental rug establishment," beneath which the thugs bring the fake Watasuki into a hall with a waiting assembly of scores of men who are apparently white. But wait!

A gong "unexpectedly reverberates" and in unison the crowd pulls off "Plastic Masks!" A white thug gleefully boasts: "When they wear one, I defy anyone to know they're really Japs!"

But as a stage curtain parts, the "Man of Tomorrow receives an even greater shock."

"No! It can't be!!"

Panels *16, 17, 18, 19, 20, 21, 22, 23, 24*

Superman cannot believe he sees "The Leer, dreaded Jap saboteur," who committed suicide in disgrace after being defeated by Superman in a previous adventure. As it turns out, however, it is not The Leer but his brother, The Sneer, who had been smuggled into the U.S. by submarine to continue the sabotage work. The Sneer speaks to the disguised Superman in Japanese, wanting to know the whereabouts of the other escapees.

The fake Watasuki "replies in his questioner's native tongue, for the Man of Tomorrow's knowledge is almost limitless and awareness of every language on earth is but one of his many accomplishments."

But suddenly, Superman's ruse is uncovered and he must subdue the whole "horde of enraged enemy Japs."

The Sneer exhorts his band, "Don't give ground! You can't lose inasmuch as you have the divine protection of Hirohito!"

Superman, however, has little trouble knocking out the subversives left and right. In one scene, Superman uses a special punch he says he reserved

158   *Chapter Six*

for "Traitors!" (The race or nationality of many of the bad-guys is not always clear.)

But before he can capture The Sneer and his cohorts, Superman is tricked away by a fake radio report that a nearby dam has been destroyed by a bomb. The Sneer escapes and Clark Kent returns to the Daily Planet.

Panels 25, 26, 27, 28, 29, 30, 31, 32

As a result of their harrowing experience in the relocation camp, Lois Lane and Clark Kent decide to collaborate on writing a series of articles emphasizing the need "for increasing resistance against the Jap foe." Their efforts come to the grateful attention of the "Chinese citizens of this city" and "Lum Wong, the 'mayor of Chinatown'" garbed in a Hollywood-style Mandarin outfit, invites them to ride a float in a bond-selling parade through Chinatown.

But the *Daily Planet* articles infuriate The Sneer who vows to stop Kent and Lane. A henchman, who is of Japanese ancestry but whose nationality is unclear, comments, "It would be much more convenient for our beloved warlords if the Allies continued to concentrate on the European front."

The saboteurs plant a subterranean bomb in Chinatown to try to blow up Kent and Lane's float in the parade, but are frustrated by Superman. Superman seizes the bomb-planters, who are forced to reveal The Sneer's lair. The Sneer, in the meantime, seizes Lois Lane and flees to the countryside. The Sneer hurtles Lois Lane down a dry well to die.

Panels 33, 34, 35

Superman saves Lane in the nick of time and then foils a henchman's effort to decapitate him with a samurai sword.

Superman eavesdrops on The Sneer's briefing of his fellow agents (again of Japanese ancestry but of unclear nationality): "You will be pleased to learn that in this safe are duplicates of the Japanese High Command's plans for an all-out attack on Allied forces in the southern Pacific area. This attack is to occur almost immediately, and it will forerun the actual invasion of America itself!"

Superman breaks into the lair.

Panels 36, 37, 38

Superman grabs the documents and flies off to Washington with The Sneer, "his slant-eyed opponent," to alert authorities about the impending offensive. Lane is left to contact the FBI who rounds up the remaining agents.

Washington officials are grateful to receive the news but are dismayed by the prospect of having little time to transfer the necessary war material to repel the invasion.

Before Superman can bop him in the face, The Sneer gloats, "It will be another example of the democracies [sic] axiom of 'Too little, too late.'"

Superman offers his help to move the supplies, inspiring one official to say that "In this case one man may save the destiny of the civilized world."

Panels 39, 40, 41, 42, 43, 44, 45, 46, 47, 48

Superman uses his extraordinary abilities to help deliver the needed military supplies to the Allies and joins the fight against the Japanese invasion force.

The threat is destroyed, showing that, as one American military man observes, "our fighting men once again demonstrate that, given the weapons with which to defend themselves, they can crush the mad plan of scheming dictators in Tokio, Berlin and Rome to dominate the world."

In denouement, Lois Lane gushes to Clark Kent, "Out of all of Superman's mighty feats in defense of democracy, I think this latest exploit ranks at the top!"

Clark Kent editorializes, "It will have served of inestimable value if only to point out to the public the importance of not belittling the Jap menace in the South Pacific."

And in the last frame (perhaps reflecting the efforts of the OWI, WRA, and John J. McCloy), Superman is given the last word after weeks of fighting the Japanese enemy. He faces the reader directly to lecture: "It should be remembered that most Japanese-Americans are loyal citizens. Many are in combat units of our armed forces, and others are working in war factories. According to government statements, not one act of sabotage was perpetrated in Hawaii or territorial U.S. by a Japanese-American."

160   *Chapter Six*

Superman's final pitch in support of loyal Japanese Americans was too little, too late and essentially irrelevant in terms of public opinion. It was symbolic of the bankruptcy of a wartime liberalism that rationalized the entire relocation policy. Moreover, the story line resonated with the deep-seated tradition of American political demonology, particularly its Yellow Peril form. The story line both drew from and confirmed deep anti-Asian prejudices and patterns of racialist thinking that made the closing generous gesture from Superman meaningless and gratuitous for Japanese Americans.

The racial and political incubus, in its Japanese wartime form, threatened to weaken and subvert the American body politic and required isolation (segregation and re-imprisonment). (The brief interlude into Metropolis' "Chinatown" accentuates these messages: the contrasting "goodness" of the allied Chinese serves to highlight the "badness" of the enemy Japanese, of course. But while the portrayed Chinese are themselves Asian and foreign, they are trivially exotic, contained, and controlled. Thus they are nonthreatening. And thus they are good for a further reason.) The Japanese enemy is both sub and superhuman. The enemy is dark, wild, cruelly animal-like and is associated with the subterranean; its behavior is deceitful; it launches attacks from behind and below, contrives traps, and intrigues. Yet it is also ingenious, arrogant, and able to overpower guileless legitimate authority. A super-being is required to frustrate the super-demon; but the superbeing is also a man (Clark Kent), and is constantly referred to as a "man" by the subversives. Superman therefore is emblematic of an idealized America itself. He becomes the counter-subversive hero and, like other counter-subversive heros in American racist folklore (the frontier scout who becomes a "savage" to hunt Indians, the Ku Klux Klan night-riders who don masks to carry out atrocities to avenge supposed atrocities, the federal agent who infiltrates the Reds) is permitted to mirror the projected behavior of the constructed foe who is being attacked. Superman strips the foe of his clothes, leaving him naked, vulnerable (clothes are power and identity—Superman is never without his costume, a modified American flag). Superman dons his enemy's outfit and assumes a new identity, his enemy's identity and license. He infiltrates the infiltrators; he impersonates the impersonators. Superman's behavior imitates the dark double to save the nation both literally and figuratively in the character of Lois Lane, the feminine America, with whom he is platonically linked. The Japanese foe, who are only male, grab and threaten her person. Ultimately, she and the nation are saved from violation by her male counterpart. In the end, Superman's sermon to the reader about the actual loyalty of Japanese Americans affirms America's self-conception of itself as a land of fair-play and democracy, but also, in so doing, legitimizes the playing of an imposter in the defense of an authentic America. Illusion and authenticity are doubly, triply confused and co-mingled both within the story line and between the story line and social reality.

There is no record of a formal Japanese American reaction to the Superman story line, although the internees sometimes did protest particularly vicious news articles that appeared in the mass media outside the camps. K.J. Takashima, chairman of the Poston Community Council (along the Colorado River in Arizona) wrote on behalf of the Council to protest to Elmer Davis, head of the OWI, inflammatory articles that appeared in the Los *Angeles Examiner* in September 1943 a few months after the Superman story line had run. He cited a story about the possibility that Poston internees might sabotage dams along the Colorado River and an article that had as its headline "ARMED JAP EVACUEES POURING INTO STATE." He feared these emotional stories would arouse public opinion against the WRA and the residents of the relocation centers, but pointed out that "any sane person would realize the fantasy" of the charges.[27] Probably unknown to Mr. Takashima, these "news" articles strangely echoed aspects of the fictional Superman story. In this case, fantasy and reality were very difficult for most Americans to unsort.

Men such as Nash, Stimson, McCloy, Eisenhower, and Myer did not consider themselves racists—some thought themselves progressive. They all believed they were solicitous, to varying degrees, of the interests of Japanese Americans and understood that many, if not most, were loyal citizens of the United States. The WRA itself acknowledged, as stated in one of its internal reports without any trace of irony, chagrin, or self-awareness, that "the rights of citizenship and the rights of law-abiding aliens are closely associated with what we are fighting for in this war."[28] The administrators distinguished themselves from the outright racists such as DeWitt, Dies, and others who believed Japanese in America were for racial reasons loyal to Tokyo and against America. The professed liberals could point to what they believed was their sensitive treatment of the Japanese, the allegedly benign and democratic functioning of the relocation camps, and the resettlement program for proven loyal Japanese Americans, as evidence of their good intentions.

162   *Chapter Six*

But these measures could not overturn the fundamental injustice of the camps or correct the horrendous message to the American public, just as Superman's closing instruction to his readers in the last frame of the story line could hardly neutralize the insidious characterizations built up over the previous weeks that resonated with traditional American political and racial demonology. The federal government, of course, subjected no other national ancestry group to indiscriminate incarceration and the laborious loyalty screening process. And thus, no matter how much the liberal administrators and officials in Washington urged public "fair" treatment for Japanese in America, those Americans who physically appeared like the racially-identified enemy could not but be looked upon with suspicion. Officials in the real Washington and the fictitious Superman both accepted incarceration on the basis of race as justified. Thus, popular animosity toward Japanese Americans remained fierce throughout the country. After all, who knew, if not the federal government, what was actually going on beneath that local "Oriental rug establishment?"

Notes

The author wishes to thank Roger Daniels, Yuji Ichioka, Bob Lee, John Liu, and the Stanford Asian American studies faculty seminar for their helpful comments on drafts of this essay.

SEVEN

Social Darwinism Versus Social Engineering: The "Education" of Japanese Americans During World War II

This chapter came from my participation in a conference at Stanford that examined state-sponsored efforts at mass population control, especially during World War II. Contributions from other participants focused principally on European experiences. My effort argued that the global war was a racialized experience in part for the United States, not just for the fascists that espoused the most extreme forms of racial chauvinism.[1]

The essay highlights two forms of racism endured by Japanese Americans in the war years. One was based on biologically based assumptions that located blood or genetics as the source of social behavior and, for the Japanese, their alleged security threat to the nation. The other was based in more "modern" and liberal notions of human malleability and state ambitions to change human behavior and identity through social engineering. Many in the administrative and teaching staff of the federal government's camps that held Japanese Americans believed they could make positive

"Social Darwinism versus Social Engineering: The 'Education' of Japanese Americans During World War II," in *Landscaping the Human Garden: 20th Century Population Management in a Comparative Framework*, edited by Amir Weiner (Stanford University Press), 2003: 189–204.

163

164   *Chapter Seven*

contributions to the war effort by transforming the prisoners into what constituted, in their view, model Americans. The state efforts were supposedly for the good of the Japanese Americans themselves. In this way, the U.S. camps were akin to many other population control mechanisms instituted by states around the world that aimed to dramatically reshape human communities and often rationalized as serving the interests of the target victims.

*

In June 1947, Donald O. Johnson, a former teacher at the War Relocation Authority (WRA) Schools at Tule Lake, California, site of one of the internment camps established by the U.S. federal government for the incarceration of persons of Japanese ancestry during World War II, ended his thesis for a Stanford master's degree with a lament tempered by a hopeful admonition for the future. Johnson, who had repeatedly expressed in the body of his unpublished paper sympathy for the internees, concluded:

> The mass evacuation [one of the many euphemisms federal authorities used during the experience] of the people of Japanese descent from the West Coast probably created more problems than it solved. . . . The [wartime security] problem seemingly could have been handled more rationally. The removal of the Japanese under the guise of "protective custody" or under any other term or reason, real or imagined, other than the established necessity for national security is questionable in the light of democratic action. But evacuation, with its resultant evils has happened, and it is only left for us to determine that if *in the future we find it necessary to control minority groups within our population, that we shall do so by democratic methods.*[2]

Evident, despite Johnson's obscurantist and qualified language, are assumptions that reflect administrative thinking that rationalized wartime internment—the interned were "people of Japanese descent" and "Japanese" (although the majority were in fact American citizens) and "national security" exigencies justified nondemocratic action. But further, Johnson, in anticipating possible similar future efforts at mass population control, betrayed no apparent awareness of his highly racialized and contradictory notions about American democracy—"we" should control "minority groups," democratically.

Johnson's way of thinking was not singular or even unusual but represented the way many of his fellow teachers, researchers, camp administrators, and political leaders had thought about wartime internment. Examining their various writings about internment offers a way of understanding not just a group of individuals who were involved in what critics even at the time of their institution called America's "concentration camps,"[3] but also more broadly racial ideologies in America and their connection to various conceptions of social control in a liberal democracy. This chapter seeks to contribute to a discussion about the ideology of social-engineering projects in the mid twentieth century.

In the early spring of 1942, several months after war began between the United States and Japan, the U.S. federal government began incarceration of what eventually numbered 120,000 persons of Japanese ancestry into ten internment centers scattered in desolate locations throughout the West and South. Sixty percent of the internees were American citizens by birth; the remainder were first-generation Japanese immigrants, whom immigration law denied, along with other Asian immigrants, the possibility of naturalized citizenship, even though most had lived in the country since their arrival in the late nineteenth and early twentieth centuries. Most of the internees had lived along the Pacific Coast, which the federal authorities after Pearl Harbor had declared a special military zone from which the army was authorized to exclude any specially designated persons for security reasons. The Western Defense Command, acting with the authority of the president, announced in April 1942 that "all persons of Japanese ancestry, both alien and non-alien" were required to report to military authorities for "evacuation" from the sensitive area into centers operated by the federal government. The duration of "relocation" was indeterminate—internees did not know if their removal was temporary or permanent.[4] With very few exceptions, the targeted population complied with the order; most lived the rest of the war years in what authorities called "assembly" and then "relocation centers," prohibited from returning to their former residences until the last months of the war. Several tens of thousands received permission to leave the camps earlier to enter the army, attend college, or work outside the exclusion zone.

166   *Chapter Seven*

The reasons for the American public's widespread support for internment varied, but many accepted the argument offered by General John L. DeWitt, commander of the Western Military Command, in his official, publicly released recommendation for internment:

> In the war in which we are now engaged racial affinities are not severed by migration. The Japanese race is an enemy race and while many second and third generation Japanese born on United States soil, possessed of United States citizenship, have become "Americanized," the racial strains are undiluted. . . . That Japan is allied with Germany and Italy in this struggle is no ground for assuming that any Japanese, barred from assimilation by convention as he is, though born and raised in the United States, will not turn against this nation when the final test of loyalty comes. It, therefore, follows that along the vital Pacific Coast over 112,000 potential enemies, of Japanese extraction, are at large today.[5]

Many in the country and especially in the West, stronghold of fears of the "yellow peril" in America, easily accepted DeWitt's assessment and proposal; many had believed that persons of Japanese ancestry were inassimilable and suspect because of a combination of genetic incompatibility with European Americans and irreconcilably hostile cultural differences. Japanese immigrants and their descendants in America were therefore considered fundamentally different from European immigrant groups, such as the Germans and Italians, neither of whom suffered any group deprivations in the war. As a *Los Angeles Times* editor urging action against Japanese Americans had written in February 1942, "A viper is nonetheless a viper wherever the egg is hatched."[6] Most American political leaders and the public, even as they embraced declared anti-aggression and antifascist purposes, had little problem endorsing the internment of persons of a racial minority at home. They had been nurtured on nineteenth-century and early-twentieth-century assumptions about a genetically based racial hierarchy of humankind and the claims of a "biology"-based social Darwinism that linked social behavior, psychology, and culture to blood.

Others who held less biologically based assumptions about race were still persuaded by the argument of "military necessity." Prominent educators and political figures with more liberal credentials fell into this category. Many in academia had come to accept the cultural rather than "race"-based explanations of social behavior that had emerged in the 1920s

Social Darwinism Versus Social Engineering 167

and 1930s, but they still found compelling the national security argument that rationalized internment. For example, faculty in Stanford University's School of Education offered this perspective not long after the implementation of internment: "Since the outbreak of war, loyal American citizens of Japanese extraction have been subjected to humiliating insults and indignities ... [although] the removal of the Japanese from the coastal region was a military necessity, both for the safety of the country and the safety of the evacuees themselves."[7] In fact, the federal government's invocation of "military necessity" was never substantiated by evidence; within the government, military intelligence and law enforcement agencies, such as the FBI, had actually opposed unselective internment of persons of Japanese ancestry. (In 1982, the federal commission appointed by President Jimmy Carter, which reviewed the history of internment, declared that it was "not justified by military necessity. The broad historical causes which shaped these decisions were race prejudice, war hysteria, and a failure of political leadership.")[8]

The view that internment was somehow even in the interests of those affected, that the national body as well as its suspect part both benefited from internment, was never offered as official rationale but did circulate widely among the public. Liberals who expressed support for the extreme measures, albeit with some regret, often believed the measures were somehow in the interests of Japanese Americans. Moreover, such support was often accompanied by forceful denunciations of the "racists," profiteers, and political demagogues, including in Congress, who publicly pressed for more extreme measures against the internees, including wholesale deportation, abolition of citizenship for the American-born, permanent segregation from the rest of the American population, separation of male and female to prevent further reproduction of the population, sterilization, and even death.[9] Such views obviously sounded uncomfortably similar to the racism of the fascist enemy and were rejected by liberal-minded Americans—nevertheless with very few exceptions, American liberals accepted and endorsed the internment order.

The remainder of this chapter will focus on this latter group of liberal, "antiracist" supporters of internment, which included many who were involved in the administration of the camps themselves. These individuals, including Dillon Myer, the director of the WRA, and many of the camp officials and personnel, often thought of themselves certainly not as

168   Chapter Seven

participants in a disreputable enterprise but as contributors to the battle for democracy and "Americanism." And more, although they may have seen internment as an unfortunate necessity, they also saw many positive possibilities in the experience, with important lessons for understanding problems in human management in the postwar world. The unassuming title of the WRA's own final public report on its work captured this faith in technomanagerialism, *The WRA: A Story of Human Conservation.*[10] Internment, which allegedly served both dominant as well as minority community interests, exemplified the ideology and method of liberal social engineering.

An individual who saw opportunity in the internment camps was John J. McCloy, assistant secretary of war, among the most responsible in government for the internment decision itself, future high commissioner of occupied Germany, and one of the most influential men in cold war America. Not long after the internment camps had opened, McCloy revealed thoughts about their possibilities; he felt sufficiently comfortable about his ideas to share them with prominent civil libertarian Alexander Meiklejohn, former president of Amherst College, McCloy's alma mater:

> We would be missing a very big opportunity if we failed to study the Japanese in these Camps at some length before they are dispersed. We have not done a very good job thus far in solving the Japanese problem in this country. I believe we have a great opportunity to give the thing intelligent thought now and to reach solid conclusions for the future. These people, gathered as they now are in these communities, afford a means of sampling their opinion and studying their customs and habits in a way we have never before had possible. We could find out what they are thinking about and we might very well influence their thinking in the right direction before they are again distributed into communities.
>
> I am aware that such a suggestion may provoke a charge that we have no right to treat these people as "guinea pigs," but I would rather treat them as guinea pigs and learn something useful than merely to treat them, or have them treated, as they have been in the past with such unsuccessful results.[11]

McCloy believed national security interests necessitated internment—as late as the 1980s McCloy continued to defend the decision, arguing that it was "entirely just and reasonable" because of the demands of wartime security—but his view of internment went further. Internment offered an

Social Darwinism Versus Social Engineering   169

opportunity for something "positive," an opportunity for those in power to study and shape the confined population in the interests of the state. The temptation was too great; the possibilities too attractive for McCloy and others to ignore. The internees, racially defined, incarcerated against their will, and in violation of constitutional practices and principles, were indeed treated as "guinea pigs." Years later after the end of the war, McCloy continued to maintain that "our Japanese/American [*sic*] population benefited from the relocation rather than suffered."[12]

Another individual with very different credentials flirted with conclusions similar to those expressed by McCloy in 1942. Carey McWilliams, chief of the Division of Immigration and Housing for the State of California in 1942, and later prolific and leading author on American minority and labor issues and editor of the *Nation,* at first criticized the idea of wholesale internment of the Japanese when the idea began to circulate publicly in early 1942. In one article for the *New Republic,* he at first characterized the idea as a "dangerous concrete proposal" and opposed it without reservation. In another article for the same journal, he declaimed that if Japanese Americans were relocated, "then obviously one group of citizens will have been discriminated against solely on the basis of race."[13]

After internment actually began, however, McWilliams adopted a very different view, one compatible with McCloy's. "Evacuation and resettlement," as McWilliams put it in the summer of 1942, "can be handled democratically and fairly for the attainment of highly desirable social objectives." He seemed to have been persuaded by what he called the "unique opportunity" relocation offered to develop underutilized lands, to "democratize" the Japanese, and to improve the economic resources of the Japanese community. "I see in the resettlement of the Japanese," McWilliams emphasized, "a unique opportunity to work out not only new community patterns . . . but the necessary administrative skills and techniques for dealing with the whole problem of rural and urban reconstruction in the post-war period." Like McCloy, he saw the possibilities that internment offered for social engineers. In a major article for *Harper's,* McWilliams, acknowledging that he had originally opposed the idea of relocation, nevertheless praised the government's actual roundup and incarceration of Japanese Americans as "a miracle of effective organization." "There is no reason why the relocation projects cannot be successful," he concluded his article, and "cannot in fact reflect great credit upon us as a nation—provided a majority of the

170   *Chapter Seven*

American people will insist upon fair treatment of the Japanese and not succumb to demagogues and race-baiters."[14]

McCloy and McWilliams in 1942 were not alone in sensing the current, and future, social-engineering lessons the camps might offer. A regiment of teachers, social scientists, and government administrators explored the possibilities in scores of internal government reports, published articles, and books. The WRA itself employed some thirty anthropologists as analysts who closely monitored the interned population and reported to camp authorities. The responsibilities of these specialists, most trained at leading research universities, was to help administrators improve social controls. According to one of these analysts, they worked at "sizing up [internment] problems which stood in the way of executing the basic policies, and to a lesser extent at devising means for solving those problems." In typical WRA bureaucratic language that obfuscated the actual social *and* racial relations between the powerless, who were incarcerated, and the authorities, the analyst concluded, "The role of Community Analysis was that of an aid in maintaining communication between a group of administrators and a group of administered people." Years later, this same analyst assumed a much more jaundiced view of the internment enterprise in which he had been involved. He came to characterize camp officials as administrative technicians steeped in the Western tradition of "getting things done." The WRA administrators made decisions for the internees "and then asked for cooperation in accomplishing what they had decided on." The result was a "paternalistic set of decisions." Though still employing euphemistic terms, the former analyst had come to sense not only the antidemocratic nature of internment but the liberal, technomanagerial ethos that imbued the entire experience.[15]

Many of the analysts, teachers, and other WRA camp staff (who were officially called "appointed personnel" or, bizarrely, "the Caucasians," to further the fiction that the camps were not prisons) believed their work carried significance beyond serving the needs of the WRA administrators and, like McCloy and McWilliams, saw their work as possibly helping address what they believed would be American needs in the postwar period. Their outlook, as revealed in their own writings, displays a confidence, even hubris, in the morality of their mission and rationality of their intentions and actions.

In these writings, the authors frequently convey an enthusiasm, a self-consciousness about involvement in what they felt was an enterprise of historic importance. This was an enthusiasm that went beyond inflation of one's contribution to the good war effort. There is the sense that, as pedestrian as some of their specific tasks may have been, they were thrilled not only by the intellectual challenge of their jobs and the research possibilities offered by access to a controlled population but also by their connection to the immense coercive power of the state and the possibilities that power offered to determine the destinies of thousands of humans. They found themselves molding, reshaping, remaking a people in ways they determined best and consistent with their own ostensibly higher values and superior way of life, regardless of the rights and sentiments of the subject population. They could have Mephisto's power but without the consequences or the guilty conscience.

The titles alone of some of their essays, many published in respected social science journals, are themselves suggestive: Emory S. Bogardus, "Relocation Centers as Planned Communities," (*Sociology and Social Research,* 1944); Bureau of Sociological Research (WRA), "The Psychiatric Approach in Problems of Community Management: From a Study of a Japanese Relocation Center" (*American Journal of Psychiatry,* 1943); Wanda Robertson, "Developing World Citizens in a Japanese Relocation Center" (*Childhood Education,* 1943); Monica Kehoe, "Japanese Become Americans: Adult Education at Gila River Relocation Project, Rivers, Arizona" (*Adult Education Journal,* 1944); John U. Provinse, "Building New Communities During War Time" (*American Sociological Review,* 1946); and Edward H. Spicer, "Reluctant Cotton-pickers: Incentive to Work in a Japanese Relocation Center," in E. H. Spicer, ed., *Human Problems in Technological Change* (1952).[16]

One administrator at the Poston Center, which contained eighteen thousand internees, enthusiastically described internment as a part of an "epic drama" testing the country's "moral import." In "Education Through Relocation," John W. Powell, a school official in the prewar years, observed that in the camps, "every relationship is educational, and every [staff] man a teacher. . . . It is hard sometimes to remember not to speak of the Project as the Campus." Education was more than formal training for the young; it sought fundamental reshaping of the lives of all the people. Powell's stated goal was to see that Poston become "a source of rich production, a school for wise and energetic Americans in years to come." In even more dramatic language that displayed his excitement in the possibilities for human

172   *Chapter Seven*

engineering that lay ahead of him and his fellow administrators, Powell explained that their goal must be "to train these people, not just to make a living or to pass the time until the war ends, but to make them ready to *hurl as projectiles* of democracy into the maelstrom of postwar readjustment."[17] Powell, as did many of his fellow administrators, objectified the internees as "docile tools," as human clay for the hands of the social engineer. Nowhere in his article does he reveal self-consciousness of any possible contradiction in his vision that the interned, placed in prison camps as a result of an authoritarian decision, could be used as agents for genuinely democratic purposes in the postwar world.

To achieve such grand ends behind barbed wire, the WRA strove to build what it believed were ideal American communities, with town councils, pseudoelections, Americanization classes, and organized celebrations of American holidays. These efforts, occurring within confinement and directed toward those who were already in fact Americans, were by nature highly contrived, artificial, prescribed, and orchestrated. An educational administrator for the camps giddily declared in an Office of Education publication during the war that the camp schools "can become, in a measure often dreamed of by educators but seldom realized, an effective instrument of community planning and building."[18] The WRA teachers' handbook stated explicitly that education should "lead each individual to practice American manners and customs." Instruction was given on proper ways to shop and recreate and on acceptable etiquette and mores. In the prison camp classrooms for children as well as for the adult education classes, teachers were to promote new gender relationships by encouraging "the American ideal of the equality of women."[19]

Although this goal of imbuing the captive Japanese American internees with the trappings of middle America (Americanizing the Americans, so to speak) was high in the minds of staff members, the *method* of attaining such ends was given no less attention. Stanford School of Education professor Paul Hanna and his graduate students helped develop the philosophy and curriculum of the camp schools. They were guided by the latest wisdom of what was known as progressive education, which stressed the integration of school and community spheres to prepare youngsters to become good, productive members of American society. For these educators, the positive opportunities seemed immense. They envisioned the internment camp as a great big school. "Education," one of the planning documents stated,

Social Darwinism Versus Social Engineering   173

"becomes a process which goes on everywhere in the Relocation Center": "The walls of a classroom cease to be educational boundaries." The whole camp was to serve "education" interests. The "Japanese Relocation Centers," Paul Hanna's associates wrote, "probably offer the greatest opportunity in the United States for the kind of service that the community school can give." Most of the educators in the camps never appreciated the cruel irony of these proposals being advanced under the banner of democracy.[20]

One who was untroubled by his work in an internment camp provides especially interesting insight into the thinking of teachers. Jerome T. Light taught at the Minidoka, Idaho, camp school and was unusually sympathetic to the internees. Light wanted to close the distance between himself and the internees, whom he acknowledged had suffered considerable dislocation and distress. He even sent his own four children to the camp school to try to live as the internees did. After the war, he completed his doctoral degree in education at Stanford, and devoted his two-volume, twelve-hundred-page thesis to an explication of his teaching experience at Minidoka. He dedicated the work to his former students at camp, praising them for conducting "a truly American high school under extremely adverse circumstances."[21]

And yet, Light pursued his educational responsibilities in camp with no self-reflection on the contradictory purposes of his job (educator *and* prison camp staff member), let alone the implications internment had for the high-minded principles continuously propagated in camp. Light, for example, reported that the camp teachers agreed that the promotion of "Americanism" should be an essential part of their teaching efforts. He proudly described their work:

The educational program itself could be expected to increase the use and appreciation of American social customs. Studies of vocations dealt with occupations in the United States. The science courses, although not exclusively American, pointed out the scientific advances made in the United States. Vocational education, including home economics and commercial courses as well as shop courses, inevitably taught American practices. The reading instruction presented American literature, the books in the library were American. . . . The American History and Government taught in grade 11 was enriched as much as possible for this same purpose. The study of World Problems in grade 12 was oriented inevitably with the American

174   *Chapter Seven*

viewpoint. In dealing with the 10th grade theme, The Community: A Human Invention to Serve Human Needs, the American communities were studied most of the time, and when foreign communities were studied they were inevitably viewed through American eyes. The theme in the 7th grade, How Man Utilizes Science and Inventions, illustrated how it was done in the United States more than elsewhere. And, the very method of instruction and the organization of the school were typically American as was realized by the students.[22]

But perhaps most intriguing was Light's description of the approach the teachers adopted in inculcating Americanism within a prison camp school:

> In keeping with these assumptions and recognized facts [the unusual circumstances of instruction, the resentment and suspicion of the pupils, Americanism as a "dynamic and growing ideology"], the faculty agreed to make no issue about Americanism in the school but to act as though there were no question about it.[23]

With these words, Light unintentionally captured much of the spirit governing the entire internment enterprise: faith in the good purpose of the project; pride in the intentions of those in authority; acceptance of the unquestioned value of propagating an idealized Americanism; obliviousness to any contradiction between those ideals and the surrounding reality; confidence in the ability to manipulate the subjects for their own good, as defined by the administrator; and a collective self-consciousness of the need to "act" to further the political ends of the authorities.

Light concluded his exhaustive account of his wartime teaching experience with a high note of optimism and convinced of the useful implications of his work. The educational program at Minidoka, Light wrote, "succeeded to a degree which would justify the repetition of its program in similar situations. . . . The experience herein described demonstrates that a program so formulated in advance can be put into successful operation despite very considerable material and administrative handicaps."[24]

Nowhere did Light reflect upon the possible reactionary consequences of what had happened to the Japanese Americans, but rather, as a good education technician, he took unquestioned pride in his work and set aside troubling questions. He was confronted with a task of managing and shaping the lives of an incarcerated human group and, even years after the original decision for internment and the appearance of wide criticism of internment, he offered his expertise as relevant to a possible, even anticipated, repeat of a similar effort. He was ready to serve the state again.

How did the targets of the social-engineering efforts respond?

The responses of Japanese Americans themselves reflected the conflicting explanations given by the state that rationalized internment and the reeducation opportunities it presented. Most Japanese Americans were confused, angry, and certainly frightened by the 1942 internment order. Their futures were completely uncertain and unguaranteed by the state. But most publicly responded to the order with relatively little opposition and protest. Some believed internment was a necessary evil demanded by a good government, and they complied and cooperated. Cooperation with whatever the state demanded could prove loyalty. For others, internment confirmed the basically racist nature of American society and resistance within the centers, which included political and cultural forms, often frustrated administrators. The differences of opinion and attitudes among the internees ran deep and produced sharp, even violent, conflicts. It was not at all clear to them whether internment was a result of a racism that assumed Japanese biological inferiority and disloyalty or of wartime overreaction to security concerns. Once in the camps, Japanese Americans did not know whether they faced possible future elimination, through deportation or physical extermination (a bleak social Darwinist "fate"), or a benign bureaucratic paternalism that wanted to bestow the blessings of Americanism (a social-engineering "project") upon them. Were they kept in what some publicly called "concentration camps" or had they been simply "evacuated" into temporary "centers" under the care of the federal government, as others described their situation? Plenty of evidence existed to argue for any of these interpretations. That there was no clear answer was itself tormenting.[25]

The recorded experience of one internee, historian Yamato Ichihashi, offers an especially useful vantage point to understand the internment dilemma. Although Ichihashi was untypical among Japanese Americans—he was not a farmer but had been a Stanford professor since 1913 and was perhaps the most eminent internee in the camps—his correspondence with Stanford friends and his diary during the war years provide a complete, day-to-day account of internment. His record is perhaps the only extant complete first-person account of the experience as events actually unfolded.

176   *Chapter Seven*

Ichihashi was also both witness as well as victim. From the beginning of his ordeal, he appreciated the historic importance of internment and recorded his experiences in order to write an account at a future point. He never got there, but his records remain for us today to consult. His observations are particularly valuable, because he was fluent in both English and Japanese, trained as a social scientist (historian and economist), and experienced in research and writing; yet his intellectual skills and wisdom did not prepare him for the years of trial in the camps. Although at the start of internment he believed himself mentally and culturally superior to the tens of thousands of other internees from plebeian backgrounds whom he had to join in the centers, he found that he could not avoid the cost of imprisonment. He thought he could rise above the mean life of camp, but by the end he too was dragged down. When he returned to Stanford in the spring of 1945, he was a bitter, cynical man whose family had disintegrated around him and whose intellectual life had died.

Examining Ichihashi's effort to try to describe his unfolding experience reveals the conflicting ideologies that controlled the camps and the difficulty he had in comprehending exactly what was happening to him and the other internees. There was no clear precedent upon which he could base his interpretation. The internment centers were not prison camps for convicted persons or prisoners of war; they were not reservations for subjugated, indigenous peoples; they were not forced labor camps; they were not reeducation centers for the politically degenerate. They were none of these but also a bit of all of them at the same time.

In one of his first letters to a Stanford colleague after he was "evacuated" to the "assembly center" at the Santa Anita racetrack, Ichihashi tried to describe his circumstances in incarceration by analogy. The choice of his words is revealing.The state, he wrote, had "established in this Center a truly classless community (a Soviet ideal unrealized as yet in Russia). Residents (inmates more appropriately) are not recognized as individuals; we are numbered for identification and are treated exactly alike." "The Camp has a population of 18,400, each of which is numbered for identification; for instance I am No. 5561A." Ichihashi described the abysmal living conditions, including multiple families forced to live in converted horse stalls. "In management of the classless community, the government has apparently adopted the lowest conceivable standard of treating human beings." He also condemned the hypocrisy of officials that administered the center. The administration was supposedly civilian, but in fact it was the army that ran the camps. Channels for complaint and communication from the internees were established, with even a "community council" composed of nominally elected representatives from among a portion of the evacuees. In fact, the administration determined their composition and manipulated their operation. Unexplained arrests, detentions, and harassment of internees were widespread, prompting Ichihashi to write in his diary (again, the language is instructive), "The present setup of the community is illogical and impossible; this is made more so by the attitude and handling of affairs by the management—autocracy enforced by a veritable Gestapo."[26]

As the months wore on, living conditions improved and administrative operations became more routinized, which provided a measure of assurance to the internees. Nevertheless, the state never produced a clear rationale about the camps; the flimsy fictions that they existed as a benign national security precaution or for the protection of the internees themselves continued. But the expressed attitudes of camp officials also regularly betrayed very different feelings toward the internees. "You can't imagine how close we came to machine-gunning the whole bunch of them," a camp official stated to the press after the suppression of a protest demonstration at the Tule Lake center. Speculating about his personal future after the war, Ichihashi wrote his closest friend at Stanford that he did not know what he and his family would do. "Who can tell whether this country will be an agreeable place for us to live, and if one were to believe what is being said at present, no Japanese are wanted here. Naturally we need not stay in a place we are not wanted; unlike the Jews, we have our native-land." (American law until 1952 denied Japanese immigrants naturalization rights, and they therefore remained Japanese citizens.)[27]

Ichihashi of course did not know what was happening to the Jews of Europe in the Nazi death camps—if he and the other Japanese Americans had known, their feelings about confinement would undoubtedly have been very different. Ignorance in their circumstances was a blessing of sorts for them. How might they have acted if they had known about the industrial murder of the confined in Europe, we of course cannot know. But we do have Ichihashi's reflection, more than a year into internment, about his experience. It is an especially insightful comment on the results of race-based confinement, official obfuscation, administrative hypocrisy and

178   *Chapter Seven*

manipulation of the internees, and brutal confinement. Ichihashi wrote a Stanford colleague in late 1943:

> I am naturally touched by the sad nature of events relative to institutions and persons. . . . [During this past year and a half] I have been forced to witness sad aspects of human life without relief; almost daily I have been encountering the death of men and women whose life history of struggle for thirty, forty, fifty years had been known to me. I have attended more funerals during this short period than I had in my lifetime. . . . But it is not death alone that saddens my heart, but the stupid behavior of young and old, resulting in the shattering of families and of controlled domestic relations, in the breaking up of true friendships. Individuals have become selfish, self-centered or egoistic or else so apathetic as to lose a balanced view of life. In brief, men and women have been washed out [of] whatsoever culture and refinement they once had possessed; they have reverted to savages and in many cases to beasts. This is the fruit of a forced communistic life as I see it.[28]

Ichihashi and his wife were finally allowed to leave internment and return to their home in the late spring of 1945. The former professor returned a greatly reduced person, in some ways as he had described others in the above commentary. He, and most of his fellow adult internees, never became "projectiles for democracy" or the model citizens wanted by the state. The ambitious social-engineering efforts never succeeded in transforming them. But this does not mean that they went untouched—they were passed by and ground down. The social engineers devoted little attention to these consequences when they reflected on the contributions internment made to the national body.

Years after internment ended, many who were involved in administration dismissed or excused their involvement by referring to the pressures of war and the demands of national mobilization. The focus of examination here, however, has not been so much about the rationalizations for internment but more about the underlying attitudes toward race and administration of internees. Except for McCloy and Myer, most of the individuals mentioned in this essay were not distinguished or unique individuals but were everyday teachers and academic researchers, with generally liberal inclinations. It is exactly their ordinariness that makes their thoughts noteworthy. In their prewar occupations, they had possessed little power in any conventional sense, but their connection to state authorities that had easily incarcerated

120,000 persons opened their visions to new possibilities and meanings for their lives. Power offered them possibilities for ambitious social engineering, possibilities that were often accepted with alacrity. (On several occasions, Ichihashi even found himself under the authority of young former students of his at Stanford.) They willingly offered their intellectual services to the state's purpose, and one wonders whether the attraction of administrative power over a captive people helped blind them to the ugliness of their endeavor and the contradiction between their expressed democratic principles and the sentiments of the targeted population. (In contrast, some were deeply troubled by their involvement. The first director of the WRA, Milton Eisenhower, was uncomfortable in his position and left the job after just a few months. When asked by Dillon Myer, his proposed replacement, about whether he should accept the position, Eisenhower said, "Yes, if you can do the job and sleep at night." Eisenhower said that had been unable to do so.)[29] The excitement of encountering "scientific possibilities" and the challenge of applying their intellectual worth to "practical" purpose were certainly part of this enthusiasm, but such is precisely the lure of projects of social control.

Functioning as good technoadministrators, as researchers consciously seeking ways to improve social control in the camps, and as conscientious teachers seeking to mold Japanese American students in their own image, these individuals believed they were playing a progressive and constructive role, not only in contributing to the war effort but in positively reshaping an entire population for their own good. They went far beyond merely trying to help a distressed group. Many took pride in their belief that they successfully fought off the racists, for the benefit of democracy and for Japanese Americans. Dillon Myer, himself, in his self-serving account of the WRA, devotes an entire chapter to "The Continuing Battle of the Racists," where he contrasts the WRA's efforts to congressional extremists. And although the differences between, on the one side, the crude racists who believed in fundamental "blood" and genetic differences among peoples and, on the other the side, the WRA educators and researchers was formidable and meaningful, the two groups also shared common ground. They shared a vision of the desirability of an America well ordered and prescribed in middle-class Euro-American values and ways, of the undesirability of Americans who did not fit those definitions, and of the possibility of using state power to reshape the target group. The liberal educators and researchers,

180   *Chapter Seven*

perhaps precisely because they held to a cultural and not genetic basis for differences in group human behavior, differed from the crude racists in their greater faith in the ability of modern forms of social control (information management, systematic education, "scientific" administration informed by the insights of social psychology) to shape a subject population. As John Embree, one of the leading academics who worked for the WRA, put it tellingly, the applied social sciences had become essential to any effective, modern management effort, whether it be "for industry, [such as] the Western Electric Company; for colonial government, [such as] the British in New Guinea and parts of Africa; and finally in our American parallel to Colonial Administration, the War Relocation Authority."[30] Dillon Myer, the director of the WRA, was appointed, appropriately, commissioner of the Bureau of Indian Affairs in the early 1950s.

One of the seeming contradictions in the internment of Japanese Americans during World War II is that political leaders such as Franklin Roosevelt and implementers such as Jerome Light were on the whole consciously "antiracist." They did not share the openly racist views of those who retained social Darwinian notions about the genetic differences among so-called racial groups. In fact, those responsible for the camps went out of their way to oppose the open racists—the assumption of the WRA's Americanization programs was that the internees could become just as American as any other people. Any yet, the entire internment enterprise and its operation were imbued with what can only be called racist policies and actions. The original internment decision, which made no distinction between the rights of alien and citizen, separated persons of Japanese ancestry from those of German or Italian descent. The camp education and Americanization campaigns sought to impose regimes that were in fact racially based and similar to efforts long directed against native Indian populations.

Scientific racism, those systematic doctrines of racial inequality and hierarchy espoused by intellectuals beginning in the nineteenth century, largely fell into disfavor by the outbreak of Wo rid War II. The mainstream of social scientists and scientists broke from open avowals of racism in the 1930s and accepted culture-based explanations of differences among peoples. The rejection of openly racist language among the educated and liberal members of the Roosevelt administration and WRA reflected this eclipse of social Darwinian notions. But, as discussed above, the emergence of a new, technocratic social-engineering mentality, replete with the jargon of

Social Darwinism Versus Social Engineering   181

racially neutral terms, code words, and unexamined assumptions, helped sanction and inspire new forms of state mistreatment of a group that was in fact racially designated, in this case Japanese Americans. They would not be alone, of course. The absence of overt racist language in intent and practice did not mean the triumph of egalitarianism but highlighted the emergence of a new faith in the malleability of social groups.[31]

Soon after internment began, the Socialist Norman Thomas publicly condemned the New Dealers and "liberals" who trumpeted the roundup of Japanese Americans solely on the authority of the president; he linked internment to the ominous general centralization of political power in the country. "For the first time in American history," he wrote, "men, committees and publications boasting of their 'liberalism' as against 'fascism' are in the vanguard in justifying the presidential assumption of dictatorial power." More troubling perhaps was the embrace of the possibilities of mass, "scientific" population control by everyday liberal Americans. The enthusiastic use of various methods of technoadministration employed by the liberals directing America's internment camps was a sign of the fascination with state manipulation of populations for their own "interests" that became ubiquitous in the postwar period.[32]

EIGHT

Asian Americans and Politics: Some Perspectives from History

One of my early writings that explicitly connected diplomatic history and Asian Americans was an essay under the title, "Asian Immigrants and American Foreign Relations."[1] It attracted the attention of the Woodrow Wilson Center for International Scholars, which was exploring ways to expand into new fields of scholarship beyond its traditional focus on high geopolitics and domestic elites. As a result, the Center, encouraged by historian Warren I. Cohen, invited me to organize a conference that eventually centered on the relationship of Asian Americans and politics, a subject that scholars were just beginning to examine seriously.

The Center provided financial and logistical support for a large gathering of scholars in Washington, D.C., in 1997. Special speakers included the pioneering Asian American congresswoman Patsy Mink. The conference members presented an array of papers that explored different historical, social, and contemporary dimensions of Asian American political behavior, participation, and prospects. Papers later appeared in a volume I edited entitled *Asian Americans and Politics: Perspectives, Experiences, Prospects*. It was

"Asian Americans and Politics: Some Perspectives from History," *Asian Americans and Politics: Perspectives, Experiences, Prospects*, edited by Gordon H. Chang (Stanford University Press and the Woodrow Wilson Press), 2002: 13–38.

183

184   *Chapter Eight*

among the first to broadly examine the subject from different disciplinary perspectives.

This chapter began the volume. Its purpose was to present historical perspectives on the subject, still hazily understood and ill-defined at the time, and as an effort to show that Asian American politics was not as novel a topic as some may have thought. Many commentators, scholars, and activists before us had also thought about the involvement of Chinese, Japanese, and other Asians in American politics and the implications of their participation. We contemporary academics—historians, sociologists, legal scholars, and political scientists—were just the latest to think about the topic.

We discussed much: Asian American voter behavior, modes of political participation other than electoral, recent victories for Asian Americans in advancing political presence (such as the gubernatorial victory of Gary Locke in Washington state), and federal actions that suppressed Asian American activism. Since the appearance of this essay, the relationship of Asian Americans and politics has become a matter of wide interest. This chapter continues to offer an important historical perspective on this still-developing dimension of Asian American life and the possible connections between the past and our present.

*

Asian Americans and politics—for many people today, these two notions seem incongruous, even contradictory. Popular belief has it that persons of Asian ancestry have not, until very recently, been generally interested in American politics. Indeed, many observers characterize Asian Americans[2] historically as laboring and economic beings, not political in any way; their alleged political disinterest stemmed from cultural differences or a conscious decision to remain inoffensive and obscure in a hostile land. Conservative economist Thomas Sowell, for example, argues that Chinese Americans "deliberately kept out of the courts and out of the political arena" and that perhaps they and Japanese Americans came to enjoy social and economic success because they, in fact, "studiously avoided political agitation." Sowell's interpretation of Chinese and Japanese American histories, however, reflects less of an interest in the experiences of these racial minorities than in constructing an argument against state efforts to remedy social and racial inequality.[3]

Another argument advanced for why Asian Americans supposedly eschewed politics, even refusing to exercise the franchise when they could, is that years of rejection and discrimination created deep distrust of the political process and pessimism about the possibility of effecting significant change.[4] Reflecting the assumption that Asians, either by "culture" or because of historical experience, have been unpolitical in America, commentators have described the increasing visibility of Asians in American politics as something of a novelty and break from an unassertive past. Titles of recent articles from across the political spectrum in the mainstream press express this attitude: "Overcome Distaste for Politics in Order to Get Their Views Heard: Asian-Americans Seek to Join Power Structure,"[5] "Have Asian Americans Arrived Politically? Not Quite,"[6] "Apathetic Asian Americans? Why Their Success Hasn't Spilled Over into Politics,"[7] "Voters of Asian Heritage Slow to Claim Voice,"[8] and "Asian Americans Head for Politics."[9]

These articles are not wrong in appreciating the emergence of Asian Americans as a political force, albeit still in its formative stages. This development is important and a turning point in the history of Asian Americans and American public life.[10] But the articles are misleading in the way they characterize this development. Suggesting a linear movement from inactivity to political involvement, from apathy to activism, from powerlessness and voicelessness to increasing influence, and even from inoffensiveness to a possible threat, may be a convenient way to view events today, but it is not a historically accurate one. Neither is it one that leads to an appreciation of the complexities of current Asian American political behavior and an understanding of its distinctive features.

This chapter does not examine the complexities of current Asian American politics. Instead, it reviews how past observers have described the relationship between Asian Americans and politics. This chapter deals, therefore, with perceptions and interpretations. But it is also about the meaning of these views, since past attitudes, assumptions, and suspicions continue to affect the ways in which current events are understood. For example, inflammatory rhetoric around the presidential campaign finance controversy of the mid-1990s echoed the fears that many in America held in the 1880s about the corrupting influence of the Chinese in American politics. The mounting assertiveness of Asian Americans in local politics around

186   *Chapter Eight*

the country has met with reactions like those seen when Japanese Americans entered Hawaiian politics in the mid-twentieth century. And many sensational comments made in 1999 about the alleged Chinese communist theft of American nuclear weapons technology fall within a tradition of questioning the loyalty of Asians to America. By contrast, the wide celebration of Asians as model and unassuming citizens also invokes another set of historically imbedded notions about the unpolitical and compliant Asian.

Understanding Asian American political activity on its own terms, without the baggage of the past, is not an easy or comfortable task for many Americans. In seeking to lighten, or at least open up, the kinds of interpretive baggage that affect much of the discussion about Asian American politics today, this chapter will examine a selection of scholarly and popular literature, principally about the relationship that Chinese and Japanese Americans, the two large, early Asian groups, have had with American politics. This literature is divided into three different periods—the mid-nineteenth century to the mid-1920s, the mid-1920s to the late 1960s, and the late 1960s to the 1990s. Changes in the social profile of the Asian American communities and in the perceptions of their relationship to politics distinguish each period.

This review will reveal that interest in the relationship of Asians to American politics is not something that emerged only toward the end of the twentieth century; it is a discussion with a long history, beginning with the arrival of significant numbers of Asians in the United States in the mid-nineteenth century. Writers have asked: What kinds of political beings are these persons of Asian ancestry? How will they participate in the political life of the country? What particular political interests will they have? What agendas will they pursue? In various forms, these questions have been posed through the years. The resulting discussion has waxed and waned, but it has always been marked by great emotion—and often by considerable prejudice. It also has been a discussion closely connected to other prominent issues of the day, including race, war, and national identity.

Mid-Nineteenth Century to the Mid-1920s

In the years immediately after the immigration of large numbers of Chinese to America, many commentators wondered about the social and cultural makeup of the new arrivals and about their political relationship to the

Republic. At first, the Chinese were frequently welcomed as positive additions to the country, and the pundits optimistically predicted that they would soon join other immigrant groups as part of the American political family. Indeed, during the grand San Francisco celebration of the admission of California to the Union in 1850, local judge Nathaniel Bennett specifically acknowledged the presence of Chinese and other immigrants in the audience: "Born and reared under different Governments and speaking different tongues, we nevertheless meet here today as brothers. . . . You stand among us in all respects as equals."[11] The participation of large numbers of Chinese in the 1852 Fourth of July festivities in San Francisco prompted the city's main daily newspaper to predict with confidence that "the China Boys will yet vote at the same polls, study at the same schools, and bow at the same altar as our own countrymen." The same year, California governor John McDougal publicly characterized the Chinese as "one of the most worthy of our newly adopted citizens."[12]

Time has shown, however, that these early writers were far off the mark in their sanguine expectations that the Chinese would slide easily into American life and society. Indeed, mounting hostility soon overwhelmed their predictions of Chinese acceptance. The Chinese as citizens, many now concluded, would be a catastrophe.

The famous decision handed down by the California Supreme Court in *People v. Hall* (1854) expressed this dark vision, which became the popular view about the Chinese and the implications of their presence in America. A jury had convicted George Hall of the murder of a Chinese, in part on the basis of the testimony of Chinese witnesses. In overturning Hall's conviction, the California Supreme Court pointed out that existing statutes maintained that "no black or mulatto person, or Indian" was allowed "to give evidence in favor of, or against a white man" in court. Chief Justice Hugh C. Murray argued that testimony from "Asiatics" also must be prohibited because the clear intent of the statutes was to distinguish whites from all others.

Murray's argument is usually cited today to illustrate the relegation of Chinese into a formal inferior racial caste along with other persons of color in America, but it is also revealing of the attitudes that would have a direct bearing on the involvement of the Chinese in American politics. "The same rule which would admit them to testify," Murray wrote, "would admit them to all the equal rights of citizenship, and we might soon see

188   *Chapter Eight*

them at the polls, in the jury box, upon the bench, and in our legislative halls." Such prospects clearly frightened the chief justice. The possibility of Chinese participation in American politics was, he argued, "not a speculation which exists in the excited and overheated imagination of the patriot and statesman, but it is an actual and present danger."[13] While Murray's own imagination may very well have been "overheated," his decision in the Hall case became a cornerstone of much subsequent California legislation and policy, and his comments were accepted as sober, judicious, and well founded.

The chief justice was not alone in his fear. Many other white Californians shared his alarm about Chinese interest in American political life. They believed the Chinese would be *hyperpolitical*—that is, inordinately, even fanatically, interested in seeking political power and influence to the detriment of established society and government. In their view, such political activity would harm, not benefit, America.

The threat of Chinese hyperpolitical activity was a common ingredient in the popular "yellow peril" literature of the last decades of the nineteenth century. Written in florid, provocative language, this literature reveals much about how the Chinese were perceived by many serious writers and a reading public.[14] One of the most well known of these polemics warned America of impending doom. Published in 1880, the future-as-history novel *Last Days of the Republic* by Pierton W. Dooner was a call to action. If the state did nothing to stop Chinese immigration, Dooner wrote, the Chinese would soon inundate California and the country as a whole. The author described a terrible future that would see nothing less than the very conquest and demise of America because of white political apathy and underappreciation of the Asian threat. The Chinese, according to Dooner, aspired to nothing less than the political conquest of America. The book ends with the Chinese seizing Washington, D.C.

Dooner was seeking to rally whites to support restrictions on Chinese immigration and Chinese access to the ballot box. His was not simple fiction, but a forecast based on evidence from real life. Dooner included, for example, long, verbatim quotes from Chief Justice Murray in the Hall murder case to remind Californians of earlier wisdom about the political dangers posed by the Chinese.[15]

Not long after publication of Dooner's book, explicit concerns about giving Chinese the right to vote were expressed throughout hearings on the federal Chinese Exclusion Act, passed by Congress in 1882. Among other things, the act made the Chinese "aliens ineligible to citizenship." This provision, more than any other single act or incident, would confirm the relegation of the Chinese in America to a political nether world and establish a precedent for the political and social marginalization of subsequent Asian immigrants. The last ethnic restrictions against Asians becoming American citizens would not be lifted until 1952.

The 1882 exclusion act was the first in a series of such acts, yet many Americans continued to express concern about the political ambitions and abilities of Chinese immigrants. In 1898, for example, the respected *North American Review* published the article "The Chinaman in American Politics," which alerted readers to the political savvy of the Chinese and the extraordinary and undesirable influence they were still having on American politics.[16] "It is the prevailing opinion that politics as a profession is unknown to the Chinese, but nothing could be farther from the truth," the article began. "As a race they are astute politicians, and, singularly, one of the most active fields for the demonstration of their skill is found, not in China, but on the American continent and among the American people." Although the Chinese were virtually without the power of the vote, the essay argued that they wielded political significance far beyond their numbers and were "more effective" than "the entire Afro-American contingent," which was many times larger in number. Blacks, it said, even with the help of "philanthropic whites," had obtained far less desired legislation than had the Chinese. As evidence, the essay pointed to the ability of the Chinese "political machine" to frustrate further legislative efforts to control their population. No one in America, it was claimed, had "ever fought a campaign with more diplomacy," "more astuteness," and more ruthless determination than had the Chinese.

But in contrast to these accounts which saw a racial conspiracy against America, considerable contemporary evidence points to a different interpretation of the political sentiments and behavior of the Chinese. Chinese leaders, writers, and organization officials regularly spoke out against the legislation that discriminated against them, but, in doing so, they argued that the Chinese had no special interests other than in seeking the rights and privileges enjoyed by others in the country. Thousands of individual Chinese turned to the courts to seek redress of grievances and to claim rights denied them. And contrary to the later notion that the Chinese were

190   *Chapter Eight*

uninterested in political democracy, many Chinese in America, inspired by the universalist declarations of American democracy, actively supported republicanism in China. Ironically, seeking to realize democracy in their faraway land of ancestry seemed a more realistic political alternative than struggling for a consistent democracy in a hostile America.[17]

But it was not just the Chinese who were characterized as hyperpolitical. In the 1920s, after two decades of Japanese immigration to America, a prominent political commentator, Montaville Flowers, raised the specter of the Japanese. He maintained that Japanese immigrants wanted

> all the rights and privileges of the American-born white man—the right of free entrance for [Japanese] nationals into the United States; the right to vote; the right to own American land anywhere, in any quantity, for any purpose; the right to be legislators and governors of states; the right to go to Congress and make the laws; the right to sit upon our Supreme Courts of State and Nation, and there to determine the very genius of our future civilization.[18]

For Flowers and many others of his day, efforts by the Japanese to seek these basic political rights was not only impudent but also evidence of another racial conspiracy. He warned that if Japanese immigrants could become citizens, they would work to end the laws restricting their economic activities. They would then concentrate their population "in certain states and in special centres in those states, and waiting, waiting for more men, for all their 'picture brides,' and for their native born children, who are American citizens by right of birth; waiting until all these vote, he [sic] will have his representatives at the capitols, control the balance of power and be master of his destiny." The Japanese effort to seize power, Flowers concluded, would be "a master stroke."

In the early twentieth century Flowers was not alone in seeing the Japanese as an outspoken racial minority in the country. The respected social scientist Jesse F. Steiner expressed a similar opinion when he observed that the Japanese, "instead of acquiescing in the position assigned them, as, on the whole, the great mass of the Negroes seem disposed to do, have taken a bold stand for their rights and insist that there shall be no discrimination against them."[19] Steiner was not the racial extremist that Flowers was, but he too warned white Americans about the changing racial balance of power in the world. In his book *The Japanese Invasion: A Study in the Psychology of*

Inter-Racial Contacts, he concludes, "We must bear in mind that the Orient will not always come to us in the attitude of a supplicant. The Orientals feel deeply that their cause is righteous, and their hands are strengthened by the consciousness of growing power." Steiner favored restrictions on immigration and other measures against the Japanese to preempt expanded racial conflict on the West Coast.

Steiner's comparison of the Japanese with African Americans may seem strange today when African American activism has set the standard for "minority politics." In the early twentieth century, however, African American leaders themselves often praised Japanese immigrants as a positive model of racial pride and political activism for the black masses. Although African American writers drew very different conclusions than Flowers and Steiner about Japanese immigrants, they too saw the Japanese as highly political people.

In those days, not just the immigrant but even the native born of Asian ancestry was suspect. In 1919, for example, influential publisher V. S. McClatchy warned California of the political danger posed by the Nisei (second-generation Japanese Americans).[20] He pointed to Hawaii where, he said, "Japanese born under the American Flag," and thus having citizenship, would soon be able to "outvote any other race; and in a generation they will probably out-vote all other races combined." If the government did not restrict their numbers and their political privileges, including naturalization, McClatchy warned, the Japanese would imperil American institutions. Echoing earlier views of the Chinese, McClatchy described the Japanese immigrants and their descendants not as unpolitical, but as hyperpolitical beings, unafraid of using their vote and public office to advance their own alleged racial agenda.

Upon their arrival in America in the early twentieth century, Asian Indians and Filipinos also encountered deep suspicions about their political loyalties. Because of their antipathy to the British colonization of their homeland, Indians, many Americans believed, were hostile not only to the British but also to the entire English-speaking world, which included America, of course. Allegedly, then, Indians would sympathize with the anti-white appeals of the Japanese and Chinese.[21] Filipino immigrants represented a different sort of problem in the eyes of commentators during the 1930s. It was feared that Filipinos, like other colonials, harbored resentments against the country that oppressed their homeland. However, unlike

192   *Chapter Eight*

other Asians, many Filipinos actually seemed to embrace America. Yet this love also was threatening to some Americans. As a specialist on Filipino immigration noted in 1931, the educated "Filipino is, if anything, *too* assimilable to accept the limitations imposed upon him by public opinion."[22] The problem here was "not that of the stranger who cannot be Americanized, but rather that of the would-be American who refuses to remain a stranger." Asians, even as putative friends, were still seen as a problem because they would not accept their subordinate place.

Thus in the view of many Americans in the first decades of the twentieth century, Asians could never become good, active citizens and join the American political family. Whether it was their different standards of morality and truth, their clannishness or cliquishness, their venality and worship of the material over principle, or their ambition and drive, Asians could not appreciate, understand, or partake of modern democracy, the argument went. They were either hyperpolitical or, as some commentators saw it, apolitical, uninterested in participating in a democracy. Though apparently contradictory, these two popular perceptions shared the assumption that Asians threatened American values and political life and could not live constructively in the country. Moreover, the loyalty and value of the Asian immigrant were suspect, according to either view. Both apolitical and hyperpolitical Asians were devoted only to advancing their own narrow interests and were unable or unwilling to accept the rules of civic participation in America.[23]

To be sure, some early observers did not view Asians in such suspicious and exaggerated ways, but they did not represent majority opinion during the period of immigration exclusion. The defenders of the Chinese and Japanese typically presented Asians as being no different from other immigrant groups in both their political behavior and attachment to America. Sociologist Mary Roberts Coolidge tried to counter the virulent anti-Chinese prejudices of her day by offering sympathetic perspectives from her own social research. In her classic 1909 work, *Chinese Immigration,* she observed that the American-born Chinese were already assuming everyday civic responsibilities.[24] "There is abundant evidence," she wrote, "that the Chinese of the second generation mean to claim their citizenship. In the smaller towns of California and in some other states they show strong patriotism, marching in Fourth of July parades and even drilling and volunteering for the army." Even the parents of these native-born Chinese, she noted, although they could not vote, were proud of the rights enjoyed by their children.

Kiyoshi K. Kawakami, a prolific, vocal defender of the Japanese in America in the pre–World War II years, argued similarly about the Japanese and suggested that the accusations about the evils of Japanese immigrant influence in America were wildly exaggerated.[25] A future historian of America examining the passions of the times, he wrote, "would no doubt wonder why there was so much ado about the naturalization of the Japanese." In his view, ending the denial of citizenship to Japanese would produce no dire results, but would simply remove a major irritant in Tokyo-Washington relations. In the views of both Coolidge and Kawakami, Chinese and Japanese Americans were really very much like any other immigrant group, and their attitudes toward politics were not fundamentally different in any way. For many years afterward, other observers would continue to frame the discussion of Asian American political behavior in a similarly simplistic way—that is, whether Asian Americans were the same or radically different from other social groups.

Mid-1920s to the Late 1960s

After passage of the Chinese Exclusion Act, designation of the "Asiatic Barred Zone" in 1917, and enactment of the Immigration Act of 1924, the United States effectively ended further immigration from Asia and classified all Asian immigrants already in America "aliens ineligible to citizenship." In view of the impossibility of naturalization and the small, slow-growing, native-born sector of the population that did enjoy citizenship rights, Americans perceived Asian American communities to be much less threatening to the dominant racial order than they had been previously. Because of harsh social discrimination, the Asian communities also were relatively isolated from the rest of society. In the end, then, the exclusion of Asians largely quieted, though did not entirely end, popular fears of the Asian presence in America and its political threat.

In fact, from the 1920s to the 1960s the perception of Asians as hyperpolitical largely disappeared. Asian Americans came to be seen as only marginal to American mainstream society and politics, and the stereotype of Asians as basically unpolitical became imbedded in America. Writings based on the "Survey of Race Relations," the first comprehensive study of

194   *Chapter Eight*

racial attitudes and the living situation of Asians in the West, reflected this view. The investigation, which involved scores of researchers in the mid-1920s, devoted little attention to the political behavior of Asians in America. For example, Stanford University's Eliot Grinnell Mears, secretary of the project, barely mentions Asian American political activity in his 1928 work *Resident Orientals on the American Pacific Coast: Their Legal and Economic Status*.[26] About all he says on the subject is that both the Chinese and Japanese in America wanted citizenship, with the Japanese more eager than the Chinese and "probably more so than the general run of American immigrants." Of the second-generation Chinese and Japanese, Mears simply describes them as "worthy Americans."

Mears's colleague at Stanford, Yamato Ichihashi, the leading authority on the Japanese in America in the prewar years, also wrote little about their political behavior in his now-classic 1932 study of Japanese immigrants.[27] Ichihashi devotes over four hundred pages to discussing their migration history, social life, economic activity, and prospects for life in America, as well as anti-Japanese agitation; three chapters are devoted especially to the situation of the Nisei. Yet in all these pages he says little about Japanese Americans and politics.

Ichihashi argues that the Japanese were as fit for residence in America as European immigrants and that, as for politics, the Japanese represented no threat. They admired America, including its political institutions, and only wanted to be given a decent chance in the country. The Nisei, he maintains, were rapidly becoming Americanized and culturally distant from their parents. In his view, it was white prejudice that prevented the full social and political assimilation of the Nisei into American life, and such prejudice was responsible, therefore, for their lingering ethnic distinctiveness.

A very different view of the future role of Japanese Americans in American politics appeared ten years later during the federal government's internment of Japanese Americans in World War II. Some social scientists and government officials linked to internment offered enthusiastic predictions about the exemplary political role Japanese Americans might play in the postwar world. They would be neither hyperpolitical threats nor apathetic citizens, these scientists and public officials asserted. Instead, they described Japanese Americans as an especially malleable human clay that could be molded for proclaimed democratic purposes. With great optimism, internment administrators and teachers often wrote about the potential of the camps as an unprecedented social engineering project for their vision of American democracy. They rejected the prewar notion that blood rendered the Japanese racial threats to America; instead, they believed that enlightened administrators could shape the Japanese into ideal citizens. One teacher wrote positively of her efforts along these lines with students at the Topaz, Utah, camp and majestically described her project as "Developing World Citizens in a Japanese Relocation Center." A leading official at the camp in Poston, Arizona, saw the internees under him as similar in potential. His challenge, he believed, was to make the Poston internment camp "a source of rich production, a school for wise and energetic Americans in years to come." He wanted to achieve nothing less than the transformation of his wards into "projectiles of democracy" who would go forward constructively into the anticipated difficult postwar world.[28] These educators saw the Japanese as compliant, without their own political identity or interests. The social engineers could make them into whatever was wanted. The Japanese would become, in a very real sense, "models," anticipating the characterization of Asian Americans two decades later.

Despite these developments, the view that the Japanese still represented a hyperpolitical threat persisted. Internment itself was the culmination of decades of racial suspicion about the loyalty of Japanese Americans. Even after the Japanese were incarcerated, hostile commentators continued to warn that Japanese Americans were waiting to exploit the political system for their own self-serving purposes. What would happen in the postwar period when the government released the internees from these camps located in sparsely populated states? What would prevent the efficient and prolific Japanese from soon dominating the politics of Nevada or Wyoming? A 1943 article in *American Legion Magazine* raised these sensational questions and challenged readers to consider "How long would it take for this fast multiplying, unresting, far-scheming race to have two Senators in Washington?"[29] The author proposed shipping all the internees to distant islands in the Pacific where they would live under direct rule from Washington without benefit of the franchise.

This thinking aside, the most common view among specialists on Japanese Americans at this time was that they were far from being the hyperpolitical threat once feared and, indeed, were notably less political, with a weaker political identity, than other Americans. Forrest E. LaViolette, a social scientist who had studied Japanese American political behavior in the

196   *Chapter Eight*

years immediately before the war, concluded that the Nisei in fact had not "participated in elections to the fullest extent."[30] Based on his own research and reports in Japanese community newspapers, LaViolette suggested that only about a third of the Nisei eligible to vote had actually registered. He characterized this behavior as "political indifference" arising from the "lack of political consciousness" among the Japanese. Continuing social segregation, isolation of the parent generation from the political arena, and the "conservative character of Japanese tradition" all contributed to this low level of political attention among young Japanese Americans. Although he pointed to developments such as the rise of the Japanese American Citizens League as evidence of changing attitudes, LaViolette saw nothing dramatic ahead. The Japanese in America, he noted, were rather conservative and few were attracted to communism or other radical politics. He predicted that neither the Chinese nor Japanese would be interested in "racial voting blocs."

Through the 1950s and into the 1960s, the view that Asians were inoffensive and without a well-formed political identity became well established in America. One of the leading scholars of the Chinese in America, sociologist Rose Hum Lee, claimed that Chinese Americans were "not politically astute, or active in American politics."[31] Critical of the perceived "apathy," Lee chastised Chinese Americans as "politically immature" and as even disdainful of politics, except for a handful of officials connected to the Chinese Nationalist Party, the Kuomintang. Lee attributed this Chinese American political indifference to influences from their immigrant parents, social isolation, or their traditional suspicion of government, and she found nothing admirable in their attitude.

Other important books published in the 1960s about Chinese Americans, such as that by S. W. Kung, *Chinese in American Life: Some Aspects of Their History, Status, Problems, and Contributions* (1962), and Betty Lee Sung's influential *Mountain of Gold: The Story of the Chinese in America* (1967), contained similar points of view. In his book, Kung devotes considerable attention to the achievements of prominent Chinese Americans, principally in the professions, but pays virtually no attention to politics, other than celebrating the election of Hiram Fong as Hawaii's U.S. senator in 1959.[32] He does acknowledge, however, that though the Chinese in America were victims of injustice that relegated them to second-class status, they "have gradually come to understand the true significance of their right to vote." Although he believes their "potential political power" was "rapidly enlarging," he ventures no prediction of how that influence might be used. Betty Lee Sung's explanation for why the "Chinese tended to shy away from American political activity or from exercising their right to vote" is that they believed their franchise was inconsequential.[33] They were, however, "gradually beginning to realize the fallacy of their thinking." In Sung's view, Chinese political inactivity was on the wane because of a decline in the sojourner mentality as well as falling social barriers and reduced discrimination. The result would be increased participation in "American life."

Authors such as Ichihashi, Lee, and Sung were highly sensitive to the past and continuing prejudices against Asians in America, and much of their writing constituted responses to the prejudiced assumptions that had dominated the discourse on Asian Americans. Indeed, their writing effectively responded to the past negative portrayals and helped introduce new, much more positive images. To counter the view that Asians represented a threat to America, these writers emphasized the inoffensiveness of Asians and focused on the developing Americanism of the Asian American communities. And to counter the view that Asian Americans were poor and unskilled and contributed little to mainstream American life, the authors offered a picture of hardworking communities that aspired to becoming assimilated and full members of middle America.

As salutary as these efforts were to ending the virulently racist views from the past, these writers helped to construct images that were one-sided in their own ways. Indeed, sometimes this was done deliberately. Yamato Ichihashi, for example, virtually omitted any discussion of politics in his prewar writings about the Japanese in America, but he knew full well the deep interest of the Issei (first-generation Japanese immigrants) and many Nisei in the politics of Japan. This interest was understandable because of the limitations they faced in the United States. Nevertheless, Ichihashi clearly crafted his accounts to create a positive and congenial image of the Japanese for his mainly Euro American audiences.[34] The writers who focused on Chinese Americans also consciously presented accounts that elided aspects of the experience that did not well serve their effort to forge a new narrative. They minimized or even entirely omitted discussion of the strong diasporic consciousness of Chinese in America and the social and political disenchantment with America that was widespread among immigrant as well as native-born generations. This scholarship helped to create

198   *Chapter Eight*

the basis for the dramatically new public attitude toward Asian Americans that had emerged by the late 1960s.[35]

Toward the end of that tumultuous decade, the periodical press featured prominent articles that consistently described Asian Americans in positive, even praiseworthy ways and endorsed the idea that Asian Americans had been and continued to be politically indifferent. Whether about Chinese or Japanese Americans, written by Asians or non-Asians, these essays presented a remarkably similar point of view, much like the "yellow peril" literature decades earlier. The 1960s literature, however, presented a triumphant story of minority immigrant communities overcoming adversity and achieving a high degree of social integration and economic success in American life. And in all these accounts, the authors suggested that Asians had eschewed political involvement, although they were beginning to show interest in electoral activity. Unlike some earlier characterizations, however, some observers now attributed *positive* qualities to this putative apoliticalness. Asian aloofness from politics was celebrated.

An example of this sort of praise appeared in the *New York Times Sunday Magazine* in 1966. In his article "Success Story, Japanese-American Style," sociologist William Petersen wrote admiringly of the ability of the Japanese, as a racial minority, to overcome social discrimination, official persecution, and economic deprivation to attain "a generally affluent and, for the most part, highly Americanized life." In venturing an explanation for their achievement, Petersen described a hardworking, frugal, unassuming people devoted to family and educational improvement. Nowhere does political activity seem to have a place in the picture; in fact, politics appears to be almost anathema to the people in Petersen's story. Petersen followed his article with a book entitled *Japanese Americans: Oppression and Success* that elaborates on the themes introduced in his article.[36] A major addition is a discussion of the Japanese experience in Hawaii, including a complimentary description of their political activity in the state. In his view, however, their new-found political visibility was an outgrowth of their social and economic success and not in any way connected to any pursuit of "ethnic politics."

One of the most widely consulted books on Japanese Americans, Bill Hosokawa's 1969 *Nisei: The Quiet Americans,* developed the success story interpretation, but paid considerable attention to the moderate political philosophy of the Japanese American Citizens League.[37] Unwavering faith in

America's basic goodness, even in the most adverse of times during World War II, sacrifice in the pursuit of democratic ideals, and triumph in advancing toward greater equality are prominent themes in this work. The politics described, however, is largely the politics of the most traditional Americanism, of a creed virtually devoid of any particular ethnic content, unless one argues that the remarkable and singular pursuit of acceptance in mainstream America is itself the unique contribution of Japanese Americans to ethnic politics. The Japanese Americans described by Hosokawa indeed seem very much like those "projectiles of democracy" promoted by the staff members of the internment centers.

This "model minority" literature appeared during a time of sharp social and political divisions in America and the emergence of assertive minority politics, especially among African Americans. While the ethnic politics of European immigrant groups was not a new subject in American intellectual life, concern about the behavior of the increasingly active African American population was.[38] And the alleged political indifference or super-Americanism of Asian Americans seemed to offer a positive contrast for writers concerned with the African American challenge. Edwin O. Reischauer, in his foreword to *Nisei: The Quiet Americans,* urged readers to appreciate the implications and message of Hosokawa's book which was that the Japanese American story was not an isolated one that concerned just one ethnic group. "It has much broader significance," Reischauer pointed out, for it offered an inspiration and, very important, a contrasting example "to others" critical of America. The Nisei showed there was another way.[39]

It was not difficult to determine who the "others" were. "The history of Japanese Americans," William Petersen had written, "challenges every such generalization about ethnic minorities." *U.S. News and World Report* wrote in a similar, but even blunter, way about Chinese Americans in 1966.[40] In the face of demands advanced by racial minorities upon the government, the Chinese American community, the magazine proclaimed, was "winning wealth and respect by dint of its own hard work." It went on to say that "still being taught in Chinatown is the old idea that people should depend on their own efforts—not a welfare check—in order to reach America's 'promised land.'"

Such commentary obviously pitted Asians against African Americans, but it also set Asians against themselves. Some activist-inclined Asian American commentators expressed impatience with the alleged political reticence

200   *Chapter Eight*

of Asians. Rather than models of behavior, they were seen as laggards in ethnic politics. In a pioneering commentary on pan-ethnic Asian political behavior written during these same years, Alfred Song, one of California's first political figures of Asian ancestry, maintained that the "evolution of noticeable political involvement by Orientals has been relatively slow compared to other minority groups."[41] He did not cite ethnic apathy or cultural difference to explain what he believed was Asian American political apathy. Rather he attributed it to Asians' pragmatic estimations of the limited significance of their vote and the continuing sensitivity to their own marginalization. But even with the passage of time, Song argued, an Asian American politics would be unlikely. "It is doubtful that there will develop any real or lasting group political solidarity among Orientals." The achievement of any future political significance by Asians in California, he predicted, would stem from individual efforts rather than from "Oriental group action." In other words, the future was unlikely to see any Asian American politics.

Late 1960s to the 1990s

At the very moment that the "success" stories about Chinese and Japanese Americans appeared, important social, political, and intellectual developments were occurring that would transform Asian American communities and make Alfred Song's prediction short-lived. In 1965 the United States ended the last vestiges of discrimination against immigration from Asia. The immigration act passed that year placed Asian immigration on the same formal basis as European immigration and sparked an unprecedented migration of Asians to the United States. Since 1965, the Asian population has grown from one million to over ten million, making Asian Americans the fastest-growing population group in America. In 1965 the majority of Asian Americans were American-born; today more than half are foreign-born. Moreover, by nationality Asian Americans have become tremendously more diverse and now include representatives of a score of different ancestries. The class base has expanded considerably as well because of immigration. Professionals and technical personnel now form a major, visible part of the Asian American population.

These demographic changes have complicated understanding the Asian American experience and the politics of Asian Americans in particular, because certain assumptions and perceptions from the past have been reinforced. For example, because many of those who have recently arrived in the country have been understandably hesitant to speak out on politics, some commentators continue to emphasize the alleged cultural or historical aloofness of Asians from politics. Yet the ethnic and class diversification of Asian Americans has made generalizing about them even more difficult than before. The fact is that Asian Americans have become increasingly involved in a wide range of political issues, including immigration legislation, social welfare and education policy, crime, racial violence, and even campaign financing at the local as well as national levels.

In addition to demographic changes, the late 1960s and early 1970s also saw the emergence of a new assertiveness by Asian Americans, which included the development of a pan-ethnic identity. Asian American intellectuals coined the term *Asian American* to help declare the birth of this self-consciousness. The designation's significance lay both in its emphasis on the commonalities shared by the different Asian ancestry groups (racial appearance, interpretation of historical experiences in America, social stigmatization, and so forth) and in its *political* claim. More than an ethnic label, the term *Asian American* also was a statement about perceived social position and group interest. Today, the term is ubiquitous. While it no longer carries the radical connotations it once did when used exclusively by activists on college campuses in the late 1960s, the designation continues to suggest a consciousness about place in American society, past and present—a consciousness that appears to be growing, not diminishing.[42]

Much of the writing about Asian Americans, which has grown tremendously in recent decades, reflects this thinking. Whether fiction or nonfiction, about the past or the present, the contemporary literature on Asian Americans largely responds to the past negative characterizations of foreignness, inferiority, danger, or marginality by casting Asian Americans as historical actors, with human agency and feeling, and as full participants in American and trans-Pacific narratives. The literature in recent decades also challenges the representations of docility, political indifference, and "success" that were constructed during the mid-twentieth century. The notions of Asians as hyperpolitical threats or apolitical exemplars, which remain deeply imbedded in American life and thinking, do not go unanswered.[43]

Researchers are also helping to construct an entirely new understanding of the Asian American experience—and Asian American politics in particular. For example, early work is under way on the important story of the

202   Chapter Eight

political activity of Asians in Hawaii;[44] the rich history of Asian American legal and civil rights activism is attracting considerable attention;[45] and the historical involvement of Asian Americans in the politics of their ancestral homelands has caught the eye of the research community.[46] Other historical work is exploring Asian American involvement in radical and labor politics,[47] and the literature on Asian Americans and certain areas of social policy, such as education, is growing[48]

As noted, many authors since the 1960s have sought to offer a corrective to the popular picture of the inoffensive and politically indifferent Asian. In the words of the author of a path-breaking study on the Chinese struggle against legal discrimination in the nineteenth century, the "conventional wisdom" about the supposed "political backwardness" of the Chinese simply needed to be "stood on its head."[49] Charles J. McClain's comment could speak for a generation of writers who have focused on the past and present activism of Asian Americans, the similarities of Asian American experiences with those of other minority groups, and Asian American challenges to the culture and politics of the dominant society. Constructing an assertive, even radical, Asian American identity has been prominent on the agenda. By contrast, relatively little attention has been devoted to topics such as political conservatism, the growth of professionalism among Asian Americans, or even partisan politics. Clearly, then, much of the work on Asian Americans in the past two decades has been as "ideological" as the earlier literature.[50]

Perhaps because of Asian Americans' interest in alternative politics and in establishing an activist identity for themselves, study of Asian American involvement in the more prosaic domain of electoral politics has been neglected until rather recently. In fact, it was not until the mid-1980s that any scholarly work that seriously explored contemporary Asian American political behavior began to appear. This scholarship is trying to define, characterize, and interpret Asian American politics, including voting patterns, ethnic interests, ideologies, specific policy concerns, and leadership approaches. Although schools of thought, controversies, and contending interpretations—a discourse—are only beginning to emerge, it might be said that the very appearance of this literature confirms intellectually the actual existence of something that can now be called Asian American politics.[51] The irony, however, is that despite the highly political circumstances under which the term *Asian American* emerged in the late 1960s and despite the politicized field of academic work known as Asian American studies, the work on Asian Americans and politics has attracted relatively little attention compared with the other fields of study about Asian Americans.[52] This will not likely continue.

Conclusion

Observations about Asian American politics have varied wildly over the past 150 years. The reasons for this have been many, including genuine clashes in culture, ignorance and fear, prejudice, political agendas, and even purposeful self-promotion on the part of some Asian Americans themselves. They have been held up as models for change as well as for moderation. They have been labeled hyperpolitical and apolitical, as well as super-threatening and super-loyal. Some commentators have branded them suspect; others have welcomed them to the body politic. Whatever the case, any discussion of Asian Americans and politics has always been highly ideological. Indeed, it has been difficult for many observers to develop a detached sense of Asian Americans and politics, because the topic is inextricably linked to sensitive and volatile experiences in race relations, in American interactions with Asia, and in conflicts over defining national identity and purpose.

One cannot transcend history and context, of course, but perhaps this review of past observations will help present-day writers avoid adopting facile, unthinking assumptions. Today's commentators are the inheritors of much intellectual and cultural baggage and would do well to leave as much of it behind as possible. Recent historical research on the past political activities of Asian Americans suggests that expanded definitions of politics and political activity are necessary to understand the past on its own terms. The same must be done today by those taking a closer look at current Asian American politics, including participation in the nation's formal political processes.

NINE

Chinese Railroad Workers and the U.S. Transcontinental Railroad in Global Perspective

Stories about the construction of the first transcontinental railroad that spanned the continent and was completed in 1869 are part of national folklore. Books about it continue to attract wide audiences. In many past accounts, the extraordinary work of Chinese railroad workers on the western portion of the line is given little attention and is sometimes omitted altogether. This is an egregious error, as the workers were indispensable in the construction of the line through some of the most difficult terrain in the continental United States. Ninety percent of the construction work force was Chinese.

The Chinese Railroad Workers in North America project at Stanford, which I co-founded in 2012 with Shelley Fisher Fishkin, aimed to remedy this lacuna and slight.[1] Some one hundred scholars from around the world worked together to compile as much historical documentation as could be located, including in China, to try to recover their history, especially their lived experience. The years of effort enabled me to write *Ghosts of Gold Mountain: The Epic Story of the Chinese Who Built the Transcontinental Railroad* (2019)

"Chinese Railroad Workers and the US Transcontinental Railroad in Global Perspective," *The Chinese and the Iron Road*, edited by Gordon H. Chang and Shelley Fisher Fishkin with Hilton Obenzinger and Roland Hsu (Stanford University Press), 2019: 27–41.

206   *Chapter Nine*

and co-edit with Shelley Fishkin a collection of research essays under the title *The Chinese and the Iron Road: Building the Transcontinental Railroad* (2019). This chapter is the opening to the latter and seeks to establish a new perspective on the history by foregrounding the work of the Chinese migrant workers and by placing the line itself in a global context. This shift in vantage point and emphasis challenges the conventional story of the railroad as a great American nationalist achievement, which narrows the significance and complexity of the history. The contributions we made to recovering the experiences of Chinese railroad workers has reshaped the narrative of the transcontinental railroad and is helping confirm the important place of Chinese in the history of the American West and beyond to global history.

*

Historical recovery is a matter of scholarly judgment and choice. Subject and interpretation, obviously, but also time and periodization, context, scale, and scope are all the historian's decision and not given by any divinity. The received history of the construction of the first transcontinental railroad across North America is a result of a writer's prerogative.

In the United States, the story of the transcontinental railroad is usually rendered within the parameters of the grand rise of the American nation. That has been the context chosen by the great majority of historians of the railroad. Begun in 1862 and completed in 1869, the first transcontinental line is celebrated in mainstream American life as well as in scholarship as one of the signal episodes of national life, elevated by some even to the level of importance of the Declaration of Independence. The railroad is honored as a "marvel" of *American* engineering and energy, as a "work of giants." It is presented as a physical and metaphoric bind that united the nation politically, economically, and socially. Linked to the recent end of the Civil War, the completion of the first transcontinental railroad is presented as a heroic contribution in overcoming the bloody division and in healing national wounds.[2]

Much is omitted from, or underplayed in, this grand narrative, and there are historians who are critical of the triumphal and celebratory account. They emphasize the terrible toll on the construction workers of all backgrounds,

Chinese Railroad Workers and the U.S. Transcontinental Railroad   207

the invasion and violent subjugation of native peoples, and the corrupt business practices of the railroad magnates in obtaining public funds to finance the project to enrich themselves at the expense of the civic good. But even these critiques are contained by narratives of national history.[3]

These accounts have been so powerfully resonant with prevailing attitudes and perspectives that they have overshadowed, even displaced, the immense international dimensions of the line. Appreciating these dimensions can lead to a vast broadening of the interpretive vision, and the railroad story can take on a very different light.

What are some of these international dimensions?

There are many: flows of international capital helped finance the construction of the line, and workers with origins in Ireland, continental Europe, Asia, and Africa contributed their blood and sweat. These people had rich histories of labor rhythms, diverse cultures, and unique skills that need to be understood and appreciated.[4]

The massive construction project also captured the imaginations of people around the world at the time. Journalists and writers traveled from Europe to witness this gigantic construction effort with their own eyes. Their published accounts in different languages helped change the way that millions of people thought about the very world itself.

Expansive thinkers in faraway settings assessed the impact of the anticipated rail line. Karl Marx considered the international implications of forming the rail connection and industrializing the New World.[5] Jules Verne produced one of the most influential pieces of literature inspired by the completion of the transcontinental railroad. The idea for his classic novel *Around the World in Eighty Days,* which was published in 1873 and made into a Hollywood movie in 1956, originated in a Paris café when Verne read about the completion, in the same year, of the rail line and the Suez Canal that connected the Mediterranean Sea and Red Sea.

Verne understood the transformative possibilities these construction projects offered for travel and the human imagination. In Verne's captivating story, an Englishman shows that the globe could be circumnavigated in less than three months, an astonishing feat at the time and one made possible especially by the two grand construction projects. Verne's story is one of the first explicit expressions of a global vision of travel, a view that offered the world for the first time within the reach of an unexceptional

208   *Chapter Nine*

person (at least a bourgeois Westerner), and not just a daring explorer or ambitious official.[6]

The development of the steam locomotive and the spread of rail lines, first in the 1830s in England, then in continental Europe and the United States, fundamentally altered the human relationship with space and time, and thus human life itself. Geography was compressed, which enormously expanded the proximate for the traveler, the businessman and merchant, and the geopolitical strategist. With the advent of the speed and power of mechanical travel using the powerful steam engine, the sense of time, the ordering of life, and the possibilities of human reach quickened and expanded in previously unimaginable ways. The US Pacific Railway, which is what the eighteen-hundred-mile western portion of the transcontinental line was called, was the first truly large-scale rail construction project. Its scale and completion astonished the world, and, as contemporary announcements of the completion of the railroad declared, the transcontinental railroad "revolutionized" the "travel and traffic of the world."[7] The Reverend John Todd, who delivered the dedication prayer at the completion ceremony at Promontory Summit, Utah, later proclaimed, "China is our neighbor now. The East and the West embrace; nay, we hardly know which is East or which is West. This one road has turned the world round."[8]

Two features establish the first transcontinental railroad's indelible and fundamental link with China. The first is the place of China in the ambition that inspired the very idea of the line itself. The line reflected an early global, not just continental, American vision of commercial and civilizational connection with China, and more generally with the Pacific. The second is that mass labor migration from China was essential to the construction of the line and other railroad projects geographically and temporally far beyond the transcontinental line. The physical presence and productive efforts of Chinese laborers connected America and Asia in a web of mental, emotional, and physical strands.

The transcontinental railroad was the realization of a long-standing vision that appeared in 1840s America. More than a national or even continental business venture, the inspiration for the building of the line was trans-Pacific. Take, for example, the ideas of the most prominent early promoter of the building of the transcontinental railroad, Asa Whitney, a relative of Eli Whitney of cotton gin fame. Asa Whitney lived in China in the

Chinese Railroad Workers and the U.S. Transcontinental Railroad 209

1840s and enriched himself in the lucrative China trade. After he returned to the United States, and for much of the rest of his life, he campaigned for the construction of a rail line that would cross the three-thousand-mile-wide continent. His most powerful argument in favor of the huge project drew not from accounting calculations but from a dramatic historical imagination that bordered on the millennialist.

In 1849 Whitney argued for the project with language such as this:

> The change of the route for the commerce with Asia has, since before the time of Solomon even, changed the destinies of Empires and States. It has, and does to this day control the world. Its march has always been westward, and can never go back to its old routes. . . . Through us [the United States] must be the route to Asia, and the change to our continent will be the last, the final change.[9]

America, Whitney declared, would be the literal, physical link of the West (the United States and Europe) to the East (China and Asia). The realization of America's providential destiny as a great nation, he maintained, required the building of this line. Whitney won thousands of prominent supporters across the country for his project, and for years they pressed Congress to back the visionary idea. It is said that a young Leland Stanford, later the president of the Central Pacific Railroad (CPRR) that constructed the western half of the transcontinental line, heard Whitney expound on his vision to Stanford's father.[10]

One of Whitney's supporters was John C. Fremont, famed explorer, merchant, and the first presidential candidate of the newly formed Republican Party. In 1854 Frémont declared, echoing Whitney, that "America will be between Asia and Europe—the golden vein which runs through the history of the world will follow the track to San Francisco, and the Asiatic trade will finally fall into its last and permanent road."[11]

The engraving on the legendary Golden Spike (or Last Spike), which ceremonially completed the line when the Central Pacific and Union Pacific Railroad Companies met head to head at Promontory Summit, Utah, captures this interplay between the national and international contexts. On May 10, 1869, Leland Stanford, presiding over a gathering of some three thousand dignitaries, railroad officials, workers, and hangers-on, tapped an eighteen-carat gold spike into the last tie. After he was done with his light labor, Chinese workers, who had laid the actual last rails to the meeting

210   *Chapter Nine*

site, replaced the ceremonial spike with a regular iron one. Inscribed on the gold one is "May God continue the unity of our Country." Following these frequently quoted words that highlight the national story are others that point to the grander vision. The engraving continues, "The Railroad unites the two great Oceans of the world." Celebratory speeches repeatedly emphasized how the line connected the West with the Far East.

Railroad supporters boasted that the transcontinental line, in the "advance of civilization," ranked "with the landing of the Pilgrims" or the "voyage of Columbus."[12] The well-known economist Henry George wondered whether the transcontinental railroad would one day elevate San Francisco to the level of the "first city," not just of the continent but of the entire world. It would surpass the importance of the great cities of Europe, of Constantinople, and of New York City, he grandly predicted. These characterizations proved to be hyperbole and widely off the mark, but they nevertheless reflected the extraordinary enthusiasm for the project and its perceived global importance.[13] Leland Stanford himself referenced the then-popular cultural phenomenon of the "Siamese twins" to declare that the transcontinental line, along with a steamship system that linked North America to Asia, formed the "ligament" "that binds the Eastern Eng and Western Chang together."[14] Stanford's close business partner, Collis P. Huntington, once suggested that California would be all the better if a half million more Chinese came over and entered the state in 1868. Newspapers reported that at the very moment of the driving of the last spike, a shipment of tea from China started eastward on the line, inaugurating the hoped-for global trade for America. That had been the animating dream, not just the opening of the resources of the US West that inspired the building of the transcontinental railroad.[15]

Another keen observer of the construction of the railroad and its international implications was Daniel Cleveland, a young attorney who had recently arrived in California from the East. He later settled in San Diego, where he made his name and fortune and is honored today as one of the city's early leaders. In 1869 the significant presence of Chinese in Northern California so fascinated him that he was moved to share what he was witnessing with others in the country. Cleveland confidentially sent his thoughts to Washington officials and also completed a four-hundred-page study on the Chinese in California meant for the general public. Although it was never published, it contains unique firsthand observations on the

Chinese and includes an entire chapter on Chinese railroad workers. Completed sometime in early 1869, it is the earliest known extended report on the Chinese involved in railroad construction. Cleveland describes the Chinese as workers, their ways of life, habits, appearance, and enormous contributions to California's economy. He saluted their presence in California in most enthusiastic terms.

Cleveland himself explicitly placed the transcontinental railroad in a global context:

> It is a singular circumstance, that the Chinese . . . should be constructing one half of the great trans-continental railroad, one of the most wonderful of the progressive achievements of this marvelous age. The two races of workmen on this road are rapidly approaching each other from the two great oceans, and will soon meet and connect [their] work. China and the United States will then strike hands, and feel more nearly drawn together in sympathy and interest than ever before. It is very appropriate that the people of the two mightiest nations of their respective continents should unite in the construction of this world's highway. May it draw and keep them close together, not only in commerce and interest, but in kindly sympathy and good offices.[16]

A New York newspaper expressed similar sentiments in its report on the laying of the last rail: "At Promontory Point, the Asiatic with his pick confronted the European with his, and the two civilizations looked into each other's eyes. There they met hand to hand. The one could point to all the Eastern half of the United States and all of Europe . . . the other had behind him the great wall of China."[17]

Soon after the transcontinental railroad was completed, a group of wealthy Bostonians traveled cross-country to San Francisco by train. According to a news report, they gathered in a solemn ceremony at the Golden Gate, where San Francisco Bay meets the Pacific. There they opened a bottle of water from the Atlantic that they had brought with them. They poured half of it into the cold surf. They then filled it back up, mixing the Atlantic water with that from the Pacific. Great cheering and celebration broke out, and reportedly some were amazed that the two waters mixed easily without problem—there was no clouding or violent chemical reaction. Then the group broke out in a rousing rendition of the song "America." The next day a young girl in the party was baptized with the mixed water, making her

212   *Chapter Nine*

what one might call perhaps the first "global soul," anointed with the waters of the two great oceans of the world.[18] The story, taken quite seriously at the time, reminds us of how the railroad helped change fundamentally the way people thought about the world and themselves, and how the Chinese workers, thousands of miles away from their own homes, facilitated the transformation.

Resources that originated far from the construction sites in the Sierra Nevada and the western deserts were required to complete the railroad. Most importantly, for the western half of the line the essential resource was the labor of thousands of workers from distant China. Their physical presence was the most dramatic manifestation of the globalized nature of the railroad construction project. Western expansion into Asia and Africa, European and American industrialization, and the explosive growth of market economies in the nineteenth century produced human movement unprecedented in scale, pace, and scope. Humans have always been migrant and mobile, but mechanized land and water transportation enabled large numbers of people to move relatively quickly and easily to destinations near and far.

Beginning in early 1864 and continuing until the laying of the last rail in May 1869, the CPRR employed directly, and indirectly through contractors, thousands of Chinese workers, up to ten thousand to twelve thousand at the high point. Some estimates place the total number of Chinese who worked on the line at more than twenty thousand due to turnover.[19] The workers formed what was likely the single largest workforce in a private enterprise in the United States until the late nineteenth century. Contemporary observers frequently expressed amazement at their sheer numbers. Hundreds labored simultaneously at different sites. Only a handful of the Chinese were citizens of the United States because federal law denied them naturalized citizenship. This alien workforce helped make possible a project celebrated as a national accomplishment.

The CPRR first hired Chinese who were already in California, having arrived in significant numbers in the early 1850s for work in mining and other sectors throughout the American West. The company later turned to recruiting labor directly from China. It advertised in newspapers and sent agents to China.[20] But Chinese had actually begun working on railroads in the New World as early as 1854, when the New York-based Panama Railway Company brought a thousand laborers from southern China to Panama to

Chinese Railroad Workers and the U.S. Transcontinental Railroad 213

construct a trans-isthmus line. When the project failed because of ghastly working conditions—50 percent of the Chinese died from accidents, disease, and suicide—the railroad company sent the survivors to Jamaica and possibly some to California.[21] Those who were moved may have joined compatriots who were working on rail lines in the 1850s and early 1860s near Sacramento and San Jose. Chinese also joined the effort to construct the San Jose-San Francisco line, today the oldest continuously operated route in the West.[22]

These railroad workers formed part of a larger stream of a globalized workers from China. From the 1830s through the early twentieth century, hundreds of thousands of Chinese left their homeland and joined construction, mining, and plantation projects throughout Southeast Asia, the Pacific, North and South America, and the Caribbean. They formed part of one of the greatest human migrations in modern history.[23] Their migration to the United States and elsewhere was a "revolution," according to a British observer, who said that its importance to world history will be greater than the "intrigues and machinations of crowned heads of wily politicians."[24]

Although many who went to Cuba and Peru endured the semislave, "coolie" trade—a system of coerced, indentured labor—the Chinese workers who came to the United States were largely free and voluntary laborers, as many observers at the time repeatedly verified. US officials in Hong Kong reportedly confirmed the voluntary nature of the contracts signed by the Chinese and determined they were consistent with federal anticoolie legislation. In contrast, many Chinese women, if they did not arrive as the wives of merchants, came into the country as bound prostitutes.[25]

Almost all the migrants were male. Most came from the Pearl River delta in southern China, where the colonies of Portuguese Macao and British Hong Kong were located. This massive migration transformed the entire region and linked it to the rest of the world. The early commercial and social histories and identities of Macao and Hong Kong as transit, processing, and embarkation sites are rooted in this system of out-migration and transpacific trade.[26]

The Chinese were differentiated by class and work responsibilities: they were unskilled and skilled workers, cooks, doctors, and contractors/business agents. Many, if not most, appear to have received some education, perhaps through village and foreign missionary schools in the Guangzhou region. They were connected to other Chinese around the American West

214   *Chapter Nine*

and in China who acted as provisioners, farmers and suppliers of food, and agents of various sorts. They formed part of a well-organized network of fellow Chinese involved with the recruitment, transport, and well-being of the workers. Non-Chinese observers at the time noted this well-organized transpacific network and its economic significance.

The Chinese workers ate food that was familiar, with many ingredients imported from their home origins. They practiced traditional customs and rituals, and engaged in distinctive leisure and nonwork activities. They and those who had come before them from China brought crop seeds and introduced new plants to America. One journalist at the time observed that, in addition to trying to cultivate silkworms, rice, and other staples common in southern China, the Chinese "introduced many of the vegetables which they cultivate at home." These they cultivated right alongside the rail line.[27] They may have even brought with them seeds of the now popular fruit known as the goji berry. Just a few years ago, hunters in Utah accidentally stumbled across wild goji plants. DNA analysis placed the plants as having originated in China, and it is believed that Chinese introduced them to the area. The plants were found near what had been one of the largest encampments of Chinese who worked on the transcontinental railroad.[28]

The Chinese workers internationalized the everyday commodities and objects they used in the US West. They used Vietnamese coins as tokens or chips in their games. They smoked opium grown in Turkey or in India and processed in Hong Kong. They wore clothing made from cotton, likely grown in South Asia. They ate rice grown in southern China from bowls made in kilns located near their homes. They consumed dried seafood from the South China Sea. They used medicinals, Chinese herbs, and ointments to maintain their health and help heal their injuries. They enjoyed Chinese gaming activities that became commonplace in the West. Their presence contributed to making the region one of the most diverse places in the world, which is another way of saying that they helped interconnect the American West with the rest of the world.[29]

In recent decades American archaeologists have located and collected an immense amount of refuse left by the Chinese along the route of the transcontinental railroad and other lines. This material evidence in the form of ceramics, food containers, cooking utensils, gaming pieces, tools, clothes, liquor bottles, and pipes displays what appears to be an uncharacteristic departure from frugality. This detritus was discarded on the ground where even the casual explorer can find it today. Did some Chinese mean to leave this garbage, this material graffiti, as markers of their presence 150 years ago? Daniel Cleveland offered a vivid description of these worker camps:

[The Chinese] live in little villages of cloth tents, containing from 50 to 500 inhabitants. As the work progresses, they fold up and remove their tents and establish their villages at other points along the line of the road. What yesterday was a noisy Chinese town is today but a barren waste, with only rubbish and debris to mark that it was once a settlement. It is to be regretted that gamblers, lottery dealers, and opium sellers always accompany them and open their shops in every Chinese camp to absorb much of the earnings of the industrious laborers.[30]

Cleveland offers an image that inspires our imaginations today. He tells us that "at night these tents are illuminated with candles, and groups of Chinese can be seen gambling, smoking opium, visiting or engaging in household labor."[31]

The Chinese workers did not just import items from Asia to the American West; they in turn sent gold and silver mined in the Americas to their families in China. This specie, especially Mexican silver dollars, formed a significant portion of the southern China economy and mightily contributed to building countless numbers of homes, schools, temples, village halls, and towers throughout the region, giving it a distinctive identity. Because of the horrible opium trade, however, much of this precious metal wound up not going to their families in China but into the coffers of the British aristocracy and mercantile and banking elite. Much of the silver in these people's opulent homes likely came from the Americas to pay for the opium brought to China by the British.

The workers sent remittances back home to support their families, and this practice itself helped establish transpacific commercial life. The early history of American banks and transport companies such as Wells Fargo & Company and the Pacific Mail Steamship Company have early connections to this remittance business. Chinese store owners and merchants too gained valuable experience and connections through facilitating the labor and remittance traffic, helping them become astute businessmen in the United States and around the world.

After the completion of the first transcontinental line, Chinese became professional railroad workers. Throughout the rest of the nineteenth century,

216   *Chapter Nine*

they joined railroad construction projects across the United States, including in the East, South, Southwest, and Northwest. More than ten thousand of them worked on the northern transcontinental line; thousands worked on the southern transcontinental route; thousands also later worked on the trans-Canada rail line. They worked on railroads in northern Mexico, beginning in 1864, and on lines to transport sugarcane in Hawaii. Thousands worked in the Andes building railroads in Peru. By the early 1880s, they were working in railroad construction in French West Africa.[32] Some workers and contractors, because of their wealth and experience, returned to China and played prominent roles in the first railroad projects there. Ten thousand Chinese workers later helped complete the trans-Siberian railroad in Russia. These tens of thousands of Chinese railroad workers occupy a central position in the development of a modern laboring class that emerged around the world in the mid- and late nineteenth century.

The American entrepreneur Henry Meiggs, who led the effort to build Peruvian railroads, considered bringing Chinese labor from California for his workforce. "For railway work they are the best men we can get," Meiggs declared in 1870. Thousands of laborers were brought from China, though the number from California is not known.[33] Chinese returned to China to build railroads in their homeland.[34] In 1869 the new journal *Scientific American* declared that the "Chinaman" was a "born railroad builder" and was destined for work not just in California but in the "whole Pacific slope."[35]

The Chinese maintained ties with their wives, families, and home villages long after their departures, in many instances for multiple generations. They established patterns of migration where the males left their homes, lived most of their lives overseas, returned to father families, and then had sons who again out-migrated. Along with the workers themselves came other linkages that tied them to their compatriots who went elsewhere. They corresponded with one another and remained linked through family and district associations. They were mobile and often traveled across many boundaries: they went back and forth from Hawaii, Canada, Mexico, the United States, the Caribbean and South America, and Southeast Asia.[36] They helped make the Guangzhou region one of the most globally connected in all of China. We wonder what important political leaders and thinkers such as Yung Wing (Rong Hong), Sun Yat-sen (Sun Zhongshan), and Liang Qichao heard from the railroad workers. These and other important figures in China's modern history were natives of the Guangzhou region and spent much time among the Chinese overseas, including in the towns and cities of the American West where many Chinese railroad workers and contractors settled. What role might any of the old railroad workers have played in stimulating Sun Yat-sen's famous passion about building railroads in China to elevate the country? Yung Wing's last effort to contribute to modernizing China was to try to build a rail line in northern China.[37]

Unfortunately, we do not know what the workers themselves said about their experiences in North America. We have no texts, besides signatures on payroll records and remittance receipts, from their hands. But we can speculate, or just imagine, what they might have said and how their experiences affected those back home. Their experiences shared from afar, or in person when they returned after their life in North America, brought new ideas and subjectivity into southern China.

Consider this: There was no mechanical travel in southern China until the latter part of the nineteenth century. Labor was almost all agricultural, conducted manually without mechanization, by families on small farms. The climate in southern China was semitropical; few Chinese railroad workers had seen snow before they arrived in the Sierra Nevada. The experience of working with thousands of other *tangren* ("people of Tang," who because of the many ethnic divisions in southern China could be almost as unfamiliar to one another as people from other countries), as well as with whites, blacks, and Native Americans, who spoke completely unfamiliar tongues, must have been bewildering. They worked for wages and in large, organized groups. They engaged in collective action to struggle for improved living and working conditions. They encountered new technologies for travel, construction, transportation, and communication. They encountered new foods, ways of daily living, and spiritual beliefs. They dealt with the unforgiving demands of business competition and construction engineering, and these demands, not the seasons and the agricultural calendar, regulated their lives. They encountered examples of private wealth and consumption unimaginable in rural southern China. Aside from some who had previously been exposed to aspects of Western life through Christian missionary schools in China, they learned for the first time about Western ways of life. Living and working in the towering Sierra Nevada in California, and in the blazing-hot deserts of Nevada and Utah, must have been a formidable, and previously unimaginable, physical, emotional, and mental challenge.

218   *Chapter Nine*

The suffering and predicaments of the Chinese deeply moved the contemporary writer Daniel Cleveland. His sympathy for them is palpable. In one section of his manuscript, Cleveland includes a harrowing report on Chinese disembarking in San Francisco and their transport into the Sierra Nevada. Cleveland invites us to imagine what the Chinese experienced.

Cleveland estimated that in the late 1860s one hundred to two hundred Chinese were on *every* steamship arriving in San Francisco, after weeks of strenuous ocean travel. Upon arrival, white labor agents and scores of assistants and strong arms interrogated them, usually on board ships, separating out those whose contracts the agents held. The contracts, which were completed in Hong Kong or China, indebted the workers for a period of time to repay the cost of their transportation. This was the so-called credit ticket system in action. The scenes Cleveland describes were chaotic, with physical violence used at times against the Chinese:

> [I] once saw a mulatto man, a petty officer on one of these boats, who had perhaps been a slave himself, taking advantage of his little brief authority to lord it over the poor Chinese. He maltreated them with a rough tyranny and keen relish as though it afforded him intense satisfaction to find human beings helpless enough to submit to his domination. The Chinese as helpless as a flock of sheep, look the picture of misery and despair, as they are huddled together upon the deck of the tug-boat listless and aimless, impotent against the force which keeps them in confinement. A small squad of resolute white men, armed with heavy bludgeons, which they are not slow to use, keep vigilant watch over the Chinese to prevent their escape.[38]

Taken by small boat directly from San Francisco Bay to Sacramento, the beginning point of the Central Pacific, the Chinese were forced by white overseers into railroad boxcars, whose doors were closed and then locked to prevent escape. "If they were culprits who had committed some heinous crime," Cleveland noted, "they would not be more closely guarded and harshly treated." During the ride, he says, some did succeed in opening the doors and tried to escape, but they died when they hit the ground. Cleveland estimated that about half of the Chinese would escape en route if such draconian measures were not taken. As it was, he estimated that 5 percent did manage to escape.

Of all the occupations that employed the Chinese in California, Cleveland claimed, none was more frightening to them than toil on the Central

Chinese Railroad Workers and the U.S. Transcontinental Railroad   219

Pacific. As the line snaked eastward through the Sierra, the Chinese became even more averse to the work, as they feared the construction would unleash powerful, evil natural forces. "They do not understand railroads and fear them," he said.

> They are utterly unknown in China and are regarded by the Chinese in America with suspicion and dread. They have a firm belief that a huge serpent of gigantic proportions is lurking in the Rocky Mountains and that someday he will dart out upon the laborers, as they work near his lair, and devour all within his reach. Americans can have no adequate conception of the terror, which this superstition inspires. Many of the Chinese in San Francisco declare and believe that terrible misfortunes will befall their countrymen who have the temerity to aid in the construction of this road.[39]

Cleveland was largely ignorant about Chinese ways and could certainly have dramatized his account for audiences on the East Coast. But we do know that the Chinese had firm beliefs in a cosmology that understood the human world as inextricably connected to supremely powerful natural forces. As late as the end of the nineteenth century, many Chinese believed railroads desecrated their natural world—the notorious antiforeign Boxer rebels in northern China targeted railroads for destruction during their uprising. Mountains, water, and trees had special meanings for the Chinese— we can wonder what they thought about what tunneling, blasting, massive tree cutting, and track laying meant for their cosmological universe, even if not being done in their native land. Accounts by whites invariably describe the many temples, worshipped gods, and spiritual practices of the Chinese wherever they went. Oh, the stories the Chinese must have told back home about the practices of the Westerners!

Even in death, these workers stimulated trade and monetary circulation: one of the most lucrative exports from the United States in the mid- to late nineteenth century was the cleaned and prepared physical remains of Chinese who had died in the United States and were returned to China for final burial. American steamship companies carried tens of thousands of containers of these remains across the Pacific. In the offensive words of an American official, sending "dead Chinamen" back to China was one of the most profitable commercial activities for Americans in the late nineteenth century.[40]

There is one more element that we might consider in thinking about the railroad and the globalized world in the 1860s and 1870s, and that is

220   *Chapter Nine*

the white backlash to the growing American interconnection with Asia. Reactive chauvinism and national exclusivity countered global moves and openings. Following the completion of the transcontinental railroad, white workers, both immigrant and native-born, raised an increasingly violent and chauvinist campaign to rid the country of the Chinese workforce. Anti-Chinese labor activists highlighted the danger the transcontinental line posed even before its completion. With a rail line across the country, a Chicago periodical warned, "Chinamen will begin to swarm through the [R]ocky [M]ountains like devouring locusts and spread out over the country this side."[41] In the fall of 1871, a white mob attacked the Los Angeles Chinatown and killed nineteen Chinese residents. Former railroad workers were likely among those lynched and shot.[42]

By 1882 white hostility had forced tens of thousands of Chinese to leave the United States and had fueled a national political movement that resulted in the passage of Chinese restriction and then exclusion acts that had far- reaching international repercussions. The Chinese were deemed to be a dangerous threat to white supremacy, and they had to be excluded to protect the nation. The Chinese "race" question and immigration became festering sore points in international relations well into the mid-twentieth century.

The history of the transcontinental railroad has always been global; it has awaited us to appreciate it as such. But we can ask, Why does the story play upon our personal and public imaginations? We are now in a new globalizing moment, marked especially by the rise of China. We are prompted to think back in time and reflect on the earlier years of relations between the United States and China. Chinese President Xi Jinping during his state visit to the United States in 2015 repeatedly invoked the memory of the Chinese railroad workers and their important contributions to the building of the American West. President Barack Obama likewise paid tribute to their contributions.[43] The leaders of China and America today hail the Chinese workers as an important, constructive early tie between the peoples of the two countries.

Historical recovery is intimately linked to our current condition. Our attitudes and viewpoints today influence the way we think about the past. We students of the past are ourselves part of a historical continuum of the railroad's global story. We have come a long way out of ignorance and neglect, but we still have a long way to go to understand the Chinese railroad workers and establish the respect they are due.

Acknowledgments

Shelley Fisher Fishkin, Roland Hsu, Hilton Obenzinger, Gabriel Wolfenstein, Teri Hessel, and others in the Chinese Railroad Workers in North America Project at Stanford University offered very helpful comments on an earlier version of this essay. I thank them.

TEN

History and Postmodernism

In my career, I occasionally engaged in scholarly controversies or discussions about the state of the fields of diplomatic history or Asian American Studies, but not often.[1] Though such examinations of historiography are commonplace and are an integral part of the profession, I contributed less frequently as the years passed. One early essay that endured is the one that follows in which I comment on the influence of postmodern intellectual theory on the writing of history, Asian American history in particular. Reading it again now many years later, it seems to me that it still has important things to say, especially to those who wonder about what it means to write history.

Once highly influential, postmodernism plays a much-reduced role in today's intellectual life, but the position I took on the importance of grounding historical scholarship, its epistemological foundations, and its purposes has much continuing value, especially in grounding Asian American Studies in actual experience.

The essay joined others in a special issue of *Amerasia Journal*, a leading academic publication dedicated to Asian American Studies, that was devoted to theory and scholarship. The essay presents the intellectual proclivities

---

"History and Postmodernism," *Amerasia Journal* (21:1–2) 1995: 89–94. © 2019 The Regents of the University of California, reprinted by permission of Informa UK Limited, trading as Taylor & Francis Group, www.tandfonline.com, on behalf of The Regents of the University of California.

224   Chapter Ten

and commitments that I followed through my career. It also speaks to those today who continue to wonder what the historical project is all about.

✳

The growth in popularity of postmodern critical theory in the field of Asian American Studies provokes mixed feelings in me as a historian (and it is from the viewpoint of a historian specializing in Asian American history that I speak in this essay). There is much that is positive in the development but much that troubles me at the same time.

As an interdisciplinary field, Asian American Studies can only benefit from the insights and originality that postmodernism, and for that matter any theoretical and analytical approach from natural science, social science, or other humanistic area, encourages among practitioners in the field. In particular, postmodern theory (I acknowledge that many different ways of thinking can be called postmodern, but in this essay, postmodernism means the current analytical concentration, posited in an epistemology of radical philosophical skepticism, on discourse) has inspired innovative work in literary criticism, creative production, and cultural analysis. At the same time, it has also promoted in the historical field a heightened sensitivity to the problematic nature of evidence, to the limits of knowledge and of truth claims, to the imbedded silences and contradictions in any effort to recover human experience, to the responsibilities of authorial voice and power, and to the complexity and variety of human experience itself, alerting us to the dangers of essentialism and overgeneralization. These effects have been all to the good.

One of the great strengths of postmodern theory is its critical power and, as such, it has furthered counterhegemonic efforts, which Marxists, ethnic studies specialists, and feminist scholars, among others, had begun in the 1960s to free historical inquiry from the dead hand of American national and consensus assumptions. Within the field of Asian American Studies itself, it has alerted us to the easy tendency to essentialize experience and ignore so-called marginal vantage points (these problems originating in the well-intentioned effort to help forge ethnic identity/identities). Indeed, the overall effect of postmodernism has been subversive, using one of its own favorite words, of all that has been intellectually established in whatever field of inquiry.[2]

But while interest in postmodernism has encouraged the counterhegemonic effort by Asian American Studies to dissemble the intellectually dominant voice, it has also contributed, ironically and less positively, to a turn away from one of the other original and still basic purposes of Asian American Studies, that is, the effort to reclaim minority voice, to uncover the "buried past," to recover collective, lived experience. Postmodernism, because of its essentially skeptical nature, questions the very legitimacy of such efforts.

Let me elaborate. "Ethnic studies," virtually by its nature, has been, and continues to be, fundamentally critical of the traditional historicism that largely omitted racial minorities. The study of their social experiences, so largely shaped as oppressed peoples, and the study of race and racism in American life, inevitably raise implicit and explicit critiques of established interpretations of the American past. Ethnic studies, by its very nature, has attacked, has been "destructive," of the notions of democracy and progress, notions that, for many, are still sacrosanct and celebrated and dominant. But "ethnic studies" has also been "constructive" in its efforts to help build minority identity by giving prominent place to the lives, ideas, perspectives, and experiences of minority peoples. It has helped legitimize, no, even more, it has helped establish these experiences in the historical record and required at least lip-service to what is called "multi-culturalism." Indeed, this latter purpose arguably serves an even more important purpose for both minority and dominant communities than the critique of race in American life. (The examination of racial thinking in America may be more important in understanding the dominant Euro-American experience, and what whites have said and thought about minorities, than in gaining insight into minority lives. For example, James S. Moy, *Marginal Sights: Staging the Chinese in America, Studies in Theatre History and Culture* and Gina Marchetti, *Romance and the "Yellow Peril": Race, Sex, and Discursive Strategies in Hollywood Fiction,* both wonderful books that are inspired to varying degrees by post-modernism, study aspects of the racism in American art and popular culture but do not extensively explore Asian-American experiences or thinking.) Postmodernism certainly can be and is used effectively to study Asian American cultural products. See for example the many impressive studies on Asian American literature that have been produced during the last several years. Still, postmodernism has yet to be proven to be useful to understanding Asian American *history,* it seems to me.

226   *Chapter Ten*

Therefore, I (and I hope others will as well) choose approaches for historical work that are by most standards rather traditional and narrative. I do so for philosophic/intellectual, social, and political reasons.

By philosophic/intellectual reasons I mean that I do not subscribe to the radical skepticism that occupies the heart of much of postmodern theory, i.e., that the representation of, or even just the search for, historical truths and realities is an impossibility and even a deception because of the constitutive role of language, in which meaning is itself ellusive; that no meaningful distinction exists between fiction and historical writing because of the subjectivity of all authors; that the absence of a unified subject makes efforts to advance historical explanation about community or individuals in history, including Asian American history, fundamentally problematic.[3]

Without going into an extended response to these specific issues, I suggest here that the historical enterprise, the effort to understand and reconstruct a knowable past, is possible when pursued in a judicious and critical way that acknowledges the limitations of evidence (whether written, oral, or artifact), the constructed and evolutionary nature of knowledge itself, and the necessity of constant discourse; discourse being necessary to critique and explore interpretation, evidence, explanation, silences, meaning, and so on in a constant effort to draw closer, to approximate but never fully capturing, truths.

Even more, the historical enterprise is not only possible but necessary as a fundamental human activity to understand ourselves, a task that has been central in Asian American Studies from its beginning, as mentioned above. To me, the need to try to know our human past as best we can, under the ever-changing circumstances and demands of life, far exceeds the sense of disempowerment and self-doubt that postmodernism seems to stimulate among some aspiring researchers. Put in another way: philosophically, I prefer a positive rather than a pessimistic epistemology.

In less abstract terms (and in more political or social terms), I choose a historiographic approach for my work that seeks to maintain a connection between intellectual activity and the social responsibility of an intellectual, in my case the demands being related to Asian American Studies. I find that while postmodern theory has enlivened the discourse of academics and artists, it has contributed little to the lives of a more general reading public, let alone a broader public interested in history. This is an audience, it seems to me, that the historian, especially the minority historian, should

History and Postmodernism 227

never ignore. My attitude should not be construed as anti-intellectual, as I acknowledge the value of postmodernism to intellectual life and the importance of intellectual life per se, but I also accept as equally, if not more, important the responsibilities that our communities and our society places on intellectuals and historians, certainly a privileged group, to understand our humanity.

And thus, I am somewhat dismayed when I review the recent programs of the annual meeting of the Association for Asian American Studies and find a decrease in historical work and a preponderance of work apparently inspired by postmodern critical theory. In my mind, and I put this following thought forward in the most provocative way possible: historical work, including the most untheoretically informed, narrative history, should/will remain the central resource for Asian American Studies, for it will be, as it always has been, an irreplaceable well-spring for artistic, critical (including postmodern criticism itself), social, anthropological and other thoughtful work. It has value in itself as well as is the "stuff" for further thought. Although they may seem highly unfashionable, I suggest that the work of Mary Roberts Coolidge, *Chinese Immigration* (1909), Yamato Ichihashi, *Japanese in the United States* (1932), and Bruno Lasker, *Filipino Immigration to Continental United States and to Hawaii* (1931), with all their flaws and "naivete," still can serve as models of historical enterprise for us today.

Lastly, there still is the question of whether those interested in Asian American history can profitably utilize postmodern theory in their investigations. My own opinion is that postmodernism would have limited use and the reason is that the thrust of Asian American history has been and will remain for the foreseeable future, social history, the effort to describe and explain the lived and felt experiences of Asian American communities. Postmodernism, because of its attention to analyzing text rather than what historians may call context, the environment that produces the text, leads away, nay, even argues against the effort to reconstruct a recognizable social experience.

However, not all Asian American history has been or must be social history. As our field develops, we should see more efforts to understand the intellectual and cultural aspects—these might be studies of journalists, religious leaders, educators, writers and others who have left extensive written legacies. Postmodernism might be helpful in understanding their materials. And certainly, postmodernism should be useful in understanding the

228   Chapter Ten

racial ideologies developed about Asian Americans. For example, Charles J. McClain has recently published a superb study of the Chinese in American courts.[4] His approach is a traditional legal historical one, but one can easily anticipate that postmodernism could be useful in exploring in different ways aspects of the story, such as court documentation, legal argument, and public opinion. And lastly, one can expect that written histories of Asian Americans will themselves gradually become subjects of postmodern criticism as these histories become part of our collective experience.[54]

A fundamental tension exists between those persuaded by the skepticism of postmodernism and those who have a desire, some may call pretention, to know and reconstruct the past. It is doubtful there can be any serious reconciliation of the two, and perhaps there should not be any effort to do so, for the conflicts between them may simply reflect the tensions inherent in the different ways we try to live socially conscious lives.

Notes

The author thanks Sue Chow and Bob Lee for their comments on an earlier draft.

PART III
Culture

ELEVEN

Emerging from the Shadows: The Visual Arts and Asian American History

My father was an accomplished artist in China and in the United States, and because of him I grew up surrounded by paintings, other artwork, furniture, and books on Chinese civilization that introduced me to Chinese history. The family spent many hours at the DeYoung Art Museum in San Francisco, which had exhibited his work on several occasions beginning in the 1940s, and I came to appreciate the world of art early in life. Visiting museums was always an essential part of family travels, but other than a memorable class in Chinese art history offered by the venerable Wen Fong when I was an undergraduate at Princeton, I did not seriously study art history until later in life.

In the early 1990s, Mark Johnson, who was the director of the Art Gallery at San Francisco State University, approached me because of his interest in my father's work. He wanted to better connect his college art space to the surrounding Asian American community, and learned that little knowledge, let alone accumulated study, of Asian American artists existed. He initiated what became a visionary project on recovering the history of art production by persons of Asian ancestry in the United States. It joined

"Emerging from the Shadows: The Visual Arts and Asian American History," *Asian American Art: A History, 1850–1970*, edited by Gordon H. Chang, Mark Dean Johnson, Paul J. Karlstrom, and Sharon Spain (Stanford University Press), 2008: ix–xv. (Illustrations accompanying the original article are not included in this volume.)

231

232   *Chapter Eleven*

the efforts of other scholars who understood the importance of appreciating their wonderful cultural contributions. What is now called the field of Asian American art history was born.

Mark, Paul J. Karlstrom (who served for many years as the West Coast regional director of the Smithsonian's Archives of American Art), Sharon Spain, an independent art curator, and I collaborated on building a project based at Stanford, to identify, document, collect, and interpret Asian American art. We engaged scores of scholars, artist family members, collectors, and interested members in the public to gather knowledge and encourage scholarship on the subject. We conducted study meetings and conferences. Our efforts resulted in the publication of a richly illustrated volume, *Asian American Art: A History, 1850–1970*, that Stanford University Press published in 2008. I am especially proud of being a part of that effort.

Since then, interest in the artistic production of persons of Asian ancestry in the United States has grown immensely. Asian American art, both contemporary and historical, has become a popular presence in museums, galleries, and other exhibition spaces. Collecting is now an avid pursuit.

Before the twenty-first century, there was little to no attention given to Asian American artists, except for a few who had caught the eye of the art establishment. The reasons for this neglect were many but included the reality that the art world in the country fixated largely on the well-known, successful artists connected to the eastern establishment. Another reason is that the aesthetics, style, subject matter, or concerns of Asian American artists, many of whom lived in the West, did not fit the established canon. Racial prejudice had led some commentators to ignore or simply dismiss the work of Asian artists. They suffered their form of exclusion from the history of art in America.

The following brief essay introduces our book, which confronts the past marginalization of the artists and asserts the extraordinary richness, variety, and importance of their artwork. I completed an essay for our art book that could not be included in this volume because of the difficulty of obtaining permissions for the illustrations that accompanied the text, but this introduction provides an overview on the book's genesis and vision.

*

Emerging from the Shadows   233

Asian American art history, not to speak of work by contemporary Asian Americans, is being recovered from the shadows of neglect. Art produced by Asian Americans years ago is now gracing the covers of important new books.[2] Several major studies about the artistic production by Asian Americans in the past and present have appeared.[3] Historical exhibitions of work by Asian American artists also are now occurring regularly. Even though much of this work was created decades ago, the public has just rediscovered it and is beginning to give it due appreciation. The artwork has waited patiently to be seen again—it has been largely invisible before the public's very eyes for years.

Why has this treasure been outside our vision?

Both art historians and social historians might address this interesting question. I am not in a position to discuss at length the reasons that mainstream art criticism neglected to study Asian American artists, other than to state perhaps the obvious, which is that the history of Asian Americans, like that of other marginalized racial groups, commanded little respect from any quarter of mainstream America. Although Asian Americans had been the objects of considerable popular and scholarly attention and speculation since their first arrival in the United States in large numbers in the mid-nineteenth century, sustained scholarship that seriously studied their lived experiences or their life as creative communities is a relatively recent development. This new attitude is a direct result of the rise of what is known popularly as "ethnic studies." Today, the study of "Asian American history" is a vigorous and growing field of investigation.

But the past scholarly neglect of Asian American art history does raise important questions of how and who determines what is "art" and who is an "artist" worth studying. These and many other questions related to art criticism, it seems to me, form a potentially large and rich area for discussion. A good number of Asian American artists received great acclaim, won prizes, and were commercial successes during their active careers, but they fell into oblivion over the years. For some, art critics and art historians never could quite understand how to label or characterize their work: Were the artists Americans, Asians, or some other sort of animal? Was their artwork American, Japanese, Chinese, or something else? Oriental? Eastern?

234   *Chapter Eleven*

Isamu Noguchi, arguably the most famous artist of Asian ancestry in America, is now widely celebrated. But during his lifetime, critics often didn't know how to refer to him. Even though he was born in the United States and spent most of his professional career here, critics often described him as Japanese, sometimes using epithets. New York critic Henry McBride dismissed him in 1935 as "wily" and predicted he would not amount to much in the public's eyes: "once an Oriental always an Oriental," he pronounced.[4] Dong Kingman, one of the most popular mid-twentieth-century artists in America, could not escape racial caricature, even when praised. "Bouncy, buck-toothed little Dong Kingman" was how *Time* magazine celebrated him in its pages in the 1940s.[5] Other artists suffered similar treatment during their careers. (One of the most bizarre may be the apparent caricature of famed painter Yasuo Kuniyoshi at the hands of author Truman Capote and film director Blake Edwards, who include a Japanese American artist, a Mr. I. Y. Yunioshi, in *Breakfast at Tiffany's*. Mickey Rooney's yellow-face portrayal of an obnoxious buffoon is one of the most racially repugnant in modern film history.) Aesthetic judgment in America was never race-free but was always racially constrained. Viewers could rarely free themselves from the assumption that art produced by persons who looked "Asian" somehow had to express something "Asian." Mainstream spectators assumed that racial or immutable cultural sensibilities indelibly marked artistic production. For many past observers, conscious or not, art was the trans-historical, transcendent materialization of race.

Kingman once commented on the confused and quixotic reaction to his art: "Western painters call me Chinese. Chinese painters say I'm very Western. I would say I'm in the middle." He also once observed, "Everyone writes that my work is half East and half West, that I'm in between." He himself wasn't quite sure what to think about this perceived "in-betweenness." "I don't know," he said. "I just want to be myself."[6]

But of course, Kingman and other Asian Americans could never be just themselves, unmarked by race, in America. Kingman in many ways endured the same ambiguities and challenges that Asians historically faced in the United States: not until 1965 did Congress lift the last of the immigration laws that overtly discriminated against Asians. The United States had deemed Chinese, Japanese, Koreans, Filipinos, and South Asians "aliens ineligible to citizenship" for much of the nineteenth and twentieth centuries.

They could not become naturalized citizens. Dominant society marginalized Asians and believed it virtually impossible for them to become acceptable members of American life. Similarly, art produced by them was rarely considered "American." At best, their art was constantly subjected to the trope of being a bridge between "Eastern" and "Western" art. Though often said in a complimentary way, the evaluation still assumed that the mainstream of American art was, as America itself, entirely Europe-derived. At worst, they were simply dismissed or not taken seriously, as they were not European American.

Also necessary to note is that prevailing trends in art criticism influenced the way past art was viewed at a particular moment in time. The fascination with modern abstraction and nonrepresentational art, especially after World War II, turned public eyes away from art that appeared to have social messages or overt ethnic connections. Art produced by Asian Americans, other racial minorities, and women in America that displayed such markers now appeared nonmodern and was eclipsed by the interest in abstraction. Art that reflected the quandary of exile (such as that suffered by Chinese diasporic artists—Wang Ya-chen, Chang Shu-chi, and Chang Dai-chien, for example—in the mid-twentieth century), displacement (such as that experienced by artists who worked in the United States during the height of racial antagonism, such as Yun Gee or Chiura Obata), and persecution (the Japanese artists who suffered internment, Eitaro Ishigaki and others, hounded because of their political beliefs) fell out of fashion. Painting techniques that appealed to abstract painters, such as calligraphy in the post–World War II period, interested some in America precisely because they could be used to pursue abstract, modernist purposes.

But one must also ask, why have historians dedicated to studying the Asian American past themselves neglected to appreciate the importance of art in Asian American lives? The historical work that Asian Americanists produced before the 1990s contains virtually no mention of Asian American art, the personal identities or experiences of any Asian American artists, or any sense of the place of art in the everyday lives of Asian Americans.

One might offer several explanations for this lacuna. For one, there is the historical circumstance of the emergence of Asian American studies. From its birth, this field of study was closely connected to the development of heightened racial and ethnic identity and self-assertion in America, and

236   *Chapter Eleven*

Asian American historians in the main attempted to reconstruct the broad outlines of this history to serve that political/ideological purpose. What is more, much of the early historical writing reflected an overriding interest in social history and in history viewed from the perspective of "from the bottom up." Evidence of mass political and social resistance to racial discrimination, laboring experiences, and social marginalization in America was given special place. Individuals, and certainly intellectuals, attracted less attention.

Art and art history, when it was considered, was often viewed as an elite, even elitist, realm, one that did not touch the lives of, and was irrelevant to, the laboring masses, the subject of much early Asian American historical imagination. Historians were interested in writing history that could help "claim America" for Asian Americans, that is, to show that Asian American experiences were an integral part of the social and political fabric of the country. They also hoped to help "claim Americanness" for Asian Americans, to assert that Asian Americans were as much American as others in the country. Asian Americanists hoped to end the stigma of perpetual foreignness placed upon people of Asian ancestry. One consequence of this effort was to downplay the transnational connections of Asian Americans and, somewhat ironically, the heritages from their lands of ancestry. Artists whose work may have displayed influences from East Asian art therefore fit less comfortably in the historical project.

But it may also simply be that Asian American art eluded attention because it is an especially challenging subject. The language of art and its interpretation (styles, themes, aims, and audiences, if one thinks of art as a "text") among Asian Americans is not easily approached. The artwork itself posed difficult questions, such as: Was it really possible to locate and define a body of art that might be called "Japanese American," "Chinese American," or even "Asian American"? How would one understand the relationship of these productions to "American art" or to "East Asian art"? Could one use established analytical tools and critical vocabulary to understand this art, or would new categories and approaches be needed? And, most of all, what "relevance" did all of this have to understanding Asian American lives in the past?

In recent years, there has been much greater understanding of the complexity of social identity in a highly racialized society. These days, the new recognition that identities are often multiple, contextual, hybrid, shifting, transnational, or unstable enables us to better appreciate the circumstances of Asian Americans past and present, including artistic production and intellectual work in general.[7] Such understanding helps us break the reification of categories such as "American" or "Eastern" art that had been constructed over many years. In addition, scholars are moving beyond the laboring masses to view other social classes among Asian Americans.[8]

One might consider the study of Asian American literature in thinking about the emerging possibilities in Asian American art history. The examination of Asian American literature began simultaneously with that of the historical project. Like history, literary study was a way to understand identities, past and present, and as a way to reclaim voices that, like Asian American historical experiences themselves, had been marginalized or even buried by the dominant society. Asian American literature seemed to be an approachable subject: it is, as has been studied, a body of texts created by people of Asian ancestry living in America writing primarily in English. The characters, contexts, and issues in this literature also tend to be clearly related to America-based experiences. The dominant concern, at least as has been interpreted to this point, is the place of the Asian in American life and her or his understanding of America. Literary scholars could engage the formal and historical qualities of these English-language literatures directly; at the same time, they relatively quickly established a discourse of interpretation that engaged older Asian American work, and American literatures more broadly, with contemporary Asian American expression. The potential to do the same was not as clear in the visual arts. In fact, to many, Asian American visual arts in the 1970s and 1980s appeared detached from any ethnic inspiration or model from the past.

What might be the value of art history to historians of the Asian American experience?

To begin with, it appears that art and artists in fact occupied a very important position in the everyday lives of many Asian Americans. The number of Asian American artists alone is impressive. The biographical survey that appears in *Asian American Art: A History, 1850–1970* [the volume in which this essay first appeared] covers 159 artists in California, just a portion of the more than 1,000 artists documented in that state alone. That survey comprises the most extensive historical study of *any* occupational or professional group of Asian Americans. The recovery of hundreds of identities will become the starting point of countless numbers of future projects in a wide variety of disciplines and interests.

238   *Chapter Eleven*

One might even argue that the visual arts were a uniquely attractive and important avenue of expression for creative Asian Americans in the past. This may have been so for a variety of reasons: ancestral traditions that highly valued visual arts; freedom from the demands of English fluency that writers faced; and mainstream interest in Asian aesthetics (Asian American artists were seen as embodying an "Oriental" talent) all may help account for the relatively large number of Asian American artists.

And apart from the artists themselves, the prominent place that the visual arts occupied in the daily lives of many Asian Americans is striking. Art production, its display in the home and community, its enjoyment in individual and in organized ways, and its celebration were all highly popular activities in Asian American communities ever since their arrival in the United States in the mid-nineteenth century. For example, Yamato Ichihashi, a Stanford history professor who studied Japanese Americans, once claimed when he was in a World War II internment camp that the Japanese were the most artistically inclined people in the world. His comment, though certainly chauvinist, did in fact highlight the special place that the display and appreciation of the arts occupied among Japanese Americans. His internment camp diary is filled with references to and descriptions of art classes and exhibitions. During incarceration, he himself spent many hours with a painter friend.[9] Important Asian American cultural figures such as Younghill Kang, Mine Okubo, Jade Snow Wong, and Chiang Yee are known mainly for their published writing, but they devoted as much or even more of their lives to art. In rereading local histories and old accounts of Chinese Americans, one is struck by the frequent mentions, brief and undeveloped as they usually are, of painting and the arts in community activities.[10]

Can one even go so far as to suggest that, given the number and productivity of Asian American artists, the special place accorded art by many people of Asian descent, and the connections of these artists with the general American art world (unacknowledged as they have been), the visual arts are an especially rich site for study of Asian American experiences? As a site of cultural and social expression, might visual art even be considered for Asian Americans akin in importance to the central place that music occupies in the African American experience? Might it be that Asian Americans have made special and unique contributions to the visual arts?

A number of other areas of study of Asian American life may benefit from a greater appreciation of the visual arts:

Emerging from the Shadows 239

THE ARTWORK AND CAREERS of the artists themselves offer fresh material to enlarge our understanding of Asian American social and intellectual history. If we understand this art as social as well as personal expression, it can help us gain insights into a wide variety of subjects, such as identity formation and projection, felt experience, perceptions of racial and ethnic identity and place, the texture of daily life, and intellectual and personal interaction with other communities, both white and minority.

ART HISTORY CAN LEAD to greater understanding of the internal organizational and institutional dynamics of Asian American communities, especially art clubs and societies, festivals, and even commerce (the ubiquitous art and curio stores, and galleries) and the business of art.

ART, IN ITS MANY forms, often played an important role in the daily lives of Asian Americans. Art, for many, was not something distant or only for the "privileged" but was an important and integral element in the home, family, and community. This recognition helps us begin to recover a sense of the actual lived experience of Asian American lives.

ART MAY LEAD US to better understand the forms of political expression. Some artists were thoroughly apolitical and detached from social activism, but a great many of the artists were profoundly affected by contemporary social movements and participated as artist activists. Asian American artists such as Yasuo Kuniyoshi and Yun Gee strongly opposed Japanese aggression in Asia during the 1930s and 1940s. Eitaro Ishigaki and Isamu Noguchi used their art to protest American racism. In the 1960s and 1970s, Lewis Suzuki, Nanying Stella Wong, Mitsu Yashima, and, of course, many younger Asian American artists used their creative talents to oppose the Vietnam War.

ASIAN AMERICAN ART OFFERS the exciting possibility of viewing the *familiar,* such as places, people, and life experiences, in *unfamiliar* ways, of seeing America with "new eyes." Chiura Obata's *Setting Sun: Sacramento Valley* and Chang Dai-chien's vision of Yosemite, *Autumn Mountains in Twilight,* offer fresh perspectives on the American landscape. We might gain new ways of understanding how others in the past have viewed traditional themes such as the "West," man and nature, the city, and, of course, race. Asian American art also might reveal the *unfamiliar* (at least for many other Americans), such as the internment experience or the attachment to heritage prompted by exile and social alienation.

240   *Chapter Eleven*

THIS ARTWORK ALSO ENCOURAGES us to think about the many ways that cultural influences from Asia have influenced America. T'eng K'uei (Teng Baiye) came from China in 1924, studied art at the University of Washington in Seattle, did graduate work at Harvard University, then returned to China in 1931. While living in the Seattle area, he became friends with Mark Tobey and gave Tobey early lessons in Chinese brushwork. One of the great influences on Tobey's own work was a trip to China and Japan in 1934, during which time he visited T'eng K'uei in Shanghai and attended lectures and classes with his friend. How have artists such as T'eng K'uei been creative agents of this influence? How did they actively explore aesthetic interaction? In what ways have Asian American artists themselves been cultural translators, transmitters, or interpreters?

THE WAYS THAT DOMINANT society received and understood Asian American artists may lead to new ways of understanding the dynamics of race and racial ideologies in America.

All in all, regardless of whatever importance Asian American art may have for the future understanding of history, these newfound artifacts from the past, these wonderful creative expressions, can now be enjoyed once again as their creators had intended: as works of emotion, of beauty, of protest, of intellectual engagement, or deeply personal sentiment. These works of art can speak to us across the divide of time. There is no Asian American aesthetic to which a work must adhere to be appreciated.[11] Exactly how we will view these works will depend on how receptive we are to challenges to our assumptions about "American art," "modern art," "Asian art," and even about Asian Americans themselves.

Notes

The author thanks Mark Johnson, Valerie Matsumoto, and Sharon Spain for their help with this foreword.

TWELVE

Chinese Painting Comes to America: Zhang Shuqi and the Diplomacy of Art

As I moved away from approaches to U.S. diplomatic history that focused on the mindsets of elites and geopolitics, I developed an interest in the ideological and cultural dimensions of the long interaction between China and America. I wanted to understand the ideological contexts of formal diplomacy as well as art itself as a vital realm of international relations. In a 1997 talk at the annual meeting of the Association for Asian Studies, for example, I presented a talk entitled "The Art of Diplomacy and the Diplomacy of Art: Art in U.S.-China Relations," in which I examined ways that the two realms were unexpectedly and often deeply interconnected. Unfortunately, the text of my talk is now lost.

Because of my family experience, art had developed as a personal arena for my exploration. My father, known in his lifetime as Shu-chi Chang (Zhang Shuqi) (1900–1957), had a successful and distinguished career in China and in the United States. He first visited the United States in the fall of 1941 and, traveling on a diplomatic passport, toured the country to promote understanding of Chinese art practice to advance the bilateral

"Chinese Painting Comes to America: Zhang Shuqi and the Diplomacy of Art," *East West Interchanges in America Art: A Long and Tumultuous Relationship,* edited by Cynthia Mills, Lee Glazer, and Amelia A. Goerlitz (Smithsonian Institution Press), 2012: 126–141. Permission of Smithsonian Institution. (Illustrations accompanying the original article are not included in this volume.)

241

Chapter Twelve

relationship. The American public at the time was sympathetic to the plight of China suffering aggression from abroad and was eager to learn about Chinese culture. After Pearl Harbor and the outbreak of war prevented his return to China, he remained in the United States and for the next five years presented his artwork throughout the country to contribute to the wartime alliance in cultural ways. After a short visit to China after the war, he returned to the United States to work and to live out his final days.

This chapter is from my participation at a Smithsonian Institution conference on trans-Pacific artistic engagements that was held in Washington, D.C. In it, I survey the history of American contact with Chinese art in the nineteenth and twentieth centuries and then turn to a description of my father's career in the United States and how technologies and performative art practices facilitated his efforts in promoting an appreciation of Chinese culture in the United States. It alludes to the difficulties American—and Chinese—art historians have had in evaluating the work he and other Asian diasporic artists produced in America. Their work often did not fit the neat categories that defined American art and thus were passed over. Recovering their legacies remains an important task in pursuing art historical study, understanding East-West interactions, and in recovering Asian diasporic cultural experiences.

Discussions of cultural interactions between Asian countries and the United States often take fixed, unexamined categories, such as "East and West" or "Asian and Euro-American," as their starting point. The categories are sometimes thought of as opposed, with the Asian construed as traditional and unchanging and the Western as modern, dynamic, and international. Recent scholarship and thinking, however, suggests that these concepts and assumptions are problematic in considering artistic interchanges in the early twentieth century, if not earlier. We now understand that artistic exchanges across the Pacific have been more complicated, mutual, and interactive than previously assumed.

Consider the first identified artist of Chinese ancestry who worked in America. Lai Yong came from southern China to California sometime in

Chinese Painting Comes to America   243

the mid-nineteenth century. During the 1860s and 1870s, he enjoyed a successful career as a portrait artist and photographer in San Francisco, where leading members of the elite sat for his Western-style oil portraits. Members of the Chinese community also served as subjects of his photographic work, which was both compelling and sensitive in approach. Lai Yong spoke out against anti-Chinese prejudices of the day and was an early proponent of equality and civil rights. But where did he learn the craft of his art, which had no putative Oriental look? Most likely, he received his training from George Chinnery (1774–1852), a noted English artist who had settled in Hong Kong and Macao, or from Chinese artists whom Chinnery had influenced. Examples of Lai Yong's work survive, but the artist himself disappeared from San Francisco and from the historical record after 1882, the year Congress passed what is known as the Chinese Exclusion Act.[2]

This essay focuses on the life and career of Zhang Shuqi (1900–1957), one of the earliest Chinese artists to have had a direct impact on large American audiences and their understanding of Chinese brush painting.[3] Under the auspices of the Chinese government, Zhang traveled to the United States in 1941 to promote Sino-American understanding and friendship. He toured the country extensively over the next five years and held solo exhibitions at major museums, where he conducted public demonstrations of his technique. The popular and art press devoted great attention to these events, which attracted thousands of people. Before his arrival in the country, the Chinese government had presented one of the artist's large compositions to President Franklin D. Roosevelt. That gift also had received extensive media coverage, making it then, and perhaps even today, the most well-known Chinese painting in America.

For most Americans (and many Asians), Zhang's work appeared to be of a traditional Chinese idiom, but his training, technique, and approach to art was fully modern in China. It combined Western and Chinese features, and he thought of himself as both an international and Chinese artist. Though highly successful in China in the 1930s and 1940s, his subtle hybrid style and life overseas have complicated historical evaluation of Zhang in China. In the United States, Zhang is not considered part of American art history at all. But for many in this country, it was Zhang Shuqi who brought Chinese painting to America. Zhang came to the United States to advance the Chinese government's practice of cultural diplomacy, reaching out to the West after Japan's invasion of China in 1937. I play with the

244 Chapter Twelve

word "diplomacy" to refer not just to the formal interaction of states but also to suggest informal artistic interpolation and mixing; both definitions are useful to understand Zhang's work and possible influence. But it was also twentieth-century modernity that enabled Chinese painting to reach a mass audience in America. Chinese paintings, like other objects, had long been found in American homes and institutions, and a few Americans had even studied them, but Chinese painting as a process or method as well as something available to wide numbers of people was virtually unknown before the mid-twentieth century. World politics and changing technologies opened new possibilities of learning, influence, and exchange.

Chinese arts and crafts had come early to the attention of Americans. In the eighteenth and nineteenth centuries, many Americans, elite and the everyday, filled their homes with Chinese porcelains, decorative ware, furniture and the like. This *chinoiserie* was widely appreciated and admired, but it was not until 1838 that the American public could view Chinese paintings firsthand. In that year, Nathan Dunn, a Philadelphia merchant enriched by the early China trade, opened what became known as the Chinese Museum to the American public. According to one estimate, more than a 100,000 people toured Dunn's collection to view 1,200 objects he had acquired when he lived in China. These items ranged from natural history specimens to garments, tools, home wares, and fine paintings. Much impressed the crowds who visited: some paintings were huge, extending nine feet wide by five feet high. But the artwork left Dunn, a Sinophile, somewhat ambivalent. He wrote in the museum catalogue that the several hundred paintings in the show provided clear evidence of Chinese artistic ability, which was even better than many had thought. But though Chinese painters could render images with "great correctness and beauty," Dunn concluded that "shading," a staple of the Western Renaissance, was something "they do not well understand." For his path-breaking efforts, the American Philosophical Society bestowed on Dunn membership in its esteemed ranks.[4]

Dunn's museum remained open for three years in Philadelphia before he moved it to London. A few years later in 1847, John R. Peters, who had been a member of the first official American delegation to China, displayed his own Chinese art collection to the American public. It was even larger than Dunn's, with 500 paintings, including some in oil color depicting everyday life in China. Other paintings presented birds and flowers "exquisitely done." Overall, Peters was more diplomatic than Dunn in his catalogue's evaluation of the artwork. "All the paintings in the Museum," he wrote, "are the work of Chinese artists, and for execution and finish speak for themselves."[5]

By the late nineteenth century, important figures in America developed a critical appreciation of Chinese painting and arts more on their own terms. Wealthy collectors began to amass important holdings of high Chinese artwork—first porcelains and then classical paintings, though little that was contemporary. Considerations of Chinese and Japanese artworks appeared in the paintings of such artists as John La Farge, James McNeill Whistler, and the European Impressionists. As historian Warren I. Cohen has noted, "East Asian art became intertwined with modernism, with avant-garde Western painting. Each prepared the way for the other."[6]

In China, a few artists from Europe had had a small presence in court arts going back at least to the sixteenth century, but they little influenced the embedded tradition until the nineteenth and early twentieth centuries. Then the challenge of the West threw everything into chaos in China. Many political reformers came to believe that Westernization, including in the arts, would be critical for China's salvation and future. Art students were sent abroad to Japan and Europe to bring back the new learning. In contrast to Europe, where realism came increasingly under fire, academic realism, Post-Impressionism, and other schools were considered to be modern in China. One of the leading apostles of the new art training in China was Liu Haisu, who styled himself as the Chinese Vincent Van Gogh. Liu founded the Shanghai Art Academy, the first fine arts college of modern China. It taught Western art techniques exclusively; no training in Chinese ink painting was even offered in its first years.[7]

Zhang Shuqi was born into this crucible of political and artistic ferment in 1900, which was also the year of the Boxer anti-foreign uprising. His birthplace in Pujiang County, Zhejiang Province, was near the art centers of Hangzhou and Shanghai. As a precocious youngster, he displayed a creative talent that impressed his artist relatives. But his first formal training came at Liu Haisu's Shanghai academy, which he entered in 1921 as one of its earliest students. His instruction was in Western techniques. "I painted day and night," he recalled, "I learned oil, water color, and charcoal. I got the foundation of painting from that school." Zhang largely trained himself, however, in techniques of Chinese brush painting and the well-established Chinese genre of birds and flowers, for which he later became most well known.[8]

246   *Chapter Twelve*

After graduation, Zhang became a practicing artist and instructor, and he taught brush painting at various schools in China, including 10 years beginning in 1930 at the National Central University in Nanjing, then the national capital. The dean of the art department, Li Yishi (1886–1942), a European-trained oil painter, completed a quick sketch of Zhang one day that captures the likeness of the young artist. But it also reflects the then-dominant Western-influenced artistic temperament at that important institution through its suggestions of direct observation of the model and use of shading to create an impression of three-dimensionality. (Zhang's inscription on the sketch, added in 1952, reads in part, "In the fall of that year, on a fine day with clear sky and crisp air, Mr. Li invited me to go to Jiming Temple [Cry of the Cock] for tea and a chat. Mr. Li drew this portrait of me ... and captured me not only in appearance but also in spirit in just a few minutes.")

Zhang and his contemporaries responded to China's political and cultural crisis in different ways. Some, such as Liu Haisu and Li Yishi, embraced Western oil painting; others such as Zhang sought to invigorate traditional Chinese painting and develop an updated, distinctive national style. His friends and associates came to include such leading artists as Fu Baoshi, Xu Beihong, Pan Tianshou, Wu Fuzhi, Zhao Shao'ang, Qi Baishi, Gao Jianfu, and Zhang Daqian. Zhang mastered the use of the Chinese brush but applied its use in compositions that reflected his Western art study. To the eyes of most contemporary observers, his work, employing the so-called boneless style of freehand ink painting technique, fell clearly in the tradition of nineteenth-century Chinese ink painters such as Ren Bonian and Wu Changshuo. At the same time, the influence of his foundation in Western techniques is clearly visible, and Chinese art commentators would sometimes compare Zhang to Van Gogh, Jean Francois Millet, and other European artists.[9]

Zhang's career developed rapidly in the 1930s, with his work included in exhibitions of contemporary Chinese painting that traveled to Paris, Berlin, and Moscow.[10] His painting also came to the attention of Chinese political elites (both Communist and Nationalist), and in 1940 the Ministry of Education asked him to complete a large composition for the occasion of Roosevelt's election to a third presidential term. As Japanese bombs fell on Chongqing, the wartime capital and Zhang's new residence, he completed his monumental *Messengers of Peace,* also known as *A Hundred Doves.* The president of the relocated National Central University, Luo Jialun, and

Chinese Painting Comes to America   247

the Chinese leader Chiang Kai-shek added inscriptions. A few days before Christmas 1940, Zhang formally presented the painting to the United States ambassador to China, Nelson T. Johnson, who forwarded it to the White House.

The painting was a good choice: it appeared to be within Chinese tradition but would appeal to American audiences. The rendering of the birds was realistic and lively, the color vibrant, and the brush strokes bold and energetic. The composition contained a Western perspective, which Johnson, a leading China specialist, specifically noted in his cover letter to Roosevelt. Conveying the sentiment as well as the energy of the painting, Johnson reported that the artist "desired to make a picture which would be symbolic of the position which the President of the United States holds in the present world situation and after choosing the dove spent three weeks working out the composition." Johnson explained: "Then in one day he painted the first fifty doves. Later others were added until he had painted 97. The last three added to make up the hundred are the dove at the extreme left, the white one in the center and the one faintly seen at the far distance coming from behind the foliage." For this painting, Zhang used gouache as well as Chinese wet colors, as he regularly did in his work.[11]

Messengers of Peace was said to have graced the White House after its acceptance, and it later was displayed in the exhibition hall of the Franklin D. Roosevelt Presidential Library and Museum in Hyde Park, New York, where it is now permanently held. The Ferargil Galleries in New York City exhibited it in 1942. Numerous newspapers, books, and periodicals reproduced the image, which became famous in the United States; to this day it is also celebrated in China.[12]

Zhang followed the painting to the United States, arriving in the fall of 1941. Traveling on a diplomatic passport with Chinese government financial support, he was presented as China's "ambassador of art and goodwill." His mission was to introduce Chinese culture to the American people and promote friendship in what quickly became a common cause after Japan's December 7 attack on Pearl Harbor. Unable to return to China, Zhang spent the next five years in the United States frenetically advancing cultural diplomacy.

He had brought 400 of his own paintings with him, but also continued to paint actively in America. He sold many of his works and participated in events to raise money for United China Relief, the non-government

248   *Chapter Twelve*

organization that rallied Americans to support the Chinese people during the war. Zhang participated in group shows of contemporary Chinese painting, such as a 1943 exhibition at the Metropolitan Museum in New York. And he held numerous large one-artist shows in museums throughout the country, including several at the de Young in San Francisco, the Seattle Art Museum, the Chicago Art Institute, the Nelson Gallery in Kansas City, the Baltimore Museum of Art, the Los Angeles County Museum of Art, and the Ontario Museum in Toronto. He exhibited at galleries and gave talks at clubs, civic organizations, and universities from Portland to Chicago to Washington, DC. Museums and collectors, such as Henry Luce, purchased his paintings. The writers Pearl Buck and Lin Yutang, the philosopher Hu Shih, and other specialists in Chinese life and culture in America admired his work. At his shows, his public demonstrations of his painting attracted large audiences of spectators who saw for the first time what Chinese brush painting was all about. Zhang returned to China after the end of World War II and then came back to the United States in 1949. He opened a studio a block away from the California College of Arts and Crafts and resided in the Oakland hills until his early death in 1957.[13]

Space does not allow a full discussion of Zhang Shuqi's work as it evolved in the conditions of life in the United States other than to present a few observations. Zhang was a serious artist who constantly studied both Chinese and Western art texts and paintings. Sometime in the early 1940s when he was in America, for example, he explored using black paper and board, which was highly unusual in the Chinese art tradition. Some of the resulting images seemed to invoke the work of John La Farge from the 1860s. La Farge had completed a composition of a water lily against a dark background after studying Japanese brush painting, and he might have inspired Zhang, who completed a similar composition and then reproduced it as a widely circulated note card in the 1940s. In China, Zhang had also become known for his "whiteism," the liberal use of white pigment, which was untraditional in Chinese painting, and he continued using white ink for his painting and even calligraphy, recalling Mark Tobey's "white writing."[14] One also wonders about possible conversations between the work of Morris Graves and Chinese bird-and-flower artists such as Zhang. In the early 1940s, Zhang exhibited his pictures and performed demonstrations of his technique at the Seattle Art Museum, which purchased his paintings for its collection and where Graves worked for a time.

Zhang never broke with representational painting—he was technically so skillful with the Chinese brush and steeped in Chinese naturalism that Western notions of abstraction never persuaded him to abandon his approach. But his work clearly evolved in the United States, and we can only speculate as to the influences that played on him.

Take, for example, one of his compositions completed on a screen, one of the traditional supports for Chinese painting. Brightly colored sunflowers evoke Van Gogh, of course, but Zhang also employs the vigorous use of black ink calligraphic brush strokes. The rendering of the flowers, in contrast, is accomplished with thick, layered pigment that may recall the impasto of western oil paints. He completed this in the United States and certainly intended it to stay in America. Other works display what he considered to be the hallmark of Chinese artwork, "rhythmic vitality" or *sheng dong*, but perhaps with even greater force, color, and abstraction than what he completed in China. He experimented with new ways to apply his paints, such as the use of kitchen and natural sponges. He sketched with ink pens and wax crayons. He worked on American watercolor cardboard, cut in dimensions for Western wood framing. He even painted on ceramics, such as tiles and lamp stands. We also see a move toward simplification, an effort to find essential formal elements, and new subject matter from the California natural and physical landscape, which he loved. He added California quail, redwood trees, and Sierra pines, along with Yosemite and Carmel, to his expanding subject repertoire.[15]

Although Zhang considered himself to be in the tradition of Chinese classical masters, he fully embraced modern technologies of reproduction and publicity. In China, he had produced note cards of his work, indicating his appreciation of the commercial potential that machine printing offered. Stranded in the United States during the war, he took the opportunity to start a business on a larger scale. He reproduced his work as fine stationery, lithographs, note cards, Christmas cards, and even as decorative items such as wallpaper, placemats, and tallies for scoring the card game of bridge (which obsessed him), as well as table napkins and paper table coverings. These reproductions sold well throughout the country and internationally, in curio stores and in fine homeware emporiums. They were marketed from the 1940s through the 1970s, circulating to tens of thousands of consumers. Zhang also authored a richly illustrated book that offered instruction on Chinese painting and its techniques, including brush use and composition.

250   *Chapter Twelve*

Viking Press published an English translation of the book in 1960 under the title *Painting in the Chinese Manner,* recognizing that it was one of the first treatises on Chinese painting in America by an actual practitioner of the art form.[16]

Another modern dimension of the presentation of his art was the live demonstration. It is unclear when Chinese painters began to offer these performances, which became more common in the latter half of the twentieth century, but we know that Liu Haisu gave public demonstrations when he toured Europe in the 1930s.[17] Within China, there was no tradition of painting in public. Live demonstrations were completely unknown, though when artists socialized they could paint with one another in friendship, often collaborating on compositions over wine or a repast. Zhang himself did so in his own homes. But in the United States, Zhang quickly added personal appearances and painting demonstrations to his exhibitions. Widely advertised, these events attracted great crowds who watched in rapt and astonished attention as he produced complicated compositions within a matter of minutes.

They were performances in every sense of the word with expectant and hushed audiences, a stage (the painting table), a charismatic figure who spoke in English with an unfamiliar inflection, and action that could not be recaptured. Art became a moment and movement, not just an object. Zhang became known for his extraordinary technical skill and speed, which *Life* magazine featured in a 1943 article about him, complete with photos of his minute-by-minute progress on a painting as a clock indicated the passing time. As the title of the *Life* photo spread declared, "Chinese Painting: Professor Chang shows how he does it in eight minutes flat." Technical speed impressed the magazine's editors, in good American style, but they were oblivious to the creative and expressive possibilities of the rapid strokes that many traditionally appreciated in Chinese painting.[18]

Many things intrigued his American audiences at the demonstrations, including his unusual handling of materials, especially the brush, the application of paints, and his composition. Zhang's rendering of simple scenes of natural beauty captivated; his birds and flowers created an "alternative reality" to the stresses of war and of daily life.[19] But there was something more, which critical observers at the time noted, implicitly, and sometimes explicitly, contrasting his work with traditional Western approaches to painting. This was the ability of the art to capture expressive gesture resulting

Chinese Painting Comes to America 251

from the interplay of trained, physical effort and contingency. Here is what Alfred Frankenstein, the well-known art critic of the *San Francisco Chronicle*, wrote in 1943 after attending one of these demonstrations:

> *Watching Chang at work is like hearing [Jascha] Heifetz play the fiddle; i.e., the results of the virtuosity are directly and immediately apparent as they seldom are in watching a Western painter at his easel. The parallel goes further in that, with Chang, one has a sense of manual dexterity trained to the last degree of subtle muscular control. He has a spiccato and a legato, he has mastered harmonics in double stops, and the right and left hand pizzicato as well. Furthermore a painting by Chang is and has to be a one-sitting performance. He can no more stop and knock off and come back than Heifetz can stop and knock off while playing the Brahms concerto in public. He works very wet, and he works entirely without model, drawing a vast stock of motifs out of memorized observation and tradition. And until you see him you do not know what a subtle, plastic and varied instrument a Chinese brush can be.*[20]

Other writers also spoke of Zhang's performances as magical and full of spirit, spontaneity, and quiet emotion. The San Francisco artist and writer John Garth witnessed Zhang at the de Young Museum and emphasized the fluid physicality of his act of painting: "The way in which Professor Chang moves his brush through its series of graceful curves, swirls and touches as the painting steadily evolves beneath his handsome hand reminds the watcher, oddly enough, of the apparent free but exactly controlled execution of a difficult dance routine by some master or mistress of the classic ballet." In a dig at some of his fellow American artists, Garth also complimented Zhang for his "calm grace of execution unknown to the western modern, who nowadays appears always to have tortured the paint on to his canvas in a frantic agony of spiritual doubt and indecision."[21]

As the *Life* photo-essay suggests, there is another technology of dissemination that we need to consider: the technology of filmic production—that is, still and moving photography. Zhang was keen on both. In China, he used photos to record his work for his own reference and for publicity. He had individual pieces photographed, as well as his exhibitions and even his gifting of *Messengers of Peace*. He understood the power of promotion and employed professional photographers to record his time in the United States and create portfolios of himself and his performances. In these portraits, he could be the gowned master draped in the silk of a Chinese scholar with

Chapter Twelve

brush in hand, or the modern international celebrity sporting a sharp, tailored wool suit, with tie, wingtips, and a casually held cigarette.

In the 1940s his work became the subject of motion picture documentaries, early examples of films showing an artist at work. His unfamiliar style, still exotic for American audiences, and his ability to paint in an energetic and intriguing way were perfect for the motion picture. Through these captivating documentaries, we can still see Zhang at work today, somewhat as his museum demonstration audiences did more than 60 years ago.

One of these films was made in 1943, a joint production of the Harmon Foundation, which is best known for supporting African American artists, and the China Institute in America, an organization that promoted the understanding of Chinese culture. American philosopher-educator John Dewey and Hu Shih, the famous Chinese intellectual, helped found the Institute in New York in 1926. The film's producer was Wango Weng, an art scholar and connoisseur who also narrated the documentary.[22] Several things about the film stand out. One is its use of Zhang's art as a way of introducing Chinese painting to an uninitiated, general American audience. In attempting to instruct, it focuses on matters that were unusual to audiences at the time: the rhythmic power of Chinese brush strokes, the effort to present nature from the mind and not from an established model, the rigorous training, and the idea of temporality in the act of painting. The film, which shows Zhang painting and completing compositions, introduces the viewer to central elements of Chinese artistic production: the sequence of brush strokes, their irretrievability, their interconnectedness and contingency, and the stylized representation of an identifiable subject. Within minutes, Zhang transforms a blank void into a virtual reality of flowers, leaves, birds, insects, and colors, visualizing a moment in imagined time. The narrator has to remind an incredulous viewer that the act of creation was occurring in "real time," not edited or mechanically quickened visually.[23]

Zhang could be presented as the prototypical Chinese artist carrying on some timeless tradition, but his actual work was a subtle interpolation within strongly held cultural assumptions. His own identity when he was alive was elusive and not transparent. Today it is still a challenge to attempt to interpret his life and work. Zhang helped to bring Chinese painting to America. He brought not just paintings as objects—which museums had long held, elite patrons admired, and scholars had studied. Under the exigencies of global conflict, he brought Chinese painting as event, as activity, and as something accessible to a broad spectrum of Americans. Technologies, market conditions, and international politics created the occasion. Artistic currents in America soon came to embrace their own versions of the gesture, the spontaneous, and the display of psychic energy. Zhang's personal style of art fit the times and opportunities.

Zhang was unique, but he was also representative. As with many of his Chinese contemporaries, he sought to reinvigorate Chinese painting while also wanting to make an impact on America and advance the internationalization of art. In China, the line between the intellectual and artistic world, on the one hand, and the political world, on the other, has been more permeable than in the West. Zhang's career was similar: his art and activity in America complemented political diplomacy to be sure, but he also helped to negotiate new, more porous boundaries between art in China and America. His was also a "diplomacy of art."

In international relations, "diplomacy" broadly refers to the formal interaction of states, while the term "art of diplomacy" honors the creative effort required to move beyond established positions and to forge new relationships. And so it is with the "diplomacy of art." Within the world of art, references are made to media, to various ways to present and articulate. But art is itself a medium, a platform that can serve to advance dialogue across various sorts of boundaries rooted in traditions, beliefs, social practices, geographies, times, and values. Art is an avenue of cultural exchange and interaction. And specific works of art can themselves embody those very conversations, with the creation of the new, unexpected, and arresting.

Zhang hoped to see the end of the East-West artistic divide, a trope that dominated the world he inhabited, and he was encouraged by the warm reception he received here and the art that he saw in America. Artists from Asia were learning from the West, he observed in the 1940s, and "occidental artists are beginning to pay attention to design by the mind much more than before"—something he believed Chinese artists had done all along. All this inspired him to "foretell a union between the East and the West." He took pride in his contributions to East-West artistic interaction and the diplomacy of art.[24]

THIRTEEN

America's Dong Kingman—Dong Kingman's America

Celebrated and demeaned, Dong Kingman (1911–2000) was one of the most important artists of Asian ancestry to work in mid-twentieth-century America. He was talented and creative and was widely appreciated during his career, but sometimes in uncomfortable ways. At times, he was diminished racially. He was emblematic of the difficult place that accomplished Asian Americans occupied in Cold War America.

Kingman's work could be accessible to a buying public, with his depictions of beautiful landscapes and cityscapes of locations all around America and beyond. Hollywood studios commissioned him to create colorful backgrounds to be displayed with the credits for lavish Hollywood film productions. Beyond the commercial work, his painting could also be visionary and even provocative, perhaps because of his experience as a member of a marginalized social group. He painted interpretations of San Francisco Chinatown and gritty urban scenes and even created visions inspired by science fiction, a genre of writing that permitted imaginative exploration.

In recent years, attention has returned to Kingman's diverse work. He is now celebrated as one of the masters of the twentieth-century American

"America's Dong Kingman—Dong Kingman's America," San Francisco Chinese Historical Society, Dong Kingman in America Catalog (2001). (Illustrations accompanying the original article are not included in this volume.)

255

256   *Chapter Thirteen*

watercolor. The following essay was written for a retrospective exhibition of his work at the San Francisco Chinese Historical Society of America Museum in 2001. Kingman is deserving of much more extensive research and writing about his life and artwork. He and other minority artists and creative figures reshaped the American cultural landscape in the critical decades after World War II.

✳

"Bouncy, buck-toothed little Dong Kingman" is how *Time* magazine described the artist in a 1945 article acclaiming his work. The feature was just the first in a long and close association between Kingman and the periodical. A few years later, *Time* used the same words again in celebrating his fresh interpretation of New York City's Times Square. The influential magazine apparently saw no problem using what seems to us now as an obviously demeaning characterization in an article meant to praise.[1] But these were years of dramatic change: America had emerged from World War II as the undisputed dominant power in the world, it promoted itself as the leader of the "free world," and the country had begun to confront its long domestic record of racial prejudice and inequality. The country, under international scrutiny, only awkwardly advanced out of its cultural parochialism.

Time was not alone in its patronizing praise of Kingman. Similar characterizations appeared in most mainstream articles about him in the 1940s and 1950s when he broke into the established art world. But it was not that the media wanted to deliberately insult Kingman; it just did not know how to praise him. Mainstream America's reaction to Kingman's early work reflected its confusion, its groping to locate a space for, and a language about, those creative individuals whose work did not fit long-established mainstream artistic styles. Where would one place a Duke Ellington, who debuted in Carnegie Hall in 1943, the same year that Congress began to dismantle the Chinese Exclusion Acts, which had denied citizenship naturalization rights to Chinese immigrants and virtually excluded them from immigrating since 1882? Where was America going in 1954 when the Supreme Court handed down its landmark decision outlawing school segregation (New York City landlords had refused to rent to Kingman himself because he was "Oriental")[2] and the

State Department selected Kingman to "sell" democracy in a U.S.-sponsored tour to non-communist Asia? Americans, conflicted and divided in many ways, did not know the answers to these difficult questions.

The story of Dong Kingman's life says much about America's acceptance of cultural diversity in the twentieth century. Kingman was born into modest and obscure circumstances in Oakland's Chinatown, but he rose from being a houseboy for the rich in San Francisco to a famed artist honored by the wealthy internationally. By the end of his career, even governments, including those of China as well as the United States, formally honored his artwork. Corporate America did too: Pan Am, IBM, Hollywood studios, and others promoted his paintings. Banks commissioned him to create murals for their offices. His art, by and large, was accessible and not challenging to prevailing politics or social sensibilities.

Early in his career, however, critics did not know exactly how to think about him *ethnically* or what to think about his work *artistically. Life* magazine, for example, thought that Kingman gave, in its words, "American scenes a lively Oriental flavor." (Unable to avoid stereotyping, the magazine ran its feature under a large photograph of the artist and his wife eating with chopsticks in a New York Chinese restaurant.)[3] Others thought they saw no "Oriental" influence in his paintings, praising his ability to transcend what they saw as the "ethnic" and offering something more "universal," which actually meant something painted in a nonprovocative, Western artistic style. Recalling the confused reception to his early shows, Kingman once noted that, "Western painters call me Chinese. Chinese painters say I'm very Western. I would say I'm in the middle."[4] Although Kingman was referring to his art, he could have been referring to the dilemma many Chinese Americans felt about their own evolving ethnic identity and ill-defined social place in America in those years.

But many observers eventually came to see Kingman's work as a meeting of "East and West," as they put it. They saw it as a synthesis of styles and sensibilities. "Everyone writes that my work is half East and half West, that I'm in between," Kingman once observed. But, then, upon further reflection, even he was not sure what to think: "I don't know," he said, "I just want to be myself."[5] Again, Kingman was speaking about his personal painting style, but he could have been expressing the frustration that many persons of color felt about trying to define their individuality and ethnicity in an increasingly race-conscious America.

258   *Chapter Thirteen*

Regardless of how the critics understood his work, the popularity of Kingman's painting reflected the fascination many Americans had with the growing interaction between Asia and America in the mid-twentieth century. To be sure, some continued to see Asia as a threat, recalling fears of the "Yellow Peril" first expressed toward the end of the nineteenth century. Others saw promise. Many open-minded Americans believed that industry, politics, art, and Western civilization generally had much to benefit from increased contact with the "East." Philosopher/historian Will Durant was one of these. In 1935, the same year that Kingman held his first one-man show in San Francisco, Durant wrote hopefully, "The future faces into the Pacific and understanding must follow it there." But Durant also knew that many other Americans saw possible discord, misunderstanding, and clash. He feared that "the theme of the twentieth century" could very well be "an all-embracing conflict between the East and the West."[6]

This promise and threat inherent in East-West interaction, as Durant described, formed the historical context for understanding much of the reception to Kingman's work. His creativity was hailed as a beneficent product of trans-Pacific contact. At the same time, many of his admirers also believed that Kingman's work could help improve East-West understanding and relations. By the latter 1950s, influential forces felt that Kingman's paintings contained a vision of a more modern and outward-looking America. His paintings, especially those of cities around the world, seemed to express what might be called a Cold War cosmopolitanism. This was a view of the world that celebrated its rich cultural diversity. But it was a limited celebration; it did not provoke one's conscience or question the assumption of America's preeminence or its goodwill in the world. There are few visible poor, radical, or angry people in Kingman's paintings. The world is at peace. It was no wonder that travel, business, and news magazines from the 1950s through the 1970s featured his colorful visions of the cities of Asia and other parts of the world in seemingly countless renditions. The world in these paintings, overall, was colorful, exciting, optimistic, and inviting.

It was a vision shared in part by his patrons, one of his first being the humanitarian and internationalist Eleanor Roosevelt, wife of the president during World War II. It was a vision expressed in print by the powerful publishing empire of Henry Luce. Luce, the son of American missionaries to China, was a passionate supporter of the China Lobby in Washington, D.C., that promoted Chiang Kai-shek's regime in Taiwan and a booster of what he called the "American Century," his nationalistic label for the twentieth century. And during the 1950s and 1960s, Hollywood studios, which increasingly produced work with international themes, regularly showcased Kingman's work.

Indeed, it may be safely said that Dong Kingman was the most renowned Chinese American of the middle decades of the twentieth century. America's cultural and media elite celebrated no other Chinese American cultural worker as enthusiastically as him. Kingman's work probably touched more Americans than any other Chinese American, whether businessman, scientist, or intellectual, in these years. And there were other important contemporary Chinese American cultural workers—actress Anna May Wong, cinematographer James Wong Howe, the essayist Pardee Lowe, and Jade Snow Wong, the celebrated writer and ceramist. They and Kingman were all grew from lowly beginnings to become the first visible and nationally honored members of what had been an invisible, silenced, and marginal community. All these artists struggled to make a place for their creativity in what had been a world deeply hostile to Chinese Americans. Their efforts, personally and artistically, were all path-breaking.

Americans may not have necessarily known Kingman's name, but they saw his work in *Fortune, Time, Holiday, McCall's,* the *New York Times,* and the *Saturday Review,* among many others. Hollywood studies commissioned him to set the visual mood in movies such as *55 Days at Peking* (1963), *The World of Suzie Wong* (1964), and *The Sand Pebbles* (1966), films that explored in some way the troubled American encounter with China.

But in addition to his well-known sketches of Hollywood celebrities and work on films for the entertainment industry, there was another side to Dong Kingman's work. One sees a populist spirit in his paintings, especially those from his early career but also beyond. Much of his work expresses an interest in, and respect for, the everyday city-dweller and the vibrant, hurly-burly life of the modern metropolis. The people who inhabit Kingman's paintings engage in commonplace activities: strolling down sidewalks, shopping for food, exercising in the park, viewing the wonders and mysteries of the city, and experiencing its energies. The scenes of his cities are as familiar to its residents as they are to the viewers of his canvases. Kingman made art from what may seem to be the mundane and the ordinary, which is why his paintings continue to speak to audiences today. His art reflects his own humble background and unassuming personality; one

260 *Chapter Thirteen*

does not need privilege, in either money or training, to enjoy his artwork and see oneself in them. His early work on San Francisco, which occupied a special place in his heart, contains these qualities in abundance. It is therefore fitting for paintings from this period of his life to be showcased in this inaugural exhibition of San Francisco's museum dedicated to the history of the Chinese in America, Dong Kingman's historical compatriots.

FOURTEEN

The Many Sides of Happy Lim: aka Hom Ah Wing, Lin Jian Fu, Happy Lum, Lin Chien Fu, Hom Yen Chuck, Lam Kin Foo, Lum Kin Foo, Hom, Lim Goon Wing, Lim Gin Foo, Gin Foo Lin, Koon Wing Lim, Henry Chin, Lim Ying Chuck, Lim Ah Wing, et al.

Much of my scholarship brings together intellectual, political, and personal sides of my life. None so more than this chapter.

In my activist days in San Francisco before my academic career, I met Hom Ah Wing (1907–1986), a.k.a. Happy Lim, the subject of this essay. He was then in the senior years in life but was still passionately committed to movements for racial justice and anti-imperialism. In his younger days, he had been a union organizer and member of the Communist Party of

"The Many Sides of Happy Lim: aka Hom Ah Wing, Lin Jian Fu, Happy Lum, Lin Chien Fu, Hom Yen Chuck, Lam Kin Foo, Lum Kin Foo, Hom, Lim Goon Wing, Lim Gin Foo, Gin Foo Lin, Koon Wing Lim, Henry Chin, Lim Ying Chuck, Lim Ah Wing, et al.," *Amerasia Journal* (34:2) 2008: 70–98. © 2019 The Regents of the University of California, reprinted by permission of Informa UK Limited, trading as Taylor & Francis Group, www .tandfonline.com, on behalf of The Regents of the University of California. (Illustrations accompanying the original article are not included in this volume.)

262   *Chapter Fourteen*

the U.S.A. He presented himself as a cultural worker, wrote short stories and poetry, and painted as a self-taught artist. He was taciturn, even enigmatic in talking about himself. He was hard to get to know despite his cheery nickname. He blended in with the many other aging men and women who frequented Portsmouth Square in the heart of San Francisco Chinatown. He was among the most prominent "proletarian intellectuals" among Chinese Americans in the mid- to late twentieth century.

After he died alone and poor in a San Francisco residence hotel, a friend of his collected his personal belongings, including a sizeable archive of writing. She shared them, and I committed myself to memorialize Happy Lim by writing a biography and publishing some of his written work. During this endeavor, I was astonished to learn from the FBI files released to me that immigration authorities believed he had entered the country in the early twentieth century under false pretenses to evade the long-standing legislation excluding Chinese. His claims, I learned, included a direct relationship with my great grandfather in California that allowed him to enter the country! We were "paper relatives." I so lamented the opportunity we might have had to really get to know one another, talk family, and share stories about activism and advancing justice.

He wrote in English and in Chinese. The poems I translated from his private manuscripts were among scores he composed from the 1930s to the 1970s. They express his bitter alienation from American life and his anguish about racism against Asians and African Americans. He admired revolutionary China and lamented his long separation from his land of ancestry. In these ways, he expressed the feelings shared by many others in his generational cohort. From his cramped quarters in bachelor hotels in Chinatown, he, as a shipyard laborer, restaurant helper, and cannery union organizer, fiercely condemned exploitation, imperialism, racism, and war. He was a remarkable voice in the cultural history of Chinese Americans in the twentieth century and a forebear to the many contemporary Asian American activists. Fighting injustice has a long lineage in Asia America, as Happy Lim exemplifies.

∗

Known to the FBI, INS, and IRS as Mr. Ah Wing Hom, he was also Lin Jian Fu, Jian Fu (Tough Guy), or just Fu to the readers of the many poems and short stories he published in Chinese over four decades in the twentieth century. And to still others, primarily English-readers of his writing, he was Happy Lim, an ironic, even tragically bizarre name, as his life was far from pleasant. On New Year's Day 1986, he died alone in a dingy San Francisco Chinatown bachelor hotel suffering from a bacterial infection and a chronic blood disorder that had required the amputation of all his toes the year before. He was seventy-eight years of age and had spent most of his life within blocks of where he died.[1]

Though he is not as widely read today as he was during his lifetime, he is still celebrated, even revered, as an inspiring voice from an older generation of Chinese American social activists and radical cultural workers. In fact, he has acquired a new audience of primarily English-readers interested in voices from the past. He wrote for more than half a century, producing an extraordinarily rich and unusual body of poetry and nonfiction writing, based loosely on his own difficult life as a poor service worker in San Francisco. He was affiliated with the organized left for most of these years and wrote about life in a capitalist society, international events, and personal tribulations. He called for revolutionary courage and sought sympathetic understanding for his own difficulties that he faced in life. Since his death, songs and odes have been written of him and pieces of his writing continue to be reproduced.[2] In the late 1960s and early 1970s, when the emerging Asian American movement searched for heroes from the past who could inspire a new generation of antiracist, anti-imperialist activists, Happy Lim and others emerged as living evidence of the history of resistance to oppression, proof that the newborn Asian American radicalism was not anomalous but deeply connected to history and community. Lim assumed an honored place alongside Yuri Kochiyama, Karl Yoneda, Carlos Bulosan, Philip Vera Cruz, and other ideological ancestors.

Unlike the others whom many of today's activists befriended or studied, Lim remained aloof and enigmatic. There were several reasons for this: for one, he communicated almost exclusively in Chinese and he preferred to keep mainly to the poor, male residents of San Francisco Chinatown. For another, even to those friends who thought they knew him, Lim always

264   *Chapter Fourteen*

remained a "mystery man." The FBI and INS, which had expended an extraordinary effort to investigate Happy Lim over many years, were also never confident they really knew who he was. One of his employers once told the INS that Lim had "no friends or enemies because he doesn't mix with anyone." An old friend of Lim, questioned by a federal agent, described him as a "lone wolf type."[3]

Happy Lim offered many accounts of his coming to America and life here, but the information he gave, such as dates and affiliations, varied widely, and not just to government agencies but to friends as well. The following biographical sketch appears to be reasonably accurate, however, and draws from family correspondence, government documents, recorded interviews with Lim, and his own writing. Still, many questions about his life remain and will probably never be fully resolved.

According to information he provided the Immigration Service on many occasions under interrogation or in legal applications and to friends, Lim was born in November 1907 in Nam How Village, Hoy Ping District, in the Pearl River Delta of Guangdong Province, China. He first came to the United States at the age of sixteen, in 1922, under the name of Hom Ah Wing, and requested admission as a United States citizen by virtue of the native-born status of his father. Lim was held at the immigration processing station at Angel Island in San Francisco Bay, where on June 22, immigration agents interrogated Lim and his father. At the hearing, Lim's father claimed, and produced considerable supporting evidence, including statements from "reputable" whites, that he, the father, had been born in 1880 in Marysville, California, the entry point to the Sierra Nevada Gold Country, and that Lim was his true son. The hearing went well and Lim was admitted to the country as a U.S. citizen. His legal status allowed him to travel out of the country easily and he visited China twice, once from 1923 to 1926 and a second time from 1927 to 1929. During the first trip, he apparently started a family, though his wife and son never came to the United States. Over the years, American officials consistently accepted his citizenship and allowed him to re-enter the country with few questions. He apparently never again left the country after 1929.[4]

Happy Lim says he lived in Marysville and San Francisco in the 1920s. He received just a few months of schooling in English in a Christian church-run school and had not much more education in China. But he decided to use Chinese as his primary language and, by personal choice, he never developed his English, even as he worked among English-speakers for most of his life. As late as the 1980s, he still spoke only rudimentary English, wrote entirely in Chinese, had a preparer complete his simple annual income tax return, and relied on the bilingual services of San Francisco's Chinese Hospital to attend to his failing health.

Little is known about his life during his early years and about how he affiliated with the left in the United States but there are some tantalizing suggestions. Late in life, Lim claimed that he had attended the famed Sun Yat-sen University for the Toilers of China in Moscow, which was a center of Soviet efforts to influence Chinese revolutionaries, for a year in the late 1920s.[5] The Russians had opened the school in the fall of 1925 to honor Sun and hundreds of hopeful and energetic Chinese traveled to Moscow to enroll; many future leaders in both the Chinese Communist and Nationalist Parties attended as students. Among them were Deng Xiaoping, Ye Jianying, Chen Bota, Yang Shangkun, and even Chiang Ching-kuo, Chiang Kai-shek's son. The school offered a general university-level curriculum as well as courses in communism but was short-lived and closed in late 1930. There is little confirming evidence for Lim's claim about attendance, but it is entirely plausible. Immigration records do show him as being away from the United States for almost two years, from 1927 to 1929 and Canton, where he went, was a center of revolutionary activity in China at this time. Students, supported by money from the Chinese Communist Party, traveled by ship from Canton to Vladisovtok and then by train to Moscow. Interestingly, Lim's family in China has no record or memory of him being in China during this time,[6] but Lim might have deliberately never informed his family of his journey. The memoirs of one who had attended the University mention that some of his fellow students had in fact come from the United States and countries other than China.[7] Though the released FBI documents on Lim do not reveal an affiliation between Lim and Sun Yat-sen University, and even mention that the CIA had nothing on Lim, the well-known Japanese American communist Karl Yoneda claimed in fact that Lim had attended Sun Yat-sen University.[8]

As for his writing, Lim recalled that he began to write poetry around 1930 and sent his work to *Chinese Vanguard*, the organ of the All-America

266   *Chapter Fourteen*

Alliance of Chinese Anti-Imperialists which began publishing in New York City in 1930. It was the "national voice" of the Chinese Marxist Left for a number of years, according to Him Mark Lai.[9] In the 1980s, Lim said that he had turned to the left because he had lived in "hunger and cold and felt deeply depressed" but was inspired by those who sought change. He said that he "admired the ambitions and progressive thoughts of this great time, as well as the people of high character who lived them." He remembered:

> I could not but believe and follow them to fight for the truth and a brighter future. I remember that on a silent night, I decided to dry my tears and start to write, epitomizing, in my poems, the rigor and bitterness of reality, as well as advocating that we must work with the suffering and progressive people of our time to strive for a better place to live. As for myself, I had to continue to write.[10]

He said that he joined the Communist Party, USA in 1930, although he later told the FBI he had been in the Party for just several years during World War II. Other sources say that he was in the Party into the 1950s and Lim himself once said that he was in the Party until 1959.[11] Although it is difficult to reconstruct an accurate history of Lim's organizational affiliations, it is clear that he affiliated himself with the Left in the early 1930s. Karl Yoneda, who joined the CP in the mid-1920s, recalled that he met Lim in Alaska, where Lim worked in the salmon canneries. Yoneda says he met Lim in a communist cell meeting in Alaska at the end of 1935 and the two often went out to have meals together. Yoneda said that Lim had already been traveling to Alaska for several years. A problem with Yoneda's account, however, is that according to his memoir, *Ganbatte,* Yoneda first went to Alaska in 1938.[12]

Lim in one of his own memoirs recalled his involvement with various leftwing Chinese organizations after the start of the Great Depression in 1929 and suggests a specific reason for his turn to the Left. The Chinese community in those years, he recalled, "was one full of economic oppression. It was a hard time to find a job and it was a time of racial discrimination." In a recollection published in 1982, Lim remembered, "many of the scenes of that time still stir up strong feelings within me. My strongest impression is one of many people out of work and little shops unable to survive. Even for myself who was single, I did not know where I would stand from one day to the next. It was this kind of hardship that threw me into struggle and led me to follow a revolutionary path." He said that he even helped organize the Chinatown contingent in the 1934 San Francisco general strike demonstration.[13]

Happy Lim remembered that young activists staged "propaganda forums on the street corners [of Chinatown] to educate people about exploitation, oppression and the unemployment suffered by workers." One of these activists was a man named Javier Dea (Ja Chong), one of the early leaders of the Chinese left in the United States who rather than face deportation left the country for the Soviet Union in 1932. In 1981, Ja Chong poignantly recalled the difficulties the Chinese community in San Francisco faced during the Depression. "Chinese were living out of Portsmouth Square and on the Streets," he wrote. "Little babies had no milk to drink." He staged street forums, which he says eventually attracted crowds of hundreds who would hear him explain that "the capitalist system caused unemployment by exploiting workers, over-production and surplus value."[14]

In October 1937, Lim and other young activists organized the Chinese Workers Mutual Aid Association, which became the most important political organization of the Left in San Francisco's Chinatown. Returned cannery workers from Alaska, like Lim, formed the core of the organization, which attracted a membership of 600. "Workers from the restaurants, laundries, sewing trades, farms, seafaring workers and longshoremen joined," Lim recalled. It was a "workers mass organization" and engaged in "propaganda and education for Chinese workers." Lim served as the organization's secretary.[15] A few years later he helped organize the New Chinese Alphabetized Language Study Society that was more cultural in orientation. The group promoted the modernization of the Chinese language and the reform of the writing system, in themselves radical propositions at the time. The group, which was the first left-wing youth group in Chinatown, quickly attracted a wide following and expanded its activities beyond language reform. The group sponsored singing and drama groups, which performed for the public, including a play named "Drifting Life." According to Lim, it told about the bitter life of the Chinese in America and received a "tremendous reception by the people," when it was staged

268   Chapter Fourteen

in Chinatown. Lim proudly remembered that "We didn't waste our time on parties or in the midst of red-and-green light drinking. We spent our youthful time [doing] some meaningful work."[16] About this same time, Happy Lim was also arrested by the San Francisco police in a Pine Street hotel for smoking opium. Though he denied the charges, he was thrown in jail overnight and placed on probation for thirty days. He never mentioned this embarrassment to interviewers later in life, but he did once say that he had been arrested for "disturbing the peace."[17] He had no other local criminal record.

Happy Lim and other Chinatown leftists engaged in a variety of political and cultural work during these years. They worked with the organized labor movement to seek improvements in the lives of Chinese working and unemployed people; they held English and Mandarin classes and organized singing, dancing, and other cultural groups to promote what they understood of the emerging revolutionary culture in China and in America. They also worked to support China's resistance to Japanese aggression. Among the prominent intellectual influences on him that Lim listed were the famous scholar of modern Chinese linguistics, Chao Yuen-ren (who later pursued his career at Harvard and UC Berkeley), and Chinese writers such as Mao Dun, Ba Jin, Guo Mojo, Lu Xun, and Mao Zedong. He admired Maxim Gorky and mourned the writer's mysterious death in 1936. Lim's "In Memory of Gorky," begins:

> As if a star has fallen from the sky,
> As if the sun has forever set.
> Gorky,
> You departed us so suddenly.

Among American writers, Lim favored Jack London and Ernest Hemingway, but it was Walt Whitman whom he most celebrated. In a preface to a collection of his own poetry that he had hoped to publish, Lim called Whitman, "the most important poet in the history of American literature." "The poet is the voice of freedom," Lim cites Whitman from the *Leaves of Grass*.[18]

In his own poetry, Lim wrote in free verse and eschewed classical Chinese styles, though in his later years he occasionally introduced classical allusions to his writing. He wrote exclusively in colloquial, simple, Chinese.

His audience, especially in his pre-1970s writing, was other leftwing "overseas Chinese" who supported the communist movement in China and were deeply alienated from America. His writings reveal one who was remarkably self-taught, widely read, and deeply devoted to the discipline of writing. Happy Lim was perhaps the most important organic intellectual among Chinese in America.

With the outbreak of war in 1941, Lim registered for the draft but never served in the military.[19] In the war years, Happy Lim found employment outside of his familiar Chinatown. He worked as kitchen help in downtown restaurants, uptown elite men's clubs, and naval shipyards at Hunter's Point, in southern San Francisco, and in Marin County. He worked in unskilled occupations (bus boy, dishwasher, fitter) his whole life. At the same time, he wrote regularly during the war years, the subject of his poems being major events such as the fall of Rome and Berlin and the liberation of Paris. He wrote about the Chinese people's resistance to Japan's invasion and the subsequent civil war between the Nationalists and Communists. He wrote about the life and struggles of Chinese in America. But it was his celebration of the victory of the Chinese Communists that appears to have brought him to the attention of the FBI, which then monitored him regularly afterward. In August 1949, Lim published "Welcoming the Free and Independent Democratic New China," which the agency translated for its records. In the long article, Lim hailed the triumph of the Chinese Communists: "The Chinese democratic revolution—opposing imperialism, feudalism and a wealthy class of officials—must complete its advance," he wrote. "The new China is being born!"[20] On October 9, a week after Mao Zedong had proclaimed the founding of the People's Republic of China, Lim and other members of the Mutual Aid Association organized a public celebration of the event at the Chinese American Citizens' Alliance Hall in San Francisco. Rightwing thugs broke up the meeting and attacked the audience. The next day, rightists passed out flyers marking fifteen leaders of the left by name for death. Happy Lim's name was prominently listed among them.[21]

Several months later, Lim published several fictional vignettes about the Korean War that broke out in June 1950. His stories encouraged support for the communist cause or sympathy for those Americans who had lost loved ones in what he saw as an unjust, imperialist war of aggression. But local federal authorities couldn't establish the basic facts about Lim's identity.

270   *Chapter Fourteen*

San Francisco FBI agents reported to their superiors in Washington that they had "encountered considerable difficulty in ascertaining the identity of Lim insofar as birth or naturalization, previous employment, and residence in the United States" and asked the central office for help. It could provide none.[22]

Nevertheless, the FBI, because of his political views, placed Lim on its "Security Index," which identified communists and other leftists the agency deemed possibly dangerous in the event of international conflict. In 1955, when Lim was placed on the Security Index, he joined 104 other "individuals of Chinese extraction," mainly in New York and San Francisco, whom the FBI determined it would monitor closely and constantly. In order to be able to "move immediately" against the thirty-six aliens and "increase and intensify the coverage" of the sixty-nine citizens, the FBI 's central office directed its field agents to report on the first of every month the "exact whereabouts of each subject" or the efforts being made to locate the subject." The FBI removed and then reinstated Lim on the list, as it was concerned about possible domestic repercussions arising from the 1955 offshore island confrontation between the United States and China. The agency kept him on the list until 1966 when it deemed he no longer fit their threat profile.[23]

In April 1956, FBI agents, seeking to gather more information on Lim, walked right into the CMWAA headquarters and directly questioned Lim. They asked a variety of probing questions of a personal and political nature. Lim tried to deflect their interrogation by claiming that he was interested only in "folk dancing" and not politics. He offered them fictions that he had a son who was in the U.S. Air Force, though he did not know his current whereabouts and had no contact with him, and two other sons, one in China and another in the United States, but had no contact with them either. He denied ever being in the Communist Party or in the Communist Political Association and said, as he had a poor memory, that he could not remember any of the names of individuals involved in the Mutual Aid Association. Lim's behavior heightened the suspicions of the agents, who reported to their superiors that they found Lim "very evasive." Though they conceded it was "unprofessional," the agents gave their own personal impressions of Lim: he was, in their way of thinking, "perhaps a 'mental case' due to his peculiar reactions, emotions, and in general, the manner in which he conducted himself physically." Years later, Happy Lim himself described this meeting with the FBI agents. He said they asked about his

The Many Sides of Happy Lim 271

financial support of the *China Daily News,* the leading Chinese leftist newspaper in the country and in which he had published, and what he thought about "New China." He said that he simply answered that he was not interested in politics, but only in literature, writing, painting, and dancing. "Good for us, good for you," the FBI agent responded, according to Lim.[24] His problematic effort to deceive the FBI however only served to increase the agency's concerns. They continued to monitor his activities, including watching his coming and going from his Chinatown residence and intercepting his personal mail.

But how he described himself was not totally false. He was deeply committed to his cultural work and was devoted to his social dancing. Karl Yoneda intimated that Lim was actually never a political leader or organizer. And many years later, one of his female dance partners shared recollections of him that provide curious insights into a part of the non-political side of his life. It was not only the FBI that found him hard to understand and enigmatic, but so did his "lady friends."

Though temporally unspecific in recollection, Helen Herrick recalled Happy Lim very well when she wrote me in 1989. He was "Happy Lim" to her when they knew each other as regular members of Changs International Folk Dancers, founded in San Francisco in 1938 as the first club devoted to understanding and practicing folk dancing from around the globe, especially from Central Europe and the Balkans.[25] As early as 1956 Lim had told the FBI that he was an "avid folk dancer" and danced "every night of the week."

At some point, Happy Lim and Herrick became regular partners at the club functions, though they seemed to have had no contact with one another away from the dance floor. "He was a quiet man, unobtrusive, but determined to learn the dances," recalled Herrick. "This he did, and when dancing with him, a partner must never question his lead. He said not a word, grimaced slightly, and led his partner where she was supposed to go without comment, a sort of a 'Pardon me, Lady, but we will do it this way.'"

He was very polite but seldom uttered a word, always smiled, and at Christmas time, came bringing (to the club's Christmas party) a card for each of his favorites, and each card, in an envelope, contained a dollar bill. If he was pathetic, he was also admirable, and though I felt many club members pitied him, I always felt that there was a very interesting story, that his life

272   Chapter Fourteen

had been beset by many problems, and that he had not always been the man I knew. I thought he was perhaps emotionally shredded by incidents in his past life, that he had been a victim of uncontrollable events, and that he was simply making the best of what was left of his person, his personality and his physical health. Happy Lim was gracious to everyone, he simply came to Changs for the recreation and it may have been his only outlet.

Herrick, herself a writer on western history and California Indians, was clearly very fond of Lim, but offered no other specifics about his life. "I am aware that many considered Happy Lim just another old Chinaman, but to me, and to my [autistic] son, he was always someone very special."[26]

Lim's platonic relationship with Herrick raises a dimension of Lim's life that has never been examined previously: his continuing infatuation with women. A good many of Lim's poems and prose are melodramatic stories of relationships he has with women, mainly white women from the physical descriptions he gives, and sometimes Asian, notably later in his life when he encountered Asian American women activists. Most of his tales are quite sentimental, even romantic, though none ever narrate or even suggest any physical involvement. Lim idealized his women friends, and embroidered them with warmth, kindness, beauty, and political sentiments that moved his heart. For him, they appeared to embody all that was good and beautiful in life. One of his poems, "Dream of a River," typically interweaves his fascination with a woman with his own political ideals, and ends:

> You deeply care for the sorrow of the destitute
> Truthful feelings spill from your heart
> On the path to go forward
> I recall the wave of your red skirt.[27]

Lim's attitude toward his women subjects is reminiscent of Carlos Bulosan's encounters with some of the white women in *America Is In The Heart,* though without the sexual component. Unlike Bulosan, almost all of Lim's female subjects are political co-travelers though occasionally a white woman appears as a grieving lover or relative of an American serviceman killed overseas. She serves as a device for Lim to condemn the price of imperialism for everyday Americans. Many of Lim's subjects appear to be flights of fancy, though some of his latter poetry does seem to be based on actual individuals. White American male subjects rarely appear in his work.

By the early 1960s, the FBI's suspicion of Happy Lim and the INS's Confession Program that sought to dismantle the elaborate historical structure based on "paper sons" and illegal entry into the country, joined together; the state began deportation proceedings against Lim on January 12, 1962. Federal agencies accused Lim of having ties with the Communist Party and related groups far beyond the World War II years and of falsely claiming United States citizenship when he first entered the country in 1922. Happy Lim, who entered the country with the name Hom Ah Wing had claimed that his father, Hom Aw Wing (aka Hom Ah Lim), had been born in the United States, which made him a native-born citizen. Happy Lim, therefore, had claimed a derived U.S. citizenship status through his alleged American-born father. The immigration authorities countered, claiming that Hom Aw Wing was a fictitious name for a man named Lim Fung Guey, who had *not* been born in the United States and in fact was himself in the country fraudulently as the "paper son" of a man named Hom Hock Fun.

Here I must interject a side-note: Hom Hock Fun is a true name and true person. In addition to being Happy Lim's claimed grandfather, he was in actuality my maternal great grandfather, who lived in Marysville, California from the 1850s until his death in 1907. He was a storekeeper and leading member of the Chinese community in Marysville for years, had had four wives, and many children, one of whom Lim said was his father. According to his claims, Happy Lim, therefore, was my granduncle. Although he and I were acquainted with one another through our involvement in the San Francisco Chinatown left in the 1970s and 1980s, we never had any idea that we were "related" and "family." I learned of the fictive relationship (the government seems to have gotten it right) only after Happy Lim had died and I had obtained his government files, which revealed that in the 1960s the INS had questioned a number of people, whose the names and identities I recognized immediately, about Happy Lim.[28] Unexpectedly reading the names of my aunts and uncles in FBI and INS reports on Happy Lim was shocking. What interesting conversations Happy Lim and I could have had!

The problem with the government's case, however, was that it had accepted Lim's claim back in 1922 when he had first entered and then twice again when he re-entered the country from trips to China. The government acknowledged that Lim had then resided in the country continuously since

274   *Chapter Fourteen*

1929. Federal authorities also considered trying to deport Lim on the basis that he was a subversive, but did not proceed as they were aware they had a weak case. The FBI was unwilling to release the most vital information it had on Lim as it was "confidential" and from sources the agency did not want to reveal. The government vigorously pursued the case for four years, during which it questioned scores of persons across the country, from New York to Oregon about what they knew about Lim. The INS interrogated Lim himself repeatedly, including in September 1964 when Him Mark Lai, then a young member of the Chinatown left and today the pioneering historian of Chinese Americans, served as his translator. Ultimately, the government dropped its case when Happy Lim conceded his questionable identity in exchange for the government accepting his own application in June 1965 for regularized, permanent resident status under provisions contained in the Immigration and Nationality Act of 1957. This legislation was popularly known as the Refugee-Escapee Act, which Congress had passed principally to assist immigrants from Communist nations, but the Act also contained provisions that allowed the Attorney General to grant permanent residency status to those individuals who had falsely claimed U.S. citizenship if they confessed their perjury and fraud. Whether Lim was troubled by his own use of provisions in this Cold War legislation is not known. As late as 1985, he told an interviewer that he was not a U.S. citizen and had no U.S. passport.[29]

The birth of a new leftwing movement in Chinatown in the late 1960s must have delighted Lim, who along with the other activists of the older generation gradually associated themselves with the various organizations that operated out of storefronts and basements along Kearny Street in San Francisco. The old and new activists embraced one another: for the old activists, the young radicals vindicated their long-held and beleaguered visions. For the new activists, some from the local community and others who came from college campuses, the old activists provided direct ties to history and community. The old and young inspired each other and shared their idealized notions of communist possibilities, which included visions of class, national, and anti-racist struggle in America and of anti-imperialist victory and socialism in Asia.

Happy Lim enjoyed the new attention he received, as one who could offer personal recollections about past struggles, old organizations, and long-held dreams. He wrote about the glory days of the Alaska cannery workers movement and the Chinese Workers Mutual Aid Association. He found new outlets for his poetry and short stories and he enjoyed the camaraderie and social life offered by the new activists. His writing, heavily influenced by the florid rhetoric from China's Cultural Revolution of the late 1960s, celebrated the so-called proletarian culture emanating from China as well as the activism of the young radicals he saw around him. But by the latter 1970s, his writing assumed a more subdued and reflective tone and he began to write nostalgically about his past experiences and his continuing hopes for a better future, long delayed. He became a contributing editor to the political/cultural periodical *East Wind* and wrote regularly for *Shidai bao,* a major left newspaper in San Francisco. In 1985, in one of his last essays before he died, he wrote, "I have long discarded decadent romanticism and any imaginary hopes to console myself. Instead, I devoted myself to calling for help for the poor and the needy while living under the same conditions they do, sharing their hardships and happiness."[30]

Though in his seventies, he continued to work as kitchen help in downtown restaurants and as a service worker at the St. Francis Hospital. He passed much of his free time frequenting the political organizations along Kearny Street beneath the International Hotel, where he cut an unusual and anomalous figure among the pea- coated, long-haired young radicals and the old-time Chinese and Filipino bachelor workers. He favored dressing smartly, favoring an early 1950s style of well-cut woolen suits, ties, and two-tone leather dress shoes. In public, he looked like he just came out of a Humphrey Bogart movie. He never spoke publicly at the many rallies, celebrations, and cultural events held along Kearny Street and often seemed a bit amused by the new, young, Left.

In the early 1980s, he appeared less and less frequently along Chinatown's streets and few knew that he was suffering from an increasingly debilitating blood disorder that destroyed his toes and his dancing feet, and eventually contributed to his death. He lived alone in Room 109 of the St. Paul's Hotel, a seedy residence hotel at 935 Kearny Street, just a block away from the famed International Hotel and where he had lived for most of the past forty years. When he died, an old friend wrote a brief obituary on him, saluting him as a longtime fighter for Chinese Americans. He was impoverished, the obituary said, and asked friends to donate funds for his funeral, as Happy Lim had lived only on a meager pension during the five years before his death. Lim, the obituary stated, "was single and had no relatives

276   *Chapter Fourteen*

by his side." His death certificate and income tax filings found in the things that he left behind provided a different story however. Lim long claimed Wan Yan Ng in China as his wife. He had a son in China too. A grandson in China wrote that Happy Lim had sent money back to China to support his wife and relatives up to a year before his death.[31] Lim was cremated and his ashes sent to China for burial.

Happy Lim wrote simply, with occasional allusions to Chinese or western canonical writing. He composed free verse poetry, vignettes of experiences, cultural commentary,[32] and memoir. His writing was strongly personal in tone and drew seemingly from personal experience and current events. Though he usually used first person voice in his writing, it is impossible to know to what extent his accounts were based on his actual experiences.

Appendix

The Poems

The following poems, all written in free verse, were among dozens that Happy Lim kept in his personal papers. In addition to poetry, Happy Lim wrote many vignettes and a few short stories, each numbering only a handful of pages. Like the verse, Lim's prose is highly personal, though it is unclear as to the extent they were closely autobiographical. Almost all his writing was written as first person narratives and most appear to be based to some degree on direct personal experience. He once wrote that his purpose in writing was to express his "inner most emotions." Much of the subject material, including certain incidents in the 1970s–1980s, is familiar to this author and conforms to his recollections about events, persons, and places. Though awkward word choices and constructions appear in his earlier pieces, Lim's writing became more sophisticated and polished through the years. Happy Lim regularly used simplified versions of characters, with occasional traditional renderings. Some characters are illegible or were incorrectly written.

These poems were selected with consideration given to presenting a sense of Happy Lim's long writing career, representative subject matter, quality of writing, style, and social and political views, in addition to their possible appeal to today's audience. Unless noted, the translations are my own, completed with the assistance of Yi-ren Chen and Philip Thai.

"Mother" and "Tokyo Elegy"

These are two of twenty-five poems that Happy Lim gathered together to publish in a volume entitled "Under the Bright Sun," though it appears never to have been completed and never published. His Introduction to the volume, which is dated November 2, 1962, says that he completed most of these poems during World War II. Several had been published before. The poems describe his longing for home (their titles provide an idea of their content: "On the Shore of the Ocean," "To the Motherland"), his feelings about the anti-fascist struggle around the world ("Mourning Rome," "An Elegy to Berlin," "Remembering Paris") and his admiration for the revolutionary movement in China and its victory in 1949 ("Unforgettable Memories," "Looking toward the Distant Motherland"). The volume ends with several poems supporting the communist forces in Korea and condemning U.S. imperialism.

It is not known when Happy Lim wrote "Mother," though it may have been in the mid- or late 1930s. In the volume that he intended to publish, he grouped it with several other poems with the same title and which expressed his anguish in hearing of Maxim Gorky's death in 1936. Gorky was a giant in Russian literature and a strong supporter of Bolshevism. He is credited as being the founder of socialist realism in writing. Gorky's novel "Mother" appeared in 1906 when Gorky was touring the United States. The story recounts a peasant woman's growing sympathy for the radical visions of her son and the rise of her own revolutionary consciousness during the Russian Revolution of 1905. "Mother" appeared in a Chinese translation at least in 1930 and Happy Lim most likely read it in Chinese. Lim probably wrote his poem sometime in the 1930s.

Mother

Outside my window the moon's dim light falls
All is still without a sound
At moments like this most are sound asleep
As I read Gorky's "Mother" I think of my own mother.

Mother, my loving, dear mother,
You are anxious for your child wandering rootless!
But your child adrift thousands of miles away
What can he do to comfort your lonely heart?

Who knows how many years have passed
Since your child left your embrace;
Who knows how many years have passed
Since your child wandered away into the distant world.

The circumstances in a foreign land
Have moved me to enter the battlefield of life;
The circumstances in a foreign land
Have also made your mark on me indelible.

Mother, my loving, dear mother,
You have nourished me;
Even though I now wander in a foreign land,
I do not forget you for a moment.

Your earnest teaching I will never forget
Your sad, gentle voice, heartfelt, I will never forget.
Oh, mother loving, dear mother
You taught me to go forth to cherish others, to have compassion
    for others, to help others.

Tokyo Elegy (August 1945)

The paper carried good news,
It says that the last fortress of the Axis powers has surrendered,
With overwhelming joy in my heart,
I read this piece of good news.

Ah, Tokyo, you were truly a wonderful, famous city,
Rich with refinement and romance,
But in the hands of the sadistic war mongers,
You walked toward the abyss of extinction.

The various war lords before boasted "bushido" before the world,
Now they all one by one shrink back like docile sheep,
Is this bravery, is this bushido?
We must wait for a later generation's judgment.

It is you war mongers who filled the sky with wind and clouds,
It is you who [filled] the wind with the stench of carrion and the rain
   of blood,
It is you who filled China's vast lands everywhere with desolation,
It is you who made World War II drag on and on.

How many people under your hands were made homeless,
How many cities were reduced to ashes under your hands,
How many children lost their fathers and mothers under your hands,
How many souls weep and cry, wailing, suffering under your hands.
Ah! You have oppressed and bullied the Chinese people for more
   than half a century,
You have used armed violence to violate China's lands for over 8 years,
However, before the powerful counter offensive of the Chinese people
and the heroic People's Liberation Army,
You finally submitted, forced to surrender.

This is a great victory for humanity,
This returns the world to light,
This is the downfall of the dark age,
This is the end of the instigators of war

Ah, Tokyo, on this day that you surrender on your knees,
The memories of cruel and savage actions from the past surface,
I do feel sadness at your disgrace,
But I also rejoice for the rebirth of the Japanese people.

Ah, Tokyo, I am now thinking about the growing ranks of the
   Japanese people,
They will stand up indomitably,
To rebuild a democratic and free Japan,
Which will protect the peace of the Far East and of the world.

280   *Chapter Fourteen*

This Happened in America

This is Happy Lim's account of the horrific murder of Emmett Till, a fourteen-year-old African American boy killed in a small Mississippi delta town in the summer of 1955. Till, who was from Chicago and unfamiliar with the racial order in the deep South, was visiting relatives when he, as the standard account goes, whistled at a white woman. Four days later in the middle of the night, the woman's husband and his half-brother drove up to the home of Till's uncle, where the boy was staying, and abducted him. Several days later, Till's brutally disfigured body was found in the Tallahatchie River. He had been shot, beaten, and his face mutilated. Till's mother returned his body to Chicago and decided to hold an open-coffin viewing to display the savagery of the racism that killed her son to the world. Thousands attended and *Jet* magazine published photographs of Till's tortured face. Their dramatic publication is now described as the initial spark of the civil rights movement. Though Till's murderers were tried, an all-white jury acquitted them. The two men later publicly admitted their guilt.

Happy Lim wrote this poem on the back on some scrap paper and it appears to be a work in progress; some words and lines were crossed-over and a few phrases are incomplete. The handwriting is quick and rough; there is no date. Although Happy Lim's account generally follows what he could have learned from reading press accounts of Till's murder, the poem also deviates significantly from the known events, especially in the description of Till's encounter with the racists and his abduction. The poem appears to have been written not long after the end of the trial, which was at the end of September 1955. I thank Chao Fen Sun for reading a version of this translation.

> **This Happened in America** (ca. 1955)
> In Mississippi's north
> The Tallahatchie River flows freely,
> Murmuring and singing,
> Reflecting images of the verdant forest along its two banks. An endless melody,
> It was early morning in late summer,
> When a child's corpse suddenly came forth from the river's depths,
> Waking the meadow from its dreamy slumber,

The Tallahatchie River is given a song of despair.
Naked, his clothes were ripped away,
His body covered with wounds,
Iron wires trussed his body,
The killers must have wanted the corpse at the river's bottom.

Aiiieee, a child of just fourteen years,
Suddenly ripped away from the warmth of life,
The river's eternal flowing
Mourned the unspeakable tragedy of his end.

Sadly, this child's name was Till,
But oh, any name would do,
Because, as it is, this happened in America,
And he is a symbol, you know, of every black person.

He was a youngster from Chicago,
Who came down South to visit his great-Uncle Wright,
He helped his Uncle Wright pick cotton
So he could bring some money back home to his mother.

One day after work
He went to Leonardo's store to buy candy,
Jeering erupted all around him as he walked the street,
His ears smothered, it seemed, by derision,
Hearing people insult him.
But he just ignored them,
And alone walked straight ahead,
With darkness descending over the town's streets,

He hoped to be able to return to his Uncle's safe home.
Then, late that night,
Violent pounding on the door woke Till from his dreams.
There was wild shouting and screaming,
Waking everyone who had been soundly sleeping.
"I'm coming!"
Uncle Wright forcefully responded from the next room.

Chapter Fourteen

He hurriedly dressed,
And went into the child's room.

"Where's that kid from Chicago?"
"Where's the little nigger who whistled at Mrs. Bryant?"
The two whites grew more and more fierce,
Like hungry wolves finding prey to satisfy their hunger.

"What are you up to?
Is whistling a crime?"
The two thugs pulled out weapons from their pockets,
And dragged Till from his bed.

Oh, the bleakness of night
Swallowed up the spirit of this young one from an oppressed race,
Only from the flashlights that the two thugs held
Could one make out the path ahead.

Uncle Wright stepped up his pace,
Rushing to follow the tracks of the wolves.
But, searching high and low,
Where could he find the boy in the darkness?

Uncle Wright's fear mounted, like a driving rain,
His heart bearing indescribable pain.
He lifted his head into the piercing wind, calling out
"Till, my boy, oh will you ever be able to return?"
He damned the threat to young Till's life.

How could one have known that in the morning three days later,
The Tallahatchie would give up a body of one from an oppressed race;
It was Till's!
Uncle Wright's suffering was unbearable, like daggers piercing his
    heart.

When the child's body was sent back to his home in Chicago,
Crowds of people surrounded the boy's corpse and mourned,

The Many Sides of Happy Lim   283

Crowds of people were furious at the brutality displayed,
Tears without end streamed down from his mother's eyes.

Child, your death was so cruel and barbaric,	Child, what crime did you commit?
How could your killer be so savage,	Your death so pointless,
How can I bear the pain!	Oh, how could the killer be so crazed?
How can I bear the pain!	How could you endure it?

Till's eyes were opened wide,
As though he might have been thinking: this atrocity must be
   avenged!
His lips were stiff and unmoving
Perhaps saying: the murderers must be brought to justice!
But incredibly the killers were found not guilty,
The police let the murderers free,
How can it be that the lives of black people are worth nothing?
How can it be that black people live to be butchered by others?

What kind of society is this? What kind of world?
I too was born unto this human world,
I too am someone!
Why is it then that I just suffer unspeakable pain and anguish?

Caribbean Dawn

In 1971, Happy Lim collected a number of his poems that he wished to
publish. "Caribbean Dawn" and "Slowly Flows the Sacramento River" are
included in the volume he entitled, "On the Soil of a Strange Land."

Caribbean Dawn (April 1959)
The good news of the Cuban revolutionaries' victory arrived today,
Before my eyes, a Caribbean tidal wave roils forward,
Thunder and lightning break out amidst the surging waves,
A windstorm sweeps over the ocean.

Ah, that struggle in the Sierra Maestra,
That declaration in Havana Square,

Chapter Fourteen

That heroic roar of the people of the entire country,
How much more can I describe the surging emotions from my
    heart!

Oh heroic Cuba!
That righteous sound plays on my ear,
My heart flies with the white clouds over the ocean,
And is together with you to hail and rejoice.

Oh fighting Cuba!
You have encountered much cruel oppression,
You have experienced a hard and bitter life,
But, you also are bringing forth revolutionary fighters.

From the time that Columbus wrote your name on the map,
For their freedom, your people have continuously struggled against
    the colonizer.
Indeed, every inch of your land
Is dyed with red blood spilled for freedom and independence.

This is it!
You have smashed Batista the dictator,
Having endured long, and bitter years,
You finally walk the glorious road of sovereignty and independence.

Ah, Cuba, you are raising the banner of revolutionary struggle,
Your banner has flicked away long years of gloom,
Your banner has strengthened the resolve of the Latin American
    people,
Your banner has beckoned the Caribbean dawn!

Ah, Cuba, I hail your new life!
You are a glorious member of the new world!
How brilliant is the example you are setting for the people of Latin
    America!
You will quickly forge ahead on the road of prosperity for the
    people!

Slowly Flows the Sacramento River

Slowly flows the Sacramento River,
Winding through the mountain passes,
Flowing along the sides of the rocky and rugged embankments,
Arriving at that distant, vast Pacific Ocean.

Slowly flows the Sacramento River,
Not far from the river bank,
There are jade-green trees,
But also houses, many and dense.

Flow, moving water, like a drifting ribbon from an auntie's
    dress,
Gently pass beneath my feet,
Then flow softly to that distant place,
Spill not even a small ripple of your torrent.

Flow, river water, send forth a sound like silver bells,
Drifting past the sides of my ears,
Just like a supple, gentle breeze,
Blowing the fragrance from atop a thicket of wild roses.

Slowly flows the Sacramento River,
The river banks hold the footprints of many of us overseas
    Chinese,
They are farmers of the fields and lumberjacks,
They are fishermen of the oceans and restaurant workers.

Tell me! Sacramento River,
In this era of "all are created equal,"
Is it that they love segregation still?
Is it that they relish yet the taste of discrimination?

Slowly flows the Sacramento River,
How long have you flowed?
How many young in the spring of life have you sent forth?
Left behind for me are unhappy memories.

I love the Sacramento River,
I love that slow moving waterway,
It endlessly weaves the beauty of nature,
Yet, the bitterness of the human world imbues it still.

Oh, slow-flowing Sacramento River,
Through your rushing waters, can you hear?
That joyous sound rising from the East,
That battle cry on the Yangzi River.
Slowly flows the Sacramento River,
Crashing through the dreary waves,
To that distant, joyful Yangzi River,
And return with the fresh scent of happiness.

Freedom

A clipping of this poem from a newspaper is in Happy Lim's papers. It may have originally appeared in the newspaper *Tuan jiebao,* perhaps in the late 1970s.

Freedom
I love life,
I believe the future should promise to eliminate sorrow and hold
    happiness in store.
But living at the turn of time,
I live a life of privation and vagrancy.

I have been abused and maltreated,
My heart is filled with many bitter memories,
I have been a victim of humiliation,
But I have never felt sorry for myself.

In the whirl and storm of struggle
I have been tempered and become stronger!
I see a majestic pine tree towering above all,
And feel that life should be as grand.

The Many Sides of Happy Lim   287

As I wander up and down the bustling street,
I seem to hear the energetic voices of progressive people,
The masses' exuberance helps dispel my melancholy,
And moves me from again indulging in self-delusion.

I am unwilling to be an oppressed slave,
I am unwilling to have my chaste body abused.
In order to obtain glorious freedom
I am willing to sacrifice all that I have for that day.

I don't know whether you are the prophet of that day,
Creating the most beautiful red clouds in the vast sky!
Or if you are a lone cold star
Illuminating only yourself.

With fervent enthusiasm
On the road of life I seek justice!
With resolution and courage
I continue to strive for freedom.

Freedom is not rhetoric,
And certainly it is not self-indulgence.
Like the penetrating light of the universe,
Freedom enters everyone's soul.

Branches and leaves will wither away in the forest,
And the human body finally will also one day decay,
But let the young enter the heat of battle,
Let our lives shine like the rosy clouds in the sky.

Why just sit quietly by yourself?
Why just feel alone and sad?
Don't you know you are an able person,
One day you will create a bright universe!

Chapter Fourteen

Watching the activists marching on the boulevard of time,
My heart feels boundless joy!
Friend! You will one day have the magnificence of freedom,
You will enjoy the dignity of freedom.

On Third Street

Happy Lim lived most of his life in a residence hotel on Kearny Street in San Francisco. About a mile's walk down Kearny one would encounter Third Street, at one time one of the seediest areas of the city. Today, after twenty years of redevelopment, the old Third Street has disappeared, replaced by the Moscone Convention Center, the Museum of Modern Art, and high-rise apartment complexes. Happy Lim would not recognize the street today.

On Third Street

The last rays of the sun have set in the west,
Fragments of sunset's glow float in the sky,
Then when twilight descends,
I walk slowly on Third Street.

I have walked along many lonely alleyways,
I have walked beneath drifting leaves on shadowed lanes,
Moonlight drapes the building facades,
The night wind plays on my body.

Here there are no skyscrapers,
Here there are no dazzling neon lights,
Here there are no fluttering skirts,
Here there are no wealthy.

I saw many poor folk,
Engaging in small-time hustling;
There were also the jobless and destitute wandering the streets,
My heart was filled with sorrow.

I walked along a small alley,
Stepping on winding stones,
In front of awnings long weathered and pealing,
A fellow in tattered clothes on the curb sings for money playing a
stringed instrument.

The fragments of the folksong,
Merge with the miserable conditions of the street;
The plaintive tune,
Cannot wipe the sorry from the pedestrian's heart.

I am not the wandering Ruan Ji,
Nor am I the grieving Byron;
But your forlorn tune
Deeply moves me.

How lonely and quiet is the night,
How dark is the night,
Following the dim street lights,
I start on the road back.

Am I So Easy to Forget

At a joyful international dance,
Amidst red flowers and light ribbons
      You flew;
But now, I don't know your
      whereabouts,
Am I so easy to forget...
By a quiet little creek,
Together we watched the sunset,
      And enjoyed a beautiful time;
But now, I can't find
      a mere trace of you,
Am I so easy to forget...
Under the blue sky, we met on the hills,

290   *Chapter Fourteen*

You called for freedom,
         adored democracy;
But now, you have drifted far away, Am I so easy to forget...
You showed boundless sympathies
         for the poor,
You expressed sincerity
         for future ideals.
You could turn darkness
         into brightness.
You could change this shape
         of this world.
Whether I am remembered or forgotten,
I am still as active as before.
My heart is filled with struggles
         against this ugly world,
Even though I still have plenty
         of memories to recall.
In front of our eyes lies reality,
         not illusions,
I give my whole life
         to the liberation of humanity.
Every effort to rid the oppressed of their miseries,
Let the sun shine all over the world.

Notes

The author especially thanks Mabel Teng for making Lim's papers available and reading a draft of this essay. Teng had collected and stored Lim's possessions from his hotel room after he had died. The author also thanks Him Mark Lai for his support and for conversations about Happy Lim.

FIFTEEN

The Life and Death of Dhan Gopal Mukerji

At one time, I planned to publish a trilogy of studies of early Stanford Asian American graduates that would include Yamato Ichihashi and Dhan Gopal Mukerji (1890–1936), a pioneering writer of South Asian descent in the United States. Both had been at Stanford in the early twentieth century.

In 2002, I republished Mukerji's out-of-print 1923 memoir, *Caste and Outcast*, which was accompanied by the following biographical essay based substantially on his personal papers provided by his surviving family members in California and France. Collaboration with anthropologists Akhil Gupta and Purnima Mankekar, who co-edited the book and contributed their own study of Mukerji and his world, advanced understanding on Mukerji and his life and times and helped the volume speak to a contemporary audience.

The third element in the envisioned trilogy was to be on Pardee Lowe, an early Chinese American writer and author of a commercially successful account of his life entitled *Father and Glorious Descendant* (1943). This study awaits completion—Lowe was a much more acerbic observer of American

---

"The Life and Death of Dhan Gopal Mukerji," in the republication of Dhan Gopal Mukerji, *Caste and Outcast*, edited and presented by Gordon H. Chang, Purnima Mankekar, and Akhil Gupta (Stanford University Press), 2002: 1–40. (Illustrations accompanying the original article are not included in this volume.)

291

life than how he presents himself in his published book. The writing from the three writers reveals their keen awareness of their trans-Pacific existences as subjects of ethnic marginalization in America and as perceived extensions of their lands of ancestry. All three devoted effort to trying to understand what it meant to be an Asian in America in the early and mid-twentieth century. *Caste and Outcast* contains some of the earliest published descriptions of the experiences of South Asian immigrants in America, who are now among the most numerous Asian Americans. Few among them, let alone the general public, know Mukerji's name and accomplishments, however. Much more needs to be done to recover this early chapter in the cultural history of Asian Americans.

A person of rare talent and broad appeal, Dhan Gopal Mukerji (1890–1936) holds the distinction of being the first author of Asian Indian ancestry who successfully wrote for American audiences about Indian life.[1] During his brilliant but tragically brief career, he produced some twenty-five published volumes of poetry, drama, fiction, social commentary, philosophy, translations, and children's stories. In his work, he drew from Indian history and literature to examine a wide range of human concerns. Few topics eluded him: he wrote about the plight of India under British colonialism and the politics of independence; in his children's work, for which he was best known, he explored humanity's relationship to the natural world and the spiritual oneness of all things, animated or not; he pondered humankind's relationship to God; he studied the Indian classics of religion and philosophy and their meaning for the contemporary world; and he examined, with a critical eye, life in his adopted country, the United States. It was here where he received his university education, married and started a family, enjoyed a hugely successful career in writing and public speaking, and then took his own life at age forty-six, out of frustration with his inability to reconcile the material and spiritual dimensions of his own existence and in anguish over his desperate effort to know God directly.

Mukerji's books sold widely. The popularity of some, such as *Gay Neck: The Story of a Pigeon,* winner of the 1927 Newberry Medal for children's literature, has kept them in print since their first appearance seventy years ago. Some works, such as *Caste and Outcast* and *The Face of Silence,* continue to receive critical attention and respect from specialists. Others have been forgotten. During his lifetime, however, his influence on American artistic and literary circles was substantial. Mukerji maintained close associations with writers and prominent figures from around the world, including the American philosophers Will and Ariel Durant, the French Nobel Prize–winning author Romain Rolland, and Jawaharlal Nehru, India's legendary political leader. Mukerji's frequent peripatetic speaking tours around the country introduced Indian philosophical and religious views to thousands of Americans. He consciously sought to serve as a cultural interpreter of "the East" for "the West." He wanted to help the West find redemption and release from what he believed was a brutal, materialistic existence by discovering what he saw as the spiritual wisdom of the East. He promoted the activities of the small circles of Hindu adherents in America, while encouraging support for the welfare of his homeland and its independence from British colonialism.

Now, more than sixty years after his death, reconsideration of Dhan Gopal Mukerji and his work is in order. There has been no major study of him since his death. His passing in midlife shocked friends and followers around the globe, but over the years he slowly slipped into obscurity. Moreover, until recently, scholars have neglected serious study of the intellectual activity of persons of Asian ancestry in America.[2] In the 1980s, however, interest in the experiences of Asian Americans and in India itself kindled renewed interest in Dhan Gopal Mukerji.[3] An examination of his work and life here will, we hope, help revitalize further interest in him and contribute to the exploration of the South Asian experience in America. Mukerji was a pivotal figure in the transmission and interpretation of Indian traditions to America in the first several decades of the twentieth century and his life offers a unique vantage point from which to consider neglected aspects of American social and intellectual history.

Dhan Gopal Mukerji was born on July 6, 1890, in Tamluk, Bengal, near Calcutta, in British colonial India. His parents, Kishorilal Mukherjee, an attorney, and Bhubanmohini Deari, were of the elite Kulin Brahmin caste and well to do. He was the youngest of five sons and had three sisters. He attended English schools established by Protestant missionaries—the Hamilton School in Tamluk and the Duff School in Calcutta, founded by the outspoken Scottish missionary Alexander Duff; he later attended the

294   *Chapter Fifteen*

University of Calcutta, where he developed a precocious facility with both written and spoken English.[4]

His family had a deep and lasting influence on the youngster. His mother's nurturing and repose appear to have deeply affected him. Throughout his life, he wrote fondly of his mother and of the peace and security of the home in which he matured. It remained in his memory an idyll in a turbulent life. His devout parents also encouraged the young Mukerji, around the age of fourteen, to leave his regular school routine to engage in a spiritual quest and become what might be called a priest initiate. Leaving home alone, he wandered the land as a mendicant, seeking to understand life and the higher power that governed it. Throughout his life, Mukerji referred to this journey as a formative experience. His pilgrimage formally ended after about a year of wandering. His early quest for spiritual understanding highlighted his cultural training, which was unique even in Indian society, but also foreshadowed his adult preoccupation with comprehending the deeper meaning of human existence.

The other enduring influence on Mukerji came from an elder brother, Jadu Gopal, an anticolonial revolutionary in Bengal. Jadu, in fact, appears to be responsible for Mukerji's original decision to leave India, although the specific reasons for Mukerji's departure remain somewhat obscure. There are two very different accounts of this important event and Mukerji himself is responsible for both—this itself suggests it was a matter of special significance for him. He apparently appreciated the implications of his migration account for his perceived persona.

The version he offered his wife and child years later in his life kindled their imaginations; it is adventuresome, even heroic, with touches of violence, spontaneity, beguiling innocence, and noble national purpose. This story begins with Jadu Gopal leading an underground movement fighting for Bengal's independence from the British. For years, his group battled the colonial authorities, even robbing banks to gather money for their cause. But the movement slowly declined as members sacrificed themselves in the fight. The younger Mukerji himself never served in the rebel ranks, but in this version acted as a courier for his brother. In 1908 or 1909, the British authorities lured Jadu out of the jungle with a promise of amnesty if he would end his crusade and surrender. Once they had him, however, the British jailed Jadu, who, in the nick of time, warned Dhan of the betrayal and urged him to go abroad to rally support

The Life and Death of Dhan Gopal Mukerji   295

for the cause and avoid imprisonment. Heeding his brother, Mukerji escaped by diving into the Ganges River in Calcutta and swimming out to seek refuge aboard a Dutch ship, which happened to be bound for Japan.[5]

Mukerji told his family that in Japan he worked for his brother's movement while enrolled in something called the "Tokyo School of Textile Engineering," which his son many years later easily recalled because of the incongruity of the image of his completely unmechanical father studying industrial arts. But without a steady income and with few friends and little sympathy from the Japanese he encountered, despite the country's promotion of pan-Asianism, Mukerji had to engage in a series of odd jobs to support himself. For reasons that remain unclear, he made his way to the docks of Yokohama and there found a "mysterious" ship moored with a file of down-and-outers trudging on board. Falling innocently into line, Mukerji discovered the ship's crew distributing what appeared to be free food for the hungry and indigent. After satisfying himself and about to take his leave, he offered eloquent and profuse thanks in his finest colonial preparatory school English for the beneficence of the ship's captain. Prevented from departing, however, Mukerji learned that by eating the meal he had incurred a debt and, being unable to pay, had to sign on for the voyage as a contract laborer. His destination was the United States. Several weeks later, Mukerji walked off his transport in North America.[6]

This family account is vague about how Mukerji next made his way to California.[7] Mukerji suggested that he may have worked as a laborer in Idaho harvesting sugar beets, and somewhere along the way his charm, intelligence, and English-language ability impressed a foreman, who encouraged him to leave the fields to get a higher education. Mukerji, who translated for the other Indian laborers, was clearly not of the same ilk as they, untutored and rough in manner. He took the foreman's advice, got out of his contract, and traveled to Berkeley, where in August 1910 he matriculated at the University of California.[8]

The contrasting migration story, distributed years later by Mukerji's longtime publisher, E. P. Dutton of New York, is a considerably more prosaic version, but one that helped create the image of the author as an earnest and hopeful intellectual making his way to America to better himself, an image much more appealing to an American reading public. According to this account, whose factual elements are more consistent with, though

296   Chapter Fifteen

not identical to, the story presented in *Caste and Outcast,* Mukerji traveled to Japan to help gather support for Indian independence and study "industrial machinery and Western methods of production" at the University of Tokyo. No mention is made of a dramatic escape from the British authorities. "Finding engineering harder than philosophy," Mukerji wrote in an autobiographical note that apparently was generated for publicity purposes, he left Japan in 1909 for the United States. Life was not easy, he recalled, and he washed dishes and harvested crops in California fields to earn enough money to study at the University of California, Berkeley, where he remained from August 1910 to March 1913.[9]

The two versions of the migration story are very different self-representations. The documentary record and sequence of events favor the latter as the more accurate one—the family story appears to be largely apocryphal. Yet, Mukerji insisted within his family that the family version was truer and that he had connived with Dutton to offer the Horatio Alger–like account because it resonated with the reassuring and familiar narrative of America as the land of opportunity for the entire world. He confided in his family that he had tailored the migration version in *Caste and Outcast* to suit the wishes of the publisher.

How might one reconcile these apparently very different accounts? Comments about the relationship of writing and truth that Mukerji once gave his son perhaps offer an explanation. Mukerji was an accomplished storyteller, much in the Indian tradition in which one discovers meaning, even high life truths, through the narration of richly elaborate stories about humans, gods, animals, and nature. According to Mukerji, storytelling permitted embellishment here and there, and even exaggeration, in order to reveal deeper, more important truths beyond a literal account. Seen in this way, the two migration stories offered by Mukerji complement each other: one offering perhaps the deeper emotional drama of his migration that emphasized his attachment to India and his belief in an unrevealed path guiding human existence; the other, the factual recounting of events and personal decision making.[10]

The two stories do converge in what happened after Mukerji entered the University of California in August 1910. School records show that he completed courses in a broad range of liberal arts subjects, including history, French, elementary Japanese, and economics and philosophy.[11] He apparently did not care for the atmosphere and people he met in Berkeley,

The Life and Death of Dhan Gopal Mukerji 297

although he seems to have taken an interest in some radicals he encountered there, including agitators from the International Workers of the World. The anarcho-syndicalist Wobblies, as they were called, militantly opposed the capitalist order and called for its revolutionary overthrow. In contrast to most other labor groups at the time, which espoused white supremacy as they appealed to the white worker, the Wobblies welcomed laborers of all colors, races, religions, and backgrounds into their ranks. Mukerji's encounter with them occupies a significant portion of *Caste and Outcast.*

Mukerji was not among the earliest Indian immigrants to America. A few dozen other South Asians had preceded him in the late eighteenth and nineteenth centuries as deckhands, servants, travelers, and merchants. Some had been indentured, and in several notorious cases others, because of their dark complexions, had been forced into chattel slavery along with Africans. But until the late nineteenth century, few Americans had ever personally encountered anyone from India. Apart from a handful of intellectuals who studied Indian literature and philosophy and an even smaller group interested in Indian religions, Americans, if they knew anything at all about India, learned it from the celebrator of British imperialism, Rudyard Kipling, whose works were widely available, and from the occasional returned missionary or traveler.[12] Mukerji himself was familiar with Kipling's immensely influential work, which included stories such as *Kim* and *The Jungle Book,* and the poem "Gunga Din."

The early twentieth century, however, saw the beginnings of a small migration of laborers and students from South Asia to Canada and the United States. They formed just a portion of the great Indian diaspora that eventually resulted in the spread of Indians around the globe, from Africa to the Caribbean, to the Pacific islands. In 1910, though, just a few thousand workers and students lived in the United States, principally in Washington State and California. From the moment of their arrival, Indians faced considerable hostility and even violence from white Americans. They endured the anti-Asian and white-supremacist attitudes that reigned throughout the country in those years, which, among other things, demanded the exclusion of nonwhite immigrants from the country. These attitudes had their culmination in 1917, when Congress passed legislation that excluded entry of persons from a so-called Asiatic Barred Zone, a region running roughly from South Asia through to the Polynesian islands. This law, along with earlier specific decisions against Chinese and Japanese, effectively ended Asian

298   *Chapter Fifteen*

immigration to the United States. After 1917, only teachers, merchants, and students (and immigrants from American possessions such as the Philippines) were exempted from the strict provisions. In 1923, the Supreme Court ruled that Asian Indians were racially prohibited from obtaining American citizenship because they were not "white persons," as required by law. Major revisions in the laws did not come until after World War II.[13]

Mukerji was one of a few dozen Indian students in Berkeley, which had become a popular destination for the few Indian students who had made their way to America. Then in September 1913, Mukerji, listing 2963 Webster Street in San Francisco as his "permanent address" (this was the location of the local Ramakrishna Center, one of the first societies dedicated to Hinduism in America), applied to and was accepted by Stanford University, some thirty miles south and across the San Francisco Bay from Berkeley.[14] At that time, the cost of attending Stanford, which required little or no tuition, was actually lower than at Berkeley. Mukerji entered shortly afterward, but decided to live off-campus on Bryant Street, in the residential area of the small town of Palo Alto. White Stanford undergraduates at this time often were not tolerant of nonwhites in their dormitories. During the year, he took courses in history, including "The History of the Far East" taught by Payson Treat, one of the first historians of Japan in America, and in English, in which he received his bachelor's degree in the summer of 1914. There is no record he personally knew the radical Sikh leaders Har Dayal and Taraknath Das, both of whom lived in Berkeley and Stanford around the same time as Mukerji, but the three young men most likely knew of one another, sharing anti-British passions as they did. Dayal was especially politically active in the Palo Alto area, where a number of Indian independence supporters lived. Stanford's president, David Starr Jordan, was himself sympathetic to India's plight and befriended a number of young Indians. Dayal's political and social iconoclasm, however, had soured his relationship with the university, where he lectured on Indian philosophy, and he formally ended his relationship with the university a year before Mukerji entered Stanford.[15] Another Indian intellectual who lived in the Stanford area was Manabendra Nath Bhattacharji, who became much better known by his later adopted name, M. N. Roy. In the latter teens through the 1950s, Roy gained a reputation as one of the most colorful international revolutionaries in the world, operating in Mexico, China, and the Soviet Union. Roy actually credits Mukerji as the original personal inspiration for his "rebirth" from an Indian nationalist into an internationalist when he was in Palo Alto.[16]

Mukerji, in contrast, remained dedicated to his intellectual work and placed political activism second. In fact, in *Caste and Outcast* he makes especially pointed criticism of several unidentified fiery Indian radicals whose espousal of violence repelled him almost as much as British colonialism. Mukerji wanted to pursue a higher academic degree and was accepted into the university's master's program in philosophy. He declared an interest in the idealism of Bernard Bosanquet, a leading contemporary English scholar of political and moral philosophy and aesthetics. But just three months later, he transferred from philosophy to English, where he wanted to explore, in his description, the "definition of tragedy." Mukerji's transcript shows he completed course work in the 1914 academic year and one semester of the following year and worked closely with Professor William Herbert Carruth, who taught "national epics," comparative literature, and the work of Alfred Lord Tennyson. Stanford's English department at the time also included Van Wyck Brooks, who later became a prominent interpreter of New England transcendentalism and one of America's leading literary critics. He and Mukerji became lifelong friends.[17] Mukerji, however, never completed his program, withdrawing from the university in the winter of 1916.[18]

During his short stay at Stanford, Mukerji distinguished himself as a literary talent. He lectured on comparative literature in the English department and before "important women's and men's clubs" in the area. He never actually taught courses at Stanford, although he held a teaching assistantship in the English department and became well known to its faculty.[19] But he found himself increasingly drawn to creative writing and away from the sedate world of academia. He had written both composed verse and drama, and his work drew the attention of Paul Elder, a prominent publisher in San Francisco, who in 1916 and 1917 published three volumes of Mukerji's work: *Rajani: Songs of the Night* (with a brief laudatory introduction by Stanford's president, David Starr Jordan) and *Sandhya: Songs of Twilight,* both collections of his poetry, and *Layla-Majnu,* a three-act play. This work explores the nature of reality, dreams, spiritual dimensions of existence, the beauty of nature, and the individual's place in a God-created world. Mukerji drew from Indian literature for the inspiration and language of these studies. He was on his way to a successful and frenetic literary career.[20]

300   *Chapter Fifteen*

Mukerji experienced another turning point in his life during his days at Stanford. He met Ethel Ray Dugan, who entered Stanford in the fall of 1914 to pursue a master's degree in history. Patty, as she liked to be called, was three years older than Mukerji and hailed from Hazelton, Pennsylvania. She had concentrated on English and history at Smith College, from which she received her bachelor's degree in 1910. Patty was proud of her lineage. Her Quaker family fled Ireland with William Penn in 1699 to escape religious persecution and remained Quakers through the centuries. One of her relatives served on the New Jersey delegation to the Continental Congress.[21] Her father, Howard Dugan, was a mining engineer who had supervised operations at the largest coal mine operation in the world in Mukden, China. Patty's family was open-minded and her parents encouraged her youthful independence and somewhat rebellious spirit. She spent a year and a half on her own at the Sorbonne in Paris before entering graduate school at Stanford, where she received her master's degree in history in 1915. She submitted a thesis on John Slidell, a Confederate diplomat to France.[22]

Mukerji and Patty made a handsome and vivacious couple, and they quickly involved themselves in California literary circles. Not long after Mukerji left Stanford, the two moved to Los Angeles. The city was both a cultural center and the location of an important and influential group of Americans interested in Indian religion.[23] The two married in Hollywood in June 1918. The marriage certificate lists Mukerji as "Caucasian," aged 28, and, for an unknown reason, a resident of Syracuse, New York. It was common for Asian Indians in these years to use the then-accepted ethnographic argument that because they were of Aryan descent, they were therefore members of the so-called Caucasian race. Mukerji was in fact dark in complexion, but claiming the racial status of Caucasian allowed him to avoid some discriminatory laws, such as California's anti-miscegenation statute, which specifically prohibited intermarriage between nonwhites and whites. Patty is listed as a resident of Los Angeles. A priest from the Church of St. Alban presided.[24]

Mukerji remained sensitive to America's racial prejudice his entire life. He makes reference to it in his published work and it affected his personal life in unexpected ways. In fact, Mukerji's decision to marry may have been connected to his frantic worry that he was about to be drafted into the U.S. army, then involved in the Great War in Europe. He condemned the fighting, labeling the war a "vast insanity." Both the Allies and Central Powers

The Life and Death of Dhan Gopal Mukerji 301

were to blame for the "imbecility," in his view. "Nothing but suffering can come out of war," he wrote a friend at Stanford.[25] He desperately appealed to friends for help in finding a way out of his predicament: he could not understand why he could be drafted even though he was not an American citizen. What is more, he heard that he might be placed into a racially segregated unit. "Many Hindus have been put into Negro regiments," he informed friend Witter Bynner, a sinologist and literary scholar at Harvard. Mukerji even proposed that Bynner take him to France to work there as an alternative to the draft. He also even thought about writing the British ambassador to see if an exemption could be arranged for him, a British subject.[26] Mukerji somehow found his way out of serving and never entered the U.S. army.

Unlike many Indian nationalists at the time, Mukerji did not harbor anti-Allied sentiment. Nevertheless, he still came under government surveillance. In 1917 and 1918, the federal government closely monitored Indian workers and intellectuals in the country because of their widespread anti-British activities. In several sensational cases, the authorities prosecuted a score of Indians and American sympathizers for agitating against Britain and undermining the war effort. The press carried lurid articles about "Hindu-German" conspiracies centered in San Francisco and New York and possibly linked to anarchists such as Emma Goldman and Alexander Berkman or communists such as Leon Trotsky. Mukerji himself came under suspicion. He knew the British were closely watching his family's activities in India and warned American friends visiting India to stay away from his relatives. Rumors swirled about that he was also a Red.[27] He adamantly rejected such characterizations, claiming he was a Brahmin interested only in spiritual matters.[28] In April 1918, however, the name of his elder brother Jadu appeared on an indictment issued in New York City. The federal government accused Jadu, along with well-known Indian activists Lajpat Rai, Taraknath Das, and Salindranath Ghose, as well as the American radical Agnes Smedley, of "attempting to stir up rebellion against British rule in India and for representing themselves as diplomats."[29] In fact, Jadu had never set foot in the United States—it seems his signature had been forged by activists in the founding of a U.S. branch of the Indian National Party. American and British intelligence agents, and public rumor, also seem to have confused Dhan Gopal with M. N. Roy, who had become a communist. It seems that personal circumstances helped confuse Mukerji

302   *Chapter Fifteen*

and Roy in the minds of intelligence agents. Both had been associated with Stanford and both married Euroamerican women. The father of Roy's wife, coincidentally, had also been a mining engineer in Asia. Publicly, Mukerji frequently expressed anti-Bolshevik sentiments, which helped to establish his true identity and shed the Red tag.[30]

Mukerji and Patty did not remain long in Los Angeles but moved to the cultural centers in the eastern United States, which is where his friends said he should be if he was serious about pursuing his literary career. Mukerji had already become, or would soon become, a friend or close associate of leading figures in American arts and letters, including writers such as Witter Bynner at Harvard; Arthur Upham Pope, a scholar of Persian art at the University of California, Berkeley; the poet Rose O'Neill; Claude Bragdon, theosophist, architect, and philosopher; stage actor Walter Hampden; Frank Jewett Mather, Jr., a Princeton art historian; Warner Fite, an ethicist and philosopher; George Waldo Brown, historian and Asianist; Patrick Geddes, the renowned urban planner; and even Kahlil Gibran, the writer-mystic from Lebanon. Mukerji also counted among his closest friends Roger Baldwin, the founder of the American Civil Liberties Union and a leader in the group Friends of India; Charles Wharton Stork, a specialist in Scandinavian literature and editor of *Contemporary Verse* who taught at Haverford College; and many of the early followers of Indian spirituality in the United States, including Josephine MacLeod and Alice Sprague.[31]

The range of interests among Mukerji's friends reflected the vibrancy of American intellectual life in the early decades of the twentieth century. Despite the persistence of the heavy hand of late-nineteenth century Victorianism, with its moral and cultural conservativism and Anglo-Saxon chauvinism, the years from just before World War I through the 1920s witnessed an extraordinary openness and creativity in American arts and intellectual life. It is true that these were years of official white supremacy, xenophobia, religious dogmatism, and Red Scares, but they were also the years of the Harlem Renaissance, cultural cosmopolitanism, and the flourishing of social and political activism of all sorts, from feminism to socialism. In many ways, Mukerji was fortunate to work in America in these years, for there was a receptivity to new ideas and hitherto neglected or even disdained sources of inspiration and learning, whether it was African-American music, the psychological "unconscious," or Asian civilizations. A "modern intellectual" in America emerged, independent, critical of a

The Life and Death of Dhan Gopal Mukerji   303

stagnant and repressive Puritanism and narrowness, and eager to engage in what has been called a political and aesthetic revolt. These were the years of Isadora Duncan, Ernest Hemingway, and the New York City Armory show of modern art in 1913; of T. S. Eliot, who studied Sanskrit in college; of Ezra Pound, who became fascinated with Chinese and Japanese poetics; and of the historian/philosophers Will and Ariel Durant, whose first installment of their ambitious and monumental *The Story of Civilization* was entitled *Our Oriental Heritage.* Will Durant wrote that the story of civilization "begins with the Orient," and with the "ascendancy of Europe" rapidly ending, "the future faces into the Pacific." Even cultural conservatives, such as the New Humanists Irving Babbit and Paul Elmer More, looked to the Hindu classics and Buddhism in their response to the moral crisis in post–World War I America.[32]

The Mukerjis stayed in Boston for a short while and then moved to New York City. Their only child, Dhan Gopal, Jr., who was called Gopal, was born in New Bedford, Massachusetts, in August 1919. But the restless, ambitious couple again went on the move. Leaving Gopal with friends in Grand Rapids, Michigan, Mukerji and Patty traveled to India in the summer of 1922. It was Mukerji's first trip back to India in twelve years and he was eager to reacquaint himself with his land of ancestry. In India, Mukerji visited relatives and collected material for his writing. He and Patty spent many days at the Ramakrishna Center in Belur. They also met Rabindranath Tagore, the great Indian poet who had won the Nobel Prize for literature in 1913;[33] Mukerji had tried to raise financial support for Tagores educational efforts in India.[34] After a visit of several months, the Mukerjis returned to New York and settled in an apartment in the center of Greenwich Village, at 2 Jane Street, where they resided for the next two years.[35] The Village had become the center of bohemian life in America—it was an exciting quarter of artists, writers, playwrights, and radicals of all kinds. Writing furiously and productively, Mukerji quickly established his reputation as a leading authority on Indian civilization, especially its literature. He wrote nonfiction, interpreting India's cultural traditions, and occasionally, its politics, translated Hindu literature and verse, and published his own poetry in prominent periodicals, including *Asia, Poetry, The American Review, The Forum, The Century Magazine,* and *The Atlantic Monthly,* which published in three consecutive issues long essays by him about contemporary Indian life, based on his recent visit.[36] In 1922, he published the first of his many

304   *Chapter Fifteen*

immensely popular children's books, *Kari the Elephant,* which drew on his own childhood experiences with animals.

Mukerji also joined the lecture circuit and became a popular speaker to university audiences, whom he impressed with his erudition. He spoke knowledgeably about the Western canon, from Yeats to Ibsen, and could draw comparisons with Indian literature. Speaking in a beautiful, sonorous English-accented voice, he could enthrall audiences with his rendition, completely from memory, of Milton's epic *Paradise Lost* and his own original verse. Nietzsche and Henri Bergson as well as the ancient Upanishads were all within his purview. He was handsome, of medium stature, and possessed a personality that endeared him to men and women alike. Witty, energetic, and direct, Mukerji easily made friends everywhere.[37] Jawaharlal Nehru once described him "as such a charming personality—so very lovable."[38] University audiences throughout the country eagerly welcomed him, and in the early 1920s he spoke at Haverford, Princeton, the University of Chicago, and the University of Washington, among other locations. Feakins, a leading booking agency in New York, represented Mukerji, and booked engagements for him throughout the United States and Europe. Indicating the regard with which he was held are the comments of Stanford's David Starr Jordan, who wrote to *The Atlantic Monthly* to correct its misidentification of Mukerji as a graduate of Berkeley. "Please do not deprive us," Jordan wrote, "of the glory reflected from our ablest Hindu graduate—philosopher and poet."[39]

Then in 1923, at the age of thirty-three, Mukerji published *Caste and Outcast,* which confirmed his reputation as a major young writer in the United States. The book is autobiographical, though not strictly so, as discussed above. It is not just his migration account that is questionable; other facts, especially about his life in America, are also difficult to substantiate. Nevertheless, the general outlines of the book appear accurate. The first half is about the author's life in India and the second about his early days in America, ending about the time he begins his writing career. It is a work of several kinds. It is in part an examination of some of the influences— spiritual, cultural, and experiential—on him as a writer. Far more than personal anecdote, though, the book is also social commentary on India as well as America. The book presented Americans with one of the first really serious and thoughtful introductions to Indian life, with its ways and beliefs, but it also offers an unusual look at the dizzy world of America in the prewar years. It implicitly compares the two civilizations he knew well. The book can also be read as a defense of India, as a response to the negative impressions many Americans had about India and Indian immigrants. Especially in the second half of the book, Mukerji deftly educates his readers about the difficult lives of Indian students and laborers in America and explains that all were not wild-eyed radicals or barbaric field hands as the popular imagination held. They shared a common humanity with others. And with light comedic touch, Mukerji reveals that Indian spiritual beliefs had more in common with the advanced ideas of the Theory of Relativity in physics than with the "spirit world" of the seance, also associated with the mystic East. Mukerji maintained he was an antimystic. At its heart, *Caste and Outcast* is an optimistic book, reflecting the authors own joy in writing and in discovering his own purpose in life, which was to serve as what one might call a literary missionary. The book is an expression of hope for the future, with a merging of positive aspects from East and West.[40]

The publication of *Caste and Outcast* marked a turning point in America's understanding of India. Most of what Americans had read previously about Indians was written by Europeans, British in particular, and by the few Americans who had traveled to India in the nineteenth century. A handful of Americans who had been attracted to Indian religion wrote brief introductions to Hinduism. There were also, of course, translations of ancient and modern Indian literary works. But Mukerji's book was the first widely read book on India and on Indians in America written by an Indian and reviewers immediately appreciated this significance. "Compared with the Occidental books that have tried to describe the life of the people of India," the reviewer for the *New York Times* wrote, "it is like seeing the interior of a richly furnished house illuminated, after getting one's impressions of that house from the pale rays of light thrown upon a poor and cheap exterior." Mukerji's effort, a reviewer observed, showed "how impossible it is for any European, and still more an American, to understand [India's] spirit and significance." Mukerji's observations about America, however, were taken less seriously by the reviewers. Few commented on his thoughts about this country. Above all, the reviewers praised *Caste and Outcast* for its vivid and lively descriptions of India and its engaging style, features that would remain with Mukerji throughout his career.[41]

Mukerji himself promoted the book's description of Indian life and deemphasized the discussion of his experiences in America. He said that

306   Chapter Fifteen

he wrote the book because after he arrived in this country, he discovered its great ignorance about India. He hoped that he could help Americans learn not only *about* his land of ancestry, but also *from* it. Adult Americans, he wrote, "had very little repose," something that he believed pervaded Indian home life. "If Americans study how we create serenity in India," he suggested, "they will be able to know serenity here in America." The East should learn activity and science from the West, whereas the West should learn "repose and meditation" from the East. The synthesis of these features was next on the agenda for human history in his view.[42] *Caste and Outcast* enjoyed not only critical but also commercial success. It went through at least five printings in the 1920s in the United States, and British, French, and even Czech editions appeared in the following years.

Mukerji's commercial success as a writer and speaker allowed him and his family to move to Europe, where many American intellectuals and writers resided for periods in their careers during these years. From late 1923 through the next two years, Mukerji and his family lived most of the time in a modest residential hotel in the old port town of Hyeres, on the French Mediterranean coast. He also spent time in Brittany, in northern France. The family did not live extravagantly, but French life and culture appealed to Mukerji and Patty, and both of them developed a deep affection for the country. Once he mused that he must have been French in a previous existence.[43] Mukerji spent most of his time in France writing, interrupted occasionally by extended speaking tours to England and the United States.[44]

In 1926, the Mukerji family moved to Geneva, where they lived for the next two years, in part to be near their son, whom they enrolled in a boarding school there. Although Mukerji was in Geneva for mainly personal reasons, he closely observed the work of the League of Nations and publicly assessed its progress later on his return to the United States.[45] Mukerji criticized the league for its preoccupation with European problems and its inattention to the "East," except for Japan. He became known in America as a reliable observer of political events in his land of ancestry.[46] But the most important consequence of his stay in Geneva was a number of new relationships with important intellectuals and writers. He became friends with Salvador de Madariaga, the celebrated Spanish scholar and leader of the League, who listened sympathetically to his presentation of India's case against the British. He had long talks with the French Nobel Prize–winning author Romain Rolland, who was developing a deep fascination

The Life and Death of Dhan Gopal Mukerji 307

with Indian philosophy and spirituality. Mukerji and Jawaharlal Nehru, Gandhi's close associate and later India's founding prime minister, also started a close friendship at this time. Nehru, accompanied by his daughter Indira, had brought his wife, Kamala, sick with tuberculosis, to Switzerland for medical treatment.[47] The later correspondence between Mukerji and Nehru reveals fascinating insights into the two that will be explored below.

The mid- and late 1920s were the most productive periods in Mukerji's career. Following *Caste and Outcast,* he published several other works of nonfiction in which he presented further observations on the politics and religion of India to American audiences. *My Brother's Face* (1924), based on his 1922 return trip to India, is offered as a record of the author's own reencounter with his land of ancestry. India had changed dramatically since his original departure as a student, he wrote, and he described the political and spiritual differences that impressed him. His story is presented almost as one of discovery, of seeing something completely new. Along with the author, the reader seems to experience new things, learns about the Gandhian nonviolent revolution, and becomes acquainted with the author's own family. The slightly naive tone adopted by the author effectively conveyed awe and wonder, which appealed to an American audience curious about an unfamiliar place. Readers were allowed to join what seemed to be an intimate, personal journey.

Displaying a writer's sensitivity to contrast, irony, and multiple meanings, the title of the book refers both to his real-life brother Jadu, whose revolutionary politics and passions he seeks to explain to the reader, and also to the "Westerner," who the author comes to realize at the end of the book is also his "brother" in a common humanity. A review in the *New York Evening Post* praised the work as "a brilliant contribution to the cause of racial understanding and comity." The Literary Review of the *Saturday Evening Post* described it as "the most important and inspiring book that has appeared in America since the war."

In 1926, Mukerji published *The Face of Silence,* one of his most important nonfiction works and one of which he was especially proud.[48] Although not the first book about the life and teachings of Ramakrishna, the great Indian spiritual leader of the mid-nineteenth century, the book profoundly influenced audiences in America and Europe. One of those most affected by Mukerji's book was Romain Rolland, who later wrote his own biography of Ramakrishna. Rolland praised Mukerji's book as having "exceptional

308   *Chapter Fifteen*

value as a work of art" and "a brilliant evocation of the figure of the Master in the atmosphere of the India of his time."[49] Although Mukerji had long been interested in Indian religious traditions, it seems, curiously, that it had been the American Josephine MacLeod in Los Angeles in 1914 who was responsible for bringing Mukerji to Ramakrishna's message.[50] In the coming years, Mukerji would become increasingly absorbed with the spiritual dimension of his own existence.[51]

Again, the title of the book is instructive. *The Face of Silence* has several meanings. Mukerji introduces the great Ramakrishna (d. 1886), a saintly, even godlike, person, revered in India, who played a pivotal role in the revitalization of Hinduism that had begun in the late eighteenth century. Breaking with the emphasis on polytheism, arcane tradition, and empty ritual that had come to burden Hinduism, Ramakrishna encouraged attention to the messages of divine unity, the spirit as the true reality, and individual meditation and god seeking. He taught detachment from the material and the passionate. In *The Face of Silence,* Mukerji introduces the reader to the "face" of Ramakrishna, to the life, teachings, and legacies of the great teacher. The book's title, however, also refers to the Silence that is Ultimate Truth, the divine that is beyond the word, knowing that is beyond expressed knowledge. As Mukerji explained in one of his novels, "Have you ever heard silence? It is not stillness which is the absence of sound. Silence is not empty, it is full of content. It is like the sky—intangible yet containing the stars, the sun, the moon, and all existence. That is Silence and it is full of tongues."[52]

The Face of Silence can be read as a twin of *My Brother's Face.* Both present sympathetic and illuminating pictures of India to Western audiences; both present their messages through dialogue, legend, and storytelling, with simple, engaging language. Each book reflected different abiding, and in some ways competing, passions of the author: one for the spiritual world, the other principally for the more temporal world of intercultural understanding and international relations. Mukerji appeared to be able to handle both spheres well at this time and believed the two were completely compatible. He and other Indian intellectuals argued that winning the country's freedom was necessary to release the messages from India's spiritual civilization to the rest of the world; at the same time, India's unique religiosity shaped its politics, best exemplified by the moral courage of Mahatma Gandhi's nonviolent revolution.

The Life and Death of Dhan Gopal Mukerji   309

Although Mukerji devoted his principal attention to his books for adults, it was his work for children that gained him more popular recognition. He published eleven volumes for young readers. These were substantial works, what one might call novels for young people. His best-known book was *Gay-Neck: The Story of A Pigeon*, for which he won the Newberry Medal in 1927 for children's literature. This engaging tale offered serious life lessons through a touching description of the trials and tribulations of a heroic little bird. The reviewer for the erudite journal *Sufi Quarterly* even praised the work, ostensibly directed at children, as in fact "good reading for philosophers."[53] Mukerji ended his tale with the instruction:

> Whatever we think and feel will colour what we say or do. He who fears, even unconsciously, or has his least little dream tainted with hate, will inevitably, sooner or later, translate these two qualities into his action. Therefore, my brothers, live courage, breathe courage and give courage. Think and feel love, so that you will be able to pour out of yourselves peace and serenity as naturally as a flower gives forth fragrance. Peace be unto all![54]

Similar wisdom about life permeated all of Mukerji's work about animals for young readers, for in his view, as he once stated, animals and humans are intimately related. Animals simply have young souls. In a gentle dig at the Protestant fundamentalism he encountered in his travels in the United States (the famous anti-Darwinian Scopes "monkey trial" took place in 1925), Mukerji suggested facetiously that he, "being a heathen," enjoyed some things that Christians could not, such as the delightful conviction that "animals are our ancestors." Animal stories therefore for him provided a venue to comprehend our own being.[55] In addition to using fables about the lives of animals, Mukerji drew from Indian legends for his other children's books such as *Rama, the Hero of India* and *Master Monkey,* which is about the monkey god Hanuman, and from his recollections of Indian daily life from his own childhood, as in *Kari the Elephant* and *Ghond the Hunter,* which he especially liked. In all his work, for both adults and children, Mukerji's devotion to what he believed was his higher calling, the propagation of the spiritual value of his Indian heritage, was clearly and consistently in evidence.

Here it may be useful to offer a brief, and certainly incomplete, introduction to Mukerji's spiritual beliefs, which occupied so prominent a place

310   *Chapter Fifteen*

in his writings and in his own personal life, and to the history of the Ramakrishna movement in America.

The history of Indian religious beliefs in America is widely underappreciated and certainly understudied. Although often identified with the turn toward alternative spiritual pursuits that emerged in the 1960s and the growing South Asian immigrant communities in the United States, Indian religious and philosophical influences appeared here early in the nineteenth century. New England intellectuals associated with the transcendentalist movement, including Ralph Waldo Emerson and Henry David Thoreau, closely studied translated classics such as the Upanishads and the Bhagavad Gita. Mukerji published his own translations of these later in his life.[56] The American intellectuals were attracted to the messages of a "universal spirit" uniting all beings and things, of seeking ultimate truths and tranquility through intuition and contemplation, of the supreme value of personal experience, of an ethical order that transcended specific religious doctrine, and of the divine power of nature. The transcendentalists, like their contemporaries the Unitarians, were also encouraged by the Indian views on the fundamental unity of all religions and the individual path to peace and enlightenment. These ideas in various forms captured the imagination of many other American writers through the years, including Walt Whitman, Josiah Royce, William James, and of course, in the 1960s, Allen Ginsberg. Whenever American authors were interested in breaking from the dominant rationalist and dualist tradition in Western thought and from its sectarian and scripture-based religious traditions, they often turned to Asian thought.[57]

The visit to America by Ramakrishna's famous disciple Vivekananda, who came from India to attend the World Parliament of Religions convened in conjunction with the 1893 Columbian Exposition of Chicago, was the turning point in the development of an organized presence of Hinduism in the United States. Although representatives from many other religions attended the convocation, Vivekananda made an especially dramatic impact. A striking figure who spoke in commanding English, he offered to his American audiences eloquent introductions to the fundamentals of Hinduism as interpreted by Ramakrishna. For the next three years and during another year-long visit in 1899–1900, Vivekananda delivered over one hundred lectures throughout the country. As a result of his work, followers organized Vedanta societies, which continue to this day in major

The Life and Death of Dhan Gopal Mukerji   311

American cities. Vedanta refers to the ancient scriptures of Hinduism called the Vedas, especially the Upanishads.[58] Mukerji once flirted with the idea of writing a biography of Vivekananda, but never completed it. "One must become pure and austere for such a task first of all," Mukerji wrote in his diary.[59]

The Ramakrishna message combines three main ideas. First, "direct experience and personal realization provide the only basis of true religion." Spirituality must be rooted in individual experience and a person's own search to know God, not in theology or philosophy. Second, differences between religions are essentially empty and unimportant. God is universal and absolute. Last, all religions are "different paths to the same goal." All religions and creeds, faithfully pursued, can in the end realize God, the fundamental and one complete reality. Prayer, yoga, and meditation may help the individual attain transcendence and renounce worldly matters and passions.[60] By the time of Mukerji's actual arrival in the United States, Vedanta societies operated in several American cities, including San Francisco and New York. After meeting Mukerji in 1914, Josephine MacLeod, perhaps Vivekananda's most important supporter in America, concluded that he, Mukerji, could be the leading voice for the Ramakrishna movement in the West.[61] During his lifetime, Mukerji may very well have been that voice.

After Dhan and Patty's return to the United States in 1928 and with the commercial and critical success of his books, Mukerji purchased a comfortable two-bedroom apartment on East Seventy-second Street in New York's Upper East Side. Patty was busy with her own career, working at the Children's University School, later known as the Dalton School. The school became known as a leader in progressive education and Patty as an important educator. She purchased a ramshackle colonial-era home in New Milford, Connecticut, where she and sometimes the couple would spend weekends.[62] Two hours from New York City, New Milford was home to a number of prominent writers and intellectuals with whom the Mukerjis socialized. Mukerji's reputation as an author soared in the late 1920s—his publisher's publicity claimed that he had attained "phenomenal popularity. In only a few years he has jumped into public favor—and more—he has won the hearts of America's children."[63] It was an embellished description, but not inaccurate. However, despite his growing success, or perhaps because of it, Mukerji was increasingly troubled by events both close to home

312   *Chapter Fifteen*

and physically distant. They had consequences for both his intellectual and emotional lives.

In early 1927, a dispute erupted between Mukerji and his longtime literary agent, Kennady and Livingston of New York, with each side hurling ugly accusations at the other regarding the control of manuscripts. Each accused the other of breach of contract and bad faith. "Your conduct," agent Paul Kennady wrote Mukerji, "was pretty thoroughly reprehensible." "You are a great proclaimer of moral precepts," Kennady continued in his personal attack, "and are inclined to make invidious comparisons between the ways of the East and the West. Some day I have the hope you will wake up to the fact that there is a certain rectitude of business conduct here in America that does not ordinarily permit the sort of treatment that you are now handing out to me." Mukerji's personal lawyer, however, supported his client and advised him that it was Kennady who had acted "in a most unbusiness-like manner."[64] The confrontation unsettled Mukerji, sincerely concerned as he was with moral conduct.

About the same time, Mukerji also became involved in one of the most bitter public debates about India that ever occurred in America. In the spring of 1927, Katherine Mayo, an American who had spent six months in India, published *Mother India,* a book based on her travels.[65] It became a wildly popular seller and remains the single most influential book on India that has ever appeared in the United States. The book, in the words of Harold Isaacs, author of a classic study of American attitudes toward India, was "a scalding and horrified recital of examples of child marriage, extreme caste practices, the plight of the untouchables, backward conditions of health and sanitation." The author presented the story from a "single plane of total revulsion and narrowly focused bias" and had "no room for qualifications."[66] Gandhi called the disparaging book a "drain pipe study."[67] An international controversy raged for years about the book, with Mukerji in the midst of the maelstrom. He publicly condemned Mayo for inaccuracy, Anglophilia, and bias. Her book, he charged, irreparably widened the divide between East and West. He claimed to have read the book five times: "The first reading was a torture of self-discipline," he stated.

> When I read it the second and third times and began to cool off about it I felt able to formulate an opinion. That opinion is this: Miss Mayo has taken the evils that undeniably exist in my country as in any other country, and

The Life and Death of Dhan Gopal Mukerji   313

with her fertile imagination has composed a book which utterly ignores the mitigating virtues of India that have made her known throughout centuries as a spiritual country and people.[68]

Within months of the appearance of Mayo's book, Mukerji published his rejoinder, *A Son of Mother India Answers,* in which he factually refuted Mayo's allegations and called on her to rewrite her work. Reviewers praised Mukerji for his reasoned and calm response.[69] His book, however, was not a commercial success, and attendance at his lectures where he spoke out against Mayo disappointed him. Unsuccessful in discrediting Mayo's negative characterization of India, Mukerji felt that he was failing in his mission as a cultural interpreter and that his efforts at encouraging East-West understanding were coming to naught. The effect on him was devastating.[70]

On top of his professional and intellectual worries, he pursued a frantic public-speaking schedule that took him back and forth across the country, mostly by train, and exhausted him mentally and physically He was worried about the very mundane matter of money, or rather the shortage of it, and saw speaking as a way to augment his income. He found himself, however, on the horns of a dilemma. His children's books and talks to popular audiences had helped make his name and earned him a good income, but he yearned for more serious intellectual engagement, which had less lucrative potential. He also had contractual commitments with his publisher and friend, John Macrae, president of E. P. Dutton of New York. The two had a close but often strained relationship. They respected each other, with Macrae often offering gentle advice and counsel to the sensitive author. Mukerji had agreed to deliver a set number of publishable manuscripts to Dutton annually and in return the publisher often advanced money to the author, but the creative as well as financial demands on Mukerji took their toll.

Macrae's frank advice to Mukerji in March 1929, before the stock market crash, highlighted the intellectual dilemma Mukerji faced. "You have the genius to write popular stuff," Macrae wrote, "[but you also have in you that] fine spiritual quality of art which comparatively few writers possess." In Macrae's words, Mukerji could travel one of two roads: "one the road of art and of the highest responsibility to the genius the gods have given you; the other is to popularize your work and bring it into the channels of more or less commercialism." Macrae did not hide what he believed best but told Mukerji that only he could decide which road to take. Still, Macrae

314   *Chapter Fifteen*

admonished him, "you cannot in the language of the farmers, play horse with your own inner soul. . . . You cannot listen to the devil and at the same time receive the blessing of the gods."[71]

Mukerji felt he could no longer bear the pressures on him. In the early summer of 1929, he confided to his close friends Charles and Elizabeth Stork that he was in poor mental health. "I have been so fragile," he wrote, "my nerves could not and will not stand any strain. I need one whole year of the Alps. It is an awful state to be in: I need silence and can't get it in America."[72] But he could not get away and he suffered a debilitating nervous breakdown, which required months of recuperation in the bucolic village of Stockbridge in the Berkshires of Massachusetts. Other writers, including his good friend Van Wyck Brooks, had recuperated there from their own breakdowns. The town was the location of the Austen Riggs Center, a respected psychiatric facility.[73] Mukerji eventually recovered sufficiently to leave, but he was never quite the same. The silence that he desired, either that of the Ultimate Truth and higher consciousness about which he wrote in his Ramakrishna book, or of simple peace and quiet, continued to elude him. He fixated on "silence," and even identified it with Indian national purpose and identity: "our country's motto ought to be," he told Nehru after he recovered from the breakdown, "*maunam Chaivasmi guhyanam*—I am the secret of secrets; I am silence."[74]

When he was finally well enough to travel, Mukerji left Patty behind at the New Milford house and took his son to Europe for school. He then left by himself for India. This was to be a pilgrimage, a seeking of answers to the life questions that tormented him. He went for spiritual renewal and creative inspiration, calling his voyage one of "soul discovery." Traveling by ship from France, he stopped at ports in the Mediterranean and Arabia along the way. He enjoyed the long voyage and the sights. Venice's architecture, he wrote in his diary, "thrilled my soul," unlike the "formless clatter of New York." He exulted in the beauty of a sunset over the Indian Ocean. In India, he found joy even in the prosaic. He described the rhythm of the daily routine "artistic": "a sweeper sweeping does it with a long sweep of his broom each time. None of your jerky quick ones of England and the U.S." And then in the holy city of Benares, the high point of his pilgrimage where he was to meet with his personal guru, he experienced disappointment as well as the sublime. Gone was the embracing spirituality he once felt there; instead, he found mostly beggars and loafers, trying to pose as holy men.[75]

Yet the wondrous beauty of Benares still captivated his poetic soul. He wrote in his diary:

> The same picturesqueness of the old city is there. The same blue water. The same yellow sandstone ghats [broad stairways leading to the river]. Pilgrims in red, blue, russet and green rising from the blue Ganges in thronging processions.

> Pigeons lift their iridescent throats against the red cornices. Monkeys lean from granite roof corners exactly like gargoyles. Over them parakeets spread on sapphire heavens their mantle of emerald.

> Sounds most amazing. Bronze groans, silver laments, drum drones, trumpet pours its fury, cymbals resound like clashing steel, then the clarion notes glide like water.

No other place in the world was like Benares for Mukerji; it had no equal in spirit or grandeur. "What one sees on gala occasions in St. Peters Square [in Rome]," he wrote for himself, "Benares offers every morning."[76]

Searching for spiritual answers to his mental crisis, he approached the Ramakrishna Center in Belur and inquired whether he might join their order to lead a monastic life. The swamis discouraged him, saying that theirs was not a world for him; he was not made for a life of seclusion, they counseled. They urged him to return to his family and work in America. He was undoubtedly disappointed in that decision.[77]

At the same time that he visited holy sites and met with spiritual leaders, Mukerji also uneasily observed the mounting political turmoil in the country. While he was in India, the movement against British rule escalated. Mukerji joined millions of other Indians who watched in rapt attention as one of Mahatma Gandhi's most dramatic acts of civil disobedience unfolded before the world. During three weeks in March and April 1930, Gandhi marched 250 miles from his Sabarmati ashram, through village after village, to Dandi at the sea, where he would make salt, an act declared illegal by the British, who held the monopoly on its production and sale. As he advanced, the crowds of followers grew in size and thousands rallied to his example. Gandhi advocated pacifism, but other Indian anticolonial protesters and the British themselves turned to violence. Hundreds were shot and scores killed; tens of thousands were jailed, including eventually

316   *Chapter Fifteen*

Gandhi himself for violating the salt law. Mukerji believed that India's salvation, and freedom, lay in Gandhi's nonviolent approach and he was dismayed by the bloodshed on both sides.[78]

During his stay he also visited Jawaharlal Nehru. The two had remained close ever since their meeting in Geneva. Their children had been playmates at the L'Ecole Internationale and Nehru had even become Gopal's godfather. The Mukerjis themselves cared for Indira in their home for extended periods of time.[79] And though the two men were very different in many respects, they were also curiously alike in others. Both Mukerji and Nehru were Indian patriots, of course, but Nehru was a man of action and took politics seriously. His faiths were socialism and secularism. He was firm willed and devoted to the independence movement. Mukerji, in contrast, was preoccupied by literary and spiritual matters and became impatient with worldly concerns. He was excitable, with an artist's temperament. However, the two men each saw something familiar in the other. They had been born within a year of one another; both were restless, driven, sensitive, and inwardly tortured. They suffered bouts of severe depression. Both were steeped in the high cultures of the West and India and passionately loved the written word. They also shared a sometimes uneasy relationship with the real India they faced. Elitists culturally and temperamentally, they were often estranged from the hundreds of millions of their compatriots who knew nothing of English literature or French philosophy. Nehru, in a long, revealing letter to Mukerji, once confessed that he was not really comfortable in India. "Unfortunately, I am a mongrel breed," he confided, "neither wholly Eastern nor Western with the result that I seldom feel at home with anybody. The modern western-educated intelligentsia in India usually bore me to extinction. The poor peasant and the worker are loveable enough but what the devil is one to do with them? I can't talk to them for long." Affectionately, Nehru concluded his confession to Mukerji, "so now I hope you will appreciate why I welcome your letters and will write to you frequently." Nehru once flirted with the idea of having Mukerji write his biography.[80]

When Mukerji finally returned to New York from abroad in June 1930, he was both inspired and depressed. He felt that he had found himself once again in India and, as he told Patty, "spiritually I am rejuvenated."[81] But he was also troubled by what he believed was the increasing radicalism, even revolutionism, as he put it, in India. He was pessimistic about finding an early, peaceful settlement to the political stalemate. Young Indians were not interested in the spirituality that mattered to him. He spoke publicly in support of India's independence movement and quickly published *Disillusioned India,* which chronicled his recent visit to India, giving special attention to explaining the Gandhian nonviolent revolution and introducing his friend Nehru to American audiences, or "Homo Americanus," the term Mukerji privately used when he wrote to Nehru. The book's title was taken from a comment made by Nehru about how Indians no longer had any faith in the promises of the British. Mukerji dedicated the book to Kamala, Nehru's dying wife.[82] Although the book is devoted to explaining the independence politics of India, it reveals Mukerji's deepening preoccupation with the spiritual. As he says in the conclusion, "the most important issue in India's struggle today is the effect that will be produced on her ancient culture."[83] And for Mukerji, the most important element of this was its religiosity. He placed his hopes in Gandhi, whom he believed exemplified India's higher morality.

Mukerji gave himself little time to rest after his return to the United States and tried to resume his furious pace of writing, especially on religious topics. In the spring of 1931, he completed a translation of the Indian classic, the Bhagavad Gita, publishing it with the title *The Song of God.* Mukerji believed that the book was the "key to the Hindu character," as well as an expression of humanity's "Universal Self." Earlier English translations were sterile, in his view, for they sacrificed emotional content and poetic force for intellectual or literal accuracy. He dedicated his book to his friend Jawaharlal Nehru.[84]

But Mukerji soon lost the peace he believed that he had found in India. Within a year after his return, the noises in his head plagued him again and he complained of mounting ailments.[85] He continued to seek help from the Ramakrishna order in India and in America, and he wrote Ramakrishna's disciple Swami Shivananda in India about his agony. Shivananda tried to help Mukerji break out of his darkness. "You are as clean, pure and unpassionate as ever," he told Mukerji. "[You are like] the shining sun covered with clouds thinking that it has become cloudy, the sun identifying itself with the passing phase of cloudiness—forgetting its own inborn shining nature. Just so in your case."[86] Mukerji also cultivated a relationship with the swami of the New York Ramakrishna Center, Swami Nikhilandanda, who attempted to provide solace.[87] But the holy men's counsel did not help him find his way.

318   *Chapter Fifteen*

Worried about his soul and worried about money, Mukerji found that writing became more and more difficult. He appealed to his publisher for financial help and, though he continued to receive advances on his books, the sympathetic John Macrae reminded Mukerji, "there is a limit in what I can do." The public in the Depression was not buying books as it once had. Macrae, changing the advice he had given Mukerji just before the advent of the Depression, told Mukerji that he had to "diversify" his writing and submit manuscripts, such as his children's stories, that would have broad commercial appeal. Books on serious topics, such as Indian religion, might be beautiful, but "it would be unwise for any one to expect that a large quantity of copies [of *The Song of God*] will be sold."[88]

Mukerji's frustrations mounted. He sent off several hastily composed manuscripts. Dutton, however, did not think much of them, believing they were repetitive, with one even "lifted almost bodily" from earlier work. Mukerji and Patty apparently also coauthored a children's book, but the work was uneven and Dutton returned it as unacceptable.[89] Unbeknownst to Mukerji, editors within E. P. Dutton privately expressed mounting impatience with the agitated and unproductive author. One even advised Macrae that Mukerji was "finished as an author, either because he is not in good health or because the well of his inspiration has run dry."[90]

Mukerji also found little comfort or strength in his family life. He had been a loving husband and father at times, but his mounting obsessions distanced him from Patty and Gopal. As he retreated from those who loved him, Patty immersed herself in her own work and regularly spent time away from Mukerji. Neither of them devoted much attention to their son, who spent most of his life in boarding schools in Europe and New England. There is a great irony in Mukerji's being known for his wise and instructive children's books but unable to be a parent close to his own son. The happiness and understanding that he brought to other families through his writing eluded his own family. Being away at school may in fact have been a blessing of sorts for Gopal, since he was spared from witnessing his father's decline. But by the time Gopal entered Phillips Exeter Academy in New Hampshire, he knew he had a troubled parent. Sometime in 1934–35, he wrote "Two Sides of My Father," a school essay that provides poignant observations about his father at this time.

Gopal began his school paper acknowledging that although every personality has different sides, there was an "amazing contrast" between

The Life and Death of Dhan Gopal Mukerji   319

how he and others outside the family viewed his father. Friends and acquaintances saw an active, public person, but in Gopal's view, his father preferred an "almost monastic seclusion" within the family. The public saw his father as a successful writer and lecturer, as a Hindu who led a colorful life, writing of the exotic and metaphysical, of the jungle, and of India's villages and cities. His audiences enjoyed him because he introduced new emotions into their lives. However, for his father, such "success is a curse, a stumbling block in the path of a spiritual life." He once desired this fame and enjoyed the public's attention, it was true, but now even though his mind and soul sought peace, he could not find it. Gopal wrote, "Revolution in India, depression in America, both took their toll of his mind and body until a nervous breakdown followed. Then I knew my father for the first time, teaching me, training me, having me meditate with him; teaching me yoga and the higher spiritual disciplines were a few of the things he did so that both he and I could not be hurt by the three greeds and terrors: desire for fame and fear of oblivion; desire for money and the fear of the lack of it; and last, the desire for all the little vanities of life, and the fear of not enjoying them." For five years, Gopal continued, he saw his father trying to train himself to be able to live on this earth without it hurting him; he wanted to discover "spiritual self-defense." No longer did he lecture for money; he refused to worry about it so that his mind might be kept pure in order to help Americans "to live in the hell of machinery and noise they had created." Gopal concluded, wisely but sadly, that his father was "a curiosity to some and a means of learning to others. He is none of these things in my eyes. He is not even my father. He is just another man hunting for the truth, trying to see god and help others do the same; helping them to live in this queer world of their own making."[91]

It seemed that Gopal wrote metaphorically about Mukerji's no longer being his father, but his father indeed had declared that he could not continue being a parent. Mukerji informed Gopal that he surrendered his son's care to a Ramakrishna monk in Boston. Other than Mukerji's repeated efforts to have Gopal communicate with the swami, however, the abandonment actually meant little. Mukerji remained as distant, or as close, to Gopal as he had ever been. During breaks from school, Gopal, encouraged by his mother, spent some time with his father typing manuscripts and attempting to cater to his eccentricities, but his father's mental disabilities

320   *Chapter Fifteen*

became impossible for the young man to endure. His father asked him to join in all-night meditations in the woods and he spoke incessantly about spiritual matters that seemed to make little sense. He spent increasing amounts of time practicing yoga. Gopal had to flee after a few weeks of contact to preserve his own emotional well-being.[92]

In the summer of 1935, Mukerji suffered another breakdown. He tried to recuperate again in Stockbridge, where he had stayed during his previous troubles. After several months of rest and therapy, he returned to his New York home and even to the speaking circuit for a short while. He delivered one of his last public talks in Detroit in March 1936. It was suggestively titled "The Conflict of Past and Present in the Far East."[93] The various conflicts within *him* also continued to churn. He attended his son's graduation from Exeter in June. He was a proud parent that day, but one devoid of energy. Soon afterward, he composed an affectionate letter to Gopal, who had hired on as a hand on an ocean freighter to get away from his unstable father. Mukerji offered helpful travel tips on getting around in Europe and ended his affectionate note assuring his son, "I have no anxiety in my heart. [God] is guiding you to the fuller revelation of your innate divinity. Rejoice. Dad." Mukerji never sent the letter.[94]

On July 14, 1936, Patty returned from a stay in New Milford and discovered her husband's body hanging in a closet in their New York apartment. He was clad in his sleeping clothes and had left no suicide note, although he had composed a final letter to the head of the Ramakrishna mission in India. A few months earlier, he had consoled his good friend Nehru on the death of his wife Kamala by saying that Kamala had finally been released from the painful disease that had afflicted her. "She is free," he wrote; she had entered the "homeland of eternity." Now, Mukerji followed.[95] Young Gopal did not learn the news for a week. He was on the Atlantic and heard about the suicide from his mother, who had hurried to London.[96]

Mukerji's death shocked his friends and literary circles around the world. The *New York Times* announced the event in an article the following day.[97] Reuters News Agency flashed the news internationally and the press throughout India ran reports. In India, after hearing the news, Jadu wrote Patty that "the whole country and the entire Indian and European press felt a wrench of the heart." Jadu confided that he had had a "peculiar dream" on the fifteenth and now understood its symbolic significance. It had meant that Dhan was united with God. Upon learning of Mukerji's death, Jawaharlal Nehru sent Patty his condolences, saying that he was "shocked and greatly upset." Years later, Nehru continued to recall Mukerji with touching fondness.[98]

How can his suicide be understood? Mukerji clearly was disturbed and emotionally tortured. Clinical history also offers insight: a history of suicide plagued the Mukerji family. Other brothers and close relatives had taken their lives. But Patty's philosophical and empathetic understanding of the death remains equally compelling. In letters to close friends, she tried to make sense of her husband's death and console those who were grief-stricken. "Don't worry about Dhan," she wrote Roger Baldwin, "he is happy at last." She reported that "life had lost its flavor and meaning to him," and he no longer found satisfaction with friends, work, or new experiences. He longed for only one thing, "to be united with the Lord." He had tried every way possible to attain spiritual union, but the longing grew too great. Finally, he "threw himself into the arms of the Lord."[99]

Patty wrote that in the days before his death, Mukerji had actually been calmer and happier than he had been for some time. He had just submitted page proofs of a new children's book, and was planning another visit to India. "He had strict views of suicide," she wrote. Hinduism did not condone suicide to escape the troubles of life, but it did allow personal sacrifice in certain instances. Her husband, she recalled, "had entire faith in the love, support and guidance of God. But the evening of his death he wrote a beautiful, poignant letter to the head of the Ramakrishna Mission in India. Probably he went into deep meditation after that. And then—he took himself to God." She continues, "How can we feel regret or sorrow? He has what he wanted—the only thing he wanted."[100]

The letter to India that Patty mentioned was in fact probably Mukerji's last communication with anyone on this earth; it revealed that several weeks earlier the Ramakrishna monks had sent him an ochre robe to honor his spiritual devotion. It was an extraordinary act, for such benefaction was usually reserved for those who had engaged in formal training under a swami's guidance. Writing in Bengali, Mukerji expressed his deep gratitude to Swami Akhandananda, ending his letter (which was later translated by Dr. Prithwindra Mukherjee, a scholar of Indian culture and a Mukerji relative) with a rambling cry of tortured resolve:

322   *Chapter Fifteen*

You ask me to write, after reflection. I find, I am prepared. My decision has been taken, on reflection. It has been decided: I am. Who decided, you know it. I am mere instrument.

The answer you promoted me to give, I have given. What guts do I have to send a reply to such a letter. Maintain grace. Maintain grace on me. Lord, maintain grace. I am prepared. I seek refuge, Lord seek refuge, Lord seek refuge.[101]

In taking his own life in New York City on a sweltering summer's night, Dhan Gopal Mukerji finally found refuge and the silence that he had desperately wanted in this world.

Tributes to Mukerji appeared around the world after his death. In India, an old friend, Ben Misra, began his public reminiscence of Mukerji in anguish: "A suicide! It is terrible! It is incredible! It is terribly incredible! It is incredibly terrible!"[102] Mukerji's associates and colleagues in literary circles could not believe that he was gone from them. The editors of *The Horn Book Magazine,* a periodical published in Boston and devoted to the study of children's literature, published a special issue entirely dedicated to Mukerji.[103] It spoke of his "wisdom," "genius," and "spirit." Elizabeth Seeger, who wrote about Asia for American readers, ended her eulogy to him observing that "the West has gained immeasurably by his coming and India cannot have lost by having so eloquent an interpreter among us."[104]

Mukerji, indeed, left a rich legacy, although his influence is difficult to appreciate fully today, many decades since his passing. During his lifetime, thousands in America and England had heard his talks. It is true that often their response frustrated him—he detested the hustle and bustle of travel and he found America culturally unattractive. "Traveling in America," he once wrote in his diary, "does not rest my eyes and ears. In each town the same speech and the same clothes, manners and houses greet my senses." And the response of his audiences sometimes even angered him. He once complained that "in the countless women's clubs" he addressed, "all that I hear is that they have 'enjoyed' my message. Think of such a horrible word applied to my art." Yet, on other occasions he received reactions that touched and deeply gratified him. Just when he thought about abandoning lecturing, "strange things happened," he once recalled. In Sioux City, Iowa, a car mechanic and his wife told Mukerji that *The Face of Silence* changed the course of their lives. A restaurant maitre d' confided that

India's spirituality guided his existence. Mukerji wondered whether he was destined to "wander the wilderness of women's clubs" so that he could hear the rare voice of a toiler reassuring him of his message?[105]

The influence of his work on other writers is also important to consider. Mukerji helped introduce Indian spirituality to Romain Rolland, who went on to write extensively about India and its beliefs for readers in Europe and America. He contributed to the creative work of the Durants. Will Durant's *The Case for India* draws in part on several of Mukerji's books.[106] The eminent specialist on Asian religions and literature Herbert H. Gowen admired Mukerji and his work. The early iconoclastic psychologist Maurice Parmelee drew from Mukerji's work as well.[107] Mukerji's opus was an integral part of a far-ranging intellectual effort in the early twentieth century that seriously studied Indian civilization and drew upon it for inspiration and direction. Those involved included such figures such as T. S. Eliot, Theodore Dreiser, Eugene O'Neill, Lewis Mumford, Luther Burbank, and Patrick Geddes.[108] Mukerji was good friends with A. J. Liebling, who, writing for the *New Yorker,* became one of America's leading journalists. Mukerji personally encouraged Van Wyck Brooks's continuing interest in India and even tried to get him to collaborate in writing a book on yoga just weeks before the suicide.[109]

Dhan Gopal Mukerji made few extended public comments about American life and culture. He was known here mainly as an interpreter of India, not America. The last chapters in *Caste and Outcast* are his most detailed published description of his life in America, and other than comments to reporters and in public addresses here and there, he did not engage in lengthy discussions of life in his adopted country. Privately, however, he made many comments about American politics—he was troubled by the dominance of Wall Street over American life and he saw the election of Herbert Hoover in 1928 as a disaster for democracy: "le regime [*sic*] democratique est fini," he wrote Patty. "Big money, big trade, and big comfort will be with us from now on." He feared the "imperial thrust" of America into the Pacific; even England had "to bow before caesar!" and "Japan must bend the knee before Rome."[110] But he differed from other writers from Asia who often made trenchant public observations, even extended critiques, of America. His contemporary Hu Shih, the Chinese intellectual who lived for many years in America, made expansive comments on what he believed were the strengths and weaknesses of the West and drew from his Confucian

324   *Chapter Fifteen*

cultural background to consider the relations between the West and East.[111] Carlos Bulosan, the Filipino author who wrote in the 1940s and whose own semiautobiographical narrative, *America Is in the Heart,* was published two decades after *Caste and Outcast,* advanced an explicitly radical political critique of America.[112] Though Mukerji condemned colonialism, race prejudice, and the arrogance of the West toward India, he never was attracted to formal political ideologies. He rejected Bolshevism vehemently and was even uncomfortable with the socialist ideas of his friend Nehru.

But seen in another way, Mukerji's entire work, taken in the context of his personal life, was thoroughly political, in that it constituted a sustained cultural critique of America, albeit made on aesthetic, even spiritual, grounds. He commented indirectly, through intimation. His fond invocations of India, with its social and natural color, rhythm of life, and values, contrasted with an America he often found devoid of human feeling and connection. He promoted Indian spirituality to address the void in America's soul. America, he saw, was lost in materialism, violence, religious narrowness, and a frantic way of living that emphasized "doing" over "being."[113] Moreover, his critique was specifically about aspects of America and not of the West or modernity generally. He regularly looked to England, France, and Switzerland for peace and aesthetic pleasure. He did not reject America out of hand—much attracted and inspired him, even as it depressed him, as America had done with others. He admired the promise of America, along with its breadth and vitality; he loved the lyricism and expansiveness of Walt Whitman and was drawn to the work of writers such as Theodore Dreiser.[114] Mukerji was undoubtedly an effective cultural interpreter, but he was more than a transmitter or a popularizer, as the notion "cultural interpreter" sometimes suggests. He was deeply committed to offering America an alternative vision, a new way of life, and a consciousness of a new civilization. Everyone would have to find his or her own answer, however. Mukerji was not a proselytizer. He only wanted to help America see beyond itself.

Part of his vision was that of the oneness of humankind, which transcended race and nation. He was proud of being Indian, but he never was an exclusivist or a chauvinist. His vision included the notion of oneness of all beings. It was a vision that had meaning for civilization as well as for the individual seeker. A chant to Silence, which he reproduced in one of his books, contained these multiple implications.

O thou River of miracles that is within me,
pour the healing waters of compassion on the
wounded body of Man and make him whole.[115]

His tragedy is that the joy and peace he undoubtedly helped others attain, the personal or social vision he inspired others to seek, ultimately eluded Dhan Gopal Mukerji himself in this world.

Appendix: Selected Work[1]

Books

Ghosts of Gold Mountain: The Epic Story of the Chinese Who Built the Transcontinental (New York: Houghton Mifflin Harcourt, 2019)

Chinese and the Iron Road: Building the Transcontinental, edited with Shelley Fisher Fishkin (Stanford: Stanford University Press, 2019)

Fateful Ties: The History of America's Preoccupation with China (Cambridge: Harvard University Press, 2015)

Asian American Art: A History, 1850–1970, edited with Mark Dean Johnson, Paul J. Karlstrom, and Sharon Spain (Stanford: Stanford University Press, 2008)

Before Internment: Essays by Yuji Ichioka, edited with Eiichiro Azuma (Stanford: Stanford University Press, 2006)

Chinese American Voices: From the Gold Rush to the Present, edited with Judy Yung and Him Mark Lai (Berkeley: University of California Press, 2006)

Dhan Gopal Mukerji, *Caste and Outcast,* edited and presented by Gordon H. Chang, Purnima Mankekar, and Akhil Gupta (Stanford: Stanford University Press, 2002)

Asian Americans and Politics: Perspectives, Experiences, Prospects, edited by Gordon H. Chang (Stanford and Washington, D.C.: Stanford University Press; Woodrow Wilson Center Press, 2001)

Morning Glory, Evening Shadow: Yamato Ichihashi and His Internment Writings, 1942–1945 (Stanford: Stanford University Press, 1997)

Friends and Enemies: The United States, China, and the Soviet Union, 1948–1972 (Stanford: Stanford University Press, 1990)

328 Appendix

Essays, Book Chapters, Other

"A 'New Normal' or Returning to the 'Old Normal': Deteriorating U.S.-China Relations, Chinese Americans, and the Future," *Journal of Chinese Overseas* (20:1), 2024, pp. 42–49

"The Railroad in the Chinese American Imagination," in *Fifty Years of Photographic Justice: Corky Lee's Asian America*, edited by Chee Wang Ng and Mae Ngai (New York: Clarkson Potter, 2024), pp. 262–263.

"Introduction" to Andy Hirsch, *The Transcontinental Railroad: Crossing the Divide* (New York: First Second, 2022), pp. i–iv

"'Labor and Capital,' 'A Note for History,' and 'The Chinese and the Stanfords': Nineteenth Century America's Fraught Relationship with the China Men," *Amerasia Journal* (45:1), 2019, pp. 3–5, 86–102

"Chinese Americans and China: A Fraught and Complicated Relationship," International Symposium to Commemorate the 40th Anniversary of the Normalization of U.S.-China Diplomatic Relations, Carter Center and Emory University, 2019 (unpublished)

"Remembering Dawn Mabalon," *Amerasia Journal* (44:3), 2019, pp. 133–135

"Recovering the Experience of Chinese Railroad Workers in North America," with Shelley Fisher Fishkin and "Chinese Railroad Workers and the U.S. Transcontinental Railroad in Global Perspective," in *Chinese Railroad Workers in North America: Recovery and Representation*, edited by Hsinya Huang (Taipei: Bookman, 2017), pp. 1–10, 11–31

"Not So Simple Life Choices," *American Quarterly* (69:3), Sept. 2017, pp. 551–557

"Preface," *Works by Chang Shu-Chi* (Hangzhou, China: Qinzhe Art Center, 2017), pp. 19–28

"Fragments of the Past: Archaeology, History, and the Chinese Railroad Workers of North America," (with Shelley Fisher Fishkin), *Historical Archaeology* (49:1), March 2015, pp. 1–3

"History of the Chinese Culture Center in the Twenty-First Century," Chinese Culture Foundation, San Francisco, 2015

"China and the Pursuit of America's Destiny: Nineteenth-Century Imagining and Why Immigration Restriction Took So Long," *Journal of Asian American Studies* (15:2), June 2012, pp. 145–169

"Trans-Pacific Composition: Zhang Shuqi Paints in California," in *Zhang Shuqi in California*, edited by Jianhua Shu (Santa Clara: Silicon Valley Art Center, 2012), pp. 20–30; revised version in *Works of Zhang Shuqi* (Hangzhou: zhejiang meishuguan, zhongguo meishu xueyuan chubanshe, 2012)

"Chinese Painting Comes to America: Zhang Shuqi and the Diplomacy of Art," in *East West Interchanges in America Art: A Long and Tumultuous Relationship*, edited by Cynthia Mills, Lee Glazer, and Amelia Goerlitz (Washington, D.C: Smithsonian Institution Press, 2012), pp. 126–141

"Jake Lee and Chinese American History," *Finding Jake Lee* (San Francisco Chinese Historical Society of America, 2012), p. 5

"Stick to Your Guns (and Don't Let Theirs Intimidate You): Reflections on Standing Up for Your Scholarship, Twenty Years After 'JFK, China, and the Bomb,'" *Passport* (43:1), April 2012, pp. 22–23

"Eternally Foreign: Asian Americans, History, and Race," in *Doing Race: 21 Essays for the Twenty-First Century,* edited by Hazel Rose Marcus and Paula M. L. Moya (New York: Norton, 2010), pp. 216–233

"The Many Sides of Happy Lim: aka Hom Ah Wing, Lin Jian Fu, Lin Chien Fu, Hom Yen Chuck, Lam Kin Foo, Lum Kin Foo, Hom, Lim Goon Wing, Lim Gin Foo, Gin Foo Lin, Koon Wing Lim, Henry Chin, Lim Ying Chuck, Lim Ah Wing, et al.," *Amerasia Journal* (34:2), 2008, pp. 70–98

"Nixon in China and Cold War I and Cold War II," *Diplomatic History* (32:3), June 2008, pp. 493–496

"Words Matter," *Diplomatic History* (31:1), January 2007, pp. 163–166

"Remembering Yuji," in *Before Internment: Essays in Prewar Japanese American History,* edited by Gordon H. Chang and Eiichiro Azuma (Stanford: Stanford University Press, 2006), pp. 301–305

"Introduction," with Mark Dean Johnson, *Asian/American/Modern Art: Shifting Currents, 1900–1970,* edited by Daniell Cornell and Mark Dean Johnson (San Francisco: Fine Arts Museums, University of California Press, 2008), pp. 9–13

"Social Darwinism versus Social Engineering: The 'Education' of Japanese Americans During World War II," in *Landscaping the Human Garden: 20th Century Population Management in a Comparative Framework,* edited by Amir Weiner (Stanford: Stanford University Press, 2003), pp. 189–204

"Whose 'Barbarism'? Whose 'Treachery'?: Race and Civilization in the Unknown United States–Korea War of 1871," *Journal of American History* (89:4), March 2003, pp. 1331–1365

"Asian Americans and Politics: Some Perspectives from History," *Asian Americans and Politics: Perspectives, Experiences, Prospects,* edited by Gordon H. Chang (Stanford, Calif., and Washington, D.C.: Stanford University Press and the Woodrow Wilson Center Press, 2002), pp. 13–38

"America's Dong Kingman—Dong Kingman's America," in *Dong Kingman in San Francisco* (San Francisco: Chinese Historical Society of America, 2001), pp. 20–24

"Writing the History of Chinese Immigrants," *South Atlantic Quarterly* (Spring/Winter 1999), pp. 135–142

330   *Appendix*

"Are There Other Ways to Think About the 'Great Interregnum'?," contribution to special issue, "Considering Opportunities: American Efforts to Reconcile U.S.-China Relations during the Great Interregnum," *Journal of American-East Asian Relations* (Spring 1998), pp. 117–122

"Who Benefited? Forty-Five Years of U.S.-China Relations," *Diplomatic History* (21:2), April 1997, 323–327

"Asian Immigrants and American Foreign Relations," in *Pacific Passage: The Study of American–East Asian Relations on the Eve of the Twenty-First Century,* edited by Warren I. Cohen (New York: Columbia University Press, 1996), pp. 103–118

"History and Postmodernism," *Amerasia Journal* (21:1–2), 1995, pp. 89–93

"Eisenhower and Mao's China," in *Eisenhower: A Centenary Assessment,* edited by Günter Bischof and Stephen E. Ambrose (Baton Rouge: Louisiana State University Press, 1995), pp. 191–205

"'Superman Is About to Visit the Relocation Centers' and the Limits of Wartime Liberalism," *Amerasia Journal* (19:1), 1993, pp. 37–59

"Indignities Suffered: The Wartime Experience of Yamato Ichihashi and His Family," *Amerasia Journal* (19:1), 1993, pp. 161–162

"Absence of War in the United States–China Confrontation over Quemoy and Matsu in 1954–55: Contingency, Luck, Deterrence?," with He Di, *American Historical Review* (98:5), December 1993, pp. 1500–1524

"Asian Americans and the Writing of Their History," *Radical History Review* (53), 1992, pp. 105–114

"JFK Twenty-Five Years after Dallas," *Reviews in American History* (18:2), 1990, pp. 249–255

"Forbidden Fruits," *Amerasia Journal* (17:1), 1991, pp. 181–186

"Interview with Su Shaozhi, Dec. 1985" and "Comments," Symposium on Marxism in China Today, *Bulletin of Concerned Asian Scholars* (20:1), 1988, pp. 11–18, 26–27

"To the Nuclear Brink: Eisenhower, Dulles, and the Quemoy-Matsu Crisis of 1954–55," *International Security* (12:4), Spring 1988, pp. 96–123

"JFK, China, and the Bomb," *Journal of American History* (74:4), 1988, pp. 1287–1310

Public Engagement

"The Long, Sickening History of Anti-Asian Violence," *Responsible Statecraft,* March 26, 2021

"Our Fifth Extreme Isolation: Why We're Thankful That We're All Here to Shelter in Place," *The American Scholar,* April 17, 2020

"'Run Them Over': The Rise of a New Sinophobia and Its Dangers to Us All," *Responsible Statecraft,* March 27, 2020

"Remember the Chinese Railroad Workers," *Los Angeles Times*, May 8, 2019

"Just How Far Will Reckless Trump Push China?," *South China Morning Post,* Jan. 20, 2017

"Historical Links Will Ensure the Sino-U.S. Relationship Endures Well Beyond the Current China Bashing," *South China Morning Post*, Aug. 21, 2016

"The Chinese Helped Build America," *Forbes.com*, May 11, 2014

"Why Become a Historian," American Historical Association, 1999. https://www .historians.org/resource/why-become-a-historian-gordon-h-chang/

"'We Almost Wept,'" *Stanford Magazine*, Nov./Dec. 1996

Recorded Lectures and Talks

"Beyond Promontory: Chinese Railroad Workers and the Rise of California," March 2023. https://huntington.org/videos-and-recorded-programs/asian -american-experiences-california-past-present-future

"Anti-Asian Violence and the New Sinophobia," Chinese Historical Society of Southern California, May 2022. https://www.youtube.com/watch?v =TsDouwhH38s&t=284s

"Chinese Workers and America's First Transcontinental Railroad, a Global Perspective," Kennedy Center, Brigham Young University, 2021. https://www .youtube.com/watch?v=Iz-CZO7aoSQ&t=34s

"Alien Chinese Railroad Workers and American National History," Clements Center for Presidential History, Southern Methodist University, 2019. https:// www.youtube.com/watch?v=bqe1uOQqSOY&t=13s

"The LONG History of America-China Relations," Stanford University, 2016. https://www.youtube.com/watch?v=vW747IAz154&t=36s

"Working on the Railroad: Chinese Workers and America's First Transcontinental Line," Chicago Humanities Festival, 2015. https://www.chicagohumanities .org/media/working-railroad/

"Chinese Painting Comes to America: Zhang Shuqi and the Diplomacy of Art," Symposium, Smithsonian American Art Museum, October, 2009. https:// www.youtube.com/watch?v=D_m8_uMtWng&t=64s

"InterChange: Conversation about *Morning Glory, Evening Shadow*," Stanford Digital Repository, October 1996. https://purl.stanford.edu/xs715rro785

Acknowledgments

Completing this volume was more challenging than I had anticipated. I found myself wondering what pieces to select, how to organize the diverse chapters, and who might be interested in them and for what reason. The answers did not come easily. Writing the introduction was also unexpectedly difficult for similar reasons and because of my reticence to speak about myself. But through it all, having to engage in self-reflection was rewarding, as it required me to think systematically about the twists and turns in my career and my life. I hope that readers will find something useful in these pages.

Countless individuals over the years helped in the writing of the work presented in this volume. Many are acknowledged in the introductory notes of the chapters, but many more are not, and I regret that it is not possible to retrieve all their names now. I am thinking of the countless students, colleagues, library staff, editors, assistants, anonymous readers, discussants, and book and journal staff workers who make scholarship possible. Scholarship is a genuinely collaborative enterprise, despite the popular image of the lone scholar toiling away in monkish isolation.

I give profuse thanks to several colleagues who helped me shape this present volume. They shared thoughts about the idea of such a volume itself, the selection of chapters, and drafts of the introduction and chapter notes. Most useful were their views about what I might say about what I have done in my career and its relationship to my activism. I sincerely appreciate their constructive candor. Among these colleagues are Calvin

334 *Acknowledgments*

Cheung-Miaw, Madeline Hsu, Evelyn Hu-DeHart, Bob Lee, Sheila Melvin, Dave Roediger, and Chris Suh. Other colleagues, including Shana Bernstein, Jennifer Gee, Kevin Kim, Koji Lau-Ozawa, Shelley Lee, Paul Nauert, Beth Lew-Williams, Lok Siu, Alastair Su, Philip Thai, Cecilia Tsu, Judy Wu, and Vivian Yan-Gonzales, have been special interlocutors over many years, and I thank them. Jerald Adamos, Aleesa Alexander, anthony lising antonio, Joel Beinin, Bart Bernstein, Al Camarillo, Clay Carson, Harry Elam, Michelle Elam, Michelle Dinh, Hien Do, Shelley Fisher Fishkin, Estelle Freedman, Allyson Hobbs, Roland Hsu, David Kennedy, Marci Kwon, Kathryn Gin Lum, Hazel Markus, Yumi Moon, Paula Moya, Stephen Murphy-Shigematsu, Cindy Ng, Hilton Obenzinger, David Palumbo-Liu, Jack Rakove, Richard Roberts, Ramon Saldivar, Steve Sano, Matt Snipp, Matt Sommer, Claude Steele, Linda Tran, Jeanne Tsai, Jun Uchida, Barbara Voss, Richard White, Christine Min Wotipka, and many others at Stanford, and Adrian Arima, Monica Arima, Eiichiro Azuma, Rick Baldoz, Jindong Cai, Yong Chen, Barre Fong, Will Gow, Hsinya Huang, Mark Johnson, Denise Khor, Don Lamm, Valerie Matsumoto, Joseph Ng, Laura Ng, Lea Anne Ng, Mae Ngai, Simei Qing, Greg Robinson, Jianhua Shu, Selia Tan, Karen Umemoto, Carolyn Wong, Eddie Wong, David Yoo, Connie Young Yu, and Helen Zia have also provided special friendship, intellectual energy, and valuable counsel over many years. I honor friends, now sadly passed, who played important roles in my life: Wilma Chan, Phil Choy, Carl Degler, Peter Duus, George Fredrickson, Hal Kahn, Emma Gee, Yuji Ichioka, Him Mark Lai, Dawn Mabalon, Lyman Van Slyke, Jean Yonemura, and Judy Yung. At the genesis of this volume, Margo Irvin, my editor at Stanford University Press who provided inestimable support in building the book series on Asian American Studies at the Press, encouraged me to pursue the project. Her invaluable comments while I was conceiving and shaping the volume helped give it concrete form, far beyond my original hazy conception. Thank you, Margo. I also thank her successor at the Press, Dylan Kyung-lim White, and the excellent production team at SUP. Also at Stanford is Ben Stone, curator of American and British History in Green Library. Ben provided enormous help with my many research projects and is present in just about every chapter. He has partnered with me in collecting a rich and growing array of archival material on Asian Americans and is making Stanford Library a place for generative research about them. Thank you, Ben. Special thanks also go to Director of

Research Sue Jester, library and museum curators, and other wonderful colleagues at the Huntington Library, Museum, and Gardens in San Marino, California, who made my year-long fellowship there in 2023–2024 a memorable and productive experience. My cohort of research fellows provided rich intellectual engagement, inspiration, and comradery that formed the social environment for the completion of this book. Thank you to everyone in the Huntington gang!

Ernie and Sharon have provided a lifetime of love and support, and I thank them. I also want to express my special appreciation to Vicki, who understood my intentions, stiffened my resolve when I wondered about why I should devote time to this book effort, shared keen insights into my work that no one else could see, and critiqued the manuscript with discernment. She has been my life partner. This book is dedicated to her and to our lovely, intelligent, and thoughtful daughters, Chloe and Maya!

Notes

Introduction

1. Theresa Sparks, *China Gold* (Fresno, Calif.: Guild Press, 1954).

2. See Gordon H. Chang, "Why Become a Historian?" AHA newsletter, n.d.

3. See, for example, Richard Leopold, *The Growth of American Foreign Policy* (New York: Knopf, 1962), which was the first text on American diplomacy that I studied. See also Alexander George and Richard Smoke, *Deterrence in American Foreign Policy: Theory and Practice* (New York: Columbia University Press, 1974), which occupied a central position in security studies when I was in graduate school.

4. For an expanded account of my life at Princeton and beyond, see William H. Tucker, *Princeton Radicals of the 1960s, Then and Now* (Jefferson, N.C.: McFarland & Company, 2015).

5. Arno Mayer, *Wilson v. Lenin: Political Origins of the New Diplomacy, 1917–1918* (New Haven, Conn.: Yale University Press, 1959).

6. See, for example, Marilyn B. Young, *The Rhetoric of Empire: American China Policy, 1895–1901* (Cambridge, Mass.: Harvard University Press, 1968); Frances FitzGerald, *Fire in the Lake: the Vietnamese and Americans in Vietnam* (New York: Little, Brown, 1972); and Stuart Creighton Miller, *"Benevolent Assimilation": The American Conquest of the Philippines, 1899–1903* (New Haven, Conn.: Yale University Press, 1982).

7. The Alice Fong Yu Papers are now housed in Special Collections, Green Library, Stanford University. My father's and mother's papers are also at Stanford under the name of Zhang Shuqi Papers.

338 *Notes to Introduction*

8. On Chinese American history, I think of Thomas Chinn, Phil Choy, William Hoy, Him Mark Lai, and Emma Louie, among others.

9. See "Guide to the Stanford University, Asian American Activities Center," Records SC0487, https://oac.cdlib.org/findaid/ark:/13030/kt9r29s431/entire_text/ (Dec. 15, 2023); and Asian American Advocacy at Stanford, https://exhibits .stanford.edu/stanford-aapi/catalog?q=SAASEI+OR+proposal+OR+program+OR +class+NOT+AIM+&search_field=search (Dec. 15, 2023).

10. See, for example, "Our Fifth Extreme Isolation: Why We're Thankful That We're All Here to Shelter in Place," *The American Scholar*, April 17, 2020.

11. For volumes in the Asian American Studies series at Stanford University Press, see https://www.sup.org/search?subjects=Asian+American+Studies.

12. An expanded but still partial list of my scholarship in books and published work is included in the appendix.

13. See "Stick to Your Guns (and Don't Let Theirs Intimidate You): Reflections on Standing Up for Your Scholarship, Twenty Years After 'JFK, China, and the Bomb,'" *Passport*, April 2012, pp. 22–23.

14. See Erez Manela, "The United States in the World," in *American History Now*, edited by Eric Foner and Lisa McGirr (Philadelphia: Temple University Press, 2011), pp. 201–219.

15. Other scholars whose work influenced my early scholarship include Gerald Horne, Reginald Horsman, Akira Iriye, Harold Isaacs, and William Appleman Williams.

16. See https://www.sup.org/books/asian-american-studies/morning-glory -evening-shadow.

17. See Gordon H. Chang, "'We Almost Wept,' the Sad Journey of Yamato Ichihashi: From Stanford to the Internment Camps," and "Professor Yamato Ichihashi was a respected scholar and member of the Stanford community but that wasn't enough to spare him the humiliation of internment," and Diane Manuel, "A Personal Journey: Biographer Gordon Chang Feels a Kinship with His Subject," *Stanford Today Magazine*, Nov./Dec. 1996, pp. 50–56.

18. See "On the Same Page 2022: Interior Chinatown," Berkeley Library, University of California, Berkeley, https://guides.lib.berkeley.edu/interiorchinatown/ voices.

19. See "Announcement," Chinese Railroad Workers in North America Project, Stanford University, Aug. 31, 2020, http://web.stanford.edu/group/ chineserailroad/cgi-bin/website/. *The Chinese and the Iron Road*, edited by Gordon H. Chang and Shelley Fisher Fishkin, with Hilton Obenzinger and Roland Hsu (Stanford, Calif.: Stanford University Press, 2019) included an important study of mine, "The Chinese and the Stanfords: Nineteenth-Century America's Fraught Relationship with the China Men." It is not included in this volume.

Notes to Introduction and Chapter 1 339

20. See https://museum.stanford.edu/AAAI; https://www.famsf.org/exhibitions/asian-american-modern-art-shifting-currents-1900-1970; and https://oac.cdlib.org/findaid/ark:/13030/kt4d5nf319/.

Chapter 1

1. See William Burr and Jeffrey T. Richelson, "Whether to 'Strangle the Baby in the Cradle': The United States and the Chinese Nuclear Program, 1960–1964," *International Security* (25:3), Winter 2000–2001, pp. 54–99; and Gordon H. Chang, "Stick to Your Guns (and Don't Let Theirs Intimidate You): Reflections on Standing Up for Your Scholarship, Twenty Years After 'JFK, China, and the Bomb,'" *Passport*, April 2012, pp. 22–23.

2. "Should We Bomb Red China's Bomb?" *National Review*, Jan. 12, 1965, pp. 8–9. The call was repeated in another editorial, "Bomb the Bang," *ibid.*, June 1, 1965, pp. 449–50.

3. "Should We Bomb Red China's Bomb?" *ibid.*, pp. 9, 10.

4. Headquarters of the Commander-in-Chief Pacific, "Pacific General War Plan (U)," Jan. 1961, p. D–9, box 44, CCS 3146 CINCPAC-CNUNC (26 Jan 1961), sec. 1, Records of the Joint Chiefs of Staff 1961, RG 218 (National Archives); Ciro E. Zoppo and Alice L. Hsieh, "The Accession of Other Nations to the Nuclear Test Ban," March 8, 1961, p. 57, box 23, CCS 3050 Disarmament (8 Mar 1961), *ibid.*; Alice Langley Hsieh, *Communist China's Strategy in the Nuclear Era* (Englewood Cliffs, 1962), 154; Walt Whitman Rostow interviewed by Gordon H. Chang, June 6,1985, Austin, Texas (in Gordon H. Chang's possession); U.S. Department of State, *Bulletin,* Sept. 18, 1961, p. 487.

5. W. Averell Harriman to John F. Kennedy, Nov. 12, Nov. 15, 1960, USSR, General, box 125, Countries, President's Office files, John F. Kennedy Papers (John F. Kennedy Library, Boston, Mass.); George F. Kennan to Kennedy, Aug. 17, 1960, p. 7, attached to Kennan interview by Louis Fischer, March 23, 1963, transcript, Oral History Program (Kennedy Library); McGeorge Bundy, "Notes on discussion of the thinking of the Soviet leadership, Cabinet Room, February 11, 1961," pp. 1–6, USSR, General 2/2/61–2/14/61, box 176, Countries, National Security files, Kennedy Papers. Charles E. Bohlen concluded early in the administration that the "Soviet Union's great fear was not United States nuclear power, it was China's possession of the atomic bomb." Charles E. Bohlen, *Witness to History, 1929–1969* (New York, 1973), 475.

6. "President's Meeting with Khrushchev, Position Papers: Progress Toward a Viable World Order," May 26, 1961, USSR-Vienna Meeting: Background Documents, 1953–1961 (G-2), box 126, President's Office files, Kennedy Papers; "Communist China," May 25, 1961, *ibid.,* "President's Meeting with Khrushchev, Position Papers: Soviet Aims and Expectations," USSR-Vienna Meeting:

340   *Notes to Chapter 1*

Background Documents, 1953–1961 (G-3), *ibid.,* "Soviet Positions on Various Disarmament Questions," 5–7, *ibid.*

7. Theodore C. Sorensen, *Kennedy* (New York, 1965), 548–49; Arthur M. Schlesinger, Jr., *A Thousand Days: John F. Kennedy in the White House* (New York, 1965), 344.

8. Charles E. Bohlen to secretary of state, March 23, 1961, USSR, General 3/23/61–5/8/61, box 180, Countries, National Security files, Kennedy Papers.

9. Arthur Krock, no. 393, Memoranda, Book III, Oct. 1961, Arthur Krock Papers (Seeley G. Mudd Library, Princeton University, Princeton, N.J.); "Summary of the President's Remarks to the National Security Council Jan. 18, 1962," National Security Council Meetings, 1962, box 313, National Security files, Kennedy Papers.

10. Sorensen, *Kennedy,* 518.

11. For background on arms negotiations during the Eisenhower administration, see Robert A. Divine, *Blowing on the Wind: The Nuclear Test Ban Debate, 1954–1960* (New York, 1978); Lincoln P. Bloomfield, Walter C. Clemens, Jr., and Franklyn Griffiths, *Khrushchev and the Arms Race: Soviet Interests in Arms Control and Disarmament, 1954–1964* (Cambridge, Mass., 1966); and National Academy of Sciences (U.S.), Committee on International Security and Arms Control, *Nuclear Arms Control: Background and Issues* (Washington, 1985), 187–90.

12. Harold Karan Jacobson and Eric Stein, *Diplomats, Scientists, and Politicians: The United States and the Nuclear Test Ban Negotiations* (Ann Arbor, 1966), 381–416; Glenn T. Seaborg, *Kennedy, Khrushchev, and the Test Ban* (Berkeley, 1981), 162–71.

13. Arthur H. Dean, *Test Ban and Disarmament: The Path of Negotiation* (New York, 1966), 90–91; Jacobson and Stein, *Diplomats,* 397–413.

14. In a December 1962 television interview, Kennedy himself linked the worsening of Sino-Soviet relations with the stand of the United States during the Cuban missile crisis. See *Public Papers of the Presidents of the United States, John F. Kennedy: Containing the Public Messages, Speeches, and Statements of the President, January 1 to December 31, 1962* (Washington, 1963), 901–2. Ray S. Cline, "Sino-Soviet Relations," cover memorandum, Jan. 14, 1963, "USSR, General 1/9/63–1/14/63," box 180, National Security files, Kennedy Papers; Central Intelligence Agency, "Sino-Soviet Relations at a New Crisis," memorandum, Jan. 14, 1963, *ibid.*

15. Central Intelligence Agency, "Sino-Soviet Relations at a New Crisis," 6.

16. William R. Tyler interview by Elizabeth Donahue, March 7, 1964, transcript, 37–39, Oral History Program (Kennedy Library); William R. Tyler to Walter LaFeber, Dec. 10, 1971, attached to transcript of Tyler oral history, *ibid.*

17. William C. Foster interview by Charles T. Morrissey, Aug. 5, 1965, transcript, 36–37, *ibid.* Sections regarding China and the test ban are still sanitized,

Notes to Chapter 1   341

including several paragraphs in which Foster describes Kennedy's "willingness to consider politically dangerous moves" against China. *Ibid.*, 37. "Mr. Hilsman's Remarks At Director's Meeting," Jan. 22, 1963, National Security—Hilsman Summary of President's Views 1/22/63, box 5, Roger Hilsman Papers (Kennedy Library).

18. Seaborg, *Kennedy, Khrushchev, and the Test Ban,* 181, 188. Arthur Dean, an architect of the Limited Test Ban Treaty, also admitted that the treaty was based on the acceptance of the possibility of Soviet cheating. Dean, *Test Ban and Disarmament,* 82.

19. U.S. Congress, Senate, Preparedness Investigating Subcommittee of the Committee on Armed Services, *Military Aspects and Implications of Nuclear Test Ban Proposals and Related Matters,* 88 Cong., 1 sess., May 7, 1963, pp. 7–11.

20. Foy Kohler to Department of State, March 16, 1963, cable, Government Agencies, State Dept.—Miscellaneous Cables, 1961–1963, box 4, Vice Presidential Security file, Lyndon B. Johnson Papers (Lyndon Baines Johnson Library, Austin, Texas); Roger Hilsman to Dean Rusk, cover memorandum, March 7, 1963, cited in Bundy, Index of Weekend Papers, 1/63–3/63, box 318, National Security files, Kennedy Papers; Hilsman to Rusk, research memorandum, March 7, 1963, *ibid.*

21. Arms Control and Disarmament Agency, *Documents on Disarmament,* 1963 (Washington, 1964), 194; *New York Times,* May 30, 1963, p. 1.

22. Thomas L. Hughes to Rusk, June 14, 1963 (Freedom of Information Act release, in Chang's possession), 1, 4. In September 1963, after the Limited Test Ban Treaty had been signed, the U.S. embassy in Moscow studied the development of Moscow's stance toward the treaty. The study stated that the Soviet attitude shifted significantly in late May because Moscow concluded that the dispute with the Chinese was not going to be resolved. American Embassy, Moscow, to Department of State, "Motivations for Moscow's Signature of the Test Ban Agreement," Sept. 6, 1963, *ibid.*

23. American Embassy, Moscow, to Department of State, "Motivations," Sept. 6, 1963, pp. 4–5.

24. Rusk to Department of State, June 25, 1963, cable (Freedom of Information Act release, in Chang's possession).

25. *New York Times,* June 25, 1963, pp. 1, 10.

26. Brady G. Barr, memorandum, meeting of Harriman and Kield Gustav Knuth-Winterfeldt, July 1, 1963 (Freedom of Information Act release, in Chang's possession); H. H. Stackhouse, memorandum, meeting of Rusk and Mongi Slim, July 15, 1963, *ibid.*

27. Harriman to Kennedy, Nov. 12, Nov. 15, 1960, USSR, General, box 125, President's Office files, Kennedy Papers; Llewellyn E. Thompson interview by Donahue, March 25, 1964, transcript, 25–28, Oral History Program (Kennedy

342   *Notes to Chapter 1*

Library); Bloomfield, Clemens, and Griffiths, *Khrushchev,* 190; State Department, "Elements For a Package Deal With Moscow," July 3, 1963, ACDA Disarmament: Harriman trip to Moscow, part III, box 265, National Security files, Kennedy Papers; Walt Whitman Rostow, "Memorandum," July 5, 1963, *ibid.*; William C. Foster, "Memorandum for the President: Political Implications of a Nuclear Test Ban," July 12, 1963, *ibid.*; Col. Wm. F. Jackson to Lyndon B. Johnson, July 9, 1963, Colonel Burris, National Security Council, 1962–63, box 5, Vice Presidential Security file, Johnson Papers; "Personal & Confidential" memo to Johnson, *ibid*; Seaborg, *Kennedy, Khrushchev, and the Test Ban,* 228; Schlesinger, *Thousand Days, 825.*

28. *Time,* July 19, 1963, pp. 24–25; *New York Times,* July 14, 1963, pp. 1, 3; *ibid.,* July 15, 1963, p. 1; *ibid.,* July 16, 1963, pp. 1, 3; *Peking Review,* July 19, 1963, p. 10.

29. Sorensen, *Kennedy,* 734–35; Benjamin H. Read interview by Joseph E. O'Connor, Feb. 22, 1966, transcript, 3, Oral History Program (Kennedy Library).

30. Kennedy to Harriman, July 15, 1963, cable (Freedom of Information Act release, in Benjamin Loeb's possession), emphasis added. Glenn T. Seaborg, chairman of the Atomic Energy Commission under Kennedy, also suggests that Kennedy's July 15 cable to Harriman indicated a possible interest in a joint preemptive strike against Chinese nuclear facilities. Seaborg, *Kennedy, Khrushchev, and the Test Ban,* 239.

31. Rusk to Department of State, June 25, 1963.

32. Hsieh, *Communist China's Strategy,* 154; Memorandum of conversation, Harriman and Penn Nouth, Aug. 19, 1963 (Freedom of Information Act release, in Chang's possession); Rusk to American ambassador, Bonn, cable, July 24, 1963, *ibid.*; Barr, memorandum, meeting of Harriman and Knuth-Winterfeldt, July 1, 1963.

33. See, Oran R. Young, "Chinese Views on the Spread of Nuclear Weapons," in *Sino-Soviet Relations and Arms Control,* ed. Morton H. Halperin (Cambridge, Mass., 1967), 22–24; Walter C. Clemens, Jr., "The Nuclear Test Ban and Sino-Soviet Relations," *ibid.,* 149–150.

34. By 1963, following the withdrawal of Soviet technicians in 1960, trade with the Soviet Union and Eastern European countries dropped to about 30% of China's total. The Soviets announced that their trade with China fell by 67% during that period. See John Gittings, *Survey of the Sino-Soviet Dispute* (London, 1968), 129–34; and *New York Times,* July 15, 1963, p. 10. Robert McNamara to John F. Kennedy, draft memorandum, Feb. 12, 1963, Disarmament Proposals, Feb. 1963, Vice Presidential Security file, box 7, Johnson Papers.

35. Defense Department. "Harriman Trip to Moscow—Briefing Book, Vol. II," 6/20/63, Tab D, ACDA Disarmament, box 265, National Security files, Kennedy Papers; Arthur Barbar, "Briefing Book on US—Soviet Non-Diffusion Agreement for Discussion at the Moscow Meeting," June 12, 1963, vol. I, pp. 1–7, ACDA Disarmament, Harriman Trip to Moscow, *ibid.*

Notes to Chapter 1   343

36. The author gratefully acknowledges Gregg Herken's sharing of this information. Gregg Herken to David Thelen, March 4, 1987 (in Chang's possession); Joseph Alsop, "Thoughts out of China—I: Go versus No Go," *New York Times Magazine*, March 11, 1973, pp. 30–31, 100–105, 108. Just before the Chinese exploded their first atomic bomb in 1964, the *New York Times* reported it had learned that Kennedy officials had approached the Soviet Union about "the possibility of cooperating to prevent Chinese Communist nuclear-weapons development" during the 1963 test ban negotiations. The newspaper gave few specifics, other than that Khrushchev's response was not positive. *New York Times,* Oct. 2, 1964, p. 13.

37. Rusk to American ambassador, Bonn, cable, July 18, 1963 (Freedom of Information Act release, in Loeb's possession); Kohler to Bundy, cable, July 21, 1963; *ibid.*; *New York Times*, July 20, 1963, pp. 1, 2; *Ibid.,* July 21, 1963, pp. 1, 2.

38. Rusk to Harriman, cable, July 24, 1963 (Freedom of Information Act release, in Chang's possession); Harriman to Kennedy, cable, no. 277, July 23, 1963 (Freedom of information Act release, in Loeb's possession); Kohler to Rusk, cable, no. 294, July 23, 1963, *ibid.* George Bunn, general counsel of the Arms Control and Disarmament Agency (ACDA) in the Kennedy administration, was struck by the attention Harriman's cables from Moscow placed on Soviet concern about China. George Bunn conversation with Chang, Sept. 17, 1987 (in Chang's possession).

39. Rusk to Harriman, cable, July 23, 1963 (Freedom of Information Act release, in Loeb's possession); Schlesinger, *Thousand Days,* 829. For other interpretations of the Kennedy administration's possible military response to China's nuclear acquisition, see Franz Schurmann, *The Logic of World Power: An Inquiry into the Origins, Currents, and Contradictions of World Politics* (New York, 1974),385–95; and Gerald Segal, *Great Power Triangle* (London, 1982), 124–25.

40. *New York Times,* July 22, 1963, p. 2. Just hours before the president was to go before the nation, Washington sent Kennedy's draft speech to Harriman for his opinion. The draft contained several references to China omitted from the final version. One of the most explicit and revealing was "I do not, of course, expect the Communist Chinese to sign this treaty. They have already denounced it as a Capitalist plot. But if the response to this treaty can serve to increase their isolation from the world community—if it can encourage other nations to apply sanctions against their nuclear development—then the outlook is not altogether gloomy." A bitterness about the Chinese pervaded the draft that was absent from the final version. The draft was also more restrained about the importance of the treaty and included comments about how the "communist split" had played a major role in bringing about the U.S.-Soviet agreement. Rusk to Harriman, cable, July 26, 1963 (Freedom of Information Act release, in Chang's possession).

41. M. Stanton Evans, "At Home," *National Review,* Aug. 20, 1963, p. 6.

344   *Notes to Chapter 1*

42. Rusk to American ambassador, Bonn, cable, July 24, 1963 (Freedom of Information Act release, in Chang's possession).

43. U.S. Congress, Senate, Committee on Foreign Relations, "Declassified Portions of *Nuclear Test Ban Treaty,*" Aug. 28, 1963, p. 71, Records of the United States Senate, RG 46 (National Archives).

44. Preparedness Investigating Subcommittee, *Military Aspects,* June 26, 1963, pp. 300–305, *ibid.,* June 27, 1963, p. 376; Seaborg, *Kennedy, Khrushchev, and the Test Ban, 228–29.*

45. U.S. Congress, Senate, Committee on Foreign Relations, *Nuclear Test Ban Treaty,* 88 Cong., 1 sess., Aug. 19, 1963, pp. 274–75, 397; Preparedness Investigating Subcommittee, *Military Aspects,* Aug. 15, 1963, pp. 738, 676–77, 707.

46. Bundy, Memorandum for the Record, Sept. 15, 1964, McGeorge Bundy—Memos to the President, vol. VI, 7/1–9/30/64, Aides files, box 2, National Security files, Johnson Papers. Stewart Alsop and Rep. L. Mendel Rivers, chairman of the House Armed Services Committee, publicly called for U.S. strikes against China's nuclear facilities at about that time. See Foster Rhea Dulles, *American Policy toward Communist China, 1949–1969* (New York, 1972), 222–23. After the Chinese test explosion, a panel headed by Under Secretary of Defense Roswell Gilpatric considered recommending a "surgical strike," among other options, to stop China's further nuclear development. See Segal, *Great Power Triangle,* 127.

47. Warren I. Cohen, *Dean Rusk* (Totowa, 1980), 169; U.S. Department of State, *Bulletin,* Nov. 26, 1962, pp. 807–11; Central Intelligence Agency, "Possibilities of Greater Militancy by the Chinese Communists—SNIE 13-4-63," July 31, 1963, Possibilities of Greater Militancy by the Chinese Communists, Vice Presidential Security file—Nations and Regions, box 11, Johnson Papers; Committee on Foreign Relations, *Nuclear Test Ban Treaty,* Aug. 15, 1963, pp. 337, 342; declassified deletions from *Nuclear Test Ban Treaty* enclosed in M. Graeme Bannerman, Staff Director, Senate Committee on Foreign Relations, to Chang, Feb. 3, 1986 (in Chang's possession).

48. Bundy, Item no. 7, Miscellaneous Papers for Hyannisport, July 21–23, 1961, Index of Weekend Papers 1/61–12/61, box 318, National Security files, Kennedy Papers; Central Intelligence Agency, Office of Current Intelligence, "The Signs of Chinese Communist Friendliness," July 17, 1961, China General 7/15/61–7/24/61, box 22, *ibid.*; Bundy, Week End Reading, vol. II, July 21, 1962, Index of Weekend Papers 1/62–6/62, box 318, *ibid.*; Hilsman to Walter P. McConaughy, July 7,1961, China General 8/1/61–8/10/61, box 22, *ibid.*; Schlesinger, *Thousand Days,* 893–918; Sorensen, *Kennedy,* 724–40.

49. Hilsman to Harriman, Aug. 13, 1963, Test Ban Treaty 7/63, box 5, Hilsman Papers.

Chapter 2

1. Press Conference of January 18, 1961, *Public Papers of the Presidents of the United States: Dwight D. Eisenhower, 1960–1961* (Washington, D.C., 1960–61), 1043.

2. Blanche Wiesen Cook, *The Declassified Eisenhower: A Divided Legacy* (Garden City, N.Y., 1981), 108.

3. Stephen E. Ambrose, *Eisenhower: Soldier, General of the Army, President-Elect, 1890–1952* (New York, 1983), 530–34.

4. Robert J. Donovan, *Eisenhower: The Inside Story* (New York, 1956), 9.

5. Herbert S. Parmet, *Eisenhower and the American Crusades* (New York, 1972), 194–95.

6. Stephen E. Ambrose, *Eisenhower: The President* (New York, 1983), 213, 229.

7. See James Shepley, "How Dulles Averted War," *Life*, January 16, 1956.

8. The following discussion of the offshore island crises is largely based on my book *Friends and Enemies: The United States, China, and the Soviet Union, 1948–1972* (Stanford, Calif., 1990), 116–42, 182–94.

9. U.S. Department of State, *Foreign Relations of the United States, 1955–57*, III, 558–66.

10. Foster Rhea Dulles, *American Policy Toward Communist China, 1949–1969* (New York, 1972), 130–87; Adam Ulam, *Expansion and Coexistence: The History of Soviet Foreign Policy, 1917–67* (New York, 1968), 613–27; Arthur M. Schlesinger, Jr., *A Thousand Days: John F. Kennedy in the White House* (Boston, 1965), 443.

11. The following is based largely on my *Friends and Enemies*, 81–174.

12. Ambrose, *Eisenhower*, 99.

13. Chang, *Friends and Enemies*, 106–107.

14. Donovan, *Eisenhower: The Inside Story*, 132; Chang, *Friends and Enemies*, 115.

15. See David Mayers, "Eisenhower and Communism: Later Findings," in Richard A. Melanson and David Mayers, eds., *Reevaluating Eisenhower: American Foreign Policy in the Fifties* (Urbana, Ill., 1987), 89–119.

16. Summary of Discussion of the 398th meeting of the NSC, March 5, 1959, box 11. Ann Whitman NSC Series, Eisenhower Papers, in Eisenhower Library, Abilene, Kansas (hereinafter cited as EL).

17. Summary of Discussion of the 399th meeting of the NSC. March 12, 1959, box 11. Ann Whitman NSC Series, Eisenhower Papers, EL. There was no discussion in the NSC on this occasion about whether the United States would have to take on the Soviet Union if there was war with China. During the offshore island crises of 1955 and 1958, administration officials contemplated war with China, but did not assume that the Soviets would become directly involved.

346   *Notes to Chapter 2*

18. Nancy B. Tucker, "John Foster Dulles and the Taiwan Roots of the 'Two Chinas' Policy," in *John Foster Dulles and the Diplomacy of the Cold War,* ed. Richard Immerman (Princeton, N.J., 1990), 235–62; Chang, *Friends and Enemies,* 144–49.

19. Harold R. Isaacs, *The New World of Negro Americans* (New York, 1964), 45–46; Michael H. Hunt, *Ideology and U.S. Foreign Policy* (New Haven, Conn., 1987), 162–64; Chang, *Friends and Enemies,* 170–74.

20. Ambrose, *Eisenhower,* 102, 125–26; Chang, *Friends and Enemies,* 171–72.

21. Dwight D. Eisenhower, *At Ease: Stories I Tell to Friends* (Garden City, N.Y., 1967), 65.

22. Eisenhower, *At Ease,* 111, 229–30.

23. Robert H. Ferrell, ed., *The Eisenhower Diaries* (New York, 1981), 11–12, 23–26; Ambrose, *Eisenhower,* 125.

24. Alfred D. Chandler, Jr., ed., *The Papers of Dwight D. Eisenhower: The War Years* (Baltimore, Md., 1981), I, 180ff.

25. *Public Papers of the Presidents of the United States: Dwight D. Eisenhower, 1954* (Washington, D.C., 1955), 182; Dwight D. Eisenhower, *The White House Years: Waging Peace* (Garden City, N.Y., 1965), 369.

26. Mao Tse-tung's name does not even appear in the indexes of two of the major biographies of Eisenhower. See Parmet, *Eisenhower and the American Cntsades,* and Ambrose, *Eisenhower.*

27. On Ike's childhood, see Ambrose, *Eisenhower,* 13–36; on Mao, see Edgar Snow, *Red Star over China* (New York, 1968), 126–38.

28. See Stuart Shram, *Mao Tse-tung* (New York, 1967), 34–37.

29. Ambrose, *Eisenhower,* 9–10.

30. See Kenneth W. Thompson, "The Strengths and Weaknesses of Eisenhower's Leadership," in *Reevaluating Eisenhower,* ed. Melanson and Mayers, 17–25.

31. See John Shy and Thomas W. Collier, "Revolutionary War," in *Makers of Modern Strategy,* ed. Peter Paret (Princeton, N.J., 1986), 839. Also see Arthur Huck, *The Security of China: Chinese Approaches to Problems of War and Strategy* (New York, 1970), 53–65; Chong-pin Lin, *China's Nuclear Weapons Strategy: Tradition Within Evolution* (Lexington, Ky., 1988), 18–21.

32. For a comparison of Eisenhower and Kennedy, see Ambrose, *Eisenhower,* 638.

33. Eisenhower occasionally became involved in decision making concerning specific military matters, such as gun emplacements, weaponry, and tactics to oppose landing forces. See Goodpaster notes of March, 1955, NSC Meeting, 16 March 1955, Ann Whitman International Series, box 9, Formosa, Visit to CiNCPAC [1955] (1), in EL.

Notes to Chapters 2, 3, and 4   347

34. Shepley, "How Dulles Averted War." Eisenhower himself once said about fearing war, "I have one great belief; nobody in war or anywhere else ever made a good decision if he was frightened to death. You have to look facts in the face, but you have to have the stamina to do it without just going hysterical." He made this statement during the 1955 offshore island crisis. Ambrose, *Eisenhower*, 239.

35. Mao Tse-tung, "Talk with the American Correspondent Anna Louise Strong," in *Selected Readings* (Peking, 1971), 345–31. Also see Mao Tse-tung, "Problems of Strategy in China's Revolutionary War," in *Selected Works* (Peking, 1963), I, 233–39.

36. Eisenhower and Mao never had any direct contact with one another. Eisenhower's public comments about Mao were always predictably disparaging. What Mao's opinions were of Eisenhower, one can only speculate. However, Mao once said to Richard Nixon, during his first trip to China, that he, Mao, liked "rightists. . . . I am comparatively happy when these people on the right come into power" (Richard Nixon, *Memoirs* [New York, 1978], 562). Mao was being his usual cryptic self, although on other occasions he suggested a reason for his preference: Rightists were less deceptive than liberals and seemed to represent the monopoly capitalists more openly.

37. *Ibid.*, 376–77.

38. Sun Tzu, *The Art of War*, trans. Samuel B. Griffith (New York, 1963), 101.

Chapter 3

1. I thank Dr. Robert A. Kapp for the invitation to the conference and for his assistance with this essay.

2. "Some Are 'Crazy Rich,' But Asians' Inequality Is Widest in the U.S.," *New York Times*, Aug. 19, 2018.

3. http://en.falundafa.org/ (accessed Sept. 24, 2018).

4. https://www.shenyunperformingarts.org/ (accessed Sept. 24, 2018).

5. https://www.theepochtimes.com/ (accessed Sept. 24, 2018).

6. The author is a member of the organization.

7. https://www.committee100.org/ (accessed Sept. 24, 2018).

Chapter 4

The author thanks the Stanford History Department Faculty Seminar, Bruce Cumings, George Fredrickson, Walter LaFeber, Hyung Suk Lee, Jacqueline Pak, Richard Roberts, Roger R. Thompson, and Cecilia Tsu for very helpful comments on earlier drafts of this essay. Shana Bernstein and Victoria Sandin helped with editing and research. Generous financial support for research and writing came from Stanford's Center for International Security and Cooperation and the Center for East Asian Studies. A fellowship from the John Simon Guggenheim

348   Notes to Chapter 4

Foundation supported the author in 1999–2000, when much of the work on this essay was completed. The author also thanks J. Michael Miller, senior archivist at the Marine Corps University Research Archives, for his assistance in locating archival and published military materials and Ruth Simmons at Rutgers University Library for her help with the William Elliot Griffis Collection.

1. Albert Castel and Andrew C. Nahm, "'Our Little War with the Heathen,'" *American Heritage*, 19 (April 1968), 18–23, 72–75; Dale L. Walker, "America's War with the Hermits," *Retired Officer* (Oct. 1980), 24–27; Joanna Nicholls Kyle, "When We Trounced Korea," *National Magazine*, 17 (Jan. 1908), 411–18. The phrase is translated variously as the "1871 American incursion" or the "1871 foreign incursion," but I believe the translation used in the text is the most accurate. See the Yonhap News Agency, *Korea-U.S.A. Centennial, 1882–1982* (Seoul, 1982), 25.

2. Dae-Sook Suh, "The Centennial: A Brief History," in *Korea and the United States: A Century of Cooperation*, ed. Youngnok Koo and Dae-sook Suh (Honolulu, 1984), 3–19. The incident is described inaccurately or neglected in F. A. McKenzie, *The Tragedy of Korea* (London, 1908); Shannon McCune, "American Image of Korea in 1882: A Bibliographic Sketch," in *U.S.-Korean Relations: 1882–1982*, ed. Tae-Hwan Kwak (Seoul, 1982), 141–56; Young Hum Kim, *East Asia's Turbulent Century, with American Documents* (New York, 1966), 15; Young Ick Lew, "The Shufeldt Treaty and Early Korean-American Interaction, 1882–1905," in *After One Hundred Years: Continuity and Change in Korean-American Relations*, ed. Sung-joo Han (Seoul, 1982), 5–6; Woonsang Choi, *The Diplomatic History of Korea* (Seoul, 1987); and Woonsang Choi, *Fall of the Hermit Kingdom* (Dobbs Ferry, 1967).

3. Tyler Dennett, *Americans in Eastern Asia: A Critical Study of United States' Policy in the Far East in the Nineteenth Century* (New York, 1922), 450.

4. For accounts that are incomplete, see James C. Thomson Jr., Peter W. Stanley, and John Curtis Perry, *Sentimental Imperialists: The American Experience in East Asia* (New York, 1981), 235; John King Fairbank, Edwin O. Reischauer, and Albert M. Craig, *East Asia: The Modern Transformation* (Boston, 1965), 375–76; Frank Gibney, *The Pacific Century: America and Asia in a Changing World* (New York, 1992); Gregory Henderson, *Korea: The Politics of the Vortex* (Cambridge, Mass., 1968); Kenneth B. Lee, *Korea and East Asia: The Story of a Phoenix* (Westport, 1997), 124–25; Stewart Lone and Gavin McCormick, *Korea since 1850* (London, 1993), 10; Robert T. Oliver, *A History of the Korean People in Modern Times: 1800 to the Present* (Newark, 1993), 45; Roger Tennant, *A History of Korea* (New York, 1996), 206; and U.S. Congress, House of Representatives, Committee on Foreign Affairs, *Background Information on the Use of United States Armed Forces in Foreign Countries,* 91 Cong., 2 sess., 1970, p. 53. For accounts that are factually wrong, see Thomas A. Bailey, *A Diplomatic History of the American People* (Englewood Cliffs, 1974), 314; Samuel Flagg Bemis, *A Diplomatic History of the*

United States (New York, 1950), 480; Edwin P. Hoyt, *Pacific Destiny: The Story of America in the Western Sea from the Early 1800s to the 1980s* (New York, 1981), 30; Geoffrey Perret, *A Country Made by War: From the Revolution to Vietnam—The Story of America's Rise to Power* (New York, 1990), 454; and Yonhap News Agency, *Korea-U.S.A. Centennial,* 25. For accounts that are one-sided, see H. A. Gosnell, "The Navy in Korea, 1871," *American Neptune,* 7 (April 1947), 107–14; K. Jack Bauer, "The Korean Expedition of 1871," *U.S. Naval Institute Proceedings,* 74 (Feb. 1948), 197–203; Glenn Howell, "Our Brief Clash with Korea," *ibid.,* 61 (Nov. 1935), 1624–36; William M. Leary Jr., "Our Other War in Korea," *ibid.,* 94 (June 1968), 47–53; Allan R. Millett, *Semper Fidelis: The History of the United States Marine Corps* (New York, 1980); Bernard C. Nalty and Truman R. Strobridge, "Our First Korean War," *American History Illustrated,* 2 (Aug. 1967), 10–19; and James Morton Callahan, "American Relations in the Pacific and the Far East, 1784–1900," *Johns Hopkins University Studies in Historical and Political Science,* 19 (Jan.–March 1901), 3–177. Among published memoirs and collected letters by Americans involved in the mission the best known is Winfield Scott Schley, *Forty-five Years under the Flag* (New York, 1904). See also Boleslaw Szczesniak, "Letters of Homer Crane Blake Concerning His Naval Expedition to China, Japan, and Korea: 1861–1872," *Monumenta Nipponica,* 13 (April–July 1957), 1–38. For a devastating critique, see Homer H. Hulbert, "Rear Admiral Schley on the Little War of 1871," *Korea Review,* 5 (March 1905), 97–106.

5. E. M. Cable, "United States–Korean Relations, 1866–1871," *Transactions of the Korea Branch of the Royal Asiatic Society,* 28 (1938); Ching Young Choe, *The Rule of the Taewongun, 1864–1873: Restoration in Yi Korea* (Cambridge, Mass., 1972); Key-Hiuk Kim, *The Last Phase of the East Asian World Order: Korea, Japan, and the Chinese Empire, 1860–1882* (Berkeley, 1980); Robert Swartout Jr., "Cultural Conflict and Gunboat Diplomacy: The Development of the 1871 Korean-American Incident," *Journal of Social Sciences and Humanities,* 43 (June 1976), 117–69. Four venerable works criticize U.S. decisions in 1871 but repeat an incomplete narrative. See Dennett, *Americans in Eastern Asia;* John W. Foster, *American Diplomacy in the Orient* (Boston, 1903); William Elliot Griffis, *Corea: The Hermit Nation* (New York, 1907); and an edited version of Homer Hulbert's 1905 work: Clarence Norwood Weems, ed., *Hulbert's History of Korea* (2 vols., New York, 1962). For the regional context, see Richard O'Connor, *Pacific Destiny: An Informal History of the U.S. in the Far East: 1776–1968* (Boston, 1969), 150–54; C. I. Eugene Kim and Han-Kyo Kim, *Korea and the Politics of Imperialism, 1876–1910* (Berkeley, 1967); Vipan Chandra, *Imperialism, Resistance, and Reform in Late Nineteenth-Century Korea: Enlightenment and the Independence Club* (Berkeley, 1988); Martina Deuchler, *Confucian Gentlemen and Barbarian Envoys: The Opening of Korea, 1875–1885* (Seattle, 1977); and Hilary Conroy, *The Japanese Seizure of Korea, 1868–1910: A Study of*

350   *Notes to Chapter 4*

Realism and Idealism in International Relations (Philadelphia, 1960). A popular novel on the events is Irving Werstein, *The Trespassers: Korea, June 1871* (New York, 1969).

6. See Fred Harvey Harrington, "An American View of Korean-American Relations, 1866–1905," in *Korean-American Relations, 1866–1997*, ed. Yur-Bok Lee and Wayne Patterson (Albany, 1999), 38–39. Rivaling the Korean conflict in destructiveness were the U.S. bombardment of Chinese forts at Guangzhou in 1856 and of Japanese fortifications in the Straits of Shimonoseki in 1864.

7. Choe, *Rule of the Taewongun*, 132–33. As recently as May 27, 2001, Koreans honored the commander in a solemn religious ceremony. See Shinmiyangyo, *Memorial* <http://www.shinmiyangyo.org/> (Aug. 5, 2002); and Pak Songjun, "Archery Led to an Encounter with Korean History," *Sisa Journal* (Seoul), May 18, 2000, pp. 78–79. I thank Jacqueline Pak for bringing this and other items to my attention. William E. Griffis, *Corea, Without and Within: Chapters on Corean History, Manners, and Religion* (Philadelphia, 1885), 202.

8. Dennett, *Americans in Eastern Asia*, vii–ix, 70–71; Michael H. Hunt, *The Making of a Special Relationship: The United States and China to 1914* (New York, 1983); Walter LaFeber, *The Clash: U.S.-Japanese Relations throughout History* (New York, 1997); Walter LaFeber, *Cambridge History of American Foreign Relations*, vol. II: *The American Search for Opportunity, 1865–1913* (New York, 1995); William Appleman Williams, *The Tragedy of American Diplomacy* (New York, 1959).

9. For general studies of race and U.S. foreign relations, see Alexander DeConde, *Ethnicity, Race, and American Foreign Policy: A History* (Boston, 1992); Gerald Horne, "Race from Power: U.S. Foreign Policy and the General Crisis of 'White Supremacy,'" *Diplomatic History*, 23 (Summer 1999), 437–61; Michael Hunt, *Ideology and American Foreign Policy* (New Haven, 1987); Paul Gordon Lauren, *Power and Prejudice: The Politics and Diplomacy of Racial Discrimination* (Boulder, 1996); and Rubin Francis Weston, *Racism in U.S. Imperialism: The Influence of Racial Assumptions on American Foreign Policy, 1893–1946* (Columbia, S.C., 1972). On race and war, see Gordon H. Chang, *Friends and Enemies: The United States, China, and the Soviet Union, 1948–1972* (Stanford, 1990); Craig M. Cameron, *American Samurai: Myth, Imagination, and the Conduct of Battle in the First Marine Division, 1941–1951* (New York, 1994); and John W Dower, *War without Mercy: Race and Power in the Pacific War* (New York, 1986). On nineteenth-century racial ideologies and American expansion, see Joseph M. Henning, *Outposts of Civilization: Race, Religion, and the Formative Years of American-Japanese Relations* (New York, 2000); and Paul A. Kramer, "Empires, Exceptions, and Anglo-Saxons: Race and Rule between the British and United States Empires, 1880–1910," *Journal of American History*, 88 (March 2002), 1315–53.

Notes to Chapter 4 351

10. See Robert H. Becker, ed., *Some Reflections of an Early California Governor Contained in a Short Dictated Memoir by Frederick F. Low, Ninth Governor of California, and Notes from an Interview between Governor Low and Hubert Howe Bancroft in 1883* (Sacramento, 1959); and David L. Anderson, "Between Two Cultures: Frederick F. Low in China," *California History*, 59 (Fall 1980), 240–54. See also Hubert Howe Bancroft, "Biography of Frederick F. Low prepared for Chroniclers of the Kings," [c. 1890], MSS C-D292, Hubert Howe Bancroft Collection (Bancroft Library, University of California, Berkeley). The Bancroft Library holds a few items from Low's personal papers, but none relevant to this study. The diary Low kept during the expedition was apparently discovered only in the late 1980s in the Buckley Collection, Dudley Knox Library, Naval Postgraduate School, Monterey, California, by Douglas E. George. What is described as a complete transcribed version appears in his thesis, Douglas E. George, "The Low-Rodgers Expedition: A Study in the Foundations of U.S. Policy in Korea" (M.A. thesis, Naval Postgraduate School, Monterey, Calif., 1988). The original handwritten diary has once again been misplaced and cannot be found, Irma Frank, of the Knox Library, Naval Postgraduate School, informed me in an October 2001 phone conversation. The only other known diary from the expedition, that of Walter Bronson, is mainly a ship's log and contains little helpful material. A typescript is available at the Marine Corps University Research Archives, Quantico, Virginia.

11. The United States later learned that the crew of the *General Sherman* was killed after attempting to advance into a prohibited area and clashing with local authorities. Another 1868 incident also stirred Korean suspicion of Americans. An American named Jenkins, formerly an interpreter in the U.S. consulate in Shanghai, led a private expedition to Korea to loot royal tombs. Although the Koreans frustrated his effort, Jenkins returned to China and his adventure became known to American authorities, who took no action against him and offered no apologies to the Koreans. See Hamilton Fish to Frederick F. Low, April 20, 1870, and enclosures, *Foreign Relations of the United States, 1870* (Washington, 1870), 334–39; Swartout, "Cultural Conflict and Gunboat Diplomacy," 146–48; and Dennett, *Americans in Eastern Asia*, 416–20. Frederick F. Low received reports from the North German Union minister in Japan, who had traveled to Korea in an unsuccessful effort to open relations in 1870. Though unimpressed by what he saw there, he reported that the Koreans "behaved themselves toward us in a more civilized manner than the brave Germans would have done toward the Coreans." Low's summary of the letter, however, focused on the negative characterizations of the Koreans. Low to Fish, Nov. 22, 1870, and enclosure, *Foreign Relations of the United States, 1870*, 73–75. On the French 1866 experience, see Soo Bock Choi, "Korea's Response to America and France in the Decade of the Taewongun, 1864–1873," in *Korea' Response to the West*, ed. Jung-Hwan Jo (Kalamazoo, 1971), 109–40.

352   *Notes to Chapter 4*

12. John Rodgers to Ann Rodgers, May 11, 1871, box 24, Rodgers Family Papers (Manuscript Division, Library of Congress, Washington, D.C.). Mail ships routinely visited American ships, including those in Korean waters. As a result, Rodgers and other Americans composed correspondence in anticipation of the mail service, and their outgoing letters contain thoughts and descriptions of events close at hand. For a hyperbolic account of American ignorance of Korea on the eve of the expedition, see W. S. Schley, "Our Navy in Korea," *Harper's Weekly,* Aug. 11, 1894, pp. 779–83. He included much of this essay in Schley, *Forty-five Years under the Flag.*

13. The missionary-scholar S. Wells Williams, later known as a friend of China, writing in 1858 during a conflict, described the Chinese as "among the most craven of people, cruel and selfish as heathenism can make men, so we must be backed by force if we wish them to listen to reason." The Koreans were seen as even more backward than the Chinese. Thomson, Stanley, and Perry, *Sentimental Imperialists,* 47.

14. Low to Fish, Nov. 22, 1870, *Foreign Relations of the United States, 1870,* 73–74; Low to Fish, May 13, 1871, *Foreign Relations of the United States, 1871* (Washington, 1871), 115. On Low as minister to China, see David L. Anderson, *Imperialism and Idealism: American Diplomats in China, 1861–1898* (Bloomington, 1985), chap. 4. As governor of California Low had publicly opposed some legislation and policies directed against the Chinese. See Theodore H. Hittell, *History of California* (San Francisco, 1897), 404–6; and Eli T. Sheppard, "Frederick Ferdinand Low, Ninth Governor of California," *University of California Chronicle,* 19 (April 1917), 109–53.

15. Choe, *Rule of the Taewongun,* 124.

16. Yur-Bok Lee, *Diplomatic Relations between the United States and Korea, 1866–1887* (New York, 1970), 17. See James B. Palais, *Politics and Policy in Traditional Korea* (Cambridge, Mass., 1975), 30–31.

17. Robert Erwin Johnson, *Rear Admiral John Rodgers, 1812–1882* (Annapolis, 1967), 305, 4, 109–13; Swartout, "Cultural Conflict and Gunboat Diplomacy," 134–35. There is only a brief account of the 1871 expedition in Asaph Hall, *Biographical Memoir of John Rodgers, 1812–1882* (Washington, 1906). On Perry's mission, see Charles Oscar Paullin, *American Voyages to the Orient, 1690–1865* (Annapolis, 1971), 128–35; and Peter Duus, *The Japanese Discovery of America* (Boston, 1997), 12–13, 90–96.

18. John Rodgers to Ann Rodgers, July 6, Sept. 2, 3, 22, Nov. 3, Dec. 17, 22, 1870, box 24, Rodgers Family Papers; John Rodgers to William Ledyard Rodgers, May 13, 1871, box 25, *ibid.*

19. John Rodgers to Ann Rodgers, April 11, 1871, box 24, *ibid.*; *North China Herald,* June 23, 1871, p. 463. On Bret Harte, see Robert McClellan, *The Heathen*

Chinee: A Study of American Attitudes toward China, 1890–1905 (Columbus, 1971), 47–49; and Ronald Takaki, *Strangers from a Different Shore: A History of Asian Americans* (Boston, 1989), 104–8.

20. John Rodgers to Ann Rodgers, April 11, 1871, box 24, Rodgers Family Papers.

21. On East Asian diplomacy at the time, see Conroy, *Japanese Seizure of Korea;* Immanuel C. Y. Hsu, "Late Ch'ing Foreign Relations, 1866–1905," in *The Cambridge History of China,* vol. XI: *Late Ch'ing, 1800–1911, Part 2,* ed. John K. Fairbank and Kwang-ching Liu (New York, 1980), 70–141; Mary C. Wright, "The Adaptability of Ch'ing Diplomacy: The Case of Korea," *Journal of Asian Studies,* 17 (May 1958), 363–81; Key-Hiuk Kim, "The Aims of Li Hung-chang's Policies toward Japan and Korea, 1870–1882," in *Li Hung-chang and China's Early Modernization,* ed. Samuel C. Chu and Kwang-ching Liu (Armonk, 1994), 145–61; Frederick Foo Chien, *The Opening of Korea: A Study of Chinese Diplomacy, 1876–1885* (Hamden, 1967); Hae-jong Chun, "Sino-Korean Tributary Relations in the Ch'ing Period," in *The Chinese World Order: Traditional China's Foreign Relations,* ed. John King Fairbank (Cambridge, Mass., 1968), 90–111; Sophia Su-fei Yen, *Taiwan in China's Foreign Relations, 1836–1874* (Hamden, 1965); and Tony Yung-yuan Teng, "Prince Kung and the Survival of the Ch'ing Rule, 1858–1898" (Ph.D. diss., University of Wisconsin, 1972).

22. *Qing ji zhong ri han guanxi shiliao* (A collection of materials on the history of relations among China, Japan, and Korea during the Qing dynasty), vol. II, ed. Guo Tinyi and Li Yushu (Taipei, 1972), 168–71. I appreciate the help of Yongling Lu with Chinese-language research and the translation of documents from the Guo and Li compilation. The British, French, Japanese, Germans, and Russians offered the Americans assistance. The British considered sending an accompanying warship. See folders March 1–16, 1871, March 17–31, 1871, April 1–15, 1871, and April 16–30, 1871, box 16, Rodgers Family Papers.

23. C. E. DeLong to John Rodgers, April 26, 1871 (2 letters), box 16, Rodgers Family Papers. On Rodgers's decision to ban a journalist he thought might be unfriendly to the mission, see Alfred Weiller to John Rodgers, May 14, 1871 (2 letters), box 17, *ibid.* See also Low Diary, in George, "Low-Rodgers Expedition," May 15, 1871. Commander of the French Fleet of the China and Japan Seas to John Rodgers, April 23, 1871, box 16, Rodgers Family Papers; Rockwell to John Rodgers, June 4, 1871, box 17, *ibid.*

24. Low Diary, May 21, 1871. Korean documentation is translated, apparently accurately, in Cable, "United States–Korean Relations, 1866–1871," 202–19. The documents appear to be from the *Chosun wang-jo sillok,* an edited compilation of high-level court-generated material compiled after the reign of King Kojong and of disputed reliability. It appears to be the main source for the account of the 1871

354   *Notes to Chapter 4*

events in Kuksa, Pyonch'an Wiwonheo (National History Compilation Committee), *Han-guk-sa* (Korean history), vol. XXXVII (Seoul, 2000). There is no other important Korean court material available on the 1871 war. I thank Hyung Suk Lee for this information. Korean and American documentation on the location and movement of the fleet largely corresponds.

25. Gosnell, "Navy in Korea, 1871," 107–14; Low Diary, May 23–27, 1871; Schley, "Our Navy in Korea," 782; Low Diary, May 30, 1871; John P. Cowles Jr. to Low, May 29, 1871, enclosure in Low to Fish, May 31, 1871, *Foreign Relations of the United States, 1871,* 116–21; dispatch of the king of Korea to the Board of Rites, Peking, n.d., enclosure in John Rodgers to George B. Robeson, Jan. 7, 1872 (microfilm: reel 257), Letters Received by the Secretary of the Navy From Commanding Officers of Squadrons (Squadron Letters), Naval Records Collection of the Office of Naval Records and Library, RG 45 (National Archives, Washington, D.C.).

26. The portion of the letter describing the drills is dated May 20, 1871, after the U.S. fleet entered Korean waters, although the letter was begun on the sixteenth. McLane Tilton to Nannie Tilton, May 16, 1871, folder 2, McLane Tilton Papers (Marine Corps University Research Archives, Quantico, Va.).

27. Choe, *Rule of the Taewongun,* 127–28; Weems, ed., *Hulbert's History of Korea,* I, 213.

28. Cable, "United States–Korean Relations, 1866–1871," 202; Choe, *Rule of the Taewongun,* 127; Griffis, *Corea,* 406–7; Low to Fish, May 31, 1871, *Foreign Relations of the United States, 1871,* 116–17; enclosure 6, *ibid.,* 120–21; Low Diary, May 30–31, 1871.

29. Low and other American officials later made much of a "tacit" approval supposedly given by the Koreans, but his official reports only vaguely describe what the Americans said and the Korean response. In his diary, Low wrote only that the Koreans "were also told that a surveying expedition would start today for Kang Hoa or beyond." Low Diary, May 31, 1871. After the clash, John Rodgers wrote his superiors that the Koreans "were informed that we wished to take soundings of their waters, and to make surveys of the shores. To this they made no objection. We expressed the hope that no molestation would be offered to our parties in landing. . . . It was further stated that twenty-four hours would be given to make this announcement to people along the river, before any movement was made. To all this they made no reply which could indicate dissent." John Rodgers to Robeson, June 3, 1871, in George B. Robeson, "Report of the Secretary of the Navy," in *Reports of the Secretary of the Navy and of the Postmaster General, 1871* (Washington, 1871), 275–77. Low to Fish, May 31, June 2, 1871, *Foreign Relations of the United States, 1871,* 116–21. A member of the expedition recollected that all along the American objective had been to reach the capital, but there is no

Notes to Chapter 4   355

corroborating evidence. See George R. Willis, *The Story of Our Cruise in the U.S. Frigate 'Colorado,' Flagship of the Asiatic Fleet—1870–'71–'72* (n.p., [1873]), 64.

30. John Rodgers to Robeson, June 3, 1871, in Robeson, "Report of the Secretary of the Navy," 275–77; Cowles to Low, June 2, 1871, enclosure with Low to Fish, June 2, 1871, *Foreign Relations of the United States, 1871,* 121–24; Homer C. Blake to John Rodgers, June 2, 1871, in Robeson, "Report of the Secretary of the Navy," 277–79. See also Willis, *Story of Our Cruise,* 67.

31. Low to Fish, June 2, 1871, *Foreign Relations of the United States, 1871,* 121–24; Choe, *Rule of the Tae-wongun,* 128–29; Willis, *Story of Our Cruise,* 69. Reports on the expedition appeared regularly in the *North China Herald,* the main English-language newspaper published in China, in June and July 1871. See, for example, "A Narrative of the U.S. Expedition in 1871," *North China Herald,* [n.d.], reprint in "Printed Matter, 1870–1871," box 31, Rodgers Family Papers.

32. Low to Fish, June 2, 1871, *Foreign Relations of the United States, 1871,* 121–24; John Rodgers to Robeson, June 3, 1871, in Robeson, "Report of the Secretary of the Navy," 275–77; John Rodgers to Ann Rodgers, June 19, 1871, box 24, Rodgers Family Papers.

33. "Our Little Battle in Corean Waters: A Naval Officer's Story," *Overland Monthly,* 8 (Aug. 1886), 125–28. The officer in charge of the surveying party may have predicted trouble; see Castel and Nahm, "'Our Little War with the Heathen,'" 23; and Peter Karsten and Thomas H. Patterson, "Comment on 'Our Other War in Korea,'" *U.S. Naval Institute Proceedings,* 792 (Feb. 1969), 112–14. For the captured Korean soldier's statement, see Cable, "United States–Korean Relations, 1866–1871," 87.

34. See articles from the *Shanghai Evening Courier,* in *American Diplomatic and Public Papers: The United States and China: Series 2, The United States, China, and Imperial Rivalries, 1861–1893: Korea, I,* ed. Jules Davids, vol. IX (Wilmington, 1979), 129–34. George F. Seward to J. C. Bancroft, June 12, 1871, *ibid.,* 124–27. George Seward may have unofficially spread criticism of the mission because of his rivalry with Low. See Low to Department of State, Nov. 25, 1871, despatch 109 (microfilm: reel 32), Despatches from United States Ministers to China, 1843–1906, Records of the Department of State, RG 59 (National Archives); and Paul Clyde, "Attitudes and Policies of George F. Seward, American Minister at Peking, 1876—1880," typescript, Aug. 18, 1932, p. 3, box 51, Payson Treat Papers (Hoover Institution Archives, Stanford, Calif.). Low's diary description of the incident is consistent with his official report. Low Diary, June 1, 1871. For a senator's critical account of the official version of the clash, based, he said, on unspecified Navy Department records, see *Congressional Record,* 45 Cong., 2 sess., April 17, 1878, pp. 2600–2601.

356   *Notes to Chapter 4*

35. John Rodgers to Robeson, June 3, 1871, in Robeson, "Report of the Secretary of the Navy," 275–77; Low to Fish, June 2, 1871, *Foreign Relations of the United States, 1871,* 121–24. As late as June 26, Low still lamented his insufficient military force to get to Seoul. See Low Diary, June 26, 1871. John Rodgers, note, [June 3, 1871?], p. 328 (reel 256), Squadron Letters, Naval Records Collection.

36. McLane Tilton to Nan Tilton, June 4, 1871, folder 2, Tilton Papers; Leary, "Our Other War in Korea," 47–53. Naval personnel studied the captured Korean weapons twenty years after they were brought to Annapolis. They were of Chinese design and manufacture. Two were of seventeenth-century vintage, a third was dated 1313. The inscriptions on the cannon were translated by Wong Chin Foo, a leading Chinese American intellectual and an outspoken critic of discrimination against the Chinese in America. See Charles R. Sanger, *The Chemical Analysis of the Three Guns at the U.S. Naval Academy, Captured in Corea by Rear-Admiral John Rodgers, U.S.N.* (Annapolis, [1892]), in Pamphlet Collection, William E. Griffis Collection (Special Collections, Rutgers University Libraries, New Brunswick, N.J.).

37. *Shanghai Evening Courier,* n.d., and other reprinted articles in "Narrative of the U.S. Expedition to the Corea, 1871," "Printed Matter, 1870–1871," box 31, Rodgers Family Papers; *Shimbun Zashi,* May 1871, in *Shim bun shusei meiji hennenshiu* (Newspaper collection of the Meiji period), ed. Nakayama Yasumasa, vol. I (Tokyo, 1934), 377. After an American ship arrived, Low noted, "The news of our first engagement appeared to excite interest in Shanghai and the whole affair was pretty fully reported in the newspapers." Low Diary, June 17, 1871.

38. Griffis, *Corea,* 409n1. See Frances Yeomans Helbig, "William Elliot Griffis: Entrepreneur of Ideas" (M.A. thesis, University of Rochester, 1966). The other early American authority on Korea, Homer B. Hulbert, similarly concluded that the American advance up the strategic passageway was provocative and that the Koreans "were evidently within their rights to fire upon our boats." Weems, ed., *Hulbert's History of Korea,* II, 214; Hulbert, "Rear Admiral Schley on the Little War of 1871," 102–4, 106.

39. The Korean court may have gained some familiarity with Western theories of international relations from a Chinese translation of Henry Wheaton, *Elements of International Law* (1836). Chinese authorities had distributed it widely, and it had reached Japan. I thank Roger Thompson for bringing this to my attention. Gerrit W. Gong, *The Standard of "Civilization" in International Society* (Oxford, Eng., 1984), 153–54.

40. McLane Tilton to Nan Tilton, June 27, 1871, folder 2, Tilton Papers; Low Diary, June 5, 1871; Schley, *Forty-Five Years under the Flag,* 85.

41. Enclosure 1, in Low to Fish, June 20, 1871, *Foreign Relations of the United States, 1871,* 130–31. Accompanying the local official's message was the king of

Korea's response to the letter Low had sent from Beijing before the expedition began. The king responded in detail to Low's inquiry about the fate of the *General Sherman* and other matters. Enclosures 4 and 5, *ibid.*, 132–34.

42. Enclosure 2, *ibid.*, 131.

43. Enclosure 6, *ibid.*, 135.

44. John Rodgers to Robeson, July 5, 1871, in Robeson, "Report of the Secretary of the Navy," 279–84; Report of Commander H. C. Blake, June 17, 1871, *ibid.*, 285–87.

45. John Quincy Adams, "On the Opium War," *Proceedings of the Massachusetts Historical Society*, 43 (Feb. 10, 1910), 303–26.

46. Low Diary, June 5, 9, 1871.

47. "Narrative of the U.S. Expedition in 1871"; Schley, "Our Navy in Korea," 782, 783. Chinese reports put the Korean losses as double the number claimed by the United States. Li Hongzhang to the Zongli Yamen, July 17, 1871, in *Qing ji zhong ri han*, II, ed. Guo and Li, 185–86.

48. Low to Fish, June 20, 1871, *Foreign Relations of the United States, 1871*, 128–29. Low did not accompany the fighting force. His diary records the events as he witnessed them from shipboard. McLane Tilton to Nan Tilton, June 21, 1871, folder 2, Tilton Papers; *New York Times*, Aug. 25, 1871, p. 1; "Narrative of the U.S. Expedition in 1871"; Leary, "Our Other War in Korea," 47–53. See also Willis, *Story of Our Cruise*, 77, 79. John Rodgers to Ann Rodgers, May 20, 1871, box 24, Rodgers Papers. The papers contain documents from officers involved in the battle, including descriptions of the fighting. See June 1–15, 1871, Official Correspondence, box 17, *ibid.* McLane Tilton to Nan Tilton, June 27, 1871, folder 2, Tilton Papers; Griffis, *Corea*, 417; Low Diary, June 14, 1871.

49. Cable, "United States–Korean Relations, 1866–1871," 207–17.

50. Enclosures 15 and 16, in Low to Fish, June 20, 1871, *Foreign Relations of the United States, 1871*, 139–41.

51. McLane Tilton to Nan Tilton, June 27, 1871, folder 2, Tilton Papers; enclosure 1, in Low to Fish, July 6, 1871, *Foreign Relations of the United States, 1871*, 148 49.

52. Low to Fish, July 6, 1871, *Foreign Relations of the United States, 1871*, 142–48; John Rodgers to Robeson, July 1, 1871 (reel 256), Squadron Letters, Naval Records Collection.

53. *New York Times*, July 17, 1871, p. 3; *ibid.*, Aug. 22, 1871, p. 1; *ibid.*, Aug. 23, 1871, p. 4; *New York Herald*, Aug. 7, 1871, p. 4; "Corea," *Harper's Weekly*, July 8, 1871, p. 624; "The Corean War," *ibid.*, Sept. 9, 1871, pp. 840–42. See also *Illustrated London News*, June 24, 1871, p. 606. *New York Herald*, July 20, 1871, p. 4; *ibid.*, July 17, 1871, p. 5.

358   *Notes to Chapter 4*

54. "Comments made at the North-China Branch of the Royal Asiatic Society," clipping, *North China Daily News,* [Jan. 1884], scrapbook 19, Griffis Collection; *New York Daily Tribune,* July 17, 1871, p. 4.

55. Fish to Low, Sept. 20, 1871, *Foreign Relations of the United States, 1871,* 153. John Rodgers's superior, Adm. David D. Porter, wrote, "Your squadron seems the most efficient afloat. I cannot pay you a higher compliment." John Rodgers to Ann Rodgers, Oct. 26, 1871, quoted in Robert Erwin Johnson, *Far China Station: The U.S. Navy in Asian Waters, 1800–1898* (Annapolis, 1979), 167. For Ulysses S. Grant's statement, see James D. Richardson, comp., *A Compilation of the Messages and Papers of the Presidents,* vol. IX (New York, 1911), 4099–100.

56. Becker, ed., "Some Reflections of an Early California Governor," 51; Low to T Eli Sheppard, March 30, 1873, box 52, Sheppard (Eli, T.) Papers (Bancroft Library); *San Francisco Chronicle,* July 22, 1894, p. 11; Anderson, "Between Two Cultures"; U.S. Congress, Joint Special Committee, *Report of the Joint Special Committee to Investigate Chinese Immigration,* 44 Cong., 2 sess., Feb. 27, 1877, pp. 65–92, 1024–28. See also John Rodgers, memorandum on restricting Chinese immigration, Jan. 21, 1878, John Rodgers Official Correspondence, 1878, box 20, Rodgers Family Papers.

57. King of Korea to Board of Rites, Peking, n.d., enclosure in John Rodgers to Robeson, Jan. 7, 1872 (reel 257), Squadron Letters, Naval Records Collection.

58. *Ibid.*

59. Cable, "United States–Korean Relations, 1866–1871," 188; Choe, *Rule of the Taewongun,* 132–33; Choi, "Korea's Response to America and France," 126–27; Palais, *Politics and Policy in Traditional Korea,* 177; Frederick C. Drake, *The Empire of the Seas: A Biography of Rear Admiral Robert Shufeldt, USN* (Honolulu, 1984), 179, 240–41.

60. Memorial from the Zongli Yamen to the emperor, Dec. 24, 1871, in *Qing ji zhong ri han,* II, ed. Guo and Li, 296; Hsu, "Late Ch'ing Foreign Relations," 102–3; Prince Gong to Low, Dec. 23, 1871, enclosure 1, in Low to Fish, Jan. 11, 1872, in *American Diplomatic and Public Papers,* IX, ed. Davids, 243–50.

61. Robert Shufeldt to King of Korea, May 4, 1880, box 24, Robert Wilson Shufeldt Papers (Manuscript Division, Library of Congress); Robert Shufeldt, "Comments," [1880?], Personal Comments, box 25, *ibid.*; Drake, *Empire of the Seas,* 115–17, 238–56, 346 47, 355–62; Robert Wilson Shufeldt, *The Relation of the Navy to the Commerce of the United States; A Letter Written by Request to Hon. Leopold Morse* (Washington, 1878), pamphlet, box 32, Shufeldt Papers.

62. Robeson, "Report of the Secretary of the Navy," 4.

63. Low to Fish, July 6, 1871, *Foreign Relations of the United States, 1871,* 142–49.

64. A. V. Wadhams to William Elliot Griffis, Nov. 20, 1877, Jan. 21, 1878, in scrapbook 20, Corea Section 2, Griffis Collection; Mary Rose Catalfamo to

Gordon H. Chang, June 27, 2000 (in Gordon H. Chang's possession); Nalty and Strobridge, "Our First Korean War," 10–19; Charles Oscar Paullin, *Diplomatic Negotiations of American Naval Officers, 1778–1883* (Baltimore, 1912), 282; Bauer, "Korean Expedition of 1871," 197–203; Millett, *Semper Fidelis,* 105–6; Truman R. Strobridge and Bernard C. Nalty, "Mission to Peking, 1870: Captain McLane Tilton's Letter Describing His Trip with the Seward Party to Peking," *American Neptune,* 25 (April 1965), 116–22.

65. See, for example, Castel and Nahm, "'Our Little War with the Heathen'"; Nalty and Strobridge, "Our First Korean War"; and Kim Won-mo, *Sajin uro pon paengnyon chon ui hanguk: Kundae hanguk, 1871–1910* (Korea one hundred years ago in photographs) (Seoul, 1986); and Jacqueline Pak to Chang, June 16, 2000 (in Chang's possession).

66. For biographical information and descriptions of Felice Beato's work, see David Harris, *Of Battle and Beauty: Felice Beato's Photographs of China* (Santa Barbara, 1999); Stephen White, "Felix Beato and the First Korean War, 1871," *Photographic Collector,* 3 (Spring 1982), 76–85; Terry Bennett, *Korea: Caught in Time* (Reading, 1997), 1–25; Frances Fralin, *The Indelible Image: Photographs of War, 1846 to the Present* (New York, 1985), 34–35; and Regine Thiriez, *Barbarian Lens: Western Photographers of the Qianlong Emperor's European Palaces* (Amsterdam, 1998), 8–9.

67. Low Diary, June 23, 1871; Bennett, *Korea,* 7. Beato's Korea images are described and their sale announced in *North China Herald,* July 7, 1871. The volume is entitled "Photographs of the Korean Punitive Expedition," 200(s) KWG-19, Still Pictures Branch (National Archives, College Park, Md.). U. S. Grant III to Wayne C. Grover, Aug. 8, 1953, Disposition I, RG 273, *ibid.* The photos do not appear in chronological order, and the captions (apparently in Beato's handwriting) that accompany many of the photos are often inaccurate, according to the description of events in Low's daily diary. Not all the photos Beato took while with the expedition appear in the album; others were made available singly. The reproductions that accompany this essay were made from original prints held in Special Collections and University Archives, Stanford University Libraries (RBCDS915.P4f). The Stanford set contains several photos not at the National Archives, with some captions differing from those at the archives.

Chapter 5

1. *Banquet to His Excellency Anson Burlingame and His Associates of the Chinese Embassy by the Citizens of New York on Tuesday, June 23, 1868* (New York: Sun Book and Job Printing House, 1868), 47.

2. *Reception and Entertainment of the Chinese Embassy by the City of Boston* (Boston: Alfred Mudge & Son, 1868), 19.

360   *Notes to Chapter 5*

3. The 1882 act is officially titled the Act to Execute Certain Treaty Stipulations Relating to Chinese and was first known commonly as the Chinese Restriction Act. Only later was it called the Exclusion Act. See Beth Lew-Williams, "The Chinese Must Go: Immigration, Deportation and Violence in the 19th Century Pacific Northwest" (PhD diss., Stanford University, 2011); Charles J. McClain, *In Search of Equality: The Chinese Struggle against Discrimination in Nineteenth-Century America* (Berkeley: University of California Press, 1994), 147–49; and Elmer Clarence Sandmeyer, *The Anti-Chinese Movement in California* (Urbana: University of Illinois Press, 1939), 96–108.

4. The literature on Chinese exclusion includes Andrew Gyory, *Closing the Gates: Race, Politics and the Chinese Exclusion Act* (Chapel Hill: University of North Carolina Press, 1998); Gwendolyn Mink, *Old Labor and New Immigrants in American Political Development: Union, Party, and State, 1875–1920* (Ithaca, N.Y.: Cornell University Press, 1986); Erika Lee, *At America's Gate: Chinese Immigration during the Exclusion Era, 1882–1943* (Chapel Hill: University of North Carolina Press, 2005); Alexander Saxton, *The Indispensable Enemy: Labor and the Anti-Chinese Movement in California,* 2nd ed. (Berkeley: University of California Press, 1995); and Shih-shan Henry Tsai, *China and the Overseas Chinese in the United States, 1868–1911* (Fayetteville: University of Arkansas Press, 1983).

5. See Moon Ho Jung, *Coolies and Cane: Race, Labor, and Sugar in the Age of Emancipation* (Baltimore: Johns Hopkins University Press, 2006), 33–38.

6. Karen Kupperman, *The Jamestown Project* (Cambridge, Mass.: Harvard University Press, 2007), 152–59; Frederick Jackson Turner, "The West and American Ideals," commencement address, University of Washington, June 17, 1914, in *The Frontier in American History* (New York: Henry Holt, 1920), 290–310.

7. Thomas Jefferson, *Writings of Thomas Jefferson,* ed. Paul Leicester Ford, (New York: Putnam's Sons, 1892–1899)8:194. On Jefferson's global vision, see Alan Taylor, "Jefferson's Pacific: The Science of Distant Empire, 1768–1811," in *Across the Continent: Jefferson, Lewis and Clark, and the Making of America,* ed. Douglas Seefeldt, Jeffrey L. Hantman, and Peter S. Onuf (Charlottesville: University of Virginia Press, 2005), 16–44.

8. Foster Rhea Dulles, *China and America: The Story of Their Relations since 1784* (Princeton, N.J.: Princeton University Press, 1946), 32; Charles H. Ambler, *The Life and Diary of John Floyd: Governor of Virginia, an Apostle of Secession, and the Father of the Oregon Country* (Richmond, Va.: Richmond Press, 1918), 65–75.

9. Robert Russel, *Improvement of Communication with the Pacific Coast as an Issue in American Politics* (Cedar Rapids, Iowa: Torch Press, 1948), 11; and Foster Stockwell, *Westerners in China: A History of Exploration and Trade, Ancient Times*

through the Present (Jefferson, N.C.: McFarland, 2003); Dulles, *China and America*, 33–34.

10. James K. Polk, "Third Annual Address," December 7, 1847; Michael P. Riccards, *The Presidency and Middle Kingdom: China, the United States, and Executive Leadership* (Lanham, Md.: Lexington Books, 2000), 18.

11. Asa Whitney, *Project for a Railroad to the Pacific* (New York: George W. Wood, 1849).

12. Ibid.

13. "China and the Indies—Our 'Manifest Destiny' in the East," *DeBow's Review* 15, no. 6 (December 1853): 541–71.

14. Peter Parker, Diary, box 4, journal 5, April 1, 1832, Peter Parker Collection, Yale University.

15. David Abeel, *Journal of a Residence in China and the Neighboring Countries* (New York: J. Abeel Williamson, 1836), 141–43.

16. Clifton J. Phillips, "The Student Volunteer Movement and Its Role in China Missions, 1886–1920," in *The Missionary Enterprise in China and America*, ed. John K. Fairbank (Cambridge, Mass.: Harvard University Press, 1974), 91–109; Barlow and Eddy quotes from Arthur Schlesinger, Jr., "Missionary Enterprise and Imperialism," in Fairbank, *Missionary Enterprise,* 356.

17. Charles Ernest Scott, *China from Within: Impressions and Experiences* (New York: Fleming H. Revell, 1917), 10, 90.

18. Kupperman, *Jamestown Project,* 156, 312; William Speer, *The Oldest and the Newest Empire: China and the United States* (Hartford, Conn.: S.S. Scranton, 1870), 24.

19. Jack Kuo Wei Tchen, *New York before Chinatown: Orientalism and the Shaping of American Culture, 1776–1882* (Baltimore: Johns Hopkins University Press, 1999), 76–79; James R. Fichter, *So Great a Profit: How the East Indies Trade Transformed Anglo-American Capitalism* (Cambridge, Mass.: Harvard University Press, 2010), 51–52; and Karen Eppler-Sanchez, "Copying and Conversion: A Connecticut Friendship Album from 'a Chinese Youth,'" *American Quarterly* 59 (June 2007): 301–39.

20. Quoted in John H. Schroeder, "Rep. John Floyd, 1817–1829: Harbinger of Oregon Territory," *Oregon Historical Quarterly* 70, no. 4 (December 1969): 341.

21. Dulles, *China and America,* 33.

22. *Congressional Globe* 29, no. 1 (1846): 917–18.

23. "Survey of the Arctic and Pacific Oceans," July 29, 1852, in *The Works of William H. Seward, 1801–1872* (New York: Houghton Mifflin, 1887), 1:236–53.

24. Speer, *Oldest and Newest Empire,* 3–6.

25. Ibid., 25–26, 36–41.

26. Ibid., 28–31.

362   *Notes to Chapters 5 and 6*

27. Ibid., 437–92, 638, 664.

28. The Burlingame Treaty is named for Anson Burlingame, the leader of the first *Chinese* diplomatic mission to Washington, D.C. President Lincoln had appointed Burlingame as American minister to China, but the Qing court so appreciated his respectful and helpful attitude that, after he retired as the U.S. representative, it appointed Burlingame as its "envoy extraordinaire and minister plenipotentiary" to represent China to the United States and European nations. Burlingame and Seward were close personally and professionally, and Seward actually drafted the treaty that Burlingame presented to the Grant administration and to the Qing court.

29. "Hon. William H. Seward: His Departure from Hong-Kong—Reception and Speech at the American Consulate," *New York Times*, February 25, 1871, 2.

30. Gordon H. Chang, "Whose 'Barbarism'? Whose 'Treachery'?: Race and Civilization in the Unknown United States-Korea War of 1871," *Journal of American History* 89, no. 4 (March 2003): 1331–65.

31. Hollister quote from Tsai, *Chinese Experience in America* (Bloomington: Indiana University Press, 1986), 58.

32. Tsai, *Chinese Experience in America,* 57–58; Hayes, Veto Message, March 1, 1879, HeinOnline, 9 Comp. Messages & Papers Pres. n.s. 4466 1897. Hayes received much support for the veto. The well-known missionary/diplomat S. Wells Williams had the entire faculty of Yale College sign his petition to Hayes that condemned the passenger bill. Hayes's veto message reproduced several of the arguments Williams advanced. "The needlessness, the unwisdom, the ridiculousness, and the dishonor of the Bill are all about equal," Williams believed. "It is all a bid for votes from the lowest strata on the Pacific coast." See Frederick Wells Williams, *The Life and Letters of Samuel Wells Williams* (New York: Putnam, 1889), 427–31.

33. Veto Message, April 4, 1882, HeinOnline, 11 Comp. Messages & Papers Pres. 4699 1897.

34. George F. Seward, *Chinese Immigration in Its Social and Economic Aspects* (New York: Scribner, 1881), 260.

35. Milton R. Konvitz, *The Alien and the Asiatic in American Law* (Ithaca, N.Y.: Cornell University Press, 1946), 10–12.

36. Gyory, *Closing the Gates,* 215–16, 248–59; Lew-Williams, "Chinese Must Go," 44–47; Delber L. McKee, *Chinese Exclusion versus the Open Door Policy, 1900–1906* (Detroit: Wayne State University Press, 1977), 15–27.

Chapter 6

1. Nash to Palmer Hoyt, June 28, 1943, OWI Files—Alphabetical Files, Nash Files, Papers of Harry S. Truman.

The Harry S. Truman Library in Independence, Missouri contains a large amount of material relevant to the study of the World War II relocation camps. The files of Philleo Nash, contained in the papers of Harry S. Truman, have federal government press releases and reports on the camps, clippings from newspapers around the country on Japanese Americans and Japanese in American, and internal government memoranda. Nash also monitored race relations in the U.S. and in the armed services generally during the war. The Nash files also have War Relocation Authority-generated material, public as well as internal. Useful material includes Department of Justice bi-weekly summaries of the camp press in 1942 and 1943. Translation of some Japanese-language articles appear in these. The summaries ran regular sections entitled "Ideological Aspects," "Grievances and Redress of Grievances," and "Organizational Activities." These provide insight into government knowledge and attitudes about camp life. The Nash files contain WRA population studies on Japanese Americans, studies of local popular attitudes toward Japanese Americans, and WRA reports on camp conditions and experiences. Most of the above material is found in Boxes 16, 23, 26, 27, 34, 50, 51, 52.

The Truman Library also holds the papers of Dillon S. Myer, Director of the War Relocation Authority. The Myer papers hold official and personal correspondence, including from the WRA years, memoranda and reports, news clippings and speeches. One half of Box 1 is of this material. Another useful collection is that of Tom C. Clark, who served in the Department of Justice during the relocation years and was later Supreme Court Justice. Scattered material on the relocation camps appears in oral histories, including that of Karl Bendetsen, Tom C. Clark, and H. B. Morrison, the Stephen J. Spingarn papers, and Harry S. Truman papers (Senate papers and President's Secretary File—Official File).

Archivists at the Truman Library say that few researchers have used the above material.

2. Slater Brown, "The Coming of Superman," *New Republic,* September 2, 1940, 301; Dennis Dooley, "The Man of Tomorrow and the Boys of Yesterday," in *Superman at Fifty,* eds. Dennis Dooley and Gary Engle (Cleveland, Ohio: Octavia Press, 1987), 19–34; M. Thomas Inge, *Comics as Culture* (Jackson, Mississippi: University Press of Mississippi, 1990), 140, 141; Ron Goulart, *The Great Comic Book Artists* (New York: St. Martin's Press, 1986), 94.

3. Brown, "Coming of Superman," ed. Peter Nicholls, *The Science Fiction Encyclopedia* (New York: Doubleday & Company, 1979), 581–83; E. Nelson Bridwell, "Introduction," *Superman: From the Thirties to the Seventies* (New York: Crown Publishers, Inc., 1971), 7–15. Also see David B. Guralnik, "Superstar, Supermom, Super Glue, Superdooper, Superman," in *Superman at Fifty,* 103–107.

4. Steve M. Barkin, "Fighting the Cartoon War: Information Strategies in World War II," *Journal of American Culture* (Spring/Summer 1984), 113–117. On

364   *Notes to Chapter 6*

racism in the Pacific War, see John Dower, *War Without Mercy: Race and Power in the Pacific War* (New York: Pantheon, 1986)

5. OWI, "When Radio Writes for War," quoted in Elaine Lu, "Antithetical Self-Identification and Yellow Peril: Chinese and Japanese Stereotypes in American Comic Art, 1869–1949," unpublished senior thesis, Department of History, Stanford University, 1989, 64.

6. John Morton Blum, *V Was for Victory: Politics and American Culture During World War II* (New York: Harcourt, Brace, Jovanovich, 1976), 21–39; Allan M. Winkler, *The Politics of Propaganda: The Office of War Information, 1942–1945,* (New Haven, Connecticut: Yale University Press, 1978).

7. Superman comic book cover cited in Lu, "Antithetical Self-Identification," 70.

8. *Washington Post,* October 13, 1987, B6; Marshall to Edith Nash, October 21, 1987, Box 1, Memoir: "Science, Politics and Human Values," Nash Files. On other fronts, Nash actively opposed discrimination. He opposed segregation in the armed services, civil service, and education. He and his wife opened one of the first racially integrated schools in the Washington, D.C. area in 1945.

9. Chicago *Herald American,* September 21, 1942, 1.

10. Gary Okihiro, "Japanese Resistance in America's Concentration Camps: A Re-evaluation," *Amerasia Journal* 2:1 (1973): 20–34.

11. War Relocation Authority, "Evacuee Resistances to Relocation," Community Analysis Report No. 5, June 1943, Nash Papers.

12. Richard Drinnon, *Keeper of Concentration Camps: Dillon S. Myer and American Racism* (Berkeley and Los Angeles: University of California Press, 1987), 64; Roger Daniels, *Asian American: Chinese and Japanese in the United States Since 1850* (Seattle, Washington: University of Washington Press, 1988), 250; Peter Irons, *Justice at War* (New York: Oxford University Press, 1983), 201, 207–210.

13. Irons, *Justice at War,* 214–216; Los *Angeles Times,* June 27, 1943, Part I, 10.

14. Nash to Hoyt, June 28, 1943.

15. Drinnon, *Keeper of Concentration Camps,* 63–64, 266–269.

16. Nash to Hoyt, June 28, 1943.

17. Franklin Roosevelt created the Office of War Information in June 1942. Its top officials included Elmer Davis a veteran journalist, Archibald MacLeish, Robert Sherwood, Milton Eisenhower, and Gardner Cowles, Jr. The staff of the OWI was an uneasy amalgam of liberal intellectuals who wanted the OWI to play an education role in informing the American public about the aims, ideals, and realities of the war and Madison Avenue executives who wanted to apply their advertising methods to wartime propaganda. The advertisers eventually triumphed. Blum, *V Was for Victory,* 30–39; Polenberg, *War and Society,* 53–54.

18. Handwritten memo, Jan Allen to Nash, n.d. and n.a., Nash Files, Box 23, OWI Files—Alphabetical Files.

19. Cable, Lewis to McCloy, July 1, 1943 and Anderson to McCloy, June 30, 1943 in Nash Files, Box 23, OWI Files—Alphabetical Files.

20. McCloy to Elmer Davis, July 6, 1943, Nash Files, Box 23, OWI Files—Alphabetical Files.

21. Scobey to Eisenhower, July 30, 1943, Nash Files, Box 23, OWI Files—Alphabetical Files.

22. People's World, "Regarding the Japanese Evacuation," June 30, 1942 and "The Manzanar Camp Riot Has a Lesson," December 9, 1942, both clippings in Karl Yoneda Papers, University of California, Los Angeles, Box 8, Folder 3 and Folder 5; Karl Yoneda, Ganbatte: Sixty-Year Struggle of a Kibei Worker (Los Angeles: Asian American Studies Center, UCLA, 1983), 115–116.

23. The following are all found in Common Ground. See, among a number of articles on the camps, Carey McWilliams, "Japanese Evacuation: Policy and Perspectives" (Summer, 1942), 65–72; Robert L. Brown, "Manzanar – Relocation Center," and Mary Oyama, "This Isn't Japan" (Autumn, 1942) 27–32 and 32–34; Dillon Myer, "Democracy in Relocation" (Winter, 1943), 43–48; and "What Happened at Manzanar—A Report" (Spring, 1943), 83–88; M. Margaret Anderson, "Get the Evacuees Out!" (Summer, 1943), 65–66. McWilliams's modified views appear in "Race Tensions: Second Phase" (Autumn, 1943), 7–12; and "The Nisei Speak" (Summer, 1944), 61–74.

24. See, Yoneda, Ganbatte, 213–215.

25. Copies of the first four panels of the Superman story line can be found in the Nash Files, Box 23, OWI Files—Alphabetical Files. The remaining story unfolded in syndicated form in newspapers across the country, including the Washington Post. I used the San Francisco Chronicle.

26. The following paragraph is inspired by Michael Rogin, Ronald Reagan, the Movie: And Other Episodes in Political Demonology (Berkeley: University of California Press, 1987).

27. Takashima to Davis, December 11, 1943, Papers of Harry S. Truman, Philleo Nash Files, Box 23, OWI Files—Alphabetical Files, Minorities, Publications – General, Japanese-Americans, Memoranda, 1943, 1944.

28. War Relocation Authority, "Evacuee Resistances to Relocation," Community Analysis Report No. 5, June 1943, Nash Papers.

Chapter 7

1. My effort was inspired in part by the interpretation advanced by historian John Dower in his classic work, War Without Mercy (New York: W.W. Norton, 1986).

366 Notes to Chapter 7

2. Donald O. Johnson, "The War Relocation Authority Schools of Tule Lake, California," unpublished master's thesis, School of Education, Stanford University, June 1947, 93–94 (emphasis added).

3. For example, see Roger Daniels, *Concentration Camps USA: Japanese Americans and World War II* (New York: Holt, Rinehart and Winston, 1972); Richard Drinnon, *Keeper of Concentration Camps: Dillon S. Myer and American Racism* (Berkeley: University of California Press, 1987); Michi Weglyn, *Years of Infamy: The Untold Story of America's Concentration Camps* (New York: William Morrow, 1976). A few respected journals condemned the internment camps as concentration camps at the time of their inception. See, for example, Michael Evans, "Concentration Camp—USA Style," *Coronet* 12 (October 1942): 43–51; Ted Nakashima, "Concentration Camp: U.S. Style," *New Republic* 106 (June 15, 1942): 822–23; "Life in a California Concentration Camp; Excerpts from Letters," *Nation* 154 (June 6, 1942): 666.

4. United States Commission on Wartime Relocation and Internment of Civilians, *Personal Justice Denied: Report of the Commission on Wartime Relocation and Internment of Civilians* (Washington, D.C.: GPO, 1982), 110–12.

5. Commission on Wartime Relocation, *Personal Justice Denied*, 6.

6. The *Los Angeles Times* editor wrote in February 1942 about what he called "our American-born Japanese":

> A viper is nonetheless a viper wherever the egg is hatched. A leopard's spots are the same and its disposition is the same wherever it is whelped.
>
> So a Japanese-American, born of Japanese parents, nurtured upon Japanese traditions, living in a transplanted Japanese atmosphere and thoroughly inoculated with Japanese thoughts, Japanese ideas and Japanese ideals, notwithstanding his nominal brand of accidental citizenship, almost inevitably and with the rarest exceptions grows up to be a Japanese, not an American, in his thoughts, in his ideas and in his ideals, and himself is a potential and menacing, if not an actual, danger and, as it were, hamstrung.
>
> [Thus I favor their control because] I cannot escape the conclusion that such treatment, as a matter of national and even personal defense, should be accorded to each and all of them while we are at war with their race. Los Angeles Times, February 2, 1942, part 2, page 4.

Leading journalists, civic leaders, and politicians throughout the Western states expressed like views through the early months of 1942. Although the top political leaders of the country did not express such virulent racism publicly, many shared the same ideas privately Discussion of the biologically based racist thinking of men such as John J. McCloy, Henry L. Stimson, and Franklin Roosevelt are in Drinnon, *Keeper of Concentration Camps,* 30, 33–34, 254–56.

Notes to Chapter 7   367

7. Stanford University, School of Education, *Education in Wartime and After* (New York: D. Appleton-Century, 1943), 66. On the rise of cultural relativist views of human difference, see Carl Degler, *In Search of Human Nature: The Decline and Revival of Darwinism in American Social Thought* (New York: Oxford University Press, 1991).

8. Commission on Wartime Relocation, *Personal Justice Denied*, 18.

9. Drinnon, *Keeper of Concentration Camps*, 64–65.The extremists included U.S. senators and congressmen and journalists with the Hearst and McClatchy newspaper chains. For more on popular notions about internment and the limited opposition to the internment order, see Gordon H. Chang, "'Superman is about to visit the relocation centers' and the Limits of Wartime Liberalism," *Amerasia Journal* 19, no. 1 (1993): 37–59.

10. Although public support for internment was enthusiastic, some public figures condemned the decision, offering a decidedly different interpretation of the action. The Quakers, the Socialist Norman Thomas, and individual Japanese Americans spoke out vigorously. Some individuals involved in the internment project actually expressed misgivings in private, revealing some understanding of the ignominy of the decision. Secretary of War Henry Stimson, before his energetic endorsement of internment, confided in his diary that the move would "make a tremendous hole in our constitutional system." Top officials in the Department of Justice, including Attorney General Francis Biddle, feared the constitutional implications of the internment decision but acquiesced and then later presented evidence in the Supreme Court they knew was false. Their rationales persuaded the top court to uphold the internment decision. Because of the exposure of the machinations of the Justice Department in the challenge cases, the Court thirty years later vacated its early decisions on internment.

11. McCloy to Meiklejohn, September 30, 1942, Japanese American Evacuation and Resettlement Study, 67/14, E1.020, Bancroft Library, U.C. Berkeley, and Drinnon, *Keeper of Concentration Camps*, 36. Directed by sociologist Dorothy Swaine Thomas, the JERS wartime project involved social scientists in an independent investigation of internment and its immediate aftermath. This project has been discussed elsewhere: see Yuji Ichioka, ed., *Views from Within: The Japanese American Evacuation and Resettlement Study* (Los Angeles: Asian American Studies Center, UCLA, 1989).

12. John J. McCloy to Jane B. Kaihatsu, April 12, 1984, reproduced in Roger Daniels, Sandra C. Taylor, and Harry H. L. Kitano, eds., *Japanese Americans: From Relocation to Redress* (Salt Lake City: University of Utah Press, 1986), 213–14.

13. Carey McWilliams, "California and the Japanese," *New Republic* 106 (March 3, 1942): 295–97, and "Japanese Out of California," *New Republic*, 106 (April 6, 1942): 456–57.

368   *Notes to Chapter 7*

14. Carey McWilliams, "Japanese Evacuation: Policy and Perspectives," *Common Ground* 2 (Summer 1942): 65–72; and "Moving the West-Coast Japanese," *Harper's* 185 (September 1942): 359–69. Months later, McWilliams again changed his views and focused his comments on the sentiments raging against Japanese Americans. He eventually came to be identified as a vocal opponent of their relocation. In his memoir many years later, McWilliams avoids mentioning his 1942 flirtation with the internment project and implies he had always opposed the idea. See his "Racism on the West Coast," *New Republic* 110 (May 29, 1944): 732–33; Prejudice, Japanese-Americans: Symbol of Racial Intolerance (Boston: Little, Brown, 1944); and The Education of Carey McWilliams (Boston: Simon and Schuster, 1978), 101–7.

15. Edward H. Spicer, "The Use of Social Scientists by the War Relocation Authority," *Applied Anthropology* 5, no. 2 (Spring 1946): 19, 35–36; and Spicer et al., *Impounded People: Japanese-Americans in the Relocation Centers* (Tucson: University of Arizona Press, 1969), 18–21. Also see Peter T. Suzuki, "Anthropologists in the Wartime Camps for Japanese Americans: A Documentary Study," *Dialectical Anthropology* 6, no. 1 (1981): 23–60.

16. Bogardus, 28:218–34; Bureau of Sociological Research, 100:328–33; Robertson, 20, no. 2, 66–71; Kehoe, 3:55–59; Provinse, 11:4, 396–410; and Spicer (New York: Russell Sage Foundation, 1952).

17. John W. Powell, "Education Through Relocation," *Adult Education Journal* 1, no. 4 (October 1942): 154–57 (emphasis added).

18. Thomas James, *Exile Within: The Schooling of Japanese Americans, 1942–1945* (Cambridge, Mass.: Harvard University Press, 1987), 39–40.

19. Quotes from James, *Exile Within*, 137.

20. "Proposed Curriculum Procedures for Japanese Relocation Centers," Summer 1942, box 153, folder 11, pp. 11, 4–5, Paul Hanna Papers, Hoover Institution, Stanford.

21. Jerome T. Light, "The Development of a Junior-Senior High School Program in a Relocation Center for People of Japanese Ancestry During the War with Japan," unpublished Ph.D. dissertation, School of Education, Stanford University, April 1947.

22. Light, "Development of a Program," 498–99.

23. Light, "Development of a Program," 496.

24. Light, "Development of a Program," 589.

25. Discussion of internee reaction to internment draws heavily from my book *Morning Glory, Evening Shadow: Yamato Ichihashi and His Internment Writings, 1942–1945* (Stanford, Calif.: Stanford University Press, 1997). Also see Yuji Ichioka, ed., *Views from Within: The Japanese American Evacuation and Resettlement Study* (Los Angeles: Asian American Studies Center, UCLA, 1989); Lane Ryo

Hirabayashi, ed., *Inside an American Concentration Camp: Japanese American Resistance at Poston, Arizona* (Tucson: University of Arizona Press, 1995); and Charles Kikuchi, *The Kikuchi Diary: Chronicle from an American Concentration Camp. The Tanforan Journals of Charles Kikuchi,* ed. John Modell (Urbana: University of Illinois Press, 1973).

26. Chang, *Morning Glory,* 111, 124.

27. Chang, *Morning Glory,* 184, 215.

28. Chang, *Morning Glory,* 286.

29. Dillon Myer, *Uprooted Americans: The Japanese Americans and the War Relocation Authority During World War II* (Tucson: University of Arizona Press, 1971), 3.

30. Quotation from Light, *Exile Within,* 93–94. One anthropologist wrote an entire book on the administrative lessons offered by internment: Alexander H. Leighton, *The Governing of Men: General Principles and Recommendations Based on Experience at a Japanese Relocation Camp* (Princeton, N.J.: Princeton University Press, 1945).

31. In this respect, my interpretation is a modification of the view in the fine book by Elazar Barkan, *Retreat of Scientific Racism: Changing Concepts of Race in Britain and the United States Between the World Wars* (New York: Cambridge University Press, 1992).

32. Norman Thomas, "Dark Day for Liberty," *Christian Century* 59 (July 29, 1942): 929–31. Also see his *Democracy and Japanese Americans* (New York: Post War World Council, 1942).

Chapter 8

1. "Asian Immigrants and American Foreign Relations," in *Pacific Passage: The Study of American-East Asian Relations on the Eve of the Twenty-First Century,* edited by Warren I. Cohen (New York: Columbia University Press), pp. 103–118.

2. For discussion purposes, this chapter assumes the existence of a social group called Asian Americans, but it makes no effort to define the group or to attribute particular characteristics to it. The term is used to refer to persons whose ancestry is in Asia.

3. Thomas Sowell, *Ethnic America: A History* (New York: Basic Books, 1981). More specifically, Sowell says that Chinese Americans were able to keep out of the courts and the political arena "because the Chinese in America lived in tight-knit communities of people from one district of one province in China. In those enclaves, they kept alive and intact a culture, a set of traditions and values, that was eroding in China itself" (p. 140). Finding praiseworthy similarities between the Chinese and Japanese American communities, Sowell concludes, "Despite the supposed prerequisite of political cohesion, some of the most remarkable advances

370   *Notes to Chapter 8*

in the face of adversity were made by groups that deliberately avoided politics—notably the Chinese and Japanese" (p. 274).

4. Betty Lee Sung, *Mountain of Gold: The Story of the Chinese in America* (New York: Macmillan, 1967), 278–280.

5. Lee May, "Overcome Distaste for Politics in Order to Get Their Views Heard: Asian-Americans Seek to Join Power Structure," *Los Angeles Times,* February 17, 1985, A15.

6. Bob Gurwitt, "Have Asian Americans Arrived Politically? Not Quite," *Governing* (November 1990): 32–38.

7. Stanley Karnow, "Apathetic Asian Americans? Why Their Success Hasn't Spilled Over into Politics," *Washington Post,* November 29, 1992, C1.

8. George Skelton, "Voters of Asian Heritage Slow to Claim Voice," *Los Angeles Times,* August 19, 1993, A3.

9. John J. Miller, "Asian Americans Head for Politics," *American Enterprise* 6 (March/April 1995): 56–58.

10. See, for example, the significance given to Asian Americans in Peter Beinart, "The Lee Rout," *New Republic,* January 5, 12, 1998, 11–12.

11. *Daily Alta* (San Francisco), October 31, 1850.

12. Mary Roberts Coolidge, *Chinese Immigration* (New York: Henry Holt, 1909), 22.

13. See *People v. Hall* in W. Cheng-tau, *"Chink!"* (New York: World Publishing, 1972), 36–43. On how the case is employed, see Ronald Takaki, *Strangers from a Different Shore* (Boston: Little, Brown, 1989), 102.

14. "Yellow peril" literature includes many obscure writers but also well-known authors such as Jack London and H. G. Wells.

15. P. W. Dooner, *Last Days of the Republic* (San Francisco: Alta California Publishing, 1880). The Hall case is discussed on pages 185–187.

16. Charles Frederick Holder, "The Chinaman in American Politics," *North American Review* (February 1898): 226–233.

17. See many of the fine essays in: Sucheng Chan, ed., *Entry Denied: Exclusion and the Chinese Community in America, 1882–1943* (Philadelphia: Temple University Press, 1991); and K. Scott Wong and Sucheng Chan, eds., *Claiming America: Constructing Chinese American Identities during the Exclusion Era* (Philadelphia: Temple University Press, 1998). Also see Charles J. McClain, *In Search of Equality: The Chinese Struggle against Discrimination in Nineteenth-Century America* (Berkeley: University of California Press, 1994); and Lucy E. Salyer, *Laws Harsh as Tigers: Chinese Immigrants and the Shaping of Modern Immigration Law* (Chapel Hill: University of North Carolina Press, 1995).

18. Montaville Flowers, *The Japanese Conquest of American Opinion* (New York: George H. Doran, 1917), 52–53.

19. Jesse Frederick Steiner, *The Japanese Invasion: A Study in the Psychology of Inter-Racial Contacts* (Chicago: A. C. McClurg, 1917), 184–185, 208–209.

20. V. S. McClatchy, *The Germany of Asia; Japan's Policy in the Far East, Her "Peaceful Penetration" of the United States, How American Commercial and National Interests Are Affected* (Sacramento: 1919), 26–28, 37–41.

21. See Kalyan Kumar Banerjee, "The U.S.A, and Indian Revolutionary Activity: Early Phase of the Gadar Movement," *Modern Review* 97 (February 1965): 97–101. Also see the work by the Anglophile Ernest H. Fitzpatrick, *The Coming Conflict of Nations; or, the Japanese-American War* (Springfield, Ill.: H. W. Rokker, 1909).

22. Bruno Lasker, citing the work of Emory S. Bogardus, *Filipino Immigration to Continental United States and to Hawaii* (Chicago: University of Chicago Press, 1931), 267, 331.

23. See Samuel Gompers and Herman Gutstadt, "Meat vs. Rice—American Manhood against Asiatic Coolieism: Which Shall Survive?" Reprinted, with an introduction by the Asiatic Exclusion League, San Francisco, 1908. For a recent and influential recapitulation of the view of Chinese as inassimilable and uninterested in American life, albeit without the overt racism, see Gunther Barth, *Bitter Strength: A History of the Chinese in the United States, 1850–1870* (Cambridge: Harvard University Press, 1964).

24. Coolidge, *Chinese Immigration*, 442–443. Also see Patrick J. Healy and Ng Poon Chew, *A Statement for Non-Exclusion* (San Francisco: 1905). The authors observed that during the anti-Chinese agitation of the 1870s in San Francisco "the Chinese by no means slept on their rights. They prepared abundant and cogent arguments to refute the lying charges made against them by the ignorance and viciousness of the self-seeking demagogues" (p. 75).

25. Kiyoshi K. Kawakami, *The Japanese Question* (San Francisco: Japanese-American News, n.d.), 2, 3.

26. Eliot Grinnell Mears, *Resident Orientals on the American Pacific Coast: Their Legal and Economic Status* (Chicago: University of Chicago Press, 1928), 104–106, 113, 117–118, 397.

27. Yamato Ichihashi, *Japanese in the United States: A Critical Study of the Problems of the Japanese Immigrants and Their Children* (Stanford: Stanford University Press, 1932), 319–363. Also see Gordon H. Chang, *Morning Glory, Evening Shadow: Yamato Ichihashi and His Wartime Writings, 1942–1945* (Stanford: Stanford University Press, 1997), 11–87.

28. Wanda Robertson, "Developing World Citizens in a Japanese Relocation Center," *Childhood Education* 20 (October 1943): 66–71; and John W. Powell, "Education through Relocation," *Adult Education Journal* 1 (October 1942): 154–157.

372   *Notes to Chapter 8*

29. Frederick G. Murray, "Japs in Our Yard," *American Legion Magazine* 34 (June 1943): 12–13, 42, 46.

30. Forrest E. LaViolette, *Americans of Japanese Ancestry: A Study of Assimilation in the American Community* (Toronto: Canadian Institute of International Affairs, 1945), 148–161. Also see LaViolette's "Political Behavior of the American-Born Japanese," *Research Studies of the State College of Washington* 8 (March 1940): 11–17.

31. Rose Hum Lee, *The Chinese in the United States of America* (Hong Kong: Hong Kong University Press, 1960), 178–180.

32. S. W. Kung, *Chinese in American Life: Some Aspects of Their History, Status, Problems, and Contributions* (Seattle: University of Washington Press, 1962), 261–262.

33. Sung, *Mountain of Gold,* 278–285.

34. Chang, *Morning Glory,* 52–72; Yuji Ichioka, "Japanese Immigrant Nationalism: The Issei and the Sino-Japanese War, 1937–1941," *Pacific Historical Review* 46 (1977): 409–437; the entire issue of *Amerasia Journal* 23 (winter 1997–1998); and Brian Hayashi, *"For the Sake of Our Japanese Brethren": Assimilation, Nationalism, and Protestantism among the Japanese of Los Angeles, 1895–1942* (Stanford: Stanford University Press, 1995).

35. Contrast the perspectives in the following essays with those found in works on Chinese Americans produced in the 1950s and 1960s: Him Mark Lai, "Roles Played by Chinese in America during China's Resistance to Japanese Aggression and during World War II," *Chinese America: History and Perspectives* (1997): 75–125; Him Mark Lai, "China and the Chinese American Community: The Political Dimension," *Chinese America: History and Perspectives* (1999): 1–32; Shihshan Henry Tsai, *China and the Overseas Chinese in the United States, 1868–1911* (Fayetteville: University of Arkansas Press, 1983); and Renqiu Yu, *To Save China, To Save Ourselves: The Chinese Hand Laundry Alliance of New York* (Philadelphia: Temple University Press, 1992).

36. William Petersen, "Success Story, Japanese-American Style," *New York Times Sunday Magazine,* January 9, 1966, 20ff.; and William Petersen, *Japanese Americans: Oppression and Success* (New York: Random House, 1971).

37. Bill Hosokawa, *Nisei: The Quiet Americans* (New York: Morrow, 1969).

38. See the pioneering book edited by Lawrence H. Fuchs, *American Ethnic Politics* (New York: Harper and Row, 1968). No essay on any Asian group appears among the thirteen entries, although there are two on African Americans. In his useful bibliographic essay, Fuchs observes that little work had been done on Chinese and "Spanish-speaking Americans" (p. 288).

39. Edwin O. Reischauer, foreword to *Nisei: The Quiet Americans,* by Bill Hosokawa (New York: Morrow, 1969).

40. "Success Story of One Minority Group in U.S.," *U.S. News and World Report,* December 26, 1966, 73–76.

41. Alfred H. Song, "Politics and Policies of the Oriental Community," in *California Politics and Policies,* ed. Eugene P. Dvorin and Arthur J. Misner (Reading, Mass.: Addison-Wesley, 1966), 387–411.

42. "New Sense of Race Arises among Asian-Americans," *New York Times,* May 30, 1996; "Asian Americans Scarce in U.S. Corridors of Power," *Los Angeles Times,* October 21, 1997; and "Asian American Programs Are Flourishing at Colleges," *New York Times,* June 9, 1999.

43. Several general histories and anthologies contain considerable material about Asian Americans and politics that span categories. See Amy Tachiki et al., *Roots: An Asian American Reader* (Los Angeles: Asian American Studies Center, University of California, 1971); Emma Gee, ed., *Counterpoint* (Los Angeles: Asian American Studies Center, 1976); Sucheng Chan, *Asian Americans: An Interpretive History* (Boston: Twayne, 1991); Roger Daniels, *Asian America: Chinese and Japanese in the United States since 1850* (Seattle: University of Washington Press, 1988); Ronald Takaki, *Strangers from a Different Shore: A History of Asian Americans* (Boston: Little, Brown, 1989); Shih-shan Henry Tsai, *The Chinese Experience in America* (Bloomington: Indiana University Press, 1986); Yuji Ichioka, *The Issei: The World of the First Generation Japanese Immigrants* (New York: Free Press, 1988); and Gary Oki-hiro, *Margins and Mainstreams: Asians in American History and Culture* (Seattle: University of Washington Press, 1994). Many articles about Asian Americans and politics, broadly defined, appear in *Amerasia Journal,* published by the UCLA Asian American Studies Center and in the *Journal of Asian American Studies.*

44. Tom Coffman, *Catch a Wave: A Case Study of Hawaii's New Politics* (Honolulu: University of Hawaii Press, 1973); Ronald Takaki, *Pau Hana: Plantation Life and Labor in Hawaii* (Honolulu: University of Hawaii Press, 1983); and Vincent N. Parrillo, "Asian Americans in American Politics," in *America's Ethnic Politics,* ed. Joseph S. Roucek and Bernard Eisenberg (Westport, Conn.: Greenwood Press, 1982), 89–112.

45. Peter Irons, *Justice at War: The Story of the Japanese American Internment Cases* (New York: Oxford University Press, 1983); McClain, *In Search of Equality,* Salyer, *Laws Harsh as Tigers;* and Leslie Hatamiya, *Righting a Wrong: Japanese Americans and the Passage of the Civil Liberties Act of 1988* (Stanford: Stanford University Press, 1993). The literature on activism during internment is growing. For example, see Richard Nishimoto, *Inside an American Concentration Camp: Japanese American Resistance at Poston, Arizona,* ed. Lane Hirabayashi (Tucson: University of Arizona Press, 1995).

374   *Notes to Chapter 8*

46. See, for example, Eve Armentrout Ma, *Revolutionaries, Monarchists, and Chinatowns: Chinese Politics in the Americas and the 1911 Revolution* (Honolulu: University of Hawaii Press, 1990); Yu, *To Save China, To Save Ourselves*; Joan Jensen, *Passage from India: Indian Pioneers in America* (New Haven: Yale University Press, 1988); Delber McKee, "The Chinese Boycott of 1905–1906 Reconsidered: The Role of Chinese Americans," *Pacific Historical Review* 55 (1986); and several essays in S. Chandrasekhar, *From India to America: A Brief History of Immigration; Problems of Discrimination; Admission and Assimilation* (La Jolla, Calif.: Population Review Publications, 1982). Many of the recent studies on Asian diasporas offer comparative perspectives on the activities and lives of Asians dispersed in various countries. See, for example, Hyung-chan Kim, ed. *The Korean Diaspora: Historical and Socio-logical Studies of Korean Immigration and Assimilation in North America* (Santa Barbara, Calif.: ABC-Clio, 1977); and Lynn Pan, *Sons of the Yellow Emperor: A History of the Chinese Diaspora* (New York: Kodansha International, 1994).

47. See, for example, Peter Kwong, *Chinatown, New York, Labor and Politics, 1930–1950* (New York: Monthly Review Press, 1979); Peter Kwong, *The New Chinatown* (New York: Hill and Wang, 1996); Robert G. Lee, "The Hidden World of Asian Immigrant Radicalism," in *The Immigrant Left in the United States,* ed. Paul Buhle and Dan Georgakas (Albany: State University of New York, 1996), 256–288; Karl Yoneda, *Ganbatte! Sixty Year Struggle of a Kibei Worker* (Los Angeles: UCLA Asian American Studies Center, 1983); Him Mark Lai, "A Historical Survey of Organizations of the Left among the Chinese in America," *Bulletin of Concerned Asian Scholars* 4 (fall 1972): 10–21; Him Mark Lai, "The Chinese Marxist Left in America to the 1960's," *Chinese America: History and Perspectives* (1992): 3–82; Karin Aguilar San-Juan, ed., *The State of Asian American: Activism and Resistance in the 1990s* (Boston: South End Press, 1994); Craig Scharlin and Lilia V. Villanueva, *Philip Vera Cruz: A Personal History of Filipino Immigrants and the Farmworkers Movement* (Los Angeles: UCLA Labor Center, 1992); and Chris Friday, *Organizing Asian American Labor: The Pacific Coast Canned-Salmon Industry, 1870–1942* (Philadelphia: Temple University Press, 1994).

48. See Victor Low, *The Unimpressible Race: A Century of Educational Struggle by the Chinese in San Francisco* (San Francisco: East/West Publishing Co., 1982); Don T. Nakanishi and Tina Yamano Nishida, eds., *The Asian American Educational Experience: A Source Book for Teachers and Students* (New York: Routledge, 1995); and Dana Takagi, *The Retreat from Race: Asian-American Admissions and Racial Politics* (New Brunswick, N.J.: Rutgers University Press, 1992).

49. McClain, *In Search of Equality,* 3.

50. See, for example, the following which have implications for thinking about the politics of Asian American studies: Gary Okihiro's interpretive history in

Margins and Mainstreams; Sylvia Yanagisako's critical essay, "Transforming Orientalism: Gender, Nationality, and Class in Asian American Studies," in *Naturalizing Power: Essays in Feminist Cultural Analysis,* ed. Sylvia Yanagisako and Carol Delany (New York: Routledge, 1995), 275–298; and Henry Yu's "The 'Oriental Problem' in America, 1920–1960: Linking the Identities of Chinese American and Japanese American Intellectuals," in *Claiming America: Constructing Chinese American Identities during the Exclusion Era,* ed. K. Scott Wong and Sucheng Chan (Philadelphia: Temple University Press, 1998), 191–214.

51. See, for example, Timothy P. Fong, *The First Suburban Chinatown: The Remaking of Monterey Park, California* (Philadelphia: Temple University Press, 1994), and Chapter 8 in Fong's *The Contemporary Asian American Experience: Beyond the Model Minority* (Upper Saddle River, N.J.: Prentice-Hall, 1997); John Horton, *The Politics of Diversity: Immigration, Resistance, and Change in Monterey Park, California* (Philadelphia: Temple University Press, 1995); Leland T. Saito, *Race and Politics: Asian Americans, Latinos, and Whites in a Los Angeles Suburb* (Urbana: University of Illinois Press, 1998); Stephen S. Fugita and David J. O'Brien, *Japanese American Ethnicity: The Persistence of Community* (Seattle: University of Washington Press, 1991), especially Chapter 9; Yung-Hwan Jo, "Problems and Strategies of Participation in American Politics," in *Koreans in Los Angeles: Prospects and Promises* (Los Angeles: Koryo Research Institute, 1982), 203–218; Angelo N. Ancheta, *Race, Rights, and the Asian American Experience* (New Brunswick, N.J.: Rutgers University Press, 1998); Jere Takahashi, *Nisei/Sansei: Shifting Japanese American Identities and Politics* (Philadelphia: Temple University Press, 1997); Yung-Hwan Jo, ed., *Political Participation of Asian Americans: Problems and Strategies* (Chicago: Pacific/Asian American Mental Health Research Center, 1980); Moon H. Jo, "The Putative Political Complacency of Asian Americans," *Political Psychology* 5 (1984): 583–605; Don T. Nakanishi, "Asian American Politics: An Agenda for Research," *Amerasia Journal* 12 (1985–1986): 1–27; L. Ling-chi Wang, "The Politics of Ethnic Identity and Empowerment: The Asian American Community since the 1960s," *Asian American Policy Review* 2 (1991): 43–56; Bruce E. Cain, "Asian American Electoral Power: Imminent or Illusory?" *Election Politics* 9 (1988): 27–30; Wendy Tam, "Asians—A Monolithic Voting Bloc?" *Political Behavior* 17 (1995): 223–249; Pei-te Lien, *The Political Participation of Asian Americans: Voting Behavior in Southern California* (New York: Garland Publishing, 1997); and Yen Le Esperitu, *Asian American Panethnicity* (Philadelphia: Temple University Press, 1992). Also see the seven editions of the *National Asian Pacific American Political Almanac* (Los Angeles: UCLA Asian American Studies Center).

52. Important work on cultural politics and Asian Americans includes that by: Dorinne Kondo, *About Face: Performing Race in Fashion and Theater* (New York: Routledge, 1997); Robert G. Lee, *Orientals: Asian Americans in Popular Culture*

376 *Notes to Chapters 8 and 9*

(Philadelphia: Temple University Press, 1999); Lisa Lowe, *Immigrant Acts: On Asian American Cultural Politics* (Durham: Duke University Press, 1996); David Li, *Imagining the Nation: Asian American Literature and Cultural Consent* (Stanford: Stanford University Press, 1998); and David Palumbo-Liu, *Asian/American: Historical Crossings of a Racial Frontier* (Stanford: Stanford University Press, 1999).

Chapter 9

1. Identifying all of the many colleagues who contributed to the project is impossible to do here, but I must thank the other project core leaders: Hilton Obenzinger, Roland Hsu, Denise Khor, Gabriel Wolfenstein, Teri Hessel, Barbara Voss, Erik Steiner, and Connie Young Yu. For more information, visit https://web.stanford.edu/group/chineserailroad/cgi-bin/website/. Acknowledgments: Shelley Fisher Fishkin, Roland Hsu, Hilton Obenzinger, Gabriel Wolfenstein, Teri Hessel, and others in the Chinese Railroad Workers in North America Project at Stanford University offered very helpful comments on an earlier version of this essay. I thank them.

2. Wesley S. Griswold, *A Work of Giants: Building the First Transcontinental Railroad* (New York: McGraw-Hill, 1962); Stephen E. Ambrose, *Nothing Like It in the World: The Men Who Built the Transcontinental Railroad, 1863–1869* (New York: Simon & Schuster, 2001).

3. David Haward Bain, *Empire Express: Building the First Transcontinental Railroad* (New York: Penguin Books, 2000); Richard White, *Railroaded: The Transcontinentals and the Making of Modern America* (New York: W. W. Norton, 2012).

4. Ryan Dearinger, *The Filth of Progress: Immigrants, Americans, and the Building of Canals and in the West* (Berkeley: University of California Press, 2015).

5. See Greg Robinson, "*Les fils du Ciel:* European Travelers' Accounts of Chinese Railroad Workers," in *The Chinese and the Iron Road,* edited by Gordon H. Chang and Shelley Fisher Fishkin (Palo Alto, Stanford University Press, 2019).

6. Although Jules Verne does not mention Chinese in the fictional account, he was well aware of their presence in California, which he reveals in "Tribulations of a Chinaman in China" (1879), a short story that he published later. In that work, the storyline revolves around financial connections between China and California.

7. See Wolfgang Schivelbusch, *Railway Journey: The Industrialization of Time and Space in the 19th Century* (New York: Urizen Books, 1979), foreword, 89, 90; Edgar B. Schieldrop, *The Railway: Conquest of Space and Time* (London: Hutchinson, 1939), 29, 228, 229; Union Pacific Railroad Company, *Around the World by Steam, via the Pacific Railroad* (London: Union Pacific Railroad Co., 1871), 4.

8. John Todd, *The Sunset Land; or, The Great Pacific Slope* (Boston: Lee & Shepard, 1870), 261.

Notes to Chapter 9   377

9. Asa Whitney, *A Project for a Railroad to the Pacific* (New York: George W. Wood, 1849).

10. *Memorial Addresses on the Life and Character of Leland Stanford* (Washington, DC: US Government Printing Office, 1894), 11.

11. John C. Frémont, letter to the editor, *National Intelligencer,* June 15, 1854, cited in Hoyt Williams, *A Great and Shining Road: The Epic Story of the Transcontinental Railroad* (Lincoln: University of Nebraska Press, 1988), 17, 18. See also "China and the Indies—Our 'Manifest Destiny' in the East," *DeBow's Review* (December 1853): 541–571; and Sidney Dillon, "Historic Moments: Driving the Last Spike of the Union Pacific," *Scribner's* 12 (September 1892): 253–259.

12. The speeches, including the one made by Leland Stanford, and celebratory messages offered for the completion of the line highlight its global significance. See "Transcontinental Railroad Postscript," *San Francisco News Letter and California Advertiser,* May 15, 1869; and "Pacific Railroad Inauguration," *Sacramento Daily Union,* January 9, 1863.

13. Dillon, "Historic Moments"; Henry George, "What the Railroad Will Bring Us," *Overland Monthly* 1, no. 4 (October 1868): 297–306.

14. "The China Mail Line," *Sacramento Daily Union,* January 3, 1867.

15. Edwin L. Sabin, *Building the Pacific Railway* (Philadelphia: J. B. Lippincott, 1919), 228, 229; C. P. Huntington to E. B. Crocker, October 3, 1867, *Letters from Collis P. Huntington to Mark Hopkins, Leland Stanford, Charles Crocker, E. B. Crocker, Charles F. Crocker, and D. D. Colton from August 20, 1867 to March 31, 1876,* microfilm (Berkeley: University of California Photographic Services).

16. Daniel Cleveland, "The Chinese as Railroad Laborers," a chapter in his 1869 unpublished manuscript, "The Chinese in California," Daniel Cleveland Manuscripts, 1868–1929, mss. HM 72175-72177, Huntington Library, San Marino, CA; see also in the same collection Daniel Cleveland to J. Ross Browne, US Minister to China, July 27, 1868. Cleveland had worked on the manuscript for a year and had arranged for its publication by Bancroft, the largest publisher in the West. It is not clear why the book was never issued. Cleveland to Benson J. Lossing, February 10, 1869, Bancroft Library, UC Berkeley, BANCMSS C-B-858.

17. "The Chinese," *Commercial Advertiser* (New York), July 6, 1869.

18. "Mixing the Waters of the Atlantic and Pacific," *Frank Leslie's Illustrated,* July 2, 1870, 245.

19. William F. Chew, *Nameless Builders of the Transcontinental Railway: The Chinese Workers of the Central Pacific Railroad* (Victoria, BC: Trafford, 2004), 40–45.

20. Russell H. Conway, *Why and How: Why the Chinese Emigrate, and the Means They Adopt for the Purpose of Reaching America* (Boston: Lee & Shepard,

378   *Notes to Chapter 9*

1871); "Mass Laborers Hiring in San Francisco," *Feilong* (California *China Mail and Flying Dragon*), January 1, 1867.

21. Lucy M. Cohen, "The Chinese of the Panama Railroad: Preliminary Notes on the Migrants of 1854 Who 'Failed,'" *Ethnohistory* 18, no. 4 (Autumn 1971): 309–320; Lok C. D. Siu, *Memories of a Future Home: Diasporic Citizenship of Chinese in Panama* (Stanford, CA: Stanford University Press, 2005), 38, 39; *The Railroad Record*, May 26, 1859, 162; Minutes of the Meetings of the Board of Directors, June 28, 1854, Records of the Panama Canal Panama Railroad Company, National Archives, Washington, DC.

22. Gilbert Olsen and Richard Floyd, "The San Jose Railroad and Crocker's Pets," in *Chinese Argonauts: An Anthology of the Chinese Contributions to the Historical Development of Santa Clara County*, edited by Gloria Sun Hom (Los Altos Hills, CA: Foothill Community College District/California History Center, 1971), 132–142; *Report of the Joint Special Committee to Investigate Chinese Immigration*, Sen. Rpt. 689, 44th Cong., 2d sess. (Washington, DC: US Government Printing Office, 1877), 667.

23. Philip A. Kuhn, *Chinese among Others: Emigration in Modern Times* (Lanham, MD: Rowman & Littlefield, 2008). Eric Hobsbawm offers his own historical perspective on Chinese migration in *The Age of Capital: 1848–1875* (New York: Vintage, 1996), 63.

24. Special correspondent, "From the Pacific," *Standard* (London), November 17, 1869, 5.

25. "Chinamen as Free Immigrants," *Massachusetts Spy*, July 30, 1869, 2; Diana Lary, *Chinese Migrations: The Movement of People, Goods, and Ideas over Four Millennia* (Lanham, MD: Rowman & Littlefield, 2012), 91; Aristide R. Zolberg, "The Great Wall against China: Responses to the First Immigration Crisis, 1885–1925," in *Migration, Migration History, History: Old Paradigms and New Perspectives*, ed. Jan Lucassen and Leo Lucassen (Bern, Switzerland: Peter Lang, 1999), 291–316.

26. Elizabeth Sinn, *Pacific Crossing: California Gold, Chinese Migration, and the Making of Hong Kong* (Hong Kong: Hong Kong University Press, 2013); Madeline Hsu, *Dreaming of Gold, Dreaming of Home: Transnationalism and Migration between the United States and South China, 1882–1943* (Stanford, CA: Stanford University Press: 2000).

27. "How Our Chinamen Are Employed," *Overland Monthly* 2, no. 3 (March 1869): 231. This long article records the wide variety in the types of work performed by the Chinese throughout the West.

28. Alexandra Kichenik DeVarenne, "Goji Farm USA Brings Superfruit to Sonoma County," *Edible* 29 (Spring 2016): 67–70.

29. See Patricia Nelson Limerick, *Legacy of Conquest: The Unbroken Past of the American West* (New York: Norton, 1987). See also J. Ryan Kennedy, Sarah

Notes to Chapter 9   379

Heffner, Virginia Popper, Ryan P. Harrod, and John J. Crandall, , "The Health and Well-Being of Chinese Railroad Workers," in *The Chinese and the Iron Road,* edited by Gordon H. Chang and Shelley Fisher Fishkin (Palo Alto, Stanford University Press, 2019).

30. Cleveland, "The Chinese as Railroad Laborers," in "The Chinese in California."

31. Other writers provided similar descriptions of the Chinese labor camps. See, for example, James Ross, *From Wisconsin to California and Return, as Reported for the "Wisconsin State Journal"* (Madison, WI: Ross, James, 1869), 33–35.

32. Raymond B. Craib, *Chinese Immigrants in Porfirian Mexico* (Albuquerque: University of New Mexico Press, 1996), 6; Jacques Meniaud, *Les pionniers du Soudan* (Paris: Société des Publications Modernes, 1931), 99, 100; Watt Stewart, *Chinese Bondage in Peru: A History of the Chinese Coolie in Peru, 1849–1874* (Durham, NC: Duke University Press, 1951), 75, 89; Watt Stewart, *Henry Meiggs: Yankee Pizarro* (Durham, NC: Duke University Press, 1946), 161–163; and Sophia V. Schweitzer and Bennet Hymer, *Big Island Journey* (Honolulu, HI: Mutual Publishing, 2009), 74.

33. Stewart, *Henry Meiggs*, 161–163. On the development of the modern worker in the mid-nineteenth century, see Hobsbawm, *Age of Capital*, 213–229.

34. See Beth Lew-Williams, "The Remarkable Life of a Sometimes Railroad Worker: Chin Gee Hee, 1844–1929," in *The Chinese and the Iron Road,* edited by Gordon H. Chang and Shelley Fisher Fishkin (Palo Alto, Stanford University Press, 2019).

35. "The Chinaman as a Railroad Builder," *Scientific American* (July 31, 1869): 75.

36. "Chinamen as Free Immigrants," *Massachusetts Spy,* July 30, 1869. See also Hsu, *Dreaming of Gold.* See essays by Yuan Ding/Roland Hsu, Zhang Guoxiong/Roland Hsu, and Liu Jin/Roland Hsu in *The Chinese and the Iron Road,* edited by Gordon H. Chang and Shelley Fisher Fishkin (Palo Alto, Stanford University Press, 2019).

37. Yung Wing, *My Life in China and America* (New York: Henry Holt, 1909), 237, 238.

38. Cleveland, "The Chinese as Railroad Laborers," in "The Chinese in California."

39. Cleveland, "The Chinese as Railroad Laborers," in "The Chinese in California."

40. Edwards Pierrepont, "Banquet to His Excellency Anson Burlingame," June 23, 1868. One estimate in 1870 put the number at 1,200 Chinese bodies sent back annually at a cost of $100 gold each. Todd, *The Sunset Land,* 280.

380   *Notes to Chapters 9 and 10*

41. *Workingman's Advocate,* February 6, 1869, quoted in Liping Zhu, *The Road to Chinese Exclusion: The Denver Riot, 1880 Election, and Rise of the West* (Lawrence: University of Kansas Press, 2013), 17–20, 34, 35.

42. Scott Zesch, *The Chinatown War: Chinese Los Angeles and the Massacre of 1871* (New York: Oxford University Press, 2012), 6–14.

43. Acknowledgment of the importance of the railroad workers in United States–China relations by political leaders is not altogether new. The famous nineteenth-century Chinese diplomat Wu Tingfang acknowledged the importance of the workers in his *America through the Spectacles of an Oriental Diplomat* (New York: Frederick A. Stokes, 1914), 44, 45. American presidents did so in the nineteenth century when they opposed passage of anti-Chinese immigration acts. See Gordon H. Chang, *Fateful Ties: A History of America's Preoccupation with China* (Cambridge, MA: Harvard University Press, 2015), 78. Annelise Heinz, "Report on Chinese Immigration Pamphlets," Chinese Railroad Workers in North America Project (unpublished paper) which examines references to the railroad workers in the 1870s–1880s public debate over Chinese immigration restriction.

Chapter 10

1. A few exceptions are: "Asian Immigrants and American Foreign Relations," in *Pacific Passage: The Study of American–East Asian Relations on the Eve of the Twenty-First Century*, edited by Warren I. Cohen (New York: Columbia University Press, 1996), pp. 103–118; "Writing the History of Chinese Immigrants to America," *South Atlantic Quarterly* (98:1/2), Winter 1999, pp. 135–142; "Asian Americans and the Writing of Their History," *Radical History Review* (53), 1992, pp. 105–114; "Are There Other Ways to Think about the 'Great Interregnum'?" *Journal of American-East Asian Relations* (7:2), Spring 1998, pp. 117–122.

2. A book that makes a valiant stab at combining postmodern theory and structuralism is Elizabeth Buck, *Paradise Remade: The Politics of Culture and History in Hawaii* (Philadelphia: Temple University Press: 1993). I am not persuaded however that postmodernism added much more to understanding the story than what other careful and serious ethnographic histories of Hawai'i had presented previously.

3. In understanding postmodernism and history, I have found helpful, Joyce Appleby, Lynn Hunt and Margaret Jacob, *Telling the Truth About History* (New York: Norton, 1994), especially pages 198–270.

4. Charles J. McClain, *In Search of Equality: The Chinese Struggle Against Discrimination in Nineteenth-Century America* (Berkeley: University of California Press, 1994).

5. See, Elaine Kim's criticism of Ronald Takaki's *Strangers From A Different Shore* in *Amerasia Journal* 16:2 (1990): 101–111.

Chapter 11

1. "Emerging from the Shadows: The Visual Arts and Asian American History," *Asian American Art: A History, 1850–1970*, edited by Gordon H. Chang, Mark Dean Johnson, Paul J. Karlstrom, and Sharon Spain (Stanford University Press), 2008: ix–xv.

2. A photograph from San Francisco Chinatown's May's Photo Studio is on the dust jacket for Yong Chen, *Chinese San Francisco, 1850–1943: A Trans-Pacific Community* (Stanford: Stanford University Press, 2000); a painting by Jade Fon Woo is on the front of Lon Kurashige and Alice Yang Murray, eds., *Major Problems in Asian American History* (New York: Houghton Mifflin, 2003); a Jack Chikamichi Yamasaki painting is reproduced on Mae M. Ngai, *Impossible Subjects: Illegal Aliens and the Making of Modern America* (Princeton: Princeton University Press, 2004); and a Henry Sugimoto painting is reproduced for Brian Masaru Hayashi, *Democratizing the Enemy: The Japanese American Internment* (Princeton: Princeton University Press, 2004).

3. For multi-artist studies, see, for example, Deborah Gesensway and Mindy Roseman, *Beyond Words: Images from America's Concentration Camps* (Ithaca, NY: Cornell University Press, 1987); Michael D. Brown, *Views from Asian California, 1920–1965* (San Francisco: Michael D. Brown, 1992); Alice Yang, *Why Asia? Contemporary Asian and Asian American Art* (New York: New York University Press, 1998); Margo Machida et al., *Asia/America: Identities in Contemporary Asian American Art* (New York: The Asia Society Galleries, 1994); Amy Ling, ed., *Yellow Light: The Flowering of Asian American Arts* (Philadelphia: Temple University Press, 1999); Elaine H. Kim (with Margo Machida and Sharon Mizota), *Fresh Talk/Daring Gazes: Conversations on Asian American Art* (Berkeley and Los Angeles: University of California Press, 2003); Jeffrey Wechsler, ed., *Asian Traditions/Modern Expressions: Asian American Artists and Abstraction, 1945–1970* (New York: Abrams in association with the Jane Vorhees Zimmerli Art Museum, Rutgers, the State University of New Jersey, 1997); Irene Poon, *Leading the Way: Asian American Artists of the Older Generation* (Wenham, MA: Gordon College, 2001); and Karin M. Higa, *The View from Within: Japanese American Art from the Internment Camps, 1942–1945* (Los Angeles: Japanese American National Museum, 1992). Studies on individual artists are also increasing.

4. Quoted in Masayo Duus, *The Life of Isamu Noguchi: Journey Without Borders*, trans. Peter Duus (Princeton: Princeton University Press, 2004), 151–152.

5. "Dashing Realist," *Time* 46, no. 10 (September 3, 1945).

6. Quoted in Leonard Slater, "Sight and Sound," *McCall's,* September 1961, 12; and "Meeting of East & West," *Time* 53, no. 16 (April 18, 1949).

382　　*Notes to Chapters 11 and 12*

7. See, for example, the essays in Wanni W. Anderson and Robert G. Lee, eds., *Displacements and Diasporas: Asians in the Americas* (New Brunswick, NJ: Rutgers University Press, 2005); Lane Ryo Hirabayashi et al., eds., *New World, New Lives: Globalization and People of Japanese Descent in the Americas and from Latin America in Japan* (Stanford: Stanford University Press, 2002); Lisa Lowe, *Immigrant Acts: On Asian American Cultural Politics* (Durham, NC: Duke University Press, 1996); and David Palumbo-Liu, *Asian/American: Historical Crossings of a Racial Frontier* (Stanford: Stanford University Press, 1999). An example of an emerging trans-Pacific intellectual history is August Fauni Esperitu, *Five Faces of Exile: The Nation and Filipino American Intellectuals* (Stanford: Stanford University Press, 2005).

8. Bert Winther-Tamaki, *Art in the Encounter of Nations: Japanese and American Artists in the Early Postwar Years* (Honolulu: University of Hawai'i Press, 2001).

9. Gordon H. Chang, *Morning Glory, Evening Shadow: The Internment Writing of Yamato Ichihashi, 1942–1945* (Stanford: Stanford University Press, 1995). The painter was Ernest Kare Kuramatsu, who had lived in the Monterey Bay area of California.

10. See, for example, Lisa See, *On Gold Mountain: The One-Hundred-Year Odyssey of a Chinese-American Family* (New York: St. Martin's Press, 1995). Also see photographs of building interiors reproduced in Arthur Bonner, *Alas! What Brought Thee Hither? The Chinese in New York, 1800–1950* (Madison, NJ: Fairleigh Dickinson University Press, 1997); and Marie Rose Wong, *Sweet Cakes, Long Journey: The Chinatowns of Portland, Oregon* (Seattle: University of Washington Press, 2004).

11. For a contemporary discussion, see "Is There an Asian American Aesthetics," chapter 30 in *Contemporary Asian America: A Multidisciplinary Reader,* eds. Min Zhou and James V. Gatewood (New York: New York University Press, 2000), 627–635.

Chapter 12

1. "Chinese Painting Comes to America: Zhang Shuqi and the Diplomacy of Art," *East West Interchanges in America Art: A Long and Tumultuous Relationship*, edited by Cynthia Mills, Lee Glazer, and Amelia A. Goerlitz (Smithsonian Institution Press), 2012: 126–141. Permission of Smithsonian Institution.

2. For new perspectives on East-West artistic interaction, see Gordon H. Chang, Mark Dean Johnson, and Paul J. Karlstrom, eds., *Asian American Art: A History, 1850–1970* (Stanford, CA: Stanford University Press, 2008); Alexandra Munroe, *The Third Mind: American Artists Contemplate Asia, 1860–1989* (New York: Guggenheim Museum, 2009); and Jeffrey Wechsler, ed., *Asian Traditions/*

Modern Expressions: Asian American Artists and Abstraction, 1945–1970 (New York: Harry N. Abrams, 1997). On Lai Yong, see Chang, et al., *Asian American Art,* 469–79.

3. The author of this essay is the son of the artist and draws from personal papers in the family collection for some of the source material. Zhang Shuqi's name is also rendered as Shu-chi Chang, which is how he was commonly known in America during his lifetime.

4. See Warren I. Cohen, *East Asian Art and American Culture: A Study in International Relations* (New York: Columbia University Press, 1992), 1–11, 30–32; Nathan Dunn, *A Descriptive Catalogue of the Chinese Collection in Philadelphia: With Miscellaneous Remarks Upon the Manners, Customs, Trade, and Government of the Celestial Empire* (Philadelphia, 1839), 77; and Jonathan Goldstein, *Philadelphia and the China Trade, 1682–1846: Commercial, Cultural, and Attitudinal Effects* (University Park: The Pennsylvania State University Press, 1978), 74, 77–79. In 1832, Dunn also constructed a manor on his New Jersey estate with Chinese architectural motifs, a practice common among the elite in these years. The structure still stands in Mt. Holly.

5. John R. Peters Jr., *Miscellaneous Remarks upon the Government, History, Religions, Literature, Agriculture, Arts, Trades, Manners, and Customs of the Chinese: As suggested by an examination of the articles comprising the Chinese Museum* (Philadelphia: G. B. Zieber & Co., 1847), quotes at 192–93.

6. Cohen, *East Asian Art,* 31.

7. Most scholarship on Liu Haisu is unavailable in English, but images and basic biographies may be found online. In Shanghai, the Liu Haisu Art Museum was opened in 1995 to house works he donated and to display modern Chinese art.

8. Zhang Shuqi, "The Story of My Painting Life," unpublished manuscript, ca. 1944, Chang Family collection.

9. See *Yifeng* (Art Wind) 3, no. 11 (1935). The entire issue is devoted to Zhang's work.

10. Julia F. Andrews and Kuiyi Shen, eds. *Chinese Painting on the Eve of the Communist Revolution: Chang Shu-chi and his Collection* (Stanford, CA: Cantor Center for Visual Arts, Stanford University, 2006), 5–6.

11. The Franklin D. Roosevelt Presidential Library and Museum holds documentation related to the gifting of the painting and some of its subsequent history in the Roosevelt administration. See Wendell A. Parks to Gordon H. Chang, November 13, 1997. Johnson to Franklin D. Roosevelt, December 24, 1940. Chang Family collection.

12. See, for example, *Shanghai renmin meishu chubanshe* [Shanghai People's Fine Art Publishing House], *Zhang Shuqi baigetu* ['Zhang Shuqi's One Hundred

384   *Notes to Chapter 12*

doves'] (Shanghai, 1997); and Hong Tuan, *Zhang Shuqi* (Hubei: Hubei meishu chubanshe [Hubei Fine Arts Publishing House], 2005).

13. *An Exhibition of Modern Chinese Paintings* (New York: Metropolitan Museum of Art, 1943), with introductions by Hu Shih, Kinn-Wei Shaw, Lin Yutang, and Alan Priest.

14. The La Farge painting is *The Last Waterlilies,* an 1862 oil in the collection of the Colby College Museum of Art. In 1932, Zhang and four Chinese artist friends founded the *Baishe* (White Society), which explored the use of white in painting.

15. Zhang also became active in American professional circles, including the Western Society of Artists. In 1956, he won the top award in its annual competition. He was a member of the faculty of the University of California at Berkeley.

16. Shu-chi Chang, *Painting in the Chinese Manner* (New York: Viking Press, 1960). In the book, Zhang devotes most attention to what can be called the techniques and formal qualities of Chinese painting rather than its philosophy and aesthetics. He wrote the book in Chinese, with the Chinese title "Shuqi's painting method." It was translated by his wife, who provided the English title.

17. *The Studio,* vol. 109 (1935): 50, includes a photograph of Liu Haisu painting in public at the New Burlington Galleries in London. It accompanies an article by him entitled "Aims of the Chinese Painters."

18. "Chinese Painting: Professor Chang shows how he does it in eight minutes flat," *Life,* 15 March 1943, 65–66. The ideal of speed in Chinese painting is discussed in James Cahill, "Quickness and Spontaneity in Chinese Painting: The Ups and Downs of an Ideal," in his *Three Alternative Histories of Chinese Painting* (Lawrence: Spencer Museum of Art, University of Kansas, 1988), 70–99.

19. On "alternative realities," see Richard Vinograd, "Temporalities in Early Twentieth Century Chinese Painting," in Andrews and Shen, eds., *Chinese Painting,* 1–2.

20. Alfred Frankenstein, "The Chinese Send Us Chang Shu-chi," *San Francisco Chronicle,* 14 November 1943, "This World," 12.

21. John Garth, "The Art World," *San Francisco Chronicle,* 19 November 1943. Among the other Asia-trained artists who came to the United States in the first half of the twentieth century are Chiura Obata, Chiang Yee, Dong Kingman, and Paul Horiuchi. Zhang was especially close to Chiang Yee, another pioneer in introducing Chinese arts to America.

22. In 2007, the Museum of Fine Arts, Boston presented an exhibition of the Weng family's painting collection, *Through Six Generations: The Weng Collection of Chinese Painting and Calligraphy.* At least one other film showing Zhang painting was made, "A Chinese Artist: The Method and Technique of Chang Shu-chi"; it was produced by Leslie P. Thatcher for the Royal Ontario Museum of Archaeology in 1942.

Notes to Chapters 12, 13, and 14   385

23. A portion of this 10-minute-long film may be found at www.americanart.si.edu/research/symposia/2009/webcast/.

24. Zhang Shuqi, "On Occidental and Oriental Painting," unpublished manuscript, ca. 1943, Chang Family collection.

Chapter 13

1. "Dashing Realist," *Time,* Sept. 3, 1945, and "Chinese Firecrackers in Manhattan," *Time,* May 28, 1951.

2. "Official Dispatch on Scroll," *Life,* Feb. 14, 1955.

3. "Dong Kingman's U.S.A.," *Life,* May 14, 1951.

4. "Leonard Slater, "Sight and Sound," *McCall's,* Sept. 1961, p. 12.

5. "Meeting of East and West," *Time,* April 18, 1949.

6. Will Durant, *The Story of Civilization: Our Oriental Heritage* (New York: Simon and Schuster, 1935), pp. viii–ix.

Chapter 14

1. Unless noted, the sources for the biographical information on Happy Lim are federal documents released through the Freedom of Information Act. The file contains material generated principally by the FBI and by the INS. It is in the possession of the author who made the request for release in 1986. In 1991, the government began to release documents, eventually numbering approximately 1,500 heavily redacted pages. About 200 pages were withheld in their entirety. The released file contains documents from 1950 to 1966. In the interests of space, I provide citations only to major documents. All of Happy Lim's writings are in Chinese but are presented here in English translation.

2. The most recent publication is "Song of Chinese Workers" (1938) in Judy Yung, Gordon H. Chang, Him Mark Lai, *Chinese American Voices* (Berkeley: University of California Press, 2006): 196–199. In the late 1980s, The 4 in One Quartet, which included Jon Jang and Francis Wong, recorded "Hymn to Happy Lim" in its album *The Ballad or the Bullet,* which was dedicated to Malcolm X and Thelonious Monk. The song continues to be included in the background music of "Yan Can Cook" in Australia. Jon Jang to author, January 31, 2008, in author's possession.

3. Him Mark Lai, who had known Lim as part of the San Francisco Chinatown Left since the 1950s, and Mabel Teng who worked closely with him during the heyday of Kearney Street activism both recall he was very difficult to know. Memorandum, SAC, SF to Director, FBI, Oct. 6, 1950; Memorandum, Director FBI to SAC, SF, Dec. 6, 1950; and INS Report of Investigation, January 31 and March 9, 1966.

386   *Notes to Chapter 14*

4. Memorandum for File, INS, Rough Draft, n.d.; author's interview with Mabel Teng, January 1, 1990.

5. Fred Ho notes from an interview with Happy Lim on March 14, 1985. Copy of notes in author's possession.

6. Application of alleged American citizen of the Chinese race for reinvestigation of status, April 26, 1927; Action Sheet, First day landings, June 12, 1929; and letter to author from Happy Lim's grandson, Xue Shengsu, Dec. 3, 1990.

7. Yueh Sheng, *Sun Yat-sen University in Moscow and the Chinese Revolution: Personal Account* (Lawrence: University of Kansas, Center for East Asian Studies, 1971): 68.

8. INS administrative page, March 9, 1966; and notes, author's interview with Karl Yoneda, September 12, 1995(?).

9. Him Mark Lai, "To Bring Forth a New China, To Build a Better America: The Chinese Marxist Left in America to the 1960s," *Chinese America: History and Perspectives* (1992): 3–82.

10. Happy Lim, "Literature, Art and Practical Struggle," (translated by Eunice Chen), *East Wind*, 1985 (Winter/Spring 1985): 18–19.

11. Ho notes; and Mabel Teng interview.

12. Karl Yoneda interview. In *Ganbatte,* Yoneda says he went to Alaska for the first time in 1938, as a union delegate of the Alaska Cannery Workers Union, AFL, 89. He recalled that he often ate there with the Chinese workers, who, because of their experience with food preparation, prepared a better table.

13. "Happy Lim," *East Wind,* 1982 (Spring/Summer): 29–31 and reprinted under the title, "Organizing Chinese Workers in the 1930's," in *Gidra* (Special Anniversary Issue) 1990: 8–9; Teng interview.

14. Typeset notes of a talk with Ja Chong [probably Xavier Dea] for *Unity,* ca. 1981, in author's possession. After living in the Soviet Union, Ja Chong joined the communist underground in China and after 1949 became a mid-level government official. He visited the United States in the 1980s to improve relations with "overseas Chinese" here. For more on the 1930s in Chinatown and Dea, see Lai, "To Bring Forth a New China," 17–21. On early communist activities among the Chinese in America, see Josephine Fowler, *Japanese & Chinese Immigrant Activists: Organizing in American & International Communist Movements, 1919–1933* (New Brunswick: Rutgers University Press, 2007).

15. "Happy Lim," *East Wind* 1982 (Spring/Summer): 29–31. Also see, "My Personal Account of the History of Chinese Workers in the US," *Chinese- American Workers: Past & Present,* n.d., 25–27.

16. Happy Lim, "Scattered Memories of the China New Language Study Group," n.d., in author's possession and Lai, "To Bring Forth a New China," 40.

17. Teng interview.

Notes to Chapter 14 387

18. "Forward" to "In Brilliant Sunshine," unpublished manuscript, Nov. 2, 1962, 1.

19. Report, SF FBI, August 1955.

20. Report, SF FBI, February 8, 1951.

21. Lai, "To Bring Forth a New China," 47 and 70–71, n.117.

22. Memorandum, SAC, San Francisco to Director, FBI, October 6, 1950 and Memorandum, Director, FBI to SAC, San Francisco, December 6, 1950.

23. Airtel, Hoover to selected SACS, March 11, 1955. Other instructions in the highly redacted document indicate that there were approximately eight subjects in San Francisco and twenty in New York. One to three subjects were identified as living in each of the cities of Albany, Cleveland, Detroit, Honolulu, Los Angeles, Newark, Philadelphia, San Diego and Seattle. Director, FBI to William F. Tompkins, Assistant Attorney General, May 5, 1955 and July 19, 1955. As of May 1962, the FBI continued to list Lim on the Security Index. The San Francisco office informed the central office that in its opinion Lim "could be a dangerous individual who would be expected to commit acts against the best interests of the United States in a time of emergency involving the United States with Red China." The reasons for this conclusion were redacted. SAC, SF to Director, FBI, May 7, 1962. Lim was removed from the list in 1965. It is unclear when the FBI first compiled a "Security Index." As early as 1946, J. Edgar Hoover sought powers to detain identified U.S. citizens in the event of war. In 1950, just after the outbreak of the Korean War, Hoover sent a plan to imprison possibly 12,000 Americans of suspect loyalty. See *New York Times,* Dec. 23, 2007, 30.

24. Report, FBI, May 4, 1956 of an "interview" with Lim on April 9, 1956; SAC, SF to Hoover, May 7, 1956; and Fred Ho notes.

25. The club was the first of its kind in California and in a few years some 400 folk dance clubs appeared in the state. The club was founded by a man known in folk dance circles as Song Chang, a Chinese American, who apparently took up folk dancing when he traveled in Europe in the early 1930s. It is said that the "warm feeling of camaraderie, the disdain for racial barriers and the fun spirit," were what attracted Chang to the pastime. The club's early activities occurred in basements and clubs around the Chinatown and North Beach areas in San Francisco. Song Chang's full name is Dai Song Chang who had studied architecture at UC Berkeley. He and his wife, Fai Sue Chang, ran the Ho-Ho Tea Room. Their son, Wah Ming Chang, became an accomplished artist in Los Angeles, Honolulu, and Carmel. Changs International Folk Dancers continues today and claims to be the oldest continuing folk dance club in the country. Larry Getchell, "A History of the Folk Dance Movement in California," http://www/folkdance.com/html/history.htm (November 17, 2006) and Michael D. Brown, *Views From Asian California, 1920–1965* (San Francisco: Michael Brown, 1992): 14.

388   *Notes to Chapters 14 and 15*

26. Helen S. Herrick to author, July 26, 1989, in author's possession. Herrick is the author of *Tales of an Old Horsetrader: The First Hundred Years,* University of Iowa Press (Iowa City, IA: 1987). Herrick's name and address were among many in Lim's personal phone book that was in his remaining possessions. The "little black book" was filled with women's names and numbers. Herrick was the only one who responded to inquiries.

27. "Dream of a River," *Gidra* (20th anniversary issue), 1990, 8.

28. Memorandum, Inspector Webber, Marysville, Dec. 5, 1906; Transcript, Inspection of Hom Ah Lim, April 7, 1920; Angel Island; Rough Draft, Memo for File, n.d.; Statement of Tom Na Hong, New York, April 3, 1962; and Transcript, Inspection of Hom Ah Lim, Angel Island, Oct. 28, 1931.

29. INS, Transcript of hearings, April 24, 1962, May 14, 1962, Nov. 12, 1964, June 9, 1965; transcripts of interviews of Tom Na Hong, April 3 and 12, 1962; Memorandum for file, n.d.; and interview with Fred Ho.

30. Happy Lim, "Literature, Art and Practical Struggle."

31. Letters from China to author.

32. See for example, "Follow Up on the *Red Detachment of Women*," "On *Swan Lake*," "War and Peace," and "I Need to Be as Strong as an Evergreen Pine," all originally in *Getting Together* and republished in translation in *Chinese- American Workers: Past & Present,* (San Francisco: Getting Together Publications, 1972): 88–94 and 98–100.

Chapter 15

I am indebted to the Mukerji family, especially to Dhan Gopal Mukerji, Jr., and Dr. Prithwindra Mukherjee, who opened their extensive collections on Dhan Gopal Mukerji to me. This essay would have been impossible without their assistance. They gave generously of their time to answer questions, provide oral histories and their own research essays, and read early drafts of this effort. I thank Dr. Chandra Mukerji for also providing me access to family papers in her possession. Manishita Dass, Akhil Gupta, Purnima Mankekar, and Sameer Pandya read early versions of this essay and provided invaluable comments; I am most appreciative of their help. I also thank Laurie Mun and Aly Remtulla for their research assistance.

1. A few Indians published earlier than Mukerji (henceforth DGM) in America, but their work had a more limited intellectual and social influence than his. Several became well known later, however, because of their radical political activities in the Indian nationalist movement. See, for example, Lajpat Rai, *Young India: An Interpretation and A History of the Nationalist Movement from Within* (New York: B. W. Huebsch, 1916), and the later work of Taraknath Das and Har

Notes to Chapter 15   389

Dayal. The eminent poet Rabindranath Tagore did not, of course, write primarily for American audiences.

2. For more on this point, see Gordon H. Chang, *Morning Glory, Evening Shadow: Yamato Ichihashi and His Internment Writings, 1942–1945* (Stanford, Calif.: Stanford University Press, 1997), 1–14; and Henry Yu, *Thinking Oriental: Migration, Contact, and Exoticism in Modern America* (New York: Oxford University Press, 2001).

3. See for example, Ronald Takaki, *Strangers from a Different Shore* (Boston: Little, Brown, 1989), which draws in part from *Caste and Outcast* to help tell the story of early South Asian immigrants. Gordon Hutner, ed., *Immigrant Voices* (New York: Signet Classic, 1999), includes pages from *Caste and Outcast*. The popular writer John Jakes draws a character closely modeled on DGM in his historical novel *California Gold* (New York: Ballantine Books, 1989), 689–724. Dr. Prithwindra Mukherjee has also completed extensive research on DGM and has published essays on him in India.

4. The surname is sometimes spelled Mukherji or Mukherjee. Early biographical information on DGM comes from the author's interview with DGM, Jr., St. Raphael, France, July 13, 1998; DGM's application to the University of California, Berkeley, in authors possession; an Autobiographical Note, c. mid-1920s; and a completed E. P. Dutton publicity questionnaire, c. mid-1920s, the last two in DGM family papers. These papers are in the possession of different family members. Much of the collection consists of photocopies of material in the papers of the publisher E. P. Dutton, held in the special collections at Syracuse University. Other materials include a diary, correspondence, and scattered manuscripts.

DGM's application to Berkeley states that he studied at Scottish Churches Collegiate School, which may have referred to the specific schools mentioned in other biographical material.

Brief published biographies of DGM include Dilly Tante, ed., *Living Authors: A Book of Biographies* (New York: H. W. Wilson, 1931), 285–86; Shyamala A. Narayan, entry, *Encyclopedia of Post-Colonial Literatures in English,* Eugene Benson and L. W. Conolly, eds. (London: Routledge, 1994), 1050–51; Jim Henry, entry, *Notable Asian Americans,* Helen Zia and Susan B. Gall, eds. (New York: Gale Research, 1995), 269–70; special issue of *Horn Book Magazine,* 4 (1937); and Susan M. Trosky, ed., *Contemporary Authors* (Detroit: Gale Research, 1992) 136: 290–92.

On Alexander Duff and his influence on British colonial education, see Gauri Viswanathan, *Masks of Conquest: Literary Study and British Rule in India* (New York: Columbia University Press, 1989), 48–65.

5. For more on Jadu Gopal Mukherjee (1886–1976), see S. P. Sen, ed., *Dictionary of National Biography* (Calcutta: Institute of Historical Studies, 1972) 3: 159–60. Jadu remained active in the Indian independence movement and was

390   *Notes to Chapter 15*

imprisoned by the British on several occasions. As a well-known revolutionary leader, he was linked to several organizations, including the Samiti Movement, Jugantar Party, and Indian National Congress. He became a well-respected medical doctor later in his life. He also associated with his cousin Jatindranath Mukherjee (1879–1915), a legendary Indian revolutionary. Sen presents a history of Jadu Gopal's early activities that differs significantly from DGM's family version.

6. Interview with DGM, Jr., July 13, 1998.

7. DGM's name does not appear on passenger lists for the ports of San Francisco or Seattle. His immigration file does not record his original port of entry. Family members speculate that he may have originally arrived in Canada.

8. Interview with DGM, Jr., July 13, 1998; DGM application to UC Berkeley. By the time of his arrival in the United States, many Indian students followed an established travel route from the Pacific Northwest to Berkeley. Joan M. Jensen, *Passage from India: Asian Indian Immigrants in North America* (New Haven, Conn.: Yale University Press, 1988), 170–71.

9. Harriet Bond Skidmore, "A Biographical Sketch of Dhan Gopal Mukerji," c. 1927, E. P. Dutton broadsheet, Faculty Bio. File, Special Collections, Green Library, Stanford University; DGM, Autobiographical Note; and application and transcript, UC Berkeley, in authors possession. A careful reading of *Caste and Outcast* reveals inconsistencies in its version of the migration account. Toward the end of Part I, DGM suggests that he traveled from Japan to San Francisco; several pages later, he implies that he entered the country at Seattle. Prithwindra Mukherjee believes that much of the family migration account is fiction; for example, DGM's description of Jadu's activities does not accord with the historical record. Letter to author, June 22, 2000.

10. Interview with DGM, Jr., July 13, 1998.

11. DGM application to Stanford University and transcript, Records, Registrar's Office, Stanford University.

12. Jensen, *Passage from India*, 12–15; and Harold R. Isaacs, *Scratches on Our Minds: American Images of China and India* (New York: John Day, 1958), 239–43, 267–68. Other surveys of the history of East Indians in the United States include: S. Chandrasekhar, ed., *From India to America: A Brief History of Immigration, Problems of Discrimination, Admission, and Assimilation* (La Jolla, Calif.: Population Review Publications, 1982); Arthur W. Helweg and Usha M. Helweg, *An Immigrant Success Story: East Indians in America* (London: Hurst and Co., 1990); and H. Brett Melendy, *Asians in America: Filipinos, Koreans, and East Indians* (Boston: Twayne, 1977).

13. Bill Ong Hing, *Making and Remaking Asian America Through Immigration Policy, 1850–1990* (Stanford, Calif: Stanford University Press, 1993), 31–32.

Notes to Chapter 15   391

Immigration from South Asia increased significantly only after passage of the 1965 Immigration Act.

14. There is no record of a formal association between DGM and the San Francisco Ramakrishna Center. Marie-Louise Burke to author, Aug. 8, 1999.

15. Jensen, *Passage from India,* 174–78; and Emily C. Brown, *Har Dayal, Hindu Revolutionary and Rationalist* (Tucson: University of Arizona Press, 1975), 97–112. In September 1912, Har Dayal resigned from his position as lecturer at Stanford. In a long letter to university president David Starr Jordan, Dayal describes the conflict between his social activism and his academic responsibilities: "All my tentative expressions of opinion and my plans and experiments in life are judged as if I had no personal life apart from 'the University' and as if 'the University' were an inquisitorial body having moral authority over me. As a 'professor,' I am also expected not to stray far from orthodox and current standards of belief and conduct in my search for new ideals. I have repeatedly been asked if 'Stanford' approves of my work for the Labor movement, or my views on the woman question, on patriotism, etc. etc. It thus appears that people take my little work in the University much more seriously than I do." Dayal felt he could no longer live with these strictures and pressures and resigned his position. Jordan immediately accepted the resignation. Dayal to Jordan, Sept. 13, 1912, and Jordan to Dayal, Sept. 17, 1912, Jordan Papers, Special Collections, Green Library, Stanford University, Box 82, F. 751.

16. M. N. Roy, "Memoirs," *The Radical Humanist,* (Feb. 1, 1953): 54–56. Roy was a comrade of DGM's famous revolutionary cousin Jatin Mukherjee and a friend of DGM's elder brother Jadu. Roy writes that his new persona, M. N. Roy, was "born" on the Stanford campus, saying that it was DGM who had encouraged him to "wipe out the past and begin a new man."

17. Helen Bosanquet, *Bernard Bosanquet: A Short Account of His Life* (London: Macmillan, 1924); Charles Capper, "'A Little Beyond': The Problem of the Transcendentalist Movement in American History," *Journal of American History* (Sept. 1998): 502–39.

18. DGM application and transcript, Stanford University, in author's possession. DGM himself described his Stanford degree as being in "metaphysics," DGM, Autobiographical Note.

19. John C. Branner to Benjamin F. Shambaugh, Nov. 9, 1915, Branner Papers, Special Collections, Green Library, Stanford University, Box 6, F.2.

20. DGM, Autobiographical Note.

21. Ethel Ray Dugan even applied for membership in the Daughters of the American Revolution in 1931. "Application for membership to the National Society," DGM family papers.

392   *Notes to Chapter 15*

22. DGM, Jr., interview, July 13, 1998; Ethel Ray Dugan transcript, Records, Registrar Office, Stanford University; DGM, Jr., to Prithwindra Mukherjee, n.d. [1987?], and Oct. 11, 1984, DGM family papers. Ethel Ray Dugan's thesis is located in Special Collections, Green Library, Stanford University.

23. Harold W. French, *The Swan's Wide Waters: Ramakrishna and Western Culture* (Port Washington, N.Y.: Kennikat Press, 1974), 97–127. Also see Pravrajika Prabuddhaprana, *Tantine: The Life of Josephine MacLeod, Friend of Swami Vivekananda* (Calcutta: Sri Sarada Math, 1990); and Paramahansa Yogananda, *Autobiography of a Yogi* (New York: The Philosophical Library, 1946).

24. Marriage certificate, DGM family papers. Before 1923 some lower courts accepted Indian claims that they were "Caucasian," even granting them United States citizenship. The U.S. Supreme Court overturned these rulings and explicitly denied naturalization rights to Indians in 1923 on the basis that Indians were not "white persons." DGM never applied for American citizenship.

25. DGM to Frederick Brasch, Oct. 16 [1916?], Brasch Family Papers, Stanford University Special Collections, Box 2, F. 13.

26. DGM to Witter Bynner, Mar. 10 [1917], Houghton Library, Harvard University, in bMS Am 1891.28 (352). There are claims that DGM actually served in the British army during World War I, but this appears to be mistaken; see his identification in the table of contents of *Asia* (Sept. 1920).

27. DGM to Witter Bynner, Oct. 8 [1918?], in Bynner Papers, Houghton Library, Harvard University; DGM to John Jay Chapman, Dec. 6 [1919?], Houghton Library, bMS Am 1854.1 (539).

28. DGM to John Jay Chapman, Dec. 10 [1919?], Houghton Library, Harvard University, bMS Am 1854.1 (539).

29. *New York Times,* Apr. 2, 1918, 8; Diwakar Prasad Singh, *American Attitude Towards the Indian Nationalist Movement* (New Delhi: Munshiram Manoharlal, 1974), 165–73; L. P. Mathur, *Indian Revolutionary Movement in the United States of America* (Delhi: S. Chand, 1970), 126–29; and Janice R. MacKinnon and Stephen R. MacKinnon, *Agnes Smedley: The Life and Times of an American Radical* (Berkeley: University of California Press, 1988), 31–50.

30. Prithwindra Mukherjee to author, Dec. 5, 1999. Roy arrived in the United States in 1916 and joined the Ghadar Party in San Francisco. Both he and his wife, Evelyn Trent, had socialist and revolutionary sympathies and later became associated with the communist movement. Roy became one of the founders of the Mexican Communist Party and later a leader in the Communist International in Moscow. Later in life, he broke with communism and founded the Radical Humanist movement. Singh, *Indian Nationalist Movement,* 171–72. The Evelyn Trent Jones Papers at the Hoover Institution, Stanford, unfortunately shed little light on this early period. In a sensational case, Evelyn Trent's father accused Roy of

Notes to Chapter 15 393

kidnapping his daughter from Stanford and had Roy arrested. Roy married Evelyn Trent in prison and was released. After federal authorities indicted Roy for conspiracy and sedition in 1917, the two left the country for Mexico, where they became involved in Mexican radical politics. See "Biography," Evelyn Trent Jones Papers, Hoover Institution, Box 1; Chandra Chakraberty, *New India* (Calcutta: Vijoya Krishna Brothers, n.d.), 34–35; and Vijaya Chandra Joshi, ed., *Lajpat Rai: Autobiographical Writings* (Delhi: University Publishers, 1965), 216–17, 247.

31. DGM to Witter Bynner, Mar. 10 [1917]; and DGM to John J. Chapman, Dec. 6 [1919?], Houghton Library, Harvard University, bMS Am 1854.1 (539); DGM, Jr., interview, July 13, 1998; Roger Baldwin to DGM, Feb. 11, 1921, Baldwin Papers, Seeley G. Mudd Manuscript Library, Princeton University; Prabuddhaprana, *Tantine*, 202.

32. Henry F. May, *The End of American Innocence: A Study of the First Years of Our Time, 1912–1917* (New York: Knopf, 1959), 279–329; J. J. Clarke, *Oriental Enlightenment: The Encounter Between Asian and Western Thought* (London: Routledge, 1997), 95–129; Stanley Coben, *Rebellion Against Victorianism: The Impetus for Cultural Change in 1920s America* (New York: Oxford University Press, 1991), 3–35, 48–68; Ann Douglas, *Terrible Honesty: Mongrel Manhattan in the 1920s* (New York: Farrar, Straus, 1995), 3–28; Will Durant, *The Story of Civilization: Our Oriental Heritage* (New York: Simon and Schuster, 1935), viii–ix; and J. David Hoeveler, Jr., *The New Humanism: A Critique of Modern America, 1900–1940* (Charlottesville: University Press of Virginia, 1976), 11, 184.

33. Prabuddhaprana, *Tantine*, 164–65; DGM, Jr., to author, July 22, 1999.

34. Roger Baldwin to DGM, Feb. 11, 1921, Baldwin Papers, Seely G. Mudd Manuscript Library, Princeton University.

35. DGM, Jr., interview, July 13, 1998.

36. See "My Brothers Face," "Indian Voices," and "The Holy One of Benares," in *The Atlantic Monthly* (June, July, and Aug. 1924). These later appeared as chapters in the book *My Brother's Face* (New York: Dutton, 1924). "Poignant Silences," Asia (May 1922): 388; "Tagore's India," *Asia* (Sept. 1920): 778–80; "Old Courtesan's Lament," *Poetry* (Oct. 1922): 27; "India's Social Revolution," *American Review* (May–June 1924): 279–82; "Saints in Benares: Talks with Holy Men in a Holy City," *Century Magazine* (Nov. 1924): 93–100; and "What is Civilization? India's Answer," *Forum* (Jan. 1925): 1–12.

37. Elizabeth Seeger, "Dhan Mukerji and His Books"; and Arthur L. Hamilton, "A Friend's Tribute to Dhan Mukerji," both in *Horn Book Magazine* 4 (1937); and Ben Misra, "Dhan Gopal Mukerji, As I Knew Him," *Contemporary India* 2 (1936): 473–81. Even DGM's detractors conceded that he was a gifted conversationalist; see for example, the comments of Boshi Sen in Prabuddhaprana, *Tantine*, 164.

Notes to Chapter 15

38. J. Nehru to Indira Nehru, Aug. 1, 1936, as cited in Sonia Gandhi, ed., *Freedom's Daughter: Letters Between Indira Gandhi and Jawaharlal, 1922–39* (London: Hodder and Stoughton, 1989), 269.

39. *The Atlantic Monthly* (Aug. 1924): 286. Revealing the close relationship between DGM and Jordan, DGM responded to Jordan from Europe, saying, "I am proud that it was you who claimed me as one of your children. I owe you more than can be set forth here. Without you I would have not been helped to bring out my first work." DGM to DSJ, July 16, 1925, Jordan Papers, Stanford University Special Collections.

40. On Indian autobiographies, see Judith E. Walsh, *Crowing Up in British India: Indian Autobiographies on Childhood and Education under the Raj* (New York: Holmes and Meier, 1983). This study, which takes a psychological approach to its subject, does not examine DGM's work.

41. "Where Literature Does Not Assume Intelligence," *New York Times,* June 3, 1923, 14; "The Ganges and the Harlem," *The New Republic* (Aug. 22, 1923): 365. About the same time that *Caste and Outcast* appeared, another Indian intellectual in the United States, Satyananda Roy, published a volume for children entitled *When I Was a Boy in India* (Boston: Lothrop, Lee and Shepard, 1924).

42. "Why I Write in English about Hindu Life," *Sufi Quarterly* (n.d.): 202–3; he explored this theme of merging "East and West" elsewhere. "The Truth About Kipling's India," *Libraries* (Oct. 1928): 395–401.

43. DGM to Patty, Feb. 25 [1930?], DGM family papers.

44. See correspondence between DGM and Charles W. Stork, editor of *Contemporary Verse,* translator of Scandinavian verse, poet, and playwright. DGM regularly wrote to Charles and Elizabeth Stork from the early days of their friendship, which began in 1921, if not earlier. DGM's letters help document his many travels. See DGM to CWS correspondence in the C. W. Stork Collection, Syracuse University Library, esp. Apr. 21, May 18, June 11, and Dec. 1, 1921; Feb 28, Apr. 2, 1923; Mar. 9, Nov. 7, 1924; Apr. 11 [1926?]. Also see Misra, "Dhan Gopal Mukerji"; and letters to Patty, Oct. 23, Nov. 6, Nov. 11, Nov. 28, and Nov. 29, 1924, DGM family papers.

45. There is a suggestion, but no firm evidence, that Nehru asked DGM to represent the Gandhian point of view for India at the League of Nations. It seems that the League occupied little of Nehru's attention when he was in Geneva. His memoirs mention that he met DGM there in 1926. J. Nehru, *Toward Freedom: The Autobiography of Jawaharlal Nehru* (New York: John Day, 1942), 121–22.

46. *New York Times,* Nov. 14, 1926, sec. 2, p. 2.

47. Communications with DGM, Jr., Mar. 27 and Mar. 29, 2000; and J. Nehru, *Toward Freedom,* 122. On Rolland and India, see R. A. Francis, *Romain Rolland* (Oxford: Berg, 1999), 132–38, 206–13.

48. After receiving the Newberry Medal, he wrote privately that he wished the "world would pay its tribute to *The Face of Silence,* the one book I am proud to have done." DGM diary, June 25, 1928, DGM family papers.

49. See excerpts from Rolland's impressions of DGM in Prabuddhaprana, *Tantine,* 203–19; Romain Rolland, *The Life of Ramakrishna,* vol. 1, trans. E. F. Malcolm Smith, 7th ed. (Calcutta: Advaita Ashrama, 1965), x, 302. The book was not without controversy, however. Rolland reports that several Ramakrishna monks were unhappy with the book, apparently because it reveals certain spiritual experiences that should not have been made public. The dispute soon settled. The book continues to be reissued in different language editions, and the New York Ramakrishna Center is arranging a new U.S. edition. DGM, Jr., to author, June 26, 2000.

50. Prabuddhaprana, *Tantine,* 202–4, 209; also see DGM dedication to MacLeod in *The Face of Silence.*

51. DGM diary, June 25, 1928, DGM family papers.

52. DGM, *Ghond the Hunter* (New York: Dutton, 1928), 69.

53. *The Sufi Quarterly* (Dec. 1928): 202–3.

54. DGM, *Gay Neck: The Story of a Pigeon,* p. 192.

55. DGM, "The Truth About Kipling's India," *Libraries* 8 (Oct. 1928): 395–401.

56. *Upanishads: Devotional Passages from the Hindu Bible* (New York: Dutton, 1929); and *The Song of God: Translation of the Bhagavad-Gita* (New York: Dutton, 1931).

57. Clarke, *Oriental Enlightenment,* 84–87, 116–18; Carl T. Jackson, *Vedanta for the West: The Ramakrishna Movement in the United States* (Bloomington: Indiana University Press, 1994), 8–10. Maxine Hong Kingston makes this point powerfully in "A Letter to Garrett Hongo upon the Publication of *The Open Boat,*" Aug. 4, 1992, *Amerasia Journal* 20.3 (1994): 25–26.

58. Jackson, *Vedanta for the West,* 30–33, 67–74.

59. DGM diary, June 25, 1928, DGM family papers.

60. Jackson, *Vedanta for the West,* 67–74.

61. Prabuddhaprana, *Tantine,* 202.

62. Prithwindra Mukherjee, DGM chronology (July 1999): 5; DGM, Jr., to author, July 22, 1999.

63. E. P. Dutton publicity broadsheet [1928?].

64. Paul Kennady to DGM, Feb. 26, 1927; Clarence B. Smith to DGM, Apr. 11, 1927, both in DGM family papers.

65. Katherine Mayo, *Mother India* (New York: Harcourt, Brace, 1927).

66. Isaacs, *Scratches,* 268–71.

67. Ibid., 289.

68. *New York Times,* Nov. 5, 1927, p. 23, col. 1.

396   *Notes to Chapter 15*

69. *New York Times,* Nov. 5, 1927, 23; Feb. 3, 1928, 23; and Feb. 6, 1928, 22. DGM, *A Son of Mother India Answers* (New York: Dutton, 1928). See clippings of reviews from newspapers including the *Milwaukee Journal,* Feb. 11, 1928; *Yale Daily,* Feb. 13, 1928; *Omaha World-Herald,* Feb. 19, 1928; *New York Herald Tribune,* n.d.; and *New York Sun,* Feb. 11, 1928, all in DGM family papers.

70. DGM, Jr., to author, July 31, 1999. At least ten books responded to Mayo's work, but DGM's was perhaps the most important. It is often cited in other work; see, for example, Ernest Wood, *An Englishman Defends Mother India: A Complete Constructive Reply to "Mother India"* (Madras: Ganesh, 1929). DGM wanted to be optimistic about India's future. "China emerges united," he wrote in his diary during its nationalist revolution, and "if China can, India will. The 19th century saw Europe shuffle off feudalism—the 20th will see Asia doing the same." DGM diary, June 25, 1928, DGM family papers.

71. John Macrae to DGM, Mar. 28, 1929, DGM family papers.

72. DGM to Lizl [*sic*] Stork, June 4, 1929, C. W. Stork Collection, Syracuse University Library, Syracuse, New York.

73. Van Wyck Brooks, *An Autobiography* (New York: Dutton, 1965), 439–41.

74. DGM to J. Nehru, Dec. 31, 1929, Nehru Papers, Nehru Museum and Library, New Delhi. DGM told Nehru of his interest in going to India as early as November 1929. DGM to J. Nehru, Nov. 17, 1929, *Jawaharlal Nehru Correspondence, 1903–1947: A Catalogue* (New Delhi: Vikas, 1988), 345.

75. DGM diary, Mar. 10, 20, and 28, 1930, DGM family papers; DGM, *Disillusioned India* (New York: Dutton, 1930), 15.

76. DGM diary, Mar. 31, 1930, DGM family papers.

77. DGM diary, Mar. 10, 1930, DGM family papers.

78. *New York Times,* June 3, 1930, 5. DGM began but never completed a manuscript on Gandhi. Partial typescript, n.d., in DGM family papers.

79. DGM, Jr., to author, July 22, 1999.

80. Nehru to DGM, June 19, 1928; July 2, 1929; Feb. 4, 1930; and Mar. 16, 1930, all in DGM family papers. Also see Stanley Wolpert, *Nehru: A Tryst with Destiny* (New York: Oxford University Press, 1996), vii–x, 3–10, 67–70.

81. DGM to Patty, May 1, 1930, DGM family papers.

82. DGM to Nehru, Mar. 30, 1929, Nehru Papers. DGM, *Disillusioned India,* 83. The book deftly hides the authors relationship with Nehru. One could not even guess at their closeness in reading the book. As he did so often, DGM wrote in a deliberately naive way, posing as an innocent, even skeptical, recorder of encounters with individuals and personal experiences. The style seduces a trusting reader.

83. DGM, *Disillusioned India,* 219.

84. DGM, *The Song of God;* J. Nehru to DGM, May 7, 1931, DGM family papers.

Notes to Chapter 15   397

85. Nehru to DGM, May 7, 1931, Aug. 19, 1931, Jan. 9, 1932, all in DGM family papers.

86. Swami Shivananda to DGM, Sept. 7, 1932, Archives of the Ramakrishna-Vivekananda Center, New York.

87. DGM, Jr., to author, July 31, 1999.

88. John Macrae to DGM, July 29, 1931, DGM family papers.

89. Typescript, DGM and Ethel Dugan Mukerji, "The Story of Nala and Dama Yanti," n.d., DGM family papers. Other unfinished work includes a play with a first scene entitled "On Board Aeroplane Going to India," n.d.; one of the characters is "Mr. Mukerji." Another unfinished work is a four-act play, "Girl with Pearl Necklace," which is in rough handwritten form. There is also evidence that DGM contemplated writing about his deeply spiritual personal experiences. In early 1933, he engaged in an extended discussion with a Dr. Millet, a psychoanalyst. The two discussed dreams, death, rituals, and universal symbols, and "Oriental" versus "Occidental" interpretations. The partial transcripts from these discussions were apparently to serve as the basis of a book. Partial transcripts of Jan. 22, 25, 29, and Feb. 8 and 20, 1933, DGM family papers.

90. DGM to John Macrae, Aug. 5, 1931, and Mar. 31, 1932; DGM to Elliot Macrae, Nov. 3, 1931; John Macrae to DGM, Mar. 29, 1932, Apr. 5, 1932; and Memo, "MSY" to EM, Mar. 25, 1932, all in DGM family papers.

91. DGM Jr., "Two Sides of My Father," n.d., DGM family papers.

92. DGM, Jr., interview, July 13, 1998; DGM to Gopal, n.d., Sept. 2, Oct. 3, Oct. 20, Nov. 7 [1934?], Aug. 15, 1934, Oct. 6, 1934, and July 3, 1936, all in DGM family papers.

93. Press release from William B. Feakins, Mar. 1936, DGM family papers.

94. DGM to Gopal, July 3, 1936, DGM family papers; DGM, Jr., to author, July 21 [31?], 1999.

95. Interview with DGM, Jr., July 13, 1998; DGM to Nehru, Apr. 23, 1936, *Jawaharlal Nehru Correspondence, 1903–1947.*

96. DGM, Jr., to author, July 31, 1999.

97. *New York Times,* July 15, 1936, 17.

98. J. Nehru to Mrs. Mukerji, July 25, 1936, DGM family papers. Nehru expressed similar shock and sorrow in letters to relatives and friends. See, for example, Nehru to Indira, Aug. 1, 1936, Gandhi, *Freedom's Daughter,* 269; and Nehru to Gobind Behari Lal, Sept. 3, 1936, *Selected Works of Jawaharlal Nehru* (New Delhi: Orient Longman, 1975) 7: 156; and J. Nehru to I. Nehru, Sept. 18, 1943, in Sonia Gandhi, ed., *Two Alone, Two Together: Letters Between Indira Gandhi and Jawaharlal, 1922–39* (London: Hodder and Stoughton, 1992), 269.

99. Patty to Roger Baldwin, Sept. 5, 1936, copy of letter. Patty sent a copy of this letter to Nehru; see *Jawaharlal Nehru Correspondence, 1903–1947,* 348.

398   *Notes to Chapter 15 and Appendix*

100. Ibid.

101. This letter was made public in the February 2000 issue of the Bengali monthly *Udbodhan,* a publication of the Ramakrishna order. Dr. Prithwindra Mukherjee translated it into English. Ramakrishna apparently accepted the taking *of* one's own life if one had had a vision of God. See Prithwindra Mukherjee to DGM, Jr., Sept. 29, 2000, and enclosures, and DGM, Jr., to author, Sept. 30, 2000.

102. Misra, "Dhan Gopal Mukerji."

103. *The Horn Book Magazine* 4 (1937). See Joan Blodgett Peterson Olson, "An Interpretive History of *The Horn Book Magazine,* 1924–1973," doctoral diss., Stanford University School of Education, 1976.

104. Seeger, "Dhan Mukerji and His Books," 199–205.

105. DGM diary, n.d. [1929?], DGM family papers.

106. *The Case for India* (New York: Simon and Schuster, 1930).

107. Herbert H. Gowen, *A History of Indian Literature: From Vedic Times to the Present Day* (New York: Greenwood, 1931), 21; Maurice Parmelee, *Oriental and Occidental Culture: An Interpretation* (New York: Century, 1928), 53, 205.

108. R. K. Gupta, *The Great Encounter: A Study of Indo-American Literature and Cultural Relations* (New Delhi: Abhinav, 1986), 146–93. Also see Clarke, *Oriental Enlightenment;* and Frank G. Novak, Jr., ed., *Lewis Mumford and Patrick Geddes: The Correspondence* (London: Routledge, 1995).

109. Brooks, *Autobiography,* 465–66.

110. DGM to Patty, Nov. 13, 1929 [?], DGM family papers. On election day, he wrote in his diary, "Between [Hoovers election] and Mr. Lindberg [presumably Charles Lindbergh] Lincoln's democracy has been buried successfully." DGM diary, Nov. 7, 1928, DGM family papers.

111. See, for example, Hu Shih, "The Civilizations of the East and the West," in Charles Austin Beard, ed., *Whither Mankind: A Panorama of Modern Civilization* (New York: Longmans, Green, 1928), 25–41.

112. There are interesting parallels to the structure and message of *Caste and Outcast* in Bulosan's *America Is in the Heart* (New York: Harcourt, Brace, 1946).

113. These themes appear in *Caste and Outcast.*

114. DGM to Theodore Dreiser, Mar. 1, 1929, Theodore Dreiser Papers, University of Pennsylvania, Special Collections, Folder 4311; DGM to Suresh C. Bannerji, Oct. 8 [1918?], Witter Bynner Papers, Harvard University.

115. DGM, *The Face of Silence,* 253–54. "Silence" is a theme that appears in *Caste and Outcast* as well.

Appendix

1. This list is partial and not complete; for example, many book reviews are not listed. Only works published in English are included.

Biographical Note

During an academic career of more than thirty years, mostly in the Department of History at Stanford University, Gordon H. Chang produced a rich collection of scholarship that ranges widely from diplomatic history to Asian American Studies to art history. This volume brings a selection of his work together in one place for the first time. Chang is a professor of history and an affiliated professor with the Department of East Asian Languages and Cultures. He is also the Olive H. Palmer Professor of Humanities at Stanford. He has served as the Director of the Center for East Asian Studies, the director of the Asian American Studies Program, and as the Senior Associate Vice Provost for Undergraduate Studies. He was one of the founding faculty members of the Center for Comparative Studies in Race and Ethnicity at Stanford and is the inaugural director of the Asian American Research Center at Stanford. He has received fellowships from the Guggenheim Foundation, National Endowment for the Humanities, American Council of Learned Societies, three times from the Humanities Center at Stanford, and from the Huntington Library in San Marino, California. He is honored with elections to the Committee of 100, the Society of American Historians, and the American Academy of Arts and Sciences. Members of the U.S. Congress and the California State Legislature awarded special recognition to him for his work on recovering the history of Chinese railroad workers.

The authorized representative in the EU for product safety and compliance is:
Mare Nostrum Group B.V.
Mauritskade 21D
1091 GC Amsterdam
The Netherlands
Email address: gpsr@mare-nostrum.co.uk

KVK chamber of commerce number: 96249943